ON INFORMATION SYSTEMS

Video training courses are available on the subjects of
James Martin ADVANCED TECHNOLOGY LIBRARY of
from Applied Learning, 1751 West Diehl Road, Naperv...

Database	Telecommunications	Networks and Data Communications	Society
AN END USER'S GUIDE TO DATABASE	TELECOMMUNICATIONS AND THE COMPUTER (third edition)	PRINCIPLES OF DATA COMMUNICATION	THE COMPUTERIZED SOCIETY
PRINCIPLES OF DATABASE MANAGEMENT (second edition)	COMMUNICATIONS SATELLITE SYSTEMS	TELEPROCESSING NETWORK ORGANIZATION	TELEMATIC SOCIETY: A CHALLENGE FOR TOMORROW
COMPUTER DATABASE ORGANIZATION (third edition)	**Distributed Processing**	SYSTEMS ANALYSIS FOR DATA TRANSMISSION	TECHNOLOGY'S CRUCIBLE
MANAGING THE DATABASE ENVIRONMENT (second edition)	COMPUTER NETWORKS AND DISTRIBUTED PROCESSING	DATA COMMUNICATION TECHNOLOGY	VIEWDATA AND THE INFORMATION SOCIETY
DATABASE ANALYSIS AND DESIGN	DESIGN AND STRATEGY FOR DISTRIBUTED DATA PROCESSING	DATA COMMUNICATION DESIGN TECHNIQUES	**SAA: Systems Application Architecture**
VSAM: ACCESS METHOD SERVICES AND PROGRAMMING TECHNIQUES	**Office Automation**	SNA: IBM's NETWORKING SOLUTION	SAA: COMMON USER ACCESS
DB2: CONCEPTS, DESIGN, AND PROGRAMMING	IBM OFFICE SYSTEMS: ARCHITECTURES AND IMPLEMENTATIONS	LOCAL AREA NETWORKS: ARCHITECTURES AND IMPLEMENTATIONS	SAA: COMMON COMMUNICATIONS SUPPORT: DISTRIBUTED APPLICATIONS
IDMS/R: CONCEPTS, DESIGN, AND PROGRAMMING		OFFICE AUTOMATION STANDARDS	SAA: COMMON COMMUNICATIONS SUPPORT: NETWORK INFRASTRUCTURE
Security		DATA COMMUNICATION STANDARDS	SAA: COMMON PROGRAMMING INTERFACE
SECURITY, ACCURACY, AND PRIVACY IN COMPUTER SYSTEMS		COMPUTER NETWORKS AND DISTRIBUTED PROCESSING: SOFTWARE, TECHNIQUES, AND ARCHITECTURE	

**OBJECT-ORIENTED
ANALYSIS AND DESIGN**

A _(signature)_ **BOOK**

THE JAMES MARTIN BOOKS

currently available from Prentice Hall

- Application Development Without Programmers
- Building Expert Systems
- Communications Satellite Systems
- Computer Data-Base Organization, Second Edition
- Computer Networks and Distributed Processing: Software, Techniques, and Architecture
- Data Communication Technology
- DB2: Concepts, Design, and Programming
- Design and Strategy of Distributed Data Processing
- An End User's Guide to Data Base
- Fourth-Generation Languages, Volume I: Principles
- Fourth-Generation Languages, Volume II: Representative 4GLs
- Fourth-Generation Languages, Volume III: 4GLs from IBM
- Future Developments in Telecommunications, Second Edition
- Hyperdocuments and How to Create Them
- IBM Office Systems: Architectures and Implementations
- IDMS/R: Concepts, Design, and Programming
- Information Engineering, Book I: Introduction and Principles
- Information Engineering, Book II: Planning and Analysis
- Information Engineering, Book III: Design and Construction
- An Information Systems Manifesto
- Local Area Networks: Architectures and Implementations
- Managing the Data-Base Environment
- Object-Oriented Analysis and Design
- Principles of Data-Base Management
- Principles of Data Communication
- Recommended Diagramming Standards for Analysts and Programmers
- SNA: IBM's Networking Solution
- Strategic Information Planning Methodologies, Second Edition
- System Design from Provably Correct Constructs
- Systems Analysis for Data Transmission
- Systems Application Architecture: Common User Access
- Systems Application Architecture: Common Communications Support: Distributed Applications
- Systems Application Architecture: Common Communications Support: Network Infrastructure
- Systems Application Architecture: Common Programming Interface
- Technology's Crucible
- Telecommunications and the Computer, Third Edition
- Telematic Society: A Challenge for Tomorrow
- VSAM: Access Method Services and Programming Techniques

with Carma McClure

- Action Diagrams: Clearly Structured Specifications, Programs, and Procedures, Second Edition
- Diagramming Techniques for Analysts and Programmers
- Software Maintenance: The Problem and Its Solutions
- Structured Techniques: The Basis for CASE, Revised Edition

OBJECT-ORIENTED ANALYSIS AND DESIGN

JAMES MARTIN

and

JAMES J. ODELL

PRENTICE HALL
Englewood Cliffs, New Jersey 07632

Library of Congress Cataloging-in-Publication Data

MARTIN, JAMES, (date)
    Object-oriented analysis and design / by James Martin and James J. Odell.
        p.   cm.
    Includes bibliographical references and index.
    ISBN 0-13-630245-9
    1. Object-oriented programming (Computer science)
    I. Odell, James J. II. Title.
QA76.64.M37 1992
005.1—dc20   91-4611
                                                      CIP

TO CORINTHIA

Editorial/production supervision: Kathryn Gollin Marshak
Liaison: Mary P. Rottino
Jacket design: Lundgren Graphics
Pre-press buyer: Mary Elizabeth McCartney
Manufacturing buyer: Susan Brunke

 Published by Prentice-Hall, Inc.
A Simon & Schuster Company
Englewood Cliffs, New Jersey 07632

The publisher offers discounts on this book when ordered
in bulk quantities. For more information, write:
        Special Sales/Professional Marketing
        Prentice-Hall, Inc.
        Professional & Technical Reference Division
        Englewood Cliffs, NJ 07632

Printed in the United States of America

10   9   8   7   6   5   4   3

ISBN 0-13-630245-9

Prentice-Hall International (UK) Limited, *London*
Prentice-Hall of Australia Pty. Limited, *Sydney*
Prentice-Hall Canada Inc., *Toronto*
Prentice-Hall Hispanoamericana, S.A., *Mexico*
Prentice-Hall of India Private Limited, *New Delhi*
Prentice-Hall of Japan, Inc., *Tokyo*
Simon & Schuster Asia Pte. Ltd., *Singapore*
Editora Prentice-Hall do Brasil, Ltda., *Rio de Janeiro*

CONTENTS

4   The Future of Software   *43*

Introduction 43; Optical Disks 44; The Need for Power Tools 44;
Evolution of Software Production 45;
Inhuman Use of Human Beings 46; Chain Reaction 47;
Repository Standards 48; Packaged Software 49; Reusability 51;
Parallelism 55; Networks and Distribution of Objects 56;
Intercorporate Computer Interaction 56; Speed of Interaction 57;
The Need for Fast Development 58;
International Standards for Reusable Classes 59;
Code Generation from the Enterprise Model 59;
The Evolution of Programming Technique 60;
Pyramids of Complexity 61; References 63

PART II   AN OVERVIEW OF ANALYSIS AND DESIGN

5   OO Models   *67*

Models of Reality 67; Tools 68; Two Types of Models 69;
The Similarity of Analysis and Design 70;
Information Engineering 72; Accommodation of Old Systems 73

6   Object Structure Analysis   *75*

Objects and Object Types 75; Object Associations 77;
Generalization Hierarchies 78; Composed-of Hierarchies 80;
Object-Relationship Diagrams 80; Object Schemas 83

7   Object Behavior Analysis   *85*

Object States 85; Events 87; Types of Events 88;
The Lifecycle of an Object 90;
Interactions between Types of Objects 91; Operations 93;
External Sources of Events 93; Trigger Rules 94;
Control Conditions 95; Event Subtypes and Supertypes 96;
Hierarchical Schemas 97; Cause-and-Effect Isolation 98;
Clear Modularization 99;
The Similarity of Analysis and Design 100;
Object-Flow Diagrams 101

8   Object Structure and Behavior Design   *107*

Class 108;
What Is the Difference between an Operation and a Method? 108;
Class Inheritance 109; Selecting a Method 112;
Polymorphism 113; "Same as, Except . . ." 113

PART III   FUNDAMENTALS OF OBJECT STRUCTURE ANALYSIS

PREFACE

Our ability to create computer software is not keeping pace with the evolution of computer hardware. An industrial revolution is needed in software.

This revolution is likely to come from object-oriented techniques combined with CASE tools, code generators, visual programming, and repository-based development. The goals are to maximize the reusability of code and to build and store complex objects.

Object-oriented techniques change I.S. analysts' view of the world. Instead of thinking about processes and the decomposition of processes, they think about objects and their behavior. The objects may be complex internally, like an electronic machine, but analysts do not need to understand that complexity (unless they design it). Knowing how the objects behave and how to use them is enough.

Events are changes in the states of objects. A business analyst naturally thinks of the events in a business and the sorts of operations triggered by events. Analysis in terms of object types and event types requires a different mindset, but it is easier and more powerful than nonobject-oriented analysis. Particularly important, end users communicate more easily in terms of events and objects than the constructs of conventional structural analysis.

Much that has been written about object-oriented techniques is anchored in object-oriented programming. A more fundamental view is necessary. Object-oriented analysis and design should be taught independently from programming languages. CASE tools should use object-oriented techniques and code generators, storing details of object types in a repository.

OO analysis and design, as described in this book, are powerful ways to think about complex systems. *Conventional* analysis and design become more difficult as systems grow more complex, until ultimately, they limit the complexity we can handle. The approach described in this book does *not* model in terms of OO programming languages; it models the way reality is understood

by *people*. The understanding and knowledge of people is the essential component in designing any system. As such, this approach to OO specification allows
us to analyze *any* area of human reality—not *just* that of data processing.

Expanding our system knowledge beyond our perspective, restricted by data
processing, extends OO analysis to support many other disciplines. As the figure
below suggests, by *first* representing our knowledge in a fundamentally object-
oriented manner, we can engineer the captured knowledge for specific target
applications. This book presents useful OO techniques that can be employed
before plunging ahead into *physical* design and programming. It emphasizes conceptual, rather than physical, object-oriented considerations for planning, analyzing, and designing systems—whether the systems are for people, machines, or
computers.

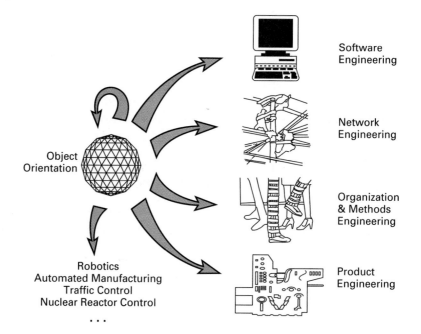

Part I of this book presents initial notions and directions of object orientation. Part II contains an overview of object-oriented analysis and design and their
recommended standards. Both Parts I and II give a useful overview for managers,
and introduce the rest of the book for the serious system developer. Part III presents ways of specifying *object structure,* with detailed, state-of-the-art techniques for modeling object types and their associations. Part IV deals with a
rigorous technique for specifying the way objects change over time. This so-
called object behavior is expressed in term of events, triggers, and operations.
Part V considers implementation by discussing some of the options and issues for
converting the analysis results to object-oriented program code. In addition, it

introduces other important issues for organizations, such as planning, management, and object-oriented database support.

In general, we have tried to avoid using too many acronyms in this book. The acronym OO for *object-oriented,* however, is visually appealing and easy to remember. So, it appears throughout the book. In addition, two other prominent abbreviations will be used: OOPL (object-oriented programming language) and OODB (object-oriented database).

PRECISION
IN DEFINITION   Precise definition of the terms used in OO analysis and design is very important. It is necessary that those in the computer industry agree on these definitions.

Many of the terms used in this book are based on those recommended by the Object Management Group (OMG) [3] and the Object-Oriented Database Task Group (OODBTG) [1, 2]. We have sometimes reworded these definitions to achieve tutorial clarity.

ACKNOWLEDGMENTS   This book includes a description of the Ptech technology which is the result of over ten years of intensive development by John Edwards in conceptual schemas and the foundations of paradigms. In particular, the Ptech technology has solved fundamental issues in formalizing the OO paradigm, and in establishing foundation methods and techniques for OO software development.

A practical application of the Ptech technology is embodied in the Ptech product set. Basic Ptech is an integrated environment that supports both enterprise modeling as well as generates executable code. Full-capability Ptech is capable of generating custom tools to support client-preferred notation, methods, and GUI across a wide variety of platforms. Ptech is a product of a Westborough, Massachusetts, company.

The authors wish to express their appreciation to Martin Fowler. Significant portions of the chapters on object-oriented design are based on his ideas and writings. The authors also wish to acknowledge the important contribution of Tim Andrews of Ontos Inc, who provided the material contained in the chapter entitled "Object-Oriented Databases." His extensive background and expertise in databases added valuable knowledge to our understanding of this area.

Other individuals also helped in this book's development. We are grateful to Dr. Bill Henneman who served as primary mentor—on call day and night. Matthew Thomas deserves special thanks for his help in refining many of the book's technical concepts. We are also indebted to Stevan Mrdalj, Brad Kain,

Ken Winter, Min-Shih Chen, Frans Van Assche, Kevin Murphy, Bill Wiley, Daniel Berry, David Orme, and Dennis de Champeaux for the effort each invested in reviewing and commenting on the manuscript. In addition, we would like to express particular appreciation to Andrea L. Matthies, who transformed the text of this book—including this acknowledgment.

Finally, we are grateful to the staff of Prentice Hall for their care and speed in producing this book—particularly, to our publisher Paul Becker, his assistant Noreen Regina, to our senior production editor Kathryn Marshak, and to Mary Rottino.

CORRECTIONS   This book's approach is based on many ideas: some go back more than two millenia, others were developed in the writing of this book. Integrating the works of Plato, Aristotle, Saint Augustine, John Duns Scotus, Alfred North Whitehead, Bertrand Russell, and many others with the contemporary notion of object orientation was a task vulnerable to errors of omission, commission, and confusion. We would appreciate your input for future editions. Comments, corrections, and suggestions should be sent to the authors care of Prentice Hall, College Editorial, Englewood Cliffs, NJ 07632, or by electronic mail to 71051,1733 (CompuServe).

REFERENCES

1. Otis, Allen, Craig Thompson and Bill Kent, eds., *ODM Reference Model,* Object-Oriented Databases Task Group (X3 ANSI/SPARC), Technical Report OODB 89-01R7, April 30, 1991.

2. Perez, Edward and Mark Sastry, eds., *ODM Glossary,* Object-Oriented Databases Task Group (X3 ANSI/SPARC), Technical Report OODB 91-07R1, July 5, 1991.

3. Soley, Richard Mark, ed., *Object Management Architecture Guide,* Object Management Group, Document 90.9.1, November 1, 1990.

James Martin
James J. Odell

PART I   WHY THE EXCITEMENT?

"Object-oriented" is going to be the most important emerging software technology of the 1990s.
—Bill Gates, Chairman, Microsoft Corp.

1 A SOFTWARE INDUSTRIAL REVOLUTION

One of the most urgent concerns in the computer industry today is the need to create software and corporate systems much faster and at lower cost. To put the ever-growing power of computers to good use, we need software of *much* greater complexity. Although more complex, this software also needs to be more reliable. High quality is essential in software development, as poor quality wastes money.

The need for better software development applies both within the software industry itself and within enterprises of all types that develop their own computer applications. Information technology organizations need to create and modify applications much faster. If applications take two or three years to build, with an application backlog of several years, businesses cannot create applications or react to competitive thrusts quickly enough. The vital ability for dynamic change is lost.

The means of achieving the quantum leap in Fig. 1.1 is probably now within sight. Instead of one technique, a combination of many tools and techniques is needed.

In software we need a quantum leap in:

- Complexity
- Design Capability
- Flexibility
- Speed of Development
- Ease of Change
- Reliability

Figure 1.1

Object-oriented techniques allow software to be constructed of *objects* that have a specified behavior. Objects themselves can be built out of other objects, that in turn can be built out of objects. This resembles complex machinery being built out of assemblies, subassemblies, sub-subassemblies, and so on.

Systems analysis in the object-oriented world is done by analyzing the objects in an environment and those events that interact with these objects. Software design is done by reusing existing object classes and, when necessary, building new classes. In modeling an enterprise, the analysts should identify its object types and the operations that cause those objects to behave in certain ways.

Throughout the history of engineering, a principle seems to emerge—*great engineering is simple engineering.* Ideas that become too cumbersome, inflexible, and problematic tend to be replaced with newer, conceptually cleaner ideas that have an aesthetic simplicity. When a programmer's diagram looks like a tangled cobweb, the time has come to rethink the entire program.

Software constantly runs the danger of becoming cumbersome, inflexible, and problematic. The linkages tend to multiply as new features are added and as users request changes. Unless the designers have conceptual clarity, they will weave a tangled web.

Object-oriented techniques can be used to simplify the design of complex systems. The system can be visualized as the collection of objects, with each object being in one of many specified states. The operations that change the state are relatively simple. Objects are built out of other objects. Systems are built out of proven components with standard-format requests invoking the operations of the component.

The term *software industrial revolution* has been used to describe the move to an era when software will be compiled out of reusable object components, creating vast libraries of such components. We must progress from an era of monolithic software packages, where one vendor builds the whole package, to an era in which software is assembled from components and packages from many vendors—just as computers or cars are assembled from components from many vendors. The components will become increasingly complex internally but simple to interact with. They will be *black boxes* which we do not look inside.

KILLER TECHNOLOGIES

Object-oriented techniques alone cannot provide the magnitude of change needed. They must be combined with other software technologies. Object-oriented techniques have existed for two decades, but the early techniques were mainly concerned with coding in languages such as Smalltalk and C++. Meanwhile, other powerful technologies have evolved, such as CASE tools, code generators, repository-based development, the inference engine, and artificial intelligence techniques. Object-oriented techniques become very powerful when combined with these other technologies.

Figure 1.2 lists a set of *killer technologies* for software development. The synergistic *combination* of these technologies will bring a revolution in software. This will require teamwork, education, and good management, along with cooperation from software companies. Standards now evolving will aid this cooperation. Box 1.1 describes the software killer technologies.

Killer Technologies for Software Development

- CASE and I-CASE
- Visual Programming
- Code Generators
- Repository and Repository Coordinator
- Repository-Based Methodologies
- Information Engineering
- Object-Oriented Databases
- Nonprocedural Languages
- Inference Engines
- Client-Server Technology
- Class Libraries which maximize reusability
- Object-Oriented Analysis and Design

Figure 1.2

BOX 1.1   A summary of the killer technologies for software development.

- **CASE (Computer-Aided Software Engineering).** Particularly important to the future of software development is the growth of the CASE industry. CASE tools are the software industry's equivalent of CAD (computer-aided design) tools for such activities as circuit layout and chip design.

  CASE tools employ graphic representations on the screen to help automate the planning, analysis, design, and generation of software.

(Continued)

BOX 1.1 *(Continued)*

- **I-CASE (Integrated CASE).** A particularly important facility of CASE tools is the code generator. Code generators should be as powerful and efficient as possible. The term I-CASE is used to mean integrated CASE, in which the tools for all stages of the lifecycle link together and drive a code generator.

> I-CASE refers to a CASE toolset that supports all lifecycle stages including complete code generation, with a single logically consistent repository.

- **Visual Programming.** Visual programming is a form of CASE that expresses the design of programs with graphics, color, and possibly sound. Objects are represented in visual form and may be thought of as physical machines that transition from state to state.

> *Visual programming* allows developers to enter, understand, think of, run, debut, and manipulate programs using primarily pictorial notations.

- **Code Generators.** Whenever possible, programs should be generated automatically from high-level designs, specifications, or images on a CASE screen. Code can be generated from decision tables, rules, action diagrams, diagrams of events, state transition diagrams, representations of objects and their properties and relationships, and so on.

> *Code generators* produce code with no syntax errors from high-level designs, charts, or specifications.

Ideal code generators would generate code as fast as designers can think and allow them to execute it.

- **Repository.** CASE tools employ a repository, which some vendors call an encyclopedia, to store the knowledge that they help the analyst create. The planning tools put information in a repository that can be used by modeling or analysis tools. These, in turn, put information in a repository that can be used by the design tools. In addition, the design tools put informa-

BOX 1.1 *(Continued)*

tion in a repository that can be used to generate code. The repository provides a seamless interface among the tools in the I-CASE toolset. I-CASE tools employ a *single, nonredundant repository.* Though logically nonredundant, physically it may employ a distributed database. Repository coordinator software uses many rules to ensure integrity of the information in the repository.

The *repository* is a mechanism for defining, storing, and managing information about an enterprise, its data and systems.

The *repository coordinator* applies methods to the data in the repository to ensure that the data and their CASE representations have consistency and integrity.

- **Repository-Based Methodologies.** Efficient software development will increasingly be repository based. An ever-growing repository stores models, specifications, designs, and reusable constructs from which software is built. Methodologies for systems development now relate to building a comprehensive collection of knowledge in a repository, where the repository drives the generation of code. A growing collection of reusable constructs are stored in the repository.

A *repository-based methodology* is designed to take full advantage of an I-CASE toolset and to maximize reusability.

Particularly important are repository-based methodologies for high-speed development.

- **Information Engineering.** Information engineering applies repository-based development to an entire enterprise to integrate the planning, design, and construction of systems that need to interoperate across the enterprise. It creates a model of the enterprise and attempts to redesign the enterprise information systems to be as effective as possible.

(Continued)

BOX 1.1 *(Continued)*

> *Information engineering* applies integrated modeling and design techniques to the enterprise as a whole (or to a large section of the enterprise) rather than to merely one project.

- **Object-Oriented Databases.** An object-oriented database is an intelligent database. It supports the object-oriented paradigm, storing data and methods, rather than just data. It is designed to be physically efficient in storing complex objects. It can prevent access to the data except via the stored methods.

> An *object-oriented database* is designed to store object data and methods with techniques that are efficient for object-oriented processing.

A CASE repository should be an object-oriented database (even when the CASE tools do not support object-oriented analysis, design, or programming).

- **Nonprocedural Languages.** With procedural languages (such as COBOL and C) we instruct the computer as to the sequence of operations it must execute. With nonprocedural languages, we define the results that we require. An interpreter or compiler generates the code.

> *Nonprocedural languages* define what is wanted, rather than how it is programmed.

Many fourth-generation languages (such as Focus and Natural) contain both procedural and nonprocedural elements.

- **Inference Engine.** An inference engine operates with a collection of rules about an area of knowledge. It selects rules and effectively chains them together to perform inferential reasoning. It may use forward chaining (input-directed reasoning) or backward chaining (goal-directed reasoning) or both. It enables a computer to make complex deductions without an application program. It is the primary technique used in artificial intelligence software.

BOX 1.1 *(Continued)*

An *inference engine* is software that makes deductions from facts and rules by using techniques of logical inference.

- **Client-Server Technology.** The computer world increasingly requires software that runs on multiple computers, such as LAN-server systems, cooperative systems, distributed computing, and parallel computers. Client-server computing can be described as a software relationship as follows.

A *client* is a software module that requests an operation.
A *server* is a software module that responds to that request.

Clients and servers can run on separate machines arranged in almost any configuration.

- **Class Libraries.** A class library contains reusable implementation of object types. Its intent should be to achieve the maximum degree of reusability in software development. Class-library software should help developers find, adapt, and use the classes they need.

A *class* is a software implementation of an object type. A class can have many subclasses.

- **Object-Oriented Analysis and Design.** The object-oriented analyst views the world as objects with data structures and methods, and events that trigger operations that change the state of objects. Operations occur as objects make requests of other objects. The analyst creates diagrams of the object structures and events that change the objects. The designer's model is similar to the analyst's model, but is taken into enough detail to create code.

Object-oriented analysis and design attempt to achieve mass reusability of object classes.

Object-oriented analysis and design model the world in terms of objects that have properties and behavior, and events that trigger operations that change the state of the objects. Objects interact formally with other objects.

INTEGRATING THE KILLER TECHNOLOGIES

Any one of the killer technologies in Fig. 1.2 is powerful. However, a software industrial revolution will not come from one of those technologies alone but all of them integrated into an object-oriented framework.

Software, like machines, will be built from reusable components. Designers will not need to know the internal workings of the components. A designer of a video-cassette recorder would not design it transistor by transistor but out of high-level components. One chip may contain a hundred-thousand transistors. In a similar way, there should be high-level software components, some containing a hundred-thousand lines of code.

A video-cassette recorder (VCR) has many components that are themselves objects, with specific operations, communicated with by specific requests. A lower-level object type, such as a circuit board, may be used in many different VCR models. To assemble a VCR, a complex bill of materials is used. Similarly, software needs a bill of materials; it should be assembled from many types of objects.

Instead of thinking in terms of loops, program steps, and procedural code, software designers will think about objects and how the objects can be accessed and modified. Some objects will become highly complex, because they are built out of objects that are built out of objects, and so on. Repositories with vast numbers of object designs will become available. Designers will have tools for finding the necessary object types and reusing and extending their behavior as appropriate. Analysts will create diagrams of events, triggers, and operations that cause objects to behave in certain ways. Business people will learn to think in terms of events, triggers, and operations that change the state of objects. Databases will contain complex objects and allow them to be manipulated only with specifically defined operations. This will help prevent misuse of data or violations of integrity.

The *methods* that objects use should be created with powerful techniques, such as declarative statements, decision tables, diagrams, rule-based inferencing, nonprocedural languages, and CASE-tool code generators.

Client-server techniques will allow objects to interact with other objects in separate machines. Object-oriented design is the key to massively distributed computing.

TAKING THE BLINDERS OFF

Software developers often become deeply immersed in one technology. They have such interesting and difficult problems to solve with that technology that they do not have time to learn other software technologies. They are like horses going around with blinders on. We talk about COBOL bigots, information engineering bigots, LISP bigots, and so on. The bigots of one technology often pour scorn on the other technologies. What we need for a software industrial revolution is integration of killer technologies, not isolated bigots. This requires vision and education. We must constantly ask How do we educate the blindered specialists? Software developers need to be moved from one technology to another, so that they grasp the power of integrating technologies.

Many of the early CASE tools were built without an understanding of object-oriented technologies. Today, the combination of object-oriented techniques with I-CASE and repository-based development can clearly change the world of software development. Similarly, fourth-generation languages and non-procedural languages were built without an object-oriented viewpoint. These languages could be more powerful if redesigned for object-oriented development.

The inferencing tools of the artificial-intelligence community evolved from *rule-based* to *frame-based,* where a frame is, essentially, an object type and the methods used by the object type are those of rule processing.

The early client-server software was primarily built without object-oriented techniques. It is now clear that the best—and in the long run perhaps the only practical—way to organize client-server interaction is with object-oriented design. An object from the client software sends a request to an object from the server software, and the latter executes one or more methods and responds.

The CASE repository is vitally important for integrating the various tools. The repository itself is (or should be) an object-oriented database. Even tools that do not support object-oriented analysis and design employ an object-oriented repository. Such repositories will contain objects of ever-increasing complexity, as objects are built out of other objects, that in turn can be built of other objects.

The corporate I.S. (Information Systems) organization has a variety of tools and techniques available to obtain the advantages of OO analysis and development. Currently, none of the tools are perfect or fully integrated, but some spectacular examples exist of success with OO methodologies.

The object-oriented viewpoint is a major paradigm shift, requiring system developers to think about the world in a different way. Nevertheless, most of today's CASE tool diagrams can be adapted to OO use. The diagrams used should be a natural extension of what is already familiar.

The main obstacle is people—not tools. A major effort is needed to reeducate the I.S. professionals, so that they understand the advantages and employ the techniques. The move to OO, with its widespread reusability of code, must be made by management. Reaping the benefits of OO techniques requires management understanding and commitment.

ALL TYPES OF COMPUTING

Object-oriented techniques are sometimes thought of in terms of what can be done with OO programming languages, such as C++ and Smalltalk. This is too restricted a viewpoint. Methods can be created with *any* appropriate technique. Sometimes, procedural languages, such as C, COBOL, and FORTRAN, are used. At other times, nonprocedural languages, such as SQL and report generators, are appropriate. Functional languages, such as LISP, solve other problems. Methods may also be implemented with an inference engine and rule-based processing or the techniques of artificial intelligence and PROLOG. Methods may be diagrammed with either action diagrams or declarative techniques.

The object-oriented approach can encompass all of the other techniques for programming. In general, the most powerful techniques must be used, which usually means employing a CASE tool for analysis and design with an integrated code generator and perhaps an inference engine.

Object-oriented programming has substantially improved software development, but does not *by itself* bring the massive improvement needed by the computer industry. Object-oriented techniques must be combined with every aspect of software automation available.

OO techniques will change:

- the entire software industry
- the way application packages are sold
- the way we use computers
- the way we use networks
- the way we analyze systems
- the way we design systems
- the way we use CASE tools
- the way we re-engineer corporations
- the job of all I.S. professionals

THE INTEGRATING PARADIGM

The software industrial revolution will gain power as object-oriented techniques spread, and we have large libraries of object classes. The libraries will link to CASE repositories so that new classes can be quickly assembled from existing classes. Most software tools will shift to using the object-oriented paradigm.

While this software revolution gathers momentum, we will see parallel computers spreading—machines with not one but many processors. A desktop workstation should have many processor chips. A LAN (local area network) server should use parallel processing. Mainframes and supercomputers will eventually be highly parallel machines.

> The first four decades of computing was the evolution of single-processor machines.
>
> The second four decades of computing is the evolution of multiprocessor machines.

Object-oriented software will allow separate objects to run on separate processors simultaneously. Object-oriented design, with CASE tools and code generators, is the key to building software for powerful parallel machines.

Object-oriented analysis and design is a general way of viewing software that will integrate all of the killer technologies, as shown in Fig. 1.3. This integration will cause a software industrial revolution. As this is recognized, the software industry will build the tools and standards that facilitate the integration.

> Object-oriented modeling and design is an integrating paradigm that should tie together all powerful tools and techniques for software creation.

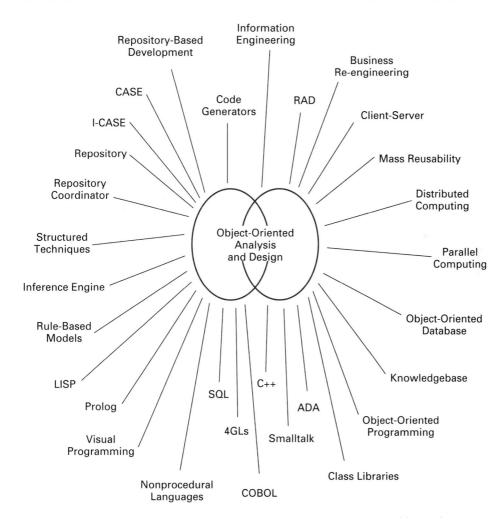

Figure 1.3   Object-oriented analysis and design should integrate and be used with the other powerful software technologies.

The sooner object-oriented analysis and design becomes widespread, the sooner software creation will progress from a cottage industry to an engineering discipline.

We need to build software as complex and trustworthy as jumbo jets or the worldwide telephone network and as rich as a legal library or an art-historian's archives. One day, software of vast complexity, flexibility, and richness will be delivered on gigabyte optical disks. This software should be developed with object-oriented analysis and design.

2 BASIC INTRODUCTION

The fundamental ideas that underlie object-oriented technology include:

- objects and classes (a class being the implementation of an object type)
- methods
- requests
- inheritance
- encapsulation

While these notions described in this chapter are the basis of object-oriented software, they are similar to notions that are the basis of all living creatures.

**WHAT IS
AN OBJECT?**
From a very early age, we form concepts. Each concept is a particular idea or understanding we have of our world. The concepts we acquire allow us to make sense of and reason about the things in our world. These things to which our concepts apply are called *objects*. An object might be real or abstract, such as the examples below:

- an invoice
- an organization
- a shape in a program for drawing (such as MacDraw)
- a screen with which a user interacts
- a field or node on the screen of a CASE tool
- a mechanism in a robotic device
- an entire engineering drawing

- a component on an engineering drawing
- a grouping of text and pictures used in a newspaper layout
- an airplane
- an airplane flight
- an airline reservation
- an icon on a screen that a user points to and "opens"
- an order-filling process
- the process of writing this line

In OO analysis and design, we are interested in the behavior of the object. If we are building software, OO software modules are based on object types. The software implementing the object contains data structures and operations that express the behavior of the object. The operations are coded as *methods*. The OO software representation of the object is thus a collection of *data types and methods*. In OO software:

> An *object* is any thing, real or abstract, about which we store data and those methods that manipulate the data.

An object may be composed of other objects. These objects, in turn, may be composed of objects—just as a machine is composed of subassemblies and its subassemblies composed of other subassemblies. This intricate structure of objects allows very complex objects to be defined.

WHAT IS AN OBJECT TYPE?   The concepts we possess apply to specific kinds of objects. For example, Employee applies to those objects who are persons employed by some organization. Instances of Employee could be Fred Collins, Margot Finkelstein, and so on. In object-oriented analysis, these concepts are called object types; their instances are called objects.

> An *object type* is a category of object.
>
> An *object* is an instance of an object type.

The database world defines *entity types,* such as Customer, Employee, and Part. There are many *instances* of each entity type. For example, *instances* of Employee are Fred Collins, Margot Finkelstein, and so on. Similarly, the object-oriented world defines *object types* and *instances* of object types. For example, an object type might be Invoice and an *object* might be Invoice #51783.

The term object, however, is fundamentally different from the term entity. *Entity* is concerned merely with the data. We typically store a record for each entity. *Object* is concerned with both the data and the methods with which the data is manipulated. In the OO world, the data structure and methods for each object type are packaged together. The data structure cannot be accessed or manipulated except with the methods that are part of the object type.

METHODS

Methods specify the way in which an object's data are manipulated. The methods in an object type reference *only* the data structures of that object type. They should not directly access the data structures of another object. To use the data structure of another object, they must send a message to that object. The object type packages together the data types and methods.

An object is thus a *thing* with its properties represented by data types and its behavior represented by methods.

A method associated with the object type Invoice might be one that computes the total of an invoice. Another might transmit the invoice to a customer. Another might check periodically to see whether the invoice has been paid and add interest to it if it has not.

ENCAPSULATION

Packaging data and methods together is called *encapsulation.* The object hides its data from other objects and allows the data to be accessed via its own methods. This is called *information hiding.* Encapsulation protects an object's data from corruption. If all programs could access the data in any way users wished, the data could easily be corrupted or misused. Encapsulation protects the object's data from arbitrary and unintended use.

Encapsulation hides the details of its internal implementation from the users of an object. Users understand what operations may be requested of the object but do not know the details of how the operation is performed. All the specifics of the object's data and the coding of its operations are tucked out of sight.

> *Encapsulation* is the result (or act) of hiding the implementation details of an object from its user.

Encapsulation is important, because it separates how an object behaves from how it is implemented. This allows object implementations to be modified without requiring the applications that use them to be modified also.

It is easier to modify programs using encapsulation, because one object type is modified at a time. If an object type is changed, only the methods and data structures associated with that object type are affected and usually only *some* of those methods and data structures. The object type's behavior can be changed and tested, independent of other object types.

Figure 2.1 illustrates an object. The data structure at the center can be used only with the methods in the outer ring.

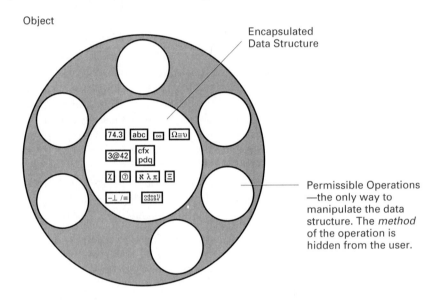

Object

Encapsulated
Data Structure

Permissible Operations
—the only way to
manipulate the data
structure. The *method*
of the operation is
hidden from the user.

Figure 2.1   Each object encapsulates a data structure and methods. A *data structure* is at the core of an object. The object is manipulated by *methods* that implement permitted operations. The data structure may be used *only* with the methods. This restriction of access is called *encapsulation*. Encapsulation protects the data from corruption.

A VCR (video cassette recorder) is an example of an object. It has certain specified types of behavior. A Sony **AH-8500 VCR** is an *object type,* and an individual machine might be an *instance of this type.* All machines of that type have the same *methods.* The VCR contains many complex components most of which themselves contain components, but you do not need to know about them.

The electronics or its data cannot be accessed directly. (It states: CAUTION. DO NOT OPEN, RISK OF ELECTRIC SHOCK.) You can use only the specified methods. Encapsulation prevents interference with the internals and also hides the complexity of the components. You are concerned only with the behavior of the VCR as described in its manual.

This object type has many methods, such as playback, recording, loading and unloading a cassette, setting the timer, audio dubbing, and tape counter functions. The data in the object cannot be used except with these methods. Telephone messages cannot be recorded on the VCR or its timer used to work the coffee machine.

MESSAGES

To make an object do something, we send it a *request*. This request causes an operation to be invoked. The operation performs the appropriate method and, optionally, returns a response. The message that constitutes the request contains the name of the object, the name of an operation, and sometimes a group of parameters.

Object-oriented programming is a form of modular design in which the world is often thought of in terms of objects, operations, methods, and messages passed among those objects as illustrated in Fig. 2.2. A message is a *request* to carry out the indicated *operation* on a given object and return the result. Consequently, OO implementations refer to messages as requests.

> A *request* asks that a specified operation be invoked using one or more objects as parameters.

Objects can be very complex, because objects can contain many subobjects, these in turn contain subobjects, and so on. Someone using the object does not need to know its internal complexity, only how to communicate with it and how it responds.

For example, you may communicate with your VCR by sending it *requests* from a hand-held controller. It responds by taking some action and displaying responses on its display. All objects of the type Sony AH-8500 VCR are controlled using the same kind of *interface*. The requests from your hand-held controller will not communicate with a JVC HR-S6600 VCR, because it requires a different type of interface.

A user of an office tool can mouse-click on the icon that represents an address-book object. The object responds by displaying a scrollable list of names on the screen. The user can employ different operations for interacting with this list—scrolling to a portion of the list and pointing to a particular person's name. The software then highlights the name. At this point, the user may request the person's address, add information, or drag the name across the screen to a telephone icon, thereby requesting the software to look up the phone number and dial it.

When object X sends a request to object Y, an operation of object X invokes an operation of object Y resulting in the data of object Y being manipulated in some way. Object Y may then return a value to object X.

For example, consider an instance of the object type Cylinder. We can send a request to obtain the height of a Cylinder object. The height operation returns its stored height value. Additionally, we can send a request to obtain the Cylinder

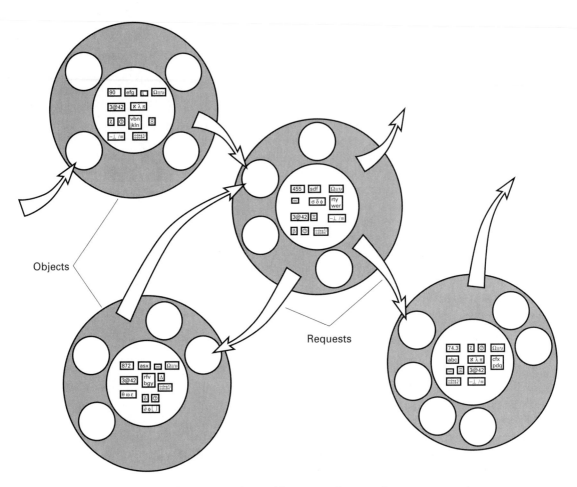

Figure 2.2   Objects communicate with requests. A *request* is a message specifying that an indicated operation be carried out using one or more objects—
and, optionally, returning a result.

object's volume. The volume operation uses the following method to compute
and return the object's **volume** value:

PI * CYLINDER.RADIUS**2 * CYLINDER.HEIGHT.

A request to a **Portfolio** object might be for its current valuation, and an
operation for accomplishing this computation is invoked.

A request to a robot vehicle might be:

VEHICLE71 MOVE TO BIN 17.

Here the object is Vehicle 71, the operation is Move To, and the parameter for that method is Bin 17.

Some of the newer OO implementations paraphrase this request in a different manner:

MOVE TO (VEHICLE71, BIN 17).

In this way, a request is not a message restricted *to* one recipient object but *for* multiple objects. Therefore, the user is not required to know which object is the recipient and which are the supporting parameters.

BLOBs

Today's computers can store large strings of bits that represent images, diagrams, speech, or possibly music or video. These are objects referred to with the acronym BLOB (Binary Large OBject). BLOBs have methods which enable them to be displayed or used. Compaction techniques are used, for example, so that images or sound can be stored in a smaller number of bits. The BLOB may have methods that enable it to be displayed on different screens. It may have methods for security, such as enciphering and deciphering. In image processing, images may be scanned quickly with low resolution, slowly with moderate resolution, and then displayed with top resolution.

The growing acceptance of image processing will increase the importance of object-oriented databases that can handle large binary objects efficiently. We will send requests to BLOBs telling them to display themselves, encipher themselves, link together for editing, and so on. In an OO database, an Invoice could be maintained in a handwritten graphic form along with the customer's spoken instructions—as well as an alphanumeric record. The handwritten graphic image is one object; the spoken instructions is another object; the alphanumeric record yet another. Together, they can compose a single Invoice object.

WHAT IS A CLASS?

The term *class* refers to the software implementation of an object type.

Object type is a conceptual notion. It specifies a family of objects without stipulating *how* the type and object are implemented. Object types are specified during OO analysis. However, when implementing object types, other terms are used.

In the Modula programming language, object types are implemented as *modules,* while Ada uses the word *package.* In object-oriented languages, object types are implemented as *classes.*

A *class* is an implementation of an object type. It specifies a data structure and the permissible operational methods that apply to each of its objects.

The class implementation specifies the data structure for each of its objects (see Fig. 2.1). For example, an Employee class would include data about exemptions, position, salary, phone extension, and so on. In addition, each class defines a set of permissible operations that allow access to and modification of object data. An Employee class could include operations such as hire, promote, and change phone extension for an Employee class. Details of the *method* of operation are specified by the class.

Figure 2.1 draws an object as though the method were part of an object. In reality, the method is stored once, and all objects of a given class share it.

The industry uses the term *class* to refer to the implementations of object types. It refers to *class libraries* as repositories of existing classes which might be employed by an analyst or designer.

INHERITANCE

A high-level object type can be specialized into lower-level object types. An object type can have subtypes. For example, the object type Person may have subtypes Civilian and Military Person. Military Person may have subtypes Officer and Enlisted Person. Officer may have subtypes Lieutenant, Captain, and Major and also subtypes such as Marine or Engineer, and Officer-on-Active-Service or Officer-on-nonActive-Service. There is a hierarchy of object types, subtypes, sub-subtypes, and so on.

A class implements the object type. A subclass *inherits* properties of its parent class; a sub-subclass inherits properties of the subclasses, and so on. A subclass may *inherit* the data structure and methods, or some of the methods, of its superclass. It also has methods and sometimes data types of its own.

Figure 2.3 shows a class and subclass. The subclass has the same methods as its superclass but also has method G. Sometimes, a class inherits properties of more than one superclass. This is called *multiple inheritance*.

PERCEPTION AND REALITY

With software we play games with reality. We can make something appear to have a certain behavior when in reality it is different. We can create a simple interface to something complex and hide the complexity.

The term *transparent* is used to mean that something appears not to exist when, in fact, it does. Many of the complex mechanisms in data storage or transmission are hidden from the programmers, so that programmers do not have to understand or even know about them. Programmers can use a *logical* record, for example, in which some fields may be hidden, and the complexities of the physical structure are hidden.

Conversely, when the word *virtual* is used to refer to computer data storage facilities, it indicates that a specified item *appears* to exist to the programmer or

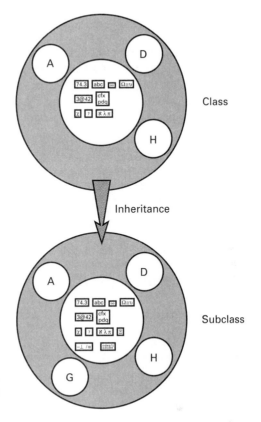

Figure 2.3 A class can have its own data structure and methods—as well as inherit them from its superclass.

user when, in reality, it does not exist in that form. We talk about virtual storage and virtual circuits.

> Something *virtual* appears to exist but in reality does not.
>
> Something *transparent* appears not to exist when in reality it does.

In OO implementations, an object is perceived as being a package of data and procedures that can be performed on these data. It *encapsulates* the data and procedures. Reality is different. The procedures are not stored in each object. This would be very wasteful, because the same procedure would have to be stored many times. Instead, the software examines each request that refers to an object and has a selection mechanism for finding the code to execute. The *method* is part of the *class*—not part of the *object*. The method may not even be part of the class; it may be part of a higher-level class in the class hierarchy. The software can find it.

Figure 2.4 illustrates the difference between how we perceive objects and how the software actually operates. Only by using transparent and virtual mechanisms can we succeed in building structures of the complexity we need.

Objects may communicate with objects: existing in one software package or in different packages; located in a processor or multiple processors; or scattered across a worldwide network (see Fig. 2.5). Programmers need not know the object's location. They merely send a request to the object and receive a response.

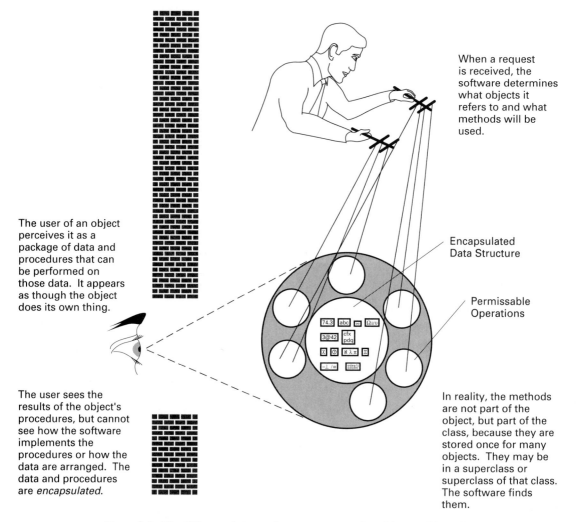

When a request is received, the software determines what objects it refers to and what methods will be used.

The user of an object perceives it as a package of data and procedures that can be performed on those data. It appears as though the object does its own thing.

Encapsulated Data Structure

Permissable Operations

The user sees the results of the object's procedures, but cannot see how the software implements the procedures or how the data are arranged. The data and procedures are *encapsulated*.

In reality, the methods are not part of the object, but part of the class, because they are stored once for many objects. They may be in a superclass or superclass of that class. The software finds them.

Figure 2.4   The difference between how we may perceive objects and how the software operates.

We perceive object-
oriented software as
consisting of objects
receiving requests and
sending responses.
The request specifies
what objects are to
carry out what operations.

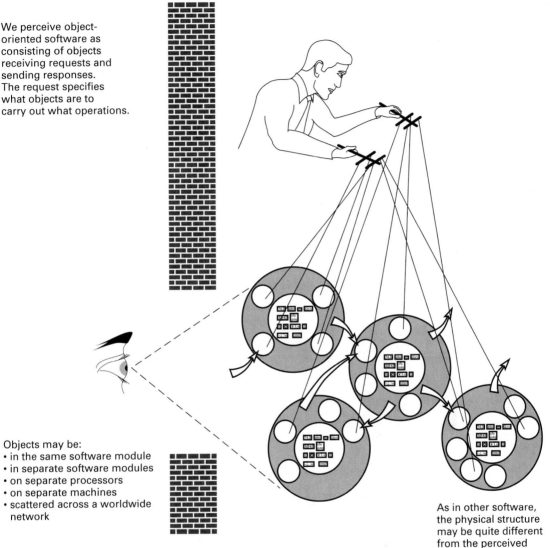

Objects may be:
• in the same software module
• in separate software modules
• on separate processors
• on separate machines
• scattered across a worldwide
  network

As in other software,
the physical structure
may be quite different
from the perceived
structure.

Figure 2.5   We often perceive that objects communicate. In reality, the OO software's selection mechanism handles requests for operations on specific objects.

**SELF-CONTAINED
CREATURES**

Some academics insist that we should avoid anthropomorphic analogies for describing software.
Software, after all, has no resemblance to biological
things. Dijkstra recommends that faculty members be fined $5 each time they use

anthropomorphic terminology [2]. However, teaching without analogy is as sterile as making films without editing. Analogies based on nature can help beginners to grasp a strange-sounding subject. So here is an analogy that could give Dijkstra a heart attack.

Think of an object as a little creature that has only one purpose in life; to apply certain methods to a specified collection of data. The creature protects its data with a vengeance, not allowing anyone to access the data except with the creature's methods.

The creature only goes into action when it receives a correctly formatted message. The message tells it what operation to use and may specify parameters. The creature performs its function and sends a message back. In a complex system, many different creatures are all doing their own thing.

There are many different types of creatures. Several different types of creatures all share the properties of a higher-level type. There are subtle variations of types just as there are in a taxonomy of plants.

Some creatures work in the same computer, waiting their turn to be active. Some work in network systems where a server creature can operate at the same time as client creatures in different machines. We are beginning to use parallel (concurrent) computers in which many creatures can be active on different processors simultaneously.

If we have vast numbers of these creatures, how do we organize them? In society, we have vast numbers of humans, and we devise ways of organizing them so that society can function—some are factory workers, some are decision makers, some are executives, and some are police. Just as we put humans into departments, so we can arrange our creatures into groups in which a collection of creatures together carry out a particular function. The group is a high-level class. Other creatures interact with this class as a whole, sending it messages and receiving messages. An enterprise has many departments. People outside of the enterprise do not know how it is structured; they request the enterprise as a whole to do something. The enterprise is complex, but outsiders can interact with it by using its catalog, placing orders, and so on.

Creatures are organized into groups, and groups are organized into entire applications. Each creature is self-contained. It executes its methods when asked without knowing why and without knowing the consequences.

As we design distributed computing, we ask: What creatures and groupings of creatures should work on what machine? When one object sends messages to another object, it does not know where that object is. It could be on the same machine or a different machine. We should usually not split a low-level object, so that its methods and data are on different machines. A high-level object may be composed of objects that *are* on different machines.

NATURE'S BUILDING BLOCKS   David Taylor points out that object-oriented design reflects the techniques of nature [3]. All living things are composed of cells. Cells are organized packages that—just as objects—combine related information and behavior. Information is contained in the DNA and protein molecules within the nucleus of the cell. The methods of the cell are carried out by structures outside the nucleus.

The cell is surrounded by a membrane that both protects and hides the internal workings of the cell from outside intrusion. Cells cannot read *each other's* protein molecules or control *each other's* structures; they can only read and control their own. Instead, they send chemical requests to one another. By packaging the information and behavior in this way, the cell is encapsulated.

Taylor comments: "This message-based communication greatly simplifies the way cells function . . . . The membrane hides the complexity of the cell and presents a relatively simple interface to the rest of the organism . . . . As you can see from the structure of the cell, *encapsulation* is an idea that's been around for a very long time."

Cells are a remarkably universal building block in nature. There are blood cells that transport chemicals, bone cells, brain cells, cells that make the eye retina work, and muscle cells that distort their shape to perform mechanical functions. The components of plants, insects, fish, and mammals are all built of cells that have a common structure and operate according to certain basic principles. All software could, in principle, be similarly built out of classes. Although cells are enormously diverse, many cells, like objects, are of similar types. One type of cell may operate in a way similar to another type, because both have inherited similar properties in evolution. Cells are grouped together into organs, such as muscles or toenails. Organs are grouped together into systems, such as the cardiovascular system.

An organism is composed of multiple systems. Although part of a complex organism, each cell acts on its own, like an object, without knowing the reason why a message was sent to it or the eventual consequences of its behavior.

The computerized enterprise is like an electronic organism. It will increasingly need complex software composed of vast numbers of objects. We need to analyze complex application areas in terms of the objects they employ and the behavior of object types.

In analyzing an enterprise, we create an *enterprise model.* At a high level, this model reflects the individual business areas. If the enterprise model is built with an object-oriented viewpoint, we ask what its object types are and specialize them into subtypes, sub-subtypes, and so on. Business rules are associated with the object types, expressing how we want the enterprise to behave.

The object types can be implemented as *classes.* Lower-level classes *inherit* behavior from higher-level classes. The classes *encapsulate* behavior, rather like biological cells encapsulating behavior. The electronic enterprise has many different encapsulated classes, linked with enterprisewide networks like a creature's nervous system.

We thus progress from a model of the enterprise with object types to a working software implementation of those object types. The classes representing object types are *active* and automatically execute their methods when requests are sent to them. Higher-level classes are composed of lower-level classes, just as the liver is composed of cells.

The world of the future will consist of many of these electronic organisms, each with its nervous system linking thousands of computers with object-oriented databases and software that make objects respond to requests. The nervous system of one enterprise will interact directly with the nervous systems of many other enterprises with EDI (electronic data interchange) systems. EDI systems are evolving from batch interaction to real-time interaction.

Two trading partners both profit from real-time EDI interaction, so financial incentives will drive the rapid interlinking of corporate computer systems. The nervous systems are becoming worldwide, high-bandwidth, and intermeshed with one another.

In one way, objects are different from the creatures we describe or biological cells. They do not *each* contain their methods; the methods are kept centrally. There would be mass redundancy if each object contains its own methods, as cells do. The methods for the object are part of the *class*. We might regard the object as something we perceive—a virtual thing that packages data and methods. The actual implementation is different, because it avoids redundant storage of methods. In this way, we can think of objects as packages of behavior, like biological cells.

Such analogies break down when pushed too far. In Part II of the book, we need to become more precise in defining object-oriented techniques. However, this somewhat cartoon-like description of object-oriented software enables us to discuss, in the next chapter, how its benefits will revolutionize the way we build systems.

REFERENCES

1. Cox, Brad J. and Andrew J. Novobilski, *Object-Oriented Programming: An Evolutionary Approach,* (2nd edition), Addison-Wesley, Reading, MA, 1991.

2. Dijkstra, Edsger W., "On the Cruelty of Really Teaching Computing Science," *Communications of the ACM,* 32:12, December 1989, pp. 1398-1404.

3. Taylor, David A., *Object-Oriented Technology: A Manager's Guide,* Addison-Wesley, Reading, MA, 1991.

3 WHY OBJECT-ORIENTED?

Object-oriented techniques improve the skill of the computer professional in surprisingly diverse ways.

Recently, Martin conducted in-depth interviews on videotape with analysts and implementors who had become proficient with OO tools and techniques [1]. He asked all of them "Why object-oriented?" "Why would you not consider going back to conventional techniques?" "Why should an enterprise go through the difficulties of changing to OO analysis and design?" Different professionals quoted completely different types of reasons why OO techniques made them more proficient. On the other hand, none of these professionals were achieving *all* of the major benefits. What made Mike so excited by object orientation had not been considered by Mary. What Chris said was the payoff was not on the wishlist of Karen.

It is desirable to understand *all* of the potential benefits of OO techniques and attempt to achieve them *all* rather than just a subset. Driving for the entire family of benefits in this chapter is likely to change the way we manage development teams and I.S. organizations.

TRUE ENGINEERING OF SOFTWARE The state of the art of most software engineering is way behind that of other areas of engineering. When most engineers complete their work and it is sold, we expect that it will work correctly. We do not expect jet engines to explode or buildings to collapse, but we are not too surprised if software does something weird. Most hardware products come with a warranty; most software products carry a *disclaimer* of warranty.

Software is sold, not when it is bug-free, but when bugs occur with suitably low frequency. When my spreadsheet tool goes berserk, I reflect that it has only 400,000 lines of code. Soon, we will use software with 50 million lines of code. Furthermore, my spreadsheet tool runs on a simple PC; we are now building software to run on parallel processors and networks with many computers running simultaneously. My spreadsheet has millions of users and has been tested endlessly. Compare that with the next generation of air traffic control software coming into use for the overcrowded skies. (Just don't think about it when you fly.)

When people are first taught to program, their teacher usually tells them to think like a computer. This technique seemed to work when we learned programming, because we wrote very simple programs. However, loops and branches give us such a vast number of combinations of paths, that we cannot think like a computer about all of them. The operation of most real software depends on conditions that are not known until the software is running. With multiprocessing the machinery is doing many things at once, and then it becomes hopeless to think like a computer.

To help deal with the complexities, structured programming came into use. It reduced the spaghetti in code, but programming was still based on the expected sequence of executing instructions. The attempt to design and debug programs by thinking through the order in which the computer does things ultimately leads to software that nobody can fully understand. Thinking like a computer is well beyond our mental capabilities.

The world of object-oriented techniques carried out with repository-based CASE tools is different. The designer thinks in terms of objects and their behavior, and code is generated. The CASE tools and code generator must be bug-free, so we have not eliminated manual programming. However, most systems can be built without having to think about loops, branches, and program control structures. The system builder learns a different style of thinking. Events cause changes in the state of objects (as we will discuss later). Most of these state changes require *small* pieces of code, so coding is less error prone. Object types are built out of simpler object types. Once the object types work well, the designer treats them as a black box which he never looks inside. (Just as you never look inside your VCR.) Software engineering then assumes more of the characteristics of hardware engineering.

Christopher Hoare, the Professor of Computing at Oxford University, comments on traditional structured design [2]:

> The attempt to build a discipline of software engineering on such shoddy foundations must surely be doomed, like trying to base chemical engineering on phlogiston theory, or astronomy on the assumption of a flat earth.

In conventional programming, data can assume any structure and processes can do anything to the data that the programmer desires. In the object-oriented world, data structures relate to objects and can be used *only* with the methods designed for that type of object.

Process orientation is eloquently described by Dan Ingalls of Smalltalk fame as responsible for "bit-grinding processors raping and plundering data structures." For him, object orientation provides a solution that leads to "a universe of well-behaved objects that courteously ask each other to carry out their various desires" [3].

The contrast between process and object orientation can be summarized in the following way. Conventional data processing focuses on the types of processes that manipulate types of data. Object orientation focuses on the types of objects whose data structure can be manipulated only with the methods of the object class. Events occur that change the state of an object. Each state change is usually simple to program by itself, so we divide programming into relatively simple pieces. Each object, in effect, performs a specific function independently of other objects. It responds to messages, not knowing why the message was sent or what the consequences of its action will be. Because objects act individually, each class can be changed largely independent of other classes. This makes the class relatively easy to test and modify. Maintenance of object-oriented systems is much easier than maintenance of conventional systems.

The object-oriented world is more disciplined than that of conventional structured techniques. It leads to a world of reusable classes, where much of the software construction process will be the assembly of existing well-proven classes.

OO techniques linked to CASE tools with a code generator and a repository that is itself object-oriented constitute the best way we know to build true software engineering.

CHARACTERISTICS OF OO TECHNIQUES

OO analysis and design have several important characteristics:

1. They change the way we think about systems. The OO way of thinking is more natural for most people than the techniques of structured analysis and design. After all, the world consists of objects. We start to learn about them in infancy and discover that they have certain types of behavior. If you shake a rattle, it makes noise. From an early age we categorize objects as we discover their behavior. End users and business people think naturally in terms of objects, events, and triggers. We can create OO diagrams that they can relate to, whereas they have difficulty with entity-relationship diagrams, structure charts, and data-flow diagrams.

2. Systems can often be built out of existing objects. This leads to a high degree of reusability, which saves money, shortens development time, and increases system reliability.

3. The complexity of the objects we can use continues to grow, because objects are built out of other objects. These in turn are built from objects, and so on.

4. The CASE repository should contain an ever-growing library of object types, some purchased and some built in-house. These object types are likely to become powerful as they grow in complexity. Most such object types will be designed, so that they can be customized to the needs of different systems.

5. Creating systems that work correctly is easier with OO techniques. This is partly because of OO classes that are designed to be reused, and partly because classes are

self-contained and neatly divided into methods. Each method is relatively easy to build, debug, and modify.

6. OO techniques have a natural fit with CASE technology. Some elegant and powerful tools exist for OO implementation. Many other CASE tools need enhancing to support OO analysis and design.

SUMMARY OF THE BENEFITS OF OO TECHNOLOGY   Box 3.1 summarizes the many benefits of OO analysis and design.

BOX 3.1   Benefits of Object-Oriented Technology

Many of these benefits are realizable only when OO analysis and design are used with repository-based OO-CASE tools that generate code.

- **Reusability.** Classes are designed so that they can be reused in many systems. To maximize reuse, classes can be built so that they can be customized. A repository should be populated with an ever-growing collection of reusable classes. Class libraries are likely to grow rapidly. A preeminent goal of OO techniques is achieving massive reusability in the building of software.

- **Stability.** Classes designed for repeated reuse become stable in the same way that microprocessors and other chips become stable. Applications are built from software chips where possible.

- **The designer thinks in terms of behavior of objects not low-level detail.** Encapsulation hides the detail and makes complex classes easy to use. Classes are like black boxes; the developer uses the black box and does not look inside it. He has to understand the behavior of the black box and how to communicate with it.

- **Classes of ever-growing complexity are built.** Classes are built out of classes, which in turn are built out of classes. Just as manufactured goods are constructed from a bill of materials of existing parts and subassemblies, so too is software created with a bill of materials of existing well-proven classes. This enables complex software components to be built which themselves become building blocks for more complex software.

- **Reliability.** Software built from well-proven stable classes is likely to have fewer bugs than software invented from scratch.

BOX 3.1 *(Continued)*

- **New software markets.** Software companies should provide libraries of classes for specific areas, easily adapted to the needs of the using organization. The era of monolithic packages is being replaced by software that incorporates classes and encapsulated packages from many different vendors.

- **Faster design.** Applications are created from preexisting components. Many components are built so that they can be customized for a particular design. The components can be seen, customized, and interlinked on the CASE tools screen.

- **Higher-quality design.** Designs are often of higher quality because they are built from well-proven components which have been tested and polished repeatedly.

- **Integrity.** Data structures can be used only with specific methods. This is particularly important with client-server and distributed systems in which unknown users might try to access a system.

- **Easier programming.** Programs are built in small pieces each of which is generally easy to create. The programmer creates one method for one class at a time. The method changes the state of objects in ways which are usually simple when considered by themselves.

- **Easier maintenance.** The maintenance programmer usually changes one method of one class at a time. Each class performs its operations independently of other classes.

- **Inventability.** Implementors proficient with the most powerful OO-CASE tools, running on a workstation, find they can generate ideas rapidly. The tools encourage them to invent and rapidly implement their inventions. The brilliant individual can be much more creative.

- **Dynamic lifecycle.** The target of system development often changes during implementation. OO-CASE tools make midlifecycle changes easier. This enables implementors to meet end users better, adapt to changes in the business, refine goals as the system comes into sharper focus, and constantly improve the design during implementation.

- **Refinement during construction.** Creative people such as writers and playwrights constantly change the design of their work while implementing it. This leads to much better end results. The best creative works are refined over and over again. OO-CASE tools give software builders the capability to refine the design as they implement it.

(Continued)

BOX 3.1 *(Continued)*

- **More realistic modeling.** OO analysis models the enterprise or application area in a way that is closer to reality than conventional analysis. The analysis translates directly into design and implementation. In conventional techniques, the paradigm changes as we go from analysis to design and from design to programming. With OO techniques, analysis, design, and implementation use the same paradigm and successively refine it.

- **Better communication between I.S. professionals and business people.** Business people more easily understand the OO paradigm. They think in terms of events, objects, and business policies that describe the behavior of objects. OO methodologies encourage better understanding as the end users and developers share a common model.

- **Intelligent enterprise models.** Enterprise models should describe business rules with which executives want to run their business. These should be expressed in terms of events and how events change the state of business objects. Application designs should be derived with as much automation as possible from the business model.

- **Declarative specifications and design.** The specifications and design, built with the formality of CASE tools, should be declarative, where possible—stating explicitly what is needed. This enables the designer to think like an end user rather than to think like a computer.

- **A user-seductive screen interface.** A graphic user interface, such as the Macintosh, should be used so that the user points at icons or pop-on menu items that relate to objects. Sometimes, the user can, in effect, see an object on the screen. To see and point is easier than to remember and type.

- **Images, video and speech.** Binary large objects (BLOBs) are stored, representing images, video, speech, unformatted text, or other long bit streams. Methods such as compression or decompression, enciphering or deciphering, and presentation techniques are used with the object.

- **Design independence.** Classes are designed to be independent of platforms, hardware, and software environments. They employ requests and responses of standard formats. This enables them to be used with multiple operating systems, database managers, network managers, graphic user interfaces, and so on. The software developer does not have to worry about the environment or wait until it is specified.

- **Interoperability.** Software from many different vendors can work together. One vendor uses classes from other vendors. A standard way exists of finding classes and interacting with classes. (The standards from the Object Management Group are discussed in Chapter 12.) Interoperability of software from many vendors is one of the most important goals of OO

BOX 3.1 *(Continued)*

standards. Software developed independently in separate places should be able to work together and appear as a single unit to the user.

- **Client-server computing.** In client-server systems, classes in the client software should send requests to classes in the server software and receive responses. A server class may be used by many different clients. These clients can only access server data with the class methods. Hence, the data is protected from corruption.

- **Massively distributed computing.** Worldwide networks will employ software directories of accessible objects. Object-oriented design is the key to massively distributed computing. Classes in one machine will interact with classes elsewhere without knowing where the classes reside. They send and receive OO messages of standard format.

- **Parallel computing.** The speed of machines will be greatly enhanced by building parallel computers. Concurrent processing will take place on multiple processor chips simultaneously. (Eventually one chip will have many processors.) Objects on different processors will execute simultaneously, each acting independently. A standard Object Request Broker will enable classes on separate processors to send requests to one another.

- **A higher level of database automation.** The data structures in OO databases are linked to methods that take automatic actions. An OO database has *intelligence* built into it, in the form of methods, whereas a basic relational database does not.

- **Machine performance.** Object-oriented databases have demonstrated much higher performance than relational databases for certain applications with very complex data structures. This and concurrent computing with OO design jointly promise major leaps in machine performance. LAN-based client-server systems will employ server machines with concurrency and object-oriented databases.

- **Migration.** Existing or non-OO applications can often be preserved by fitting them with an OO wrapper, so that communication with them is by standard OO messages.

- **Better CASE tools.** CASE tools will use graphic techniques for designing classes and their interaction and for using existing objects adapted to new applications. The tools should facilitate modeling in terms of events, triggers, object states, and so on. OO-CASE tools should generate code as soon as classes are defined and allow the designer to use and test the methods created. The tools should be designed to encourage maximum creativity and continuous refinement of the design during construction.

(Continued)

BOX 3.1   *(Continued)*

- **Industry class libraries.** Software companies sell libraries for different application areas. Application-independent class libraries are also important and these are best provided as a facility of CASE tools.

- **Corporate class libraries.** Corporations should create their own libraries of classes that reflect their internal standards and application needs. The top-down identification of business objects is an important aspect of information engineering.

PROGRAM COMPLEXITY METRICS

Program complexity is a measure of program understandability. The more complex a program, the more difficult it is to understand. Program complexity is a function of the number of possible execution paths in a program and the difficulty of tracing paths. Avoiding excessive program complexity will improve program reliability and reduce the effort needed to develop and maintain a program.

The McCabe Cyclomatic Complexity Metric, named after its creator, is the most widely used measurement of complexity. It has measured programs written in languages such as FORTRAN, COBOL, PL/1, C, and Pascal. It has been automated by many re-engineering and CASE tools. Cyclomatic complexity is a graph-theoretic complexity measure that is based on counting the number of individual logic paths contained in the program. For example, the small program shown in Fig. 3.1 has three possible logic paths depending on the IF-statement conditions.

Program analyzers that automatically measure the McCabe number reveal that many programs have a McCabe metric of 15. McCabe recommends that the number should not exceed 10. He found that modules, and indeed programs containing modules, whose cyclomatic complexity was greater than 10 were generally more troublesome and less reliable.

A study was conducted during the development of the AEGIS Naval Weapon System, which was composed of 276 modules with approximately half the modules at a complexity level above the threshold of 10. Those modules having a complexity above the recommended level had an error rate of 5.6 errors per 100 source statements. In contrast, those below 10 had an error rate of only 4.6 [7]. The error count increased significantly at the complexity level of 11.

OO design and programming give much lower McCabe metrics and, hence, make software much easier to debug and maintain. For example, the develop-

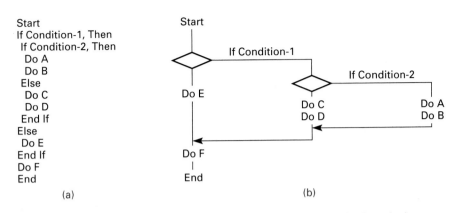

```
Start
  If Condition-1, Then
    If Condition-2, Then
      Do A
      Do B
    Else
      Do C
      Do D
    End If
  Else
    Do E
  End If
  Do F
End
```

        (a)   (b)

Figure 3.1   This simple program has a McCabe Cyclomatic Complexity Metric of 3, because there are 3 possible paths through the program. OO programming lowers the McCabe Cyclomatic Complexity Metric from figures typically in the range of 10 to 15, to an average of about 3.

ment of the COOPERATION software in NCR was a massive project done with OO techniques. The techniques resulted in a McCabe metric of 3 [1]. On previous non-OO software projects, NCR had a McCabe metric averaging above 10. The reason for the dramatically lower number is that each *method* is relatively simple and self-contained. Other software organizations also report a McCabe metric of around 3 with OO techniques.

REUSABILITY

Several organizations have reported a level of reusability above 80 percent, using OO design and programming (i.e., less than 20 percent of the system code is new; the rest comes from reusable classes). The COOPERATION project in NCR attempted to push this number from 80 percent to 90 percent [1]. With careful management of the class library and good motivation by the developers with design reviews for reusability 80 percent seems generally achievable. An overhead is required to achieve this level of reuse, but it results in faster, cheaper development and higher software quality.

Reusability is a management act. A development environment should be designed and tightly managed to achieve high reusability [6].

DIFFERENT BENEFITS

The benefits listed in Box 3.1 affect different types of developers in different ways. Let us examine the benefits as they might be perceived by five different types of I.S. professionals:

- A highly creative software inventor
- A software factory
- The corporate CIO
- An I.S. project team
- A systems integrator

A Highly Creative Software Inventor

Consider a brilliant, highly innovative, software builder. This person works alone at a powerful workstation using software creatively to solve problems. This individual would like a powerful toolset to help invent and generate code quickly. With an OO toolset this inventor can create object classes, add behavior, generate code immediately, and observe the application running. The application invention is constantly being modified. Object-oriented representation helps clarify the system being invented and makes it easy to modify or add.

If a professional programmer, the inventor might write code in C++ or Smalltalk. However, the most interesting software inventors should be people whose expertise lies in the application area rather than in professional programming. They do not want to code in C, C++, or languages of that detail. They want to create methods quickly with powerful techniques using pictures, tables, declarative statements, rules, and nonprocedural techniques. The code is created interpretively by the toolset as they add details to their application. Later, it is compiled for maximum speed. They want a rich set of classes that they can easily find and use, and customize, when necessary. Some classes are application independent and many relate to the application area.

> The software inventor would like the OO-CASE toolset to generate code as fast as he can put ideas on the screen.

A Software Factory

A software factory is different from the lone inventor. The software factory requires teamwork and discipline. All the developers should share common I-CASE tools with a common repository. A powerful repository coordinator must enforce consistency with careful version control (see Chapter 11). The repository and its coordinator should be an object-oriented database.

The software factory needs to maximize reusability. It manages a library of reusable classes. Some developers create new classes, and they are measured on the reuse of what they build. Some developers employ classes, and they are measured on how they will reuse what exists. The software factory strives to make its reusable classes as stable as possible, so that bugs are rare and maintenance costs are minimized.

> To create rich and interesting products, the software factory needs to incorporate much software from other vendors into its designs.

The era of monolithic single-vendor software is coming to an end. Software builders should make use of existing software, where possible, standing on the shoulders of others. They would like this licensed software to be object-oriented and to obey standards (see Chapter 12). Standard requests and responses should be used for communication with classes.

The software factory should steadily increase the functionality of the classes it uses—building objects out of component objects. Stable classes of ever greater complexity are desirable and are built using both in-house components and those licensed from other companies. The software should be built independently of the environment—the operating system, LAN management, database management, user interface, and so on. It should be linkable to multiple environments by means of standard class requests and responses.

The Corporate CIO (Chief Information Officer)

The CIO's major concern is making the corporation more competitive by identifying ways to streamline and automate the corporation, cut costs, and improve customer service. Business windows of opportunity are shortening, and the CIO needs an environment in which new applications can be built and changed quickly.

The CIO uses information engineering to maintain a model of the enterprise [4]. Preferably, this would be an OO model that reflects the rules used to respond to events. The business area models are in an I-CASE repository (encyclopedia) used to help drive the design of systems. The OO approach makes the enterprise model understandable to business people and easy to modify when needed. OO diagrams facilitate more realistic modeling. Most corporations need re-engineering to be efficient with 1990s technology. A realistic OO enterprise model is needed to analyze and design the potential changes to the enterprise.

> Most enterprises need redesign to make them more automated and competitive. This redesign needs a model of the enterprise that communicates as clearly as possible with the enterprise management.

The top-down approach of information engineering enables the identification of object classes that are reusable across the enterprise. Such classes are designed so that they can be adapted to specific needs. Systems are built with a RAD lifecycle by small teams with I-CASE tools linked to the corporate repository [5]. The teams employ reusable classes, either purchased or designed in the corporation.

> The goal is to assemble applications of very high quality from reusable parts as much as possible and use a generator for all new code.

The CIO would like software companies to sell class libraries and application packages designed for OO usage, to reside in the corporate repository (encyclopedia).

To make the corporate systems as easy to use as possible the CIO would like a standard graphic user interface, such as the Macintosh, MOTIF, or IBM's graphical CUA. The screen icons and menu words should relate to objects in OO design.

An I.S. Project Team

An I.S. SWAT team is a small group that works and stays together, moving from one project to another [5]. It is highly skilled and has a repository-based I-CASE toolset. Its goal is building very high-quality applications at high speed, constantly striving to improve its own measured performance. It can do this by growing its own collection of reusable classes, along with its skill in using them.

A SWAT team using an OO-CASE toolset would like the up-front design thought out in terms of objects, methods, and events that trigger operations. (Many SWAT teams work today with non-OO-CASE tools and non-OO design.)

The SWAT team works with end users, showing them pieces of the application as it is built and making modifications if necessary.

> OO-CASE tools enable the SWAT team to continually adjust or redesign the application while it is being built to meet user needs as closely as possible.

The application should be delivered while the users are still excited about it, and there should be no surprises at cutover. The users know exactly what they are going to get.

A Systems Integrator

A systems integrator is concerned with building networked systems with machines and software from different vendors. A major problem is getting the software of different vendors to work together. Standards are now emerging for enabling the interoperation of classes from any vendor who conforms to the standards (see Chapter 12).

Object-oriented analysis and design are the best way to handle distributed computing for a variety of reasons. Separate machines should have separate objects and low-level objects should normally not be split between machines. A standard Object Request Broker [8] is desirable to interlink the classes—locating the classes and sending standard-format requests to them. Applications or software that are not object-oriented should have a wrapper put around them that makes them appear object-oriented to the Object Request Broker.

A CHANGE IN THE WAY WE THINK

This chapter has described a rich set of benefits that derive from object-oriented technology. However, perhaps the most important benefit in the long run is a change in the way people think. I.S. professionals were all taught to think like computers. This breaks down when the complexity level is high—particularly when computers use highly parallel processors. OO analysis resembles the way humans naturally categorize and comprehend their world. OO-CASE tools enable us to generate code based on this more human way of thinking.

> As computers become more complex, humans should give up trying to think like computers. Instead, computers should be made to think like humans.

This fundamentally different idea about software and systems will enable us to build better systems and improve communication with end users. I.S. professionals and businesspeople need to interact with the same enterprise models that reflect business policies. OO thinking will enable us to achieve more powerful automation of highly complex enterprises.

This change in the way we think about systems is so fundamental that it needs to be taught to I.S. professionals everywhere—in universities, technical schools, and business schools. In the long run, it will change the entire computer profession and the thinking of end users who interact with that profession.

REFERENCES

1. Hazeltine, Nelson, Director of Architecture and Systems Management, Cooperative Computing Systems Division, NCR, "Principles of Object-Oriented Technology," videotaped interview series, James Martin Insight, Naperville, IL, 1991.

2. Hoare, C. A. R., "The Engineering of Software: A Startling Contradiction," *Computer Bulletin,* December, 1975.

3. Ingalls, Daniel H. H., "Design Principles Behind Smalltalk," *Byte,* 6:8, August 1981, pp. 286-298.

4. Martin, James, *Information Engineering,* Prentice-Hall, Englewood Cliffs, NJ, 1990.

5. Martin, James, *Rapid Application Development,* Macmillan, New York, 1991.

6. Martin, James, *Reusability,* videotaped training series, James Martin Insight, Naperville, IL, 1992.

7. McCabe, Thomas and Charles Butler, "Design Complexity Measurement and Testing," *Communications of the ACM,* 32:12, December 1989, pp. 1415-1425.

8. Soley, Richard Mark, ed., *Object Management Architecture Guide,* Object Management Group, Document 90.9.1, November 1, 1990.

4 THE FUTURE OF SOFTWARE

INTRODUCTION   The human brain is good at some tasks and bad at others, while the computer is good at certain tasks that the brain does badly. The challenge of computing is to forge a creative partnership using the best of both.

The electronic machine is fast and absolutely precise. It executes its instructions unerringly. Our meat machine of a brain is slow and, usually, imprecise. It cannot do long, meticulous operations of logic without making mistakes. Fortunately, it has some remarkable properties. It can invent, conceptualize, demand improvements, create visions. Humans can write music, start wars, build cities, create art, fall in love, dream of colonizing the solar system, but can not write bug-free COBOL.

The future challenge in most human endeavors will be merging human and machine capabilities—to achieve the best synergy between people and machines. This synergy will evolve rapidly, because machines are becoming more powerful and networks are growing at a furious rate.

The computers of the future will be nothing like the robots we see in the movies. They will not have the human abilities of an automated Schwarzenegger. In many ways, they will be more interesting, because they will use worldwide networks of immense bandwidth and have access to vast amounts of data and vast libraries of complex object-oriented software that are absolutely precise in their operation.

Today's software is relatively trivial. To make computers the synergistic partners for humans, they need complex software. Software of the necessary complexity probably cannot be built using traditional structured techniques alone. In the mid-1980s, authorities of structured techniques claimed that building the proposed systems of 50 million lines of code was impossible [4]. Our future requires software in which systems of 50 million lines of code will be commonplace. Object-oriented techniques with encapsulation, polymorphism, repository-based development, design automation, and code generators are essential for this.

OPTICAL DISKS

In the near future, desktop machines will have optical disks capable of holding hundreds of millions of lines of code. Billion line-of-code disks will eventually be commonplace. Software will probably be sold on optical disks, with one disk containing multiple related products—for example, a general office worker's set of tools or an I.S. professional's set of tools. If a COBOL programmer had been coding at today's average rate since the time of Christ, all the object code produced would not fill one CD-ROM.

Future developers will have CD-ROMs containing libraries of applications and objects designed for reusability These libraries will appear in I-CASE format, so that their design can be displayed on the screen, modified, and linked to other system components. Mainframe and LAN server repositories will contain much larger libraries. The tools will need search mechanisms and expert systems to help the developers find the reusable components most appropriate to their needs. Computer users will also have CD-ROMs full of software. More than 100 million lines of object code can reside on one CD-ROM. Disks will be sold with many applications and tools integrated together. Cars, tanks, planes, robots, building controllers, household machines, security devices—machines of many types will have their own optical disks of software.

THE NEED FOR POWER TOOLS

We could not build today's cities, microchips, or jet aircraft without power tools. Our civilization depends on power tools. Yet, the application of computing power to corporate systems is often done by hand methods. Design of the interlocking computer applications of a modern enterprise is no less complex than the design of a microchip or a jet aircraft. To attempt this design using hand methods is ridiculous.

Power tools change the methods of construction. Object-oriented modeling and design change the basic way we think about systems. Now that such tools exist, the entire application development process should be reexamined and improved. Advanced power tools give rise to the need for an engineering-like discipline. OO techniques are the foundation for this discipline.

Important from the business point of view is that power tools for software change *what can be constructed,* just as power tools for building enable us to create skyscrapers. These changes need to be understood by management at every level. Making the changes is a critical success factor for business. Top management needs to ensure that its I.S. organization is adopting the new solutions as quickly as possible.

EVOLUTION OF SOFTWARE PRODUCTION

Since the industrial revolution, manufacturing techniques have evolved in an extraordinary way—from hand tools to power tools, from mass production to flexible robotic factories. Software building should also evolve from hand methods; the evolution will be very much faster. In both manufacturing and software production, four phases may evolve:

Phase 1: A Craft Industry

Most software today is designed and coded with manual techniques; each program is a unique piece of craftsmanship, rather like the making of clothes in cottages before the industrial revolution or the building of guns by individual gunsmiths in the eighteenth century.

Phase 2: Power Tools and Engineering Methods

I-CASE represents the coming of power tools to software building. Designs are synthesized with the help of a computer, and code with no coding errors is generated from the designs. The tools enforce structured techniques and apply rigorous checks to the design, bringing a much needed engineering-like discipline to the building of software.

Phase 3: Mass Production

In the early use of I-CASE tools, each program is still designed on a one-off basis. Later, repositories become populated with reusable classes, and libraries of reusable classes evolve. Applications are built by assembling preexisting building blocks.

Phase 4: Robot Production

As object-oriented design matures, classes of great complexity are created. Vast libraries of reusable classes are built. Tools assist the developer in specifying requirements and then automatically select and assemble the classes and class methods that can meet the requirements. The toolset carries on a dialog with the designer, enabling him to modify the design, selecting parameters and options.

This evolution could be compared to four generations of a family business making furniture. In the first generation, each piece of furniture is built by hand. In the second generation, lathes, drills, and power tools become available (like I-CASE tools), but craftsmen still build each piece on a one-off basis. In the third generation, an inventory is built of reusable parts—table tops, legs, chair seats, and so on. Furniture is now assembled from reusable parts with minor custom work. Orders can be filled quickly. The capital required is higher, but the manufacturing cost is lower. Similarly, I-CASE tools are being used with a repository of reusable classes and minor custom work. In the fourth generation, robotic factories assemble the components and allow great variability in what can be built from the components. This is like software tools automatically synthesizing much of the design to meet high-level statements of requirements.

Software tools have not yet evolved to this fourth phase. It could be accomplished by combining object-oriented techniques with

- a standard repository capable of storing many thousands of classes
- a powerful repository coordinator
- building intelligent enterprise models that express business rules
- expert system techniques for guiding the developer in stating requirements and translating them into design

INHUMAN USE OF HUMAN BEINGS

Norbert Wiener, the great pioneer of computers, wrote a book with the memorable title *The Human Use of Human Beings* [5]. In his view, jobs that are inhuman because of drudgery should be done by machines—not people. However, among these jobs, he omitted that of the COBOL programmer.

In a sense, the programmer's job is inhuman, because programmers are required to write large amounts of complex code without errors. To build the strategic and competitive systems that business needs, we want complex new procedures programmed in three months. This is beyond the capability of COBOL-programmed systems.

Many of the tasks that I.S. professionals do are unsuited to our meat-machine brain. They need the precision of an electronic machine. Humans create program specifications that are full of inconsistencies and vagueness. Computers should help humans create specifications and check them at each step for consistency. Humans should not write programs from specifications, because they cannot do that well. A computer should generate the code needed. When humans want to make changes—a frequent occurrence—they have real problems changing the code. Seemingly innocent changes have unperceived ramifications that can cause a chain reaction of errors.

If the programs needed are *large,* we are in even worse trouble, because many people work together on them. When humans try to interact at the needed level of meticulous detail, communication errors abound. When one human makes a change, it affects the work of others. Often, however, the subtle interconnection is not perceived. Meat machines do not communicate with precision.

The end user perceives problems of the I.S. department but does not know how to solve them. A major part of the problem is that humans are so slow; they often take two years to produce results, and they are delayed by the backlog. It is rather like communicating with a development team in another solar system where the signals take years to get there and back.

Error-free coding is not natural for our animal-like brains. We cannot handle the meticulous detail and the vast numbers of combinatorial paths. Furthermore, if we want thousands of lines of code produced per day, then the job is even more inhuman. It is a job for machines, not people. Only recently have we understood how to make machines do it.

The era of code generators, specification tools, and software design automation is just at its primitive beginnings. The era of artificial intelligence is also young—with machines that can reason automatically using large numbers of rules. As these capabilities mature, machines will become vastly more powerful.

CHAIN REACTION

> The automation of software development is the beginning of a chain reaction.

As developers build software out of building blocks, they can create more complex building blocks (whether this is done with object-oriented design or other techniques). High-level constructs can be built out of primitive constructs. Still higher level ones can be built out of these and so on. Highly powerful constructs will evolve for different system types and application areas.

Essential in this is the rigor of the mechanism that enforces correct interfacing among the modules. This rigor allows pyramiding, so that modules can be built out of other modules. The rigor may be achieved by using rules and rule-based processing to enforce integrity in the designs and ensure consistency when separate components are linked. As designers of rule-based I-CASE tools have discovered, a large number of rules are needed to enforce consistency and integrity.

Essential to the chain reaction is an intelligent repository that stores a large quantity of reusable designs from which procedures can be built. Many developers will use large central repositories as well as repositories on LAN servers.

As the software pyramids grow, software must be made as easy to use as possible. The complexity of software will become formidable, but will be hidden from the users just as the complexity of the telephone network is hidden from telephone customers. Higher-level semantics will be needed for instructing computers to do complex tasks. High-level design languages will allow fast, very complex design. Decision-support dialogs will help complex decision making. Each category of professional will employ an appropriate computer dialog. Click-and-point, object-oriented dialogs using icons will be employed. Speech input and output will mature. The pyramiding of complex software will evolve along with the human-interface tools for making the software easy to use.

Libraries of constructs need to be built for different classes of applications. Some examples of application classes that need their own libraries of operations and control structures are

- commercial procedures
- financial application
- design of operating systems
- automatic database navigation
- query languages
- design of circuits with NOR, NAND gates, and so on
- control of robots
- cryptanalysis
- missile control
- building architecture
- design graphics
- network design
- avionics
- CAD/CAM, computer-aided design and manufacturing
- production control
- project management
- decision-support graphics

The list is endless.

REPOSITORY
STANDARDS

At the heart of CASE tools is the repository—providing libraries of reusable classes and facilitating reusable design. The repository is an object-oriented database, storing information about the objects that appear on the screens of I-CASE tools and using methods to validate integrity and coordinate the knowledge in the repository. The repository, containing many objects and rules, is very complex.

It is essential for the future of software that standards exist for the repository. Having no *open* standard for the repository and its tool interfaces would be like having no standard for music CDs. Sony CDs would not play on Philips equipment, and so on. An open standard for the I-CASE repository and its interfaces is as important to software development as the CD standard is to the music industry.

Open standards should incorporate the following:

- A *repository* with its contents defined in terms of the types of objects that it stores
- *Repository services* that use precisely defined methods for checking the consistency and integrity of information stored in the repository
- *Version control* for managing the separate versions of objects that are stored
- *Tool services* defining the objects that are created or modified by the tools and then stored in the repository
- *Standards formats* for object requests and responses. Standard techniques for object interoperability (such as the OMG Object Request Broker)
- A *standard GUI (Graphic User Interface)* to make CASE tools and their diagrams look and feel similar and easy to use
- *Workstation services* for enabling desktop computers to interact with the repository on a LAN server or mainframe
- Full use of existing open systems standards

Development tools will evolve and change. Diverse tools will be built by many corporations, often small, inventive corporations. The repositories ought to be usable with all these tools. Corporate repositories are already growing to a formidable size and are becoming a vital strategic resource, in some cases helping the corporation stay ahead of its competition. Repositories of reusable components will also contain a large quantity of knowledge—sometimes sold as CD-ROMs. If these repositories follow a standard format, they can be used with many different design tools.

PACKAGED SOFTWARE Object-oriented techniques in combination with standard I-CASE repositories will have a major impact on the packaged software industry. A problem with mainframe application packages is that I.S. organizations buying them often have to modify the package to adapt it to their needs. These packages are difficult and expensive to modify. One survey by EDS showed that modification and maintenance of mainframe package software averaged six times the original cost of the software. To overcome this problem, packaged software should be sold in OO-CASE form, so that it can be adapted and modified easily with code generators. Having an open standard for the repository will facilitate this greatly.

A problem with the PC software industry is that low prices are dictated by the shops and organizations that distribute software. Creating complex and interesting new software at these low prices is difficult. Only a few items like word processors and spreadsheet tools can generate enough sales to pay for a 100 person-year development effort. Many PC software companies are embroidering their own products with features of questionable value, rather than striking out for a new 100 person-year innovation. They are stuck on a sandbar related to the cost structure of the industry. This dilemma can be resolved by assembling innovative products from licensable object-oriented components. Recognizing this, Patriot Partners (originally formed by IBM and Metaphor, Inc.) envisioned a new software marketplace. In this vision, many companies create software units that become components of packages from many vendors on multiple platforms using multiple operating systems, LAN managers, network architectures, graphic user interfaces (GUIs), and so on. The initial effort of the partnership was called the Constellation project. The goal of Constellation is to build a framework that provides interfaces between platforms, networks, operating systems, and GUIs. These interfaces would shield developers from spending their time on these issues.

Patriot Partners visualized a world in which developers build software from many licensed components, rather than creating a monolithic application in house. They described the following needs:

1. The data will include all kinds of text, numbers, and graphics, even video and sound, and will most likely reside in many different locations. The new breed of user will demand comprehensive and transparent access to all these data sources, as well as means to easily organize, analyze, and synthesize the information in persuasive new contexts.

2. Users need entire suites of software tools, able to span broad-ranging, variable tasks. These tools must be built on conceptual models that match the nature of the tasks, and designed so that users do not face the disruptive transitions common today when moving from one software environment to another.

3. Users can create their own high-value application, intuitively and without coding. Business professionals are constantly confronted with context-specific tasks that cannot be satisfied by generic applications. A task may be vital one week and all but forgotten the next. We must give those users the tools to fulfill computing needs as they arise, to attack this week's or this afternoon's new problem [2].

The vision of Patriot Partners looked promising, and IBM bought Metaphor in July 1991. The Patriot Partners brochure commented:

> The industry's challenge, then, is no less than redefining what an application is, how it is developed, how it gets distributed and how it is used by a new kind of user. If this challenge seems risky, remember that the low-hanging fruit has been picked; there are no more easy million-seller generic applications out there. The greater risk lies in taking today's products from the Baroque to the Rococo, trying to grow by shaving away at competitors' market shares with feature-laden products that add marginal real value at best.

The Patriot Partners' vision is in many ways similar to that of the OMG with its Object Management Architecture. The OMG is creating an open architecture, whereas an IBM-based initiative may lead to a proprietary architecture.

REUSABILITY To a large extent, the future of software depends upon reusable components. One of the best ways to achieve reusability is with OO components designed to reside in a standard (or *de facto* standard) repository, with a repository coordinator and OO I-CASE tools. The potential value of reusable object-oriented designs is immense. Applications may one day be built largely with off-the-shelf components that can be assembled and modified very quickly. This opportunity presents a great challenge to the packaged software industry.

Conversion of the software industry to I-CASE design will not happen overnight. The investment tied up in existing software is large, and the resistance of major software companies to new methods is high. Perhaps, relatively small or new corporations will sell reusable I-CASE designs first. Patriot Partners gave two scenarios for software built from complex OO components with precisely defined protocols for interlinking the components [3]:

> **Scenario 1:** An engineer working on a jet aircraft design uses his AeroCAD package's drafting assistant, dimension engine and parametric modeling component tools. To get a 3-D rendering, he pulls in the rendering component from another favorite application, Stanford Graphics. To complete the drawing, he calls up the blend tool in Stucco Illustrator to realistically shade the aircraft skin. Since all three applications use component-and-protocol architecture, the tools interact quickly and cooperatively, without forcing the engineer to load different programs, exit applications, or import and export files.

> **Scenario 2:** A project team has a problem. The company's best seller bleach bottle is too heavy for the new molding machines and needs redesign. Manufacturing designs a bottle that meets requirements and creates wireframe and 3-D views of it. Packaging uses those images to figure how many will fit on store shelves, how they look side-by-side, and whether labels need changing. Advertising evaluates how the new design will work in ad layouts and point-of-sale displays. Finance analyzes manufacturing costs and the need for larger boxes to ship the new bottles. The brand manager reports the results of the project to management, relying on a database containing bottle images, dimensions, financials, and consumer responses. Because all project team members use component-based software, they easily share information over their network, manipulating images and data to contribute to the complete solution without recreating or reentering any material.

Box 4.1 describes desirable characteristics of future software development.

BOX 4.1 Desirable characteristics of future software development.

In the near future, desktop machines will have optical disks capable of holding hundreds of millions of lines of code. Software of far greater complexity than today's is needed and will probably be sold on optical disks. Software components from many companies will be interlinked and cross-licensed. In such a world, the following characteristics are desirable:

- *Software is built out of components from many companies.* No one company is likely to build monolithic software of the complexity required. Instead, software companies will create new applications that are assembled from existing components and some new code.

- *Components have OO design with encapsulation and polymorphism.* Components should not only be reusable but easily maintained and extendable.

- *OO components are licensed with well-structured and controllable licensing terms.* Many corporations should sell reusable classes that other corporations can use in their software.

- *Open standards* should exist to allow objects to intercommunicate.

- *Components should reside on a standard repository.* In the absence of international open standards for software repositories, *de facto* standards from large vendors (IBM, DEC, and so on) will define the repository metamodel and user interfaces.

- *A repository coordinator checks the integrity of the repository contents.* Thousands of rules are used with rule-based inferential reasoning to ensure that the repository contents fit together with integrity (as with today's major I-CASE repositories encyclopedias).

- *All development is repository based.* Integrated CASE tools facilitate the analysis and design of software and the linkage of repository components.

- *Licensed software components have OO descriptions (in the repository) that developers use when building applications.* Components are designed to work with OO I-CASE tools. All development is done with such tools.

- *Software design is generated, where possible, from rules, templates, and repository-based classes.* CASE tools should provide the maximum design automation.

- *Code is generated where possible, not hand programmed.* CASE tools should provide the most powerful code-generation capabilities.

BOX 4.1 *(Continued)*

- *Design is independent of the platform on which the code runs.* Code can be generated from the design for many major platforms.

- *Specified interfaces make platform independence possible.* Specified and standard interfaces should enable software to run with
  - multiple host machines
  - multiple operating systems
  - multiple storage subsystems
  - multiple database management systems
  - multiple network architectures
  - multiple LAN managers
  - multiple GUIs (graphic user interfaces)

- *Specified protocols allow objects to work together.* Specified and standardized protocols should exist for both static and dynamic schema linkages.

- *Specified protocols allow interprocess, interhost, and networked interaction.* The same classes may be linked within one machine, within a client-server system, or across an enterprise.

- *Specified protocols allow portability.* There should be smooth portability from small machines to large machines, and from stand-alone systems to enterprisewide systems and interenterprise systems.

- *Software is designed for multimedia platforms.* Multimedia will include text, graphics, images, animation, sound, and video. Many objects will use images, animation, sound, and video.

- *Software is designed for maximum ease of use with a GUI.* Software should be designed for a graphic user interface and be able to work with the different dominant graphic user interfaces.

- *Software is designed for highly parallel processors.* An OO event schema may be used to design how operations execute on different processors simultaneously. Parallel processors should be used for specialized functions such as database management, searching, and display generation.

- *Software is built where possible from executable specifications.* Specifications should be precise enough that code can be generated from them. They should be built with OO I-CASE tools using graphics as well as rule-based and mathematical techniques.

- *Specification techniques provide a way to think about systems that improve conceptual clarity.* The techniques should be easy to use and learn. At higher levels, they should be employed by end users—CASE tools.

(Continued)

BOX 4.1 *(Continued)*

- *Methods are mathematically based where possible.* I-CASE tools should make mathematically based techniques easy to use, achieve maximum precision in specification, and enable the regeneration of code for different platforms.

- *System design and program design use visual techniques.* CASE users should be given maximum help in visualizing and automating designs.

- *Fast iterative prototyping is used.* CASE tools should give the fastest, smoothest prototyping capability. They should allow the system developer to progress as rapidly as possible through the following stages:

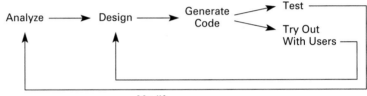

- *Expert systems help developers use libraries of components.* Developers should have access to vast libraries of components and have an expert system help them to locate the most appropriate components and use them correctly.

- *A comprehensive cataloging scheme is used for software components.* A scheme, perhaps like the Library of Congress classification for books, is needed for cataloging classes that form licensable software components.

- *Developers are able to locate and obtain software components they need via networks.* Software development and cross-licensing will be a worldwide industry using worldwide networks.

- *Enterprise models are built with OO techniques.* Enterprisewide information engineering should employ OO analysis. Business people should be able to understand the business models and request changes when needed.

- *The enterprise models form input into a design generator that employs a code generator.* Enterprisewide information engineering should have a high-level OO enterprise model driving OO business area models. These business area models are input to OO system design, where the design tools link to a code generator.

BOX 4.1   *(Continued)*

- *A seamless and automated progression moves from high-level specification to design and code.* All stages in the progression update the knowledge in a single repository.

- *End users can validate and help create the high-level specification.* Specifications may include business rules expressed in English (or other human language), equations, professional drawings, or, in general, the language of the end user. Specifications should show event schemas that users can understand.

PARALLELISM   The PC or LAN server of the future will have many processors. Processor chips of the future will be mass produced in vast quantities. When many millions of one processor chip are made, that processor can be very low in cost. Japan has plans to flood the world with low-cost processor chips. In the future, powerful computers should be built out of many small computers that yield to the economics of mass production. Examples of highly parallel machines have existed for some time, but designing software for applications that run efficiently on them has been very difficult.

The search for ways to introduce a high degree of parallelism into computing is an important one. A million-dollar computer should not be doing one thing at a time; it should be doing ten thousand things at a time. The Connection Machine, from Thinking Machines, Inc., has 65,536 small processors operating in parallel. Such machines will be built from mass-produced wafers, each with many chips.

Software for highly parallel machines will necessarily be intricate. However, analysts do not think naturally in terms of parallel processes. The culture of computing and algorithm theory relates to sequential operations, not parallel ones. To bridge the gap between how analysts think and how parallel computers should be used, we need design tools and nonprocedural languages, such as SQL and PROLOG, that can be translated by generators into parallel processing. Some types of formal decomposition indicate clearly what steps in complex procedures can take place in parallel [1]. Some processes need parallel machines to be efficient, for example, searching—large databases, high-throughput transaction processing, database machines (like Teradata), image generators, compression and decompression of digitized television signals, and possibly human speech processing.

The event schemas in Part III of this book indicate how different operations can function in parallel (i.e., simultaneously) on the same or different processors.

A challenge of the OO-CASE industry today is to evolve CASE tools that help to visualize how multiprocessor machines can be used, or to take specifications and implement them with different OO classes running on different machines. We need to evolve techniques that make it practical to use microelectronic wafers or boards containing many advanced RISC processors.

NETWORKS AND DISTRIBUTION OF OBJECTS

The first attempts at interaction between humans and computers were crude. They employed dumb terminals, slow transmission lines, and cumbersome mainframes. The personal computer brought a new world of interaction between humans and machines. Apple Computer demonstrated that computers could be made easy to use. However, personal computers had limited power. The desktop machine was needed, making use of more powerful machines. The desktop machine needed high-bandwidth links to powerful servers.

LAN technology provided the high-bandwidth link—initially, 10 million bits per second; as optical LANs spread, 100 million bits per second; and in the future, a billion or so bits per second. LANs have created islands of computing. Instead of accessing a machine on the LAN, the user accesses a machine miles away, and the transmission speed drops to low figures. A bit-mapped screen can no longer be painted with an interactive response time. Thought processes dependent on subsecond interaction with the server can no longer occur. The telecommunications companies of the world are installing optical-fiber trunks. One trunk cable contains a large number of fibers, and each fiber transmits more than half a billion bits per second. A major market for fiber-based telecommunications will be available to servers, previously limited by a LAN. Vast networks of optical fibers will be woven around the earth. People will be linked by a billion computers—the farthest one only 68 milliseconds away.

OO classes in one machine will interact with classes in many other machines. Object-oriented analysis and design is an appropriate way to think about distributed computing. A class will not necessarily know where a request comes from. Each class performs its own methods and is isolated from cause and effect elsewhere. It must, however, protect its own data types.

In conventional distributed systems, data can be accessed in ad hoc ways. There may be little or no assurance of who is doing what to the data via the network. With object-oriented systems, the data is *encapsulated,* as it is in biological cells, and is not available for random manipulation. To build distributed systems open to masses of users, without encapsulation, is dangerous. Encapsulation seems essential to protect the integrity of data.

INTERCORPORATE COMPUTER INTERACTION

Networks have created many new business opportunities. Corporations have streamlined their procedures as it became possible to transmit any information to any location.

Initially, computer network applications were built within one corporation. Then, it became clear that major business advantages could accrue from intercorporate networks. Airlines built networks linking travel-agent PCs directly into airline reservation computers. Corporations put software in their customer locations enabling customers to reorder automatically. Supermarket computers transmitted market research information direct to their supplies. Computers in one corporation became linked to computers in other corporations.

Commercial data processing is evolving through the following stages:

1. *Stand-alone Batch Processing.* Stand-alone machines process batches of work.

2. *Offline Telecommunications.* Batches are transmitted offline. Orders are sent by fax.

3. *Online Transaction Processing.* Terminals for handling transactions are linked directly to computer centers.

4. *Distributed Network Processing.* Localized processing environments, including client-server systems, are linked to computer centers in the same corporation.

5. *Simple EDI (Electronic Data Interchange).* A corporate computer center is linked directly to the terminals or PCs of customers or suppliers.

6. *EDI Networks.* Corporate computers can be connected online to computers in many possible suppliers, outlets, customers.

7. *Intercorporate Computer Interaction.* Computers in one corporation interact directly with computers in other corporations.

To achieve intercorporate computer interaction, standards are vital. The world of the future will be one of open systems and standards. Single-vendor, proprietary, vanity architectures will give way to architectures designed for open connectivity, portability, and worldwide access to databases.

Standards for electronic documents will be important, so that machines in one corporation can send electronic purchase orders, invoices, receipts, and so on, to the computers in other corporations. Where such standards are not yet adequate, corporations make contractual agreements about the format of electronically exchanged data.

SPEED OF INTERACTION

As we progress from the era of stand-alone batch processing through the above stages, business interactions tend to speed up. With online systems, events happen more quickly than with batch systems. With networks, information can flow immediately from where it originates to where it is used in decision making. With EDI, information passes between corporations quickly, facilitating immediate inventory control and continuous flow planning in manufacturing. Money passes around the world almost instantly with electronic transfer of funds.

We are progressing to a world in which the computers in one corporation interact directly with the computers of its customers, suppliers, and service providers. A manufacturer's purchasing application scans the possible supplier computers to find goods of the best price and delivery schedule. Computers in hospitals and clinics automatically reorder supplies by transmission to supplier computers (such as the pioneering system at American Hospital Supply—bought by Baxter). Travel-agent computers are online to airline computers. Later, a secretary's computer could do everything that a travel-agent's computer does. Airline computers, in turn, adjust seat fares and bargain flights in an attempt to maximize the load factors on planes.

Trading rooms in stock markets and futures markets are automated, so that traders worldwide can make deals. Brokers worldwide can make trades, and then the public can buy stocks online bypassing brokers and their commissions.

Bar scanners inform computers in stores what goods are selling, and stores adjust their prices constantly in an attempt to maximize profit. Computers in stores send details of sales to manufacturers' computers, bypassing traditional market research. Buyers' computers search for deals, and sellers' computers constantly adjust prices and terms. Both sets of machines try to maximize profits or provide the best service. When computers in one corporation interact directly with computers in another corporation, middlemen can be bypassed.

Business transactions happen instantly. The windows of opportunity are much shorter. Prices, set by computers, change constantly. Complexity increases because the interacting machines can handle complex airline fares, price structures, manufacturing schedules, and so on. An order placed in Ireland with an order-entry computer in Germany triggers a manufacturing planning system in New York to place items into a manufacturing schedule in Dallas that requires chips from Japan built into circuit boards in Taiwan for final assembly in the robotic factory in Dallas and shipment from a warehouse in England.

Society will be laced with networks for computer-to-computer interaction among separate enterprises—worldwide. These networks will decrease reaction times, decrease inventories and buffers, bypass middlemen and bureaucrats, and increase complexity as the machines handle ever more elaborate schemes to try to maximize profit. Small corporations will plug into the networks of computers that offer specialized goods or services at competitive prices.

THE NEED FOR FAST DEVELOPMENT

As commerce speeds up because of automated systems interacting worldwide, many new competitive opportunities emerge. An era of rapid change is always an era filled with new opportunities. Slow-moving corporations are bypassed. Entrepreneurs and inventive I.S. professionals will invent new systems with new ways to compete.

New competitive systems are needed. These systems need to be flexible, built quickly, and controlled by business people or end users. Avoiding the straightjacket of traditional mainframe development with its multiyear backlog and maintenance problems is vital.

To achieve fast development, new systems, as far as possible, should be built out of classes that already exist and can be adapted to circumstances. Repository-based development is needed—with automated tools. The tools should make it quick and easy to customize a standard graphic user interface. Systems should be built so that they can be changed quickly and easily, without the maintenance problems of the past.

The methodology for RAD (Rapid Application Development) is very different from traditional methodologies. It should be designed to maximize the efficiency of OO repository-based techniques. The RAD methodology will be increasingly essential for business survival [3].

INTERNATIONAL STANDARDS FOR REUSABLE CLASSES

Large enterprises will have hundreds of thousands of computers, with millions of MIPS (million instructions per second) worldwide. Managements that fail to build an efficiently functioning organism with this power will not survive. The efficient corporate organism will have repositories storing large amounts of knowledge about the enterprise, its classes, methods, and business values. The classes and operations will be designed for reusability across the enterprise. Commercial paperwork will be replaced by electronic documents in the format of international standards, because computers everywhere will exchange such documents with other computers.

Today, standards for EDI (Electronic Data Interchange) are evolving rapidly. In some cases, standards committees are starting to define documents in object-oriented terms. ODA (the Office Document Architecture) from ISO (the International Standards Organization) defines MO:DCA—the *Mixed Object Document Content Architecture*. This includes an Object Contents Architecture defining image formats, graphics, fonts, and so on, and an Object Method Architecture, defining methods for employing fonts, images, and so on.

As Stage 7 of the above seven stages becomes widespread, changing the world's patterns of commerce, standards should be established for many of the reusable classes used in commerce—customers, accounts, orders, parts, locations, and so on. Millions of transactions will pass between corporations every second. Corporations whose computers interact need not have common classes. This commonality could come from mutual agreements or from large vendors such as IBM, DEC, or possibly large telephone companies. International standards for the major classes of commerce will become increasingly desirable.

CODE GENERATION FROM THE ENTERPRISE MODEL

Executable program code should be generated from the highest-level specification possible. A major evolution in I-CASE tools will be generating code from higher level specifications. If the enterprise model contains rules expressing how the enterprise functions, code can be generated directly from the enterprise model. The enterprise model should be understood by the business managers. It should clarify thinking about how they want the enterprise to operate. A precise expression of how the enterprise operates should reside in the repository and should be discussed in workshop sessions. Code should be generated directly from this. A change in business procedures should then be directly translated into the code for implementing the procedures.

The term Code Generation from the Enterprise Model (CGEM) has been used to describe this higher-level code generation. One of the best ways to achieve it is with object-oriented analysis and design. Operational methods describe the desired behavior of objects. Events indicate changes in the state of objects.

Events, objects, and business rules provide a way of describing the enterprise that business managers and staff can understand. We have stressed that object-oriented techniques provide *a way to think about systems*—a way to think about a business. As such, the subject ought to be taught in business schools and management training courses, as well as in computer science schools and system analyst courses. At its different levels, it can be understood by both business people and computer professionals. It provides a vital way to bridge the gap between these two cultures.

Business schools should teach how businesses work with diagrams showing object types, operations, event types, and trigger rules. The courses should use CASE tools for planning and analysis. New types of charts will probably be devised that help human communication. To become a basis for system specification, they should be designed so that they have the precision that enables repository-based tools to check their integrity and consistency with other diagrams.

As we acquire the capability to generate code from the enterprise model or business area model, the development lifecycle will become faster. The libraries of reusable classes will become more mature and enterprise models will evolve—representing business rules more comprehensively. Much development will consist of the successive refinement of existing applications, rather than the creation of entirely new applications.

THE EVOLUTION OF PROGRAMMING TECHNIQUE

Generating code from the enterprise model is one example of programming techniques reflecting the way users think rather than the way the machinery works. In the beginning, humans had to program using the computer's instruction set. When computer programs changed from switches to languages, the new programs were organized around the machine instruction set.

Therefore, the first languages and machine instructions were very similar. A process-oriented programming model was the result. For example, programs for addition were organized around the machine process of addition: loading registers with numbers, executing the add instruction, and dealing with overflow and underflow. As shown in Fig. 4.1, the programming technique steadily became more remote from the way the hardware operates. It moved closer to human language, to the way humans solve problems, and to human professional disciplines. As this happened, programming became more dependent on interpreters, compilers, and then code generators and CASE tools.

Meanwhile, the machinery evolved away from an instruction set that was good for humans to technology that was as fast and cost effective as possible. We had generations of RISC (Reduced Instruction Set Computing) chips and then concurrent computers with many processors. The RISC chips drifted far from what humans could have programmed easily without software translation. Concurrent computers carried the trend further. It would be difficult for humans to write code that executed on multiple independent processors simultaneously. We have a tradition of *sequential*—not parallel—logic, mathematics, algorithms, and languages.

Object-oriented analysis and design help users to think about their world in terms that can be represented naturally on the CASE screen and help code generators to produce code for concurrent computers, leading eventually to massively parallel machines with large numbers of cheap processor chips. An object-oriented database engine may be one way to take advantage of parallelism. Corporations of the future may be run with vast networks of object-oriented database engines.

As users become familiar with using the icons and panels as objects on the computer screen, using computers and building applications becomes easier. The users should model their world in an OO fashion with tools that allow models to be expanded into detail and made to run actively. In this way, the distinction between modeling and executable systems blurs.

PYRAMIDS OF COMPLEXITY

The complexity of living things, built by nature, is awesome to a computer professional. The brain is so intricate that it cannot be mapped, imitated, or understood in detail. It is rich in diversity—yet, self-protecting and self-renewing. The things of nature are complex, because they are grown using organic components. Similarly, we can develop software and information system components and *grow* complex automated systems. However, we need disciplines and tools that facilitate and enable us to manage such growth.

> *The designers of the future must stand on the shoulders of the designers of the present.*

Figure 4.1   In the beginning, humans had to program using the machine's instruction set. The programming technique and the machine steadily diverged, the hardware becoming more cost efficient and the programming methods becoming closer to the way users think about their world.

As the pyramids of complexity grow, we will reach very high-level OO constructs, often designed for parallel RISC engines. Vast libraries of such constructs will exist. Sophisticated tools and languages will enable developers to employ the constructs they need. Many millions of computers of worldwide data networks will exchange constructs from these libraries. Knowledge-based systems will acquire ever more knowledge and become self-feeding. Intelligent network directories will allow machines and users to find the resources they need.

The programmer of handmade COBOL with his ad hoc designer will become part of the romantic past of computer history like the weavers in their cottages when the industrial revolution began.

REFERENCES

1. Hamilton, M. and S. Zeldin, "Higher Order Software: A Methodology for Defining Software," *IEEE Transactions on Software Engineering,* 2:3, March 1976, pp. 25–32.

2. Liddle, David E., *Patriot Partners: A Vision of a New Software Marketplace,* brochure from Patriot Partners, Mountain View, CA, 1991.

3. Martin, James, *Rapid Application Development,* Macmillan, New York, 1991.

4. Parnas, David L., "Software Aspects of Strategic Defense Systems," *Communications of the ACM,* 28:12, December 1985, pp. 1326–1335.

5. Wiener, Norbert, *The Human Use of Human Beings: Cybernetics and Society,* Da Capo Press, New York, 1954.

PART **II** AN OVERVIEW
OF ANALYSIS AND DESIGN

5 OO MODELS

MODELS OF REALITY

When we analyze systems, we create models of the application area that interest us. A model might involve one system, such as a production-planning system, focus on one business area, or cover an entire enterprise. Enterprise modeling is important in planning enterprise automation.

The model represents an aspect of reality and is built in such a way that it helps us to understand reality. The model is much simpler than reality, just as a model airplane is simpler than a real airplane. We can manipulate the model and this helps us to invent systems or redesign business areas.

With object-oriented analysis, the way we model reality differs from conventional analysis. We model the world in terms of object types and what happens to those object types. This also leads us to design and program systems in an object-oriented way, striving for the benefits summarized in Chapter 3.

Figure 5.1 illustrates how we build systems. The analyst creates a model of the area of interest. The model is converted into a design and then code. The model should represent how the end users perceive the area or what the users want the system to do. As far as possible, this model should be in a form that users can understand and helps them be creative about their needs. The implementor uses the model and creates a design from which code can be written or generated.

The models we build in OO analysis reflect reality more naturally than the models in traditional systems analysis. Reality, after all, consists of objects and events that change the state of those objects. Using OO techniques, we build software that more closely models the real world. When the real world changes, our software is easier to change—a real advantage. We would like to capture the end users' view of the world and translate it into software as automatically as possible. Then, when the users' needs change, the software changes with it.

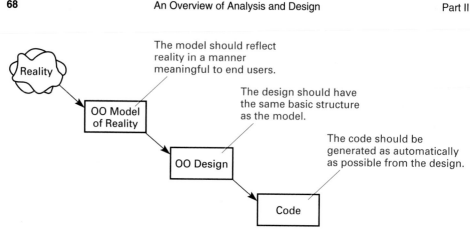

Figure 5.1

For example, business people have rules about business operations. These rules relate to objects, operations, and events that trigger operations. They have rules about backordering, rules about rating bad payers, rules about scheduling production, and selecting suppliers. With traditional systems, those rules are buried in multiple COBOL programs. When the business people change the rules, changing the programs is very difficult. With OO analysis and design, we want to express the business rules explicitly in our models and use them to create the design and code. When the rules change, we can change the design and code as automatically as possible.

TOOLS

The designer of a microchip would not dream of working without powerful computerized tools. Tools are similarly needed for the design of software. CASE tools (see Chapter 11) help the analyst to create models of the area. Using the information in the models, a design is created and methods are built. All of this information resides in a common repository.

With OO tools, design and code naturally progress from the high-level model. All of these relate to object types, the methods that objects use, and the events that trigger operations with the objects. The repository stores many classes and helps us to find those classes useful in the design. Every time we tell an advanced CASE tool about classes, inheritance, and so on, it should generate code. Code in existing classes or methods is reused. Code for new methods may be generated from declarative statements, collections of rules, decision tables, SQL statements, logic represented on action diagrams, and other means. Systems of great complexity have been built without having to program in languages, such as COBOL, C, C++, and so on. Ideally the code should be created interpretively, so that we can run it whenever we change the system, like running a spreadsheet as we grow it with a spreadsheet tool. Later, the code is compiled for machine efficiency.

TWO TYPES　　　In OO analysis, we build two types of closely interre-
OF MODELS　　　lated models: a model of the object types and their
　　　　　　　　　　structure and a model of what happens to the objects.
The models are drawn with diagrams called *schemas*—object schemas showing the object structures and event schemas showing what happens to the objects.

OO analysis and design have two aspects, illustrated in Fig. 5.2. The first aspect concerns object types, classes, relationships among objects, and inheritance, and is referred to as *Object Structure Analysis* (OSA) and *Object Structure Design* (OSD). The other aspect concerns the behavior of objects and what happens to them over time and is referred to as *Object Behavior Analysis* (OBA) and *Object Behavior Design* (OBD).

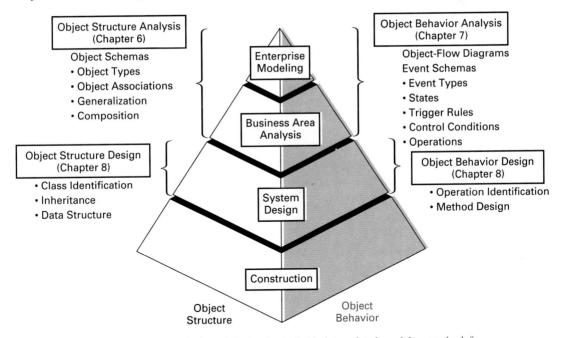

Figure 5.2 Analysis and design both divide into related models—on the left are object structure models and on the right are object behavior models.

Chapters 6 and 7 discuss Object Structure Analysis and Object Behavior Analysis. Chapter 8 deals with Object Structure and Behavior Design. Part III of this book describes Object Structure Analysis in more detail; Part IV studies Object Behavior Analysis; and Part V discusses design and implementation.

THE SIMILARITY OF ANALYSIS AND DESIGN

In traditional development methodologies, the conceptual models used for analysis differ from those used for design. Programming has yet a third view of the world. Analysts use entity-relationship models, functional decomposition, and matrices. Designers use data-flow diagrams, structure charts, and action diagrams. Programmers use the constructs of COBOL, FORTRAN, C, or ADA.

In OO techniques, analysts, designers, programmers, and, particularly important, end users all use the same conceptual model (see Fig. 5.3). They all think of object types, objects, and how the objects behave. They draw hierarchies of object types or classes in which the subtypes share the properties of their parent. They think about objects being composed of other objects and use generalization and encapsulation. They think about events changing the states of objects and triggering certain operations.

The transition from analysis to design is so natural, that specifying where analysis ends and design begins is sometimes difficult. This is especially so

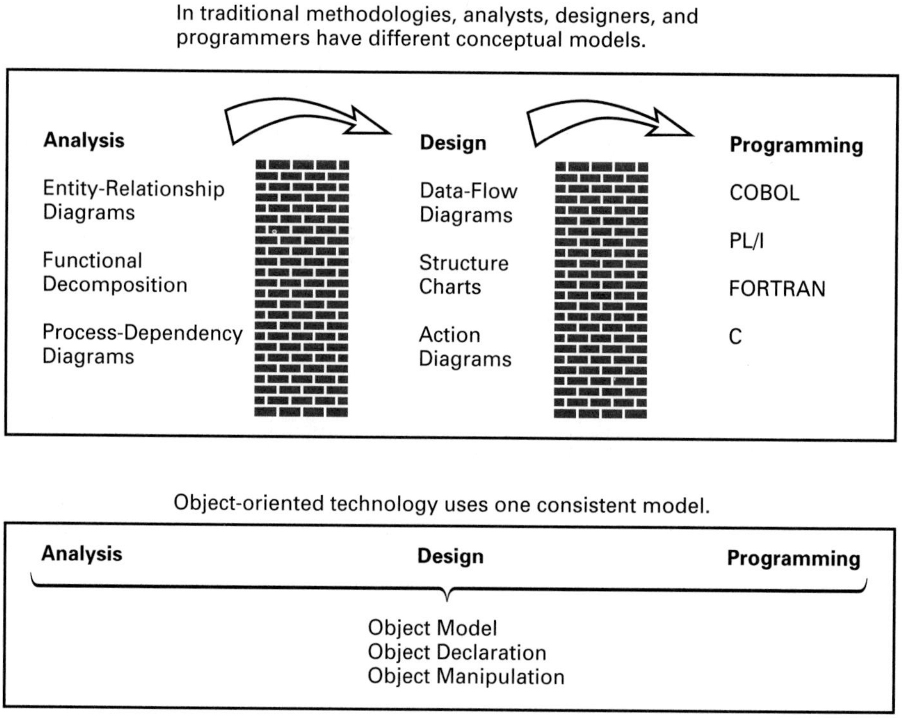

In traditional methodologies, analysts, designers, and programmers have different conceptual models.

Analysis	Design	Programming
Entity-Relationship Diagrams	Data-Flow Diagrams	COBOL
		PL/I
Functional Decomposition	Structure Charts	FORTRAN
Process-Dependency Diagrams	Action Diagrams	C

Object-oriented technology uses one consistent model.

Analysis	Design	Programming

Object Model
Object Declaration
Object Manipulation

Figure 5.3 OO techniques use the same conceptual model for OO analysis, design, and programming. OO techniques tear down the conceptual walls between analysis, design, and programming (or code generation).

where an integrated CASE tool employs the same paradigm for analysis and design, and generates code.

When traditional development crosses the walls shown in Fig. 5.3, information is often lost and misunderstandings occur. The transition is time consuming and often lowers the quality of the end product.

The employment of a single conceptual model with an integrated CASE tool for that model results in

- Higher productivity
- Fewer errors
- Better communication among users, analysts, designers, and implementors
- Better quality results
- More flexibility
- Greater inventability

Figure 5.4 shows what is of interest to the two sides of analysis and design.

Object Structure Analysis (OSA)

Concerned with Object Types and Their Associations

- Object Types and Associations
- Generalization Diagrams
- Object-Relationship Diagrams
- Composed-of Diagrams

Object Behavior Analysis (OBA)

Concerned with What Happens to the Objects over Time

- Object-Flow Diagrams
- Event Schemas
- Operation Diagrams Showing Operations and the Sequence in Which They Occur
- Object States and Object State Changes
- Trigger Rules that Link Cause and Effect

Object Structure Design (OSD)

Concerned with Classes, Methods, and Inheritance

- Classes
- Superclasses and Subclasses
- Inheritance
- Data Structures
- Database Design

Object Behavior Design (OBD)

Concerned with the Design of Methods

- Methods and Operations
- Procedural Logic
- Nonprocedural Code
- Input to Code Generators
- Screen and Dialog Design
- Prototyping

Figure 5.4   The two halves of OO analysis and design.

Object Structure Analysis is concerned with defining the kinds of objects and the way in which we associate them. We ask: What types of objects exist? What are their relations and functions? What subtypes and supertypes are useful? Is a certain kind of object composed of other objects?

As this pushes into Object Structure Design, we identify classes (the implementation of object types). Superclasses and subclasses, their inheritance paths, and the methods they use are defined. Detailed design of the data structures or database is done.

Object Behavior Analysis is concerned with modeling what happens to the objects over time. We ask: What states can the object classes be in? What types of events change these states? What succession of events occurs? What operations result in these events, and how are they triggered?

As this pushes into design, we become concerned with the detailed design of methods, either with procedural or nonprocedural techniques. The input to code generators is developed. Screen design is done, dialogs are designed and generated. Prototypes are built and evolved.

The CASE tool used should tightly integrate these aspects of analysis and design.

INFORMATION ENGINEERING

The modern enterprise needs to be highly automated. Many computerized systems need to work together as efficiently as possible. Many events happen between a customer taking an order and the finished goods being delivered. The separate systems supporting this chain of events need to fit together, so that the chain happens as effectively as possible, with minimum costs. To create this complex collection of systems, a model of the enterprise must be built: identifying the object types in the enterprise, how they interrelate, and what events occur to change the state of objects. This model is extended in greater detail as business areas are analyzed. When separate systems are built, they relate to the same model and, hence, should work together efficiently.

Figure 5.5 illustrates this process of creating an enterprise model, extending it into business-area models, and building systems that relate to the models. The process is called *information engineering*. The practice of information engineering has been evolving from entity models to object models. In the former, procedures are separated from the data. In the latter, procedures (i.e. methods) are packaged with the data to form classes.

Traditional information engineering has built detailed models of entity types, subtypes, and supertypes across the enterprise. In OO information engineering, most of these become object types. In traditional information engineering, a matrix diagram shows what processes occur and what entity types they relate to. In OO information engineering, the processes become methods packaged with the data structures. Traditional information engineering is enhanced by thinking about events. Operations cause events to occur, and rules (identified in

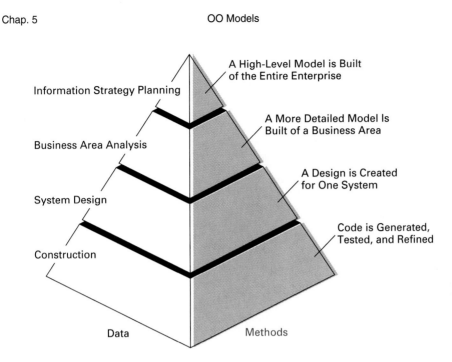

Figure 5.5 Information engineering.

traditional information engineering) govern actions taken when events occur. Event schemas, then, enhance information engineering as it assumes the object-oriented view of the world.

Object-oriented information engineering applies Object Structure Analysis and Object Behavior Analysis at various levels as shown in Fig. 5.6.

A major goal of information engineering is to achieve reusability of design and code across the enterprise. This becomes easier to accomplish, and more effective, with the formal class structures of object-oriented analysis and design.

ACCOMMODATION OF OLD SYSTEMS

Many applications already exist, so the information engineer has to make a new world of clearly designed systems fit in with the old world. (Sometimes they are called a *legacy application,* as they are a legacy from the past.) Using OO techniques, we can often put a wrapper around the old applications that enables new classes to communicate with them using the standard messages of the OO world. An old application, for example, may have its terminal dialog replaced with a graphic user interface. The user may then employ it along with the new OO application using the same style of PC interaction.

As we evolve to the new OO environment with all its benefits, we cannot scrap the old environment. For years, perhaps decades, new systems will have to coexist with the systems of the past. Where the legacy systems are expensive to maintain, they will steadily be rebuilt with repository-based OO techniques.

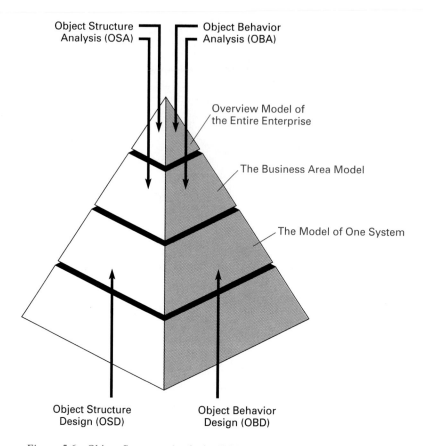

Figure 5.6   Object Structure Analysis (OSA) and Object Behavior Analysis (OBA) are used at the various levels of information engineering.

6 OBJECT STRUCTURE ANALYSIS

Object Structure Analysis (OSA) defines the kinds of objects we perceive and the ways in which we associate them. This chapter introduces the models that are created during Object Structure Analysis. These same OSA models guide the definition of classes and their data structures in Object Structure and Behavior Design (see Chapter 8).

OBJECTS AND OBJECT TYPES

During Object Structure Analysis, the analysis team is more intent on identifying the types of objects than

BOX 6.1 OSA is concerned with three basic kinds of information.

In Object Structure Analysis, the following information is identified:

- What are the object types and how are they associated? The identification of objects and their associations are represented by an object schema. This information guides the designer in class and data structure definition.

- How are the object types organized into supertypes and subtypes? Generalization hierarchies can be diagrammed and indicate directions of inheritance to the designer.

- What is the composition of complex objects? Composed-of hierarchies can be diagrammed. Composition guides the designer in defining mechanisms that properly manage objects-within-objects.

identifying the individual objects in a system. As defined in Chapter 2, *object types are categories of objects.*

Object types are important, because they create conceptual building blocks for designing systems. In object-oriented programming, these building blocks guide the designer in defining the classes and their data structures. In addition, object types provide an index for system processes. For instance, operations such as Hire, Promote, Retire, and Fire are intimately tied to the object type Employee, because they change the state of an employee. In other words, an object should only be manipulated via the operations associated with its type. Without object types, then, operations cannot be defined properly.

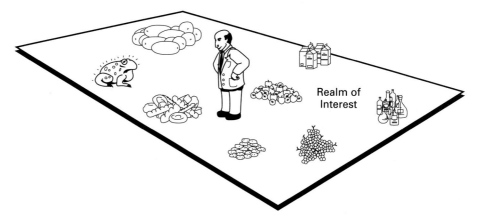

Figure 6.1   We choose how to categorize our world.

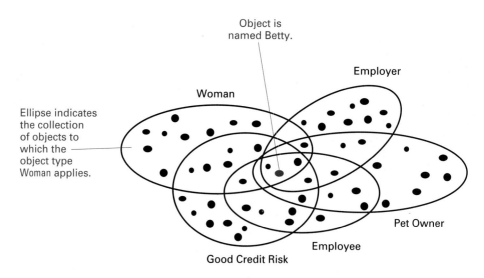

Figure 6.2   The same object can be categorized in many ways.

The object types we define and use can be varied, because we choose them based on how we understand our world (see Fig. 6.1).

While this may seem rather arbitrary, that is how our minds work. In fact, an object can be categorized in more than one way. For example, in Fig. 6.2 one person may regard the object Betty as a **Woman**. Her boss regards her as an **Employee**. The person who mows her lawn classifies her as an **Employer**. The local animal control agency licenses her as a **Pet Owner**. The credit bureau reports that Betty is an instance of the object type called **Good Credit Risk**—and so on.

Other examples of object types can be

Concrete	Intangible	Roles	Judgments
person	time	doctor	productive job
pencil	quality	patient	high pay
car	company	owner	good example

Relational	Events	Displayable	Others
marriage	sale	string	image
partnership	purchase	integer	signal
ownership	system crash	icon	gnome

OBJECT ASSOCIATIONS

As stated above, modeling the object types that classify the objects around us is vital in OO analysis. Modeling the way in which objects associate with other objects is also important. For example in Fig. 6.3(a), **Organization** objects

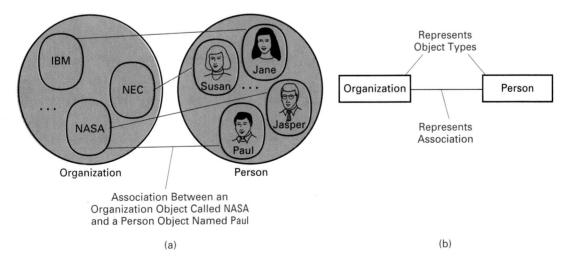

(a)   (b)

Figure 6.3   Objects of one type associate with objects of other types.

like IBM, NASA, and NEC associate with Person objects Susan, Jane, Jasper, and Paul. Figure 6.3(b) represents one way of expressing the association between these two types of objects.

While Fig. 6.3 illustrates associations between two types of objects, the *meaning* of the association is not indicated. In addition to the meaning, the number of objects with which any given object can and must associate is also not indicated. In analysis, naming associations and indicating how many objects of one type must associate with the objects of another type are useful, because they provide meaning and increase understanding (see Fig. 6.4).

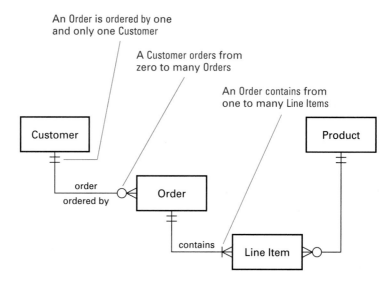

Figure 6.4 Naming associations and constraining the number of associations an object of a specific type may have are useful. They provide meaning and understanding.

GENERALIZATION HIERARCHIES   One of the common-sense ways in which humans organize their mass of knowledge is by arranging it into hierarchies from the general to the more specific. For example, Fig. 6.5 depicts a hierarchy with knowledge of the object type of Person at the top. This means that Person is a more general type of object than

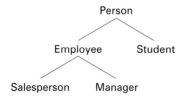

Figure 6.5   A generalization hierarchy of object types indicating that Person is a supertype of Employee and Student. In turn, Employee is a supertype of Salesperson and Manager.

Employee and Student. This means that Employee and Student are *subtypes* of Person, or conversely Person is a *supertype* of Employee and Student.

All the properties of an object type also apply to its subtypes. For example, Sony makes many video cassette recorders. VCR is an object type with certain features. AH-8500 is a subtype of VCR. Therefore, the AH-8500 has all the properties of a VCR and properties of its own. Additionally, Sony makes several models of the AH-8500. AH-8500-12 is one model. Therefore, all the properties of the AH-8500 apply to the AH-8500-12, while the AH-8500-12 also has some special properties.

Generalization is the result (or act) of distinguishing an object type as being more general, or inclusive, than another. Everything that applies to an object type also applies to its subtypes. Every instance of an object type is also an instance of its supertypes.

An object type may have subtypes, sub-subtypes, sub-sub-subtypes, and so on. For example, Acid is a subtype of Liquid, and Nitric Acid is a subtype of Acid. Product 739 is a subtype of Nitric Acid. Figure 6.6 shows this generalization hierarchy.

Figure 6.6 illustrates a hierarchy where each type has no more than one supertype. However, a type often has multiple supertypes. Generalization hierarchies, then, are not necessarily tree structures. Figure 6.7 illustrates one such hierarchy. The type Whale has two supertypes: Mammal and Water Animal. In another example, everything that applies to Flying Animals and Mammals also applies to Bats. Put another way, every instance of a Bat is also an instance of a Flying Animal and a Mammal.

Generalization hierarchies are important to the OO developer for two reasons. First, using the notion of supertypes and subtypes provides a useful tool with which we can describe the world of the application system. Second, it indicates directions of inheritance between classes in OO programming languages. Inheritance will be discussed in more detail in Chapter 8.

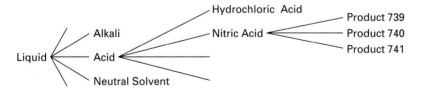

Figure 6.6 A generalization hierarchy indicating that all the properties of Nitric Acid apply to Product 739, Product 740, and Product 741, but each product has specialized properties of its own. Similarly, all the properties of Acid apply to Nitric Acid, Hydrochloric Acid, and so on.

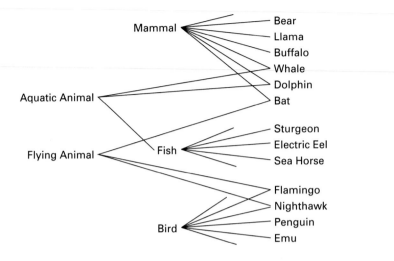

Figure 6.7 A fern diagram showing a generalization hierarchy where types can have multiple supertypes. The properties of more than one supertype can apply to any one object type. Some object-oriented CASE tools employ this type of diagram.

COMPOSED-OF HIERARCHIES

Some types of objects are described as complex. By *complex* we mean that some objects are perceived as being composed of other objects. For instance, a car can be described as consisting of a chassis, wheels, and an engine. In turn, the engine is composed of an engine block, valves, pistons, and so on. Additionally, the piston is a complex object made up of rings, a piston rod, and piston head. For anybody who is interested, this process can continue by eventually describing atomic and subatomic particles of each car part.

In OO analysis, object composition helps to describe that drawings are made up of a certain configuration of symbols, jobs are composed of specific tasks, organizations consist of other organizations, and so on. In advanced technology systems, the analyst will describe how an order can consist of not only line items, but contain verbal instructions from the customer and a handwritten diagram as well. Orders of this kind are called *complex objects*. Each order can be manipulated as a single object consisting of other objects that, in turn, can be manipulated separately, if necessary.

One way of representing the composed-of aspect of objects is by diagramming them as shown in Figure 6.8.

OBJECT-RELATIONSHIP DIAGRAMS

Object types have relationships with other object types. An **Employee** works in a **Branch Office**. A **Customer** places an **Order** for many **Products**.

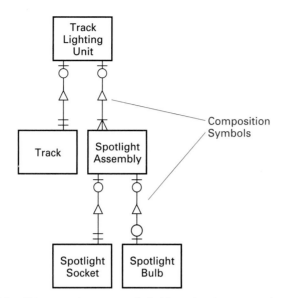

Figure 6.8 Objects can be composed of objects that, in turn, can be composed of objects.

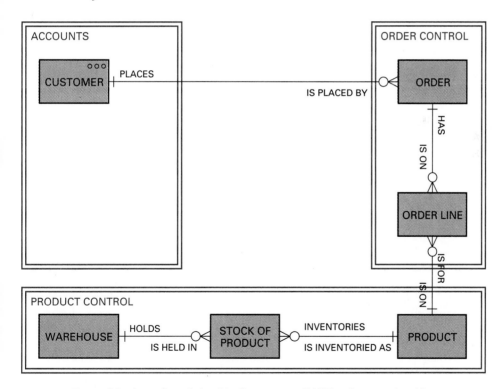

Figure 6.9 An entity-relationship diagram on a CASE tool screen. An object-relationship diagram can be represented in the same manner. (Courtesy of Texas Instruments)

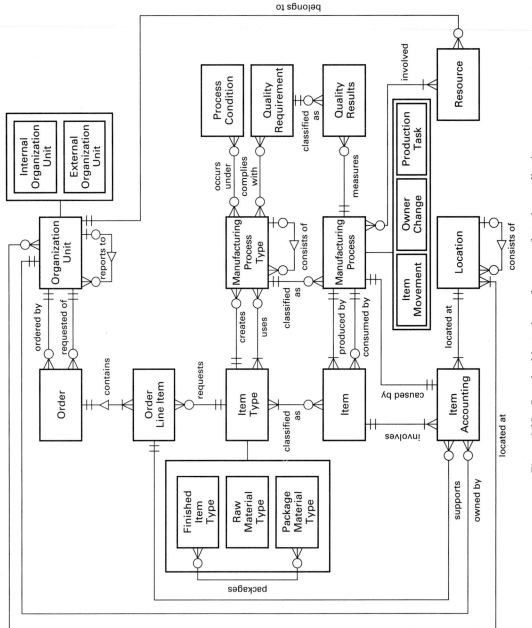

Figure 6.10 Sample object schema for a manufacturing application.

Entity-relationship diagrams have been used for many years in conventional systems analysis. They show associations among entity types. Figure 6.9 shows a portion of an entity-relationship diagram on the screen of the IEF CASE tool. Customer has three dots in its box indicating that it can be expanded to show the subtypes of customer.

An object-relationship diagram is essentially the same as an entity-relationship diagram. Each box in Fig. 6.9 could be an object type in Object Structure Analysis.

OBJECT SCHEMAS   Understanding a model is often easier when object types and relationships are represented on an object-relationship diagram; supertypes and subtypes on a generalization hierarchy diagram; and composed-of structures on a composed-of diagram. For more sophisticated users, however, expressing them all on the same diagram can be useful. This kind of diagram is called the *object schema,* as illustrated in Fig. 6.10.

7 OBJECT BEHAVIOR ANALYSIS

In Object Behavior Analysis (OSA), we draw event schemas showing events, the sequence in which they occur, and how events change the state of objects. An *event schema* represents processing scripts that change the states of objects. Event schemas, then, must be expressed in terms of object schemas, because events change the state of given types of objects. Therefore, a CASE tool for object-oriented analysis should enable its users to build object schemas and event schemas and to maintain the close relationship that exists between these two types of representation.

Box 7.1 lists the information that is identified in Object Behavior Analysis. OSA and OBA are closely related. They are not done separately but evolve together to form integrated models and designs.

OBJECT STATES An object can exist in one of many different states. For example, an Airline Booking object could be an instance of one of the following object types:

- Requested Airline Booking
- Wait-listed Airline Booking
- Confirmed Airline Booking
- Cancelled Airline Booking
- Fulfilled Airline Booking (once the plane takes off)
- Archived Airline Booking

Such object types are often perceived as possible lifecycle *states* of an object. However, an object can have many such lifecycle perspectives. For exam-

BOX 7.1

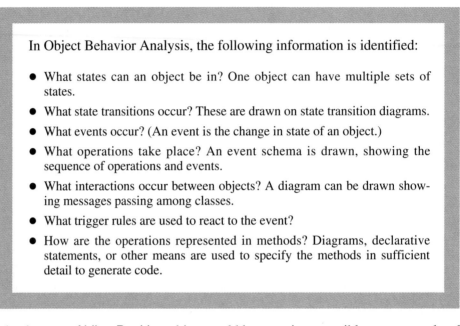

In Object Behavior Analysis, the following information is identified:

- What states can an object be in? One object can have multiple sets of states.
- What state transitions occur? These are drawn on state transition diagrams.
- What events occur? (An event is the change in state of an object.)
- What operations take place? An event schema is drawn, showing the sequence of operations and events.
- What interactions occur between objects? A diagram can be drawn showing messages passing among classes.
- What trigger rules are used to react to the event?
- How are the operations represented in methods? Diagrams, declarative statements, or other means are used to specify the methods in sufficient detail to generate code.

ple, the same **Airline Booking** object could have various possible payment-related *states* as well:

- Unpaid Airline Booking
- Deposit-paid Airline Booking
- Fully-paid Airline Booking
- Airline Booking In Need of Payment Refund
- Refunded Airline Booking

At some moment, then, an object could be both a **Wait-listed Airline Booking** and a **Fully-paid Airline Booking**. At the same moment, the same object could also be an instance of a **June Booking** and an **IBM Corporation Booking** (see Fig. 7.1). In other words, an object can be an instance of many object types simultaneously.

> The *state* of an object is the collection of object types that apply to it.

When implemented by an OO programming language, the state is recorded in the data stored about the object. It is determined by the classes and data field values associated with the object. Therefore, an alternate definition of state is commonly used by OO programmers.

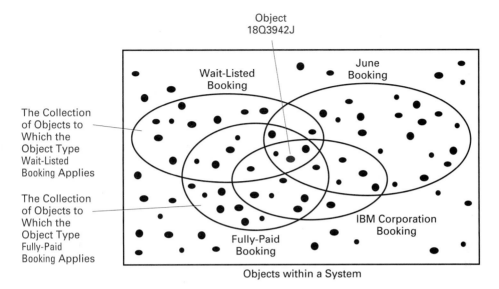

Figure 7.1   When a state change occurs, an object changes from one categorization to another.

The *state* of an object is the collection of associations that an object has.

(See Appendix E for more information on why the two definitions of state are equivalent.)

In the OO language, *requests* are sent and cause *methods* to be activated. The methods change the *state* of the object. The state is recorded in the object's data.

EVENTS

Our world is full of events. The cat has kittens. Aunt Agatha arrives unexpectedly. An airline customer requests a booking. A machine tool breaks down. A job is completed.

In object-oriented analysis, the world is described in terms of objects and their states, and events that change those states.

An *event* is a change in the state of an object.

For example in Fig. 7.2, an object's state is changed from being a **Wait-listed Airline Booking** to a **Confirmed Airline Booking**. The name for this event could be **Wait-listed Airline Booking for Object 18Q3942J Confirmed**.

In the world of astronomy or physics, changes in state are common occurrences—a star explodes, a comet's orbit is changed, a radioactive particle decays.

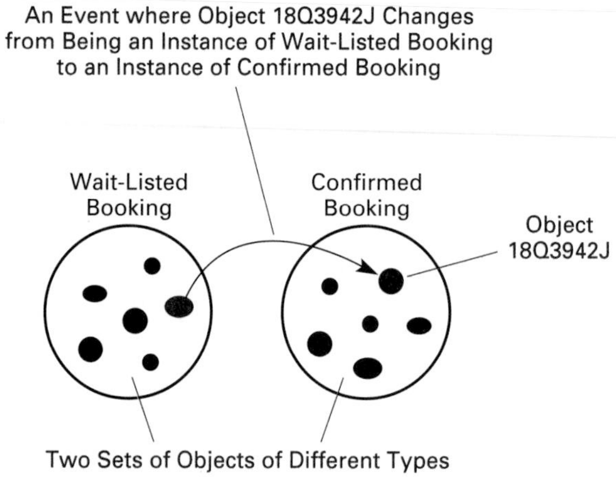

An Event where Object 18Q3942J Changes
from Being an Instance of Wait-Listed Booking
to an Instance of Confirmed Booking

Wait-Listed
Booking

Confirmed
Booking

Object
18Q3942J

Two Sets of Objects of Different Types

Figure 7.2   The state of an object changing from one object type to another.

Most of these state changes are unnoticed or undetectable by us. However, if we wish to know about and react to them in some way, their occurrence must be noted. Events, then, serve as markers for the points in time when state changes occur.

Without events, the world as we know it would not change. In a world without events, we could build and populate databases without worrying about updating them. In most applications, however, database contents do change. Since we wish to know about such changes and react appropriately to them, we must understand and model events.

TYPES OF EVENTS   The OO analyst does not wish to know about every event that occurs in an organization—only the *types* of events. Just as we talk about object types and instances of object types, so we talk about event types and instances of event types. For example, the Wait-listed Airline Booking Confirmed event type is the collection of those events where an object changes from a Wait-listed Airline Booking to a Confirmed Airline Booking. Figure 7.2 is one instance of this event type.

Event types indicate simple changes in object state, for example, when money is added to a bank account or an employee's salary is updated. Fundamentally, event types describe the following kinds of state changes:

● An object is *created.* For example, an airline booking is created.

● An object is *terminated.* For example, a product is destroyed or a contract is terminated.

- An object is *classified* as an instance of an object type. For example, a wife becomes a mother; a firm becomes a customer; an employee becomes a manager.

- An object is *declassified* as an instance of an object type. For example, a firm ceases to be a customer; a product is dropped from the sales catalog.

- An object *changes* classification. For example, a lawyer changes from associate to partner; an account changes from a normal account to an overdue account.

- An object's attribute is changed.

Events can associate one object with another. For example, in most organizations when an object is classified as an Employee, it must be associated with a Department. One event will classify the object as an Employee. A different event will create an association between the Employee object with a Department object. (Associations are objects like everything else. If named, this kind of association could be called the Employee-Department Assignment object type.) If the Employee changed Department, a new Employee-Department Assignment would be created and the old one terminated.

Updating an account balance is another example of an event. When $10 is added to account #14274, an event associates the account with a different value.

Some events require other events to occur first. For example, before a *department* can be closed, all of its *employees* must be allocated to a different *department,* the *offices* it occupied must be allocated to a different use, and so on.

Sometimes one event causes a chain reaction of other events. Changing a node on the screen of a CASE tool, for example, may require a set of changes to other objects in order to preserve integrity. Adding a circuit to the wiring of a jumbo jet may require mandatory changes to many objects.

An operation causes events to happen. We draw the operation as a round-cornered box, because events indicate points in time when an object state change occurs. Event types are represented as solid black triangles usually connected to the operation box. When represented in the following way, they seem to point to a particular kind of "point in time":

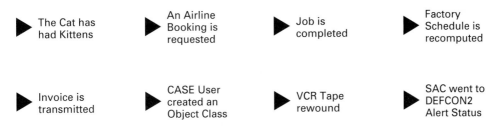

Depending on the area being modeled, more than one event can occur when an operation completes—where each can trigger separate operations:

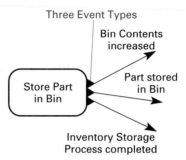

THE LIFECYCLE OF AN OBJECT   Most objects have a lifecycle in which a succession of events can happen to it, each changing its state. When the Airline Booking object is first created, it may pass through the states of being Requested Airline Booking, Wait-listed Airline Booking, Confirmed Airline Booking, Fulfilled Airline Booking, and Archived Airline Booking. Other events may happen that cause it to be Denied Airline Booking, Cancelled Airline Booking, or Modified Airline Booking.

In object-oriented analysis, we draw a diagram showing the lifecycle of an object. Figure 7.3, for example, expresses one facet of the lifecycle of an Airline Booking object. In addition to showing the possible states of the objects, the diagram also shows the permissible state changes. The diagram in Fig. 7.3 is a state-transition diagram.

In addition to those object types in Fig. 7.3, other object types may determine the state of an object. For example, the figure indicates nothing about the

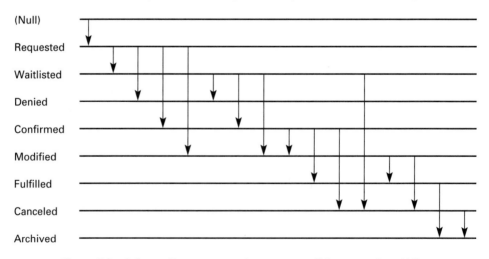

Figure 7.3   A fence diagram expressing some possible states of an Airline Booking object. The horizontal lines represent states of an Airline Booking object. The vertical lines represent transitions between states.

payment status of a booking. Another such diagram may express a payment-related lifecycle of an Airline Booking object: Unpaid Airline Booking, Deposit Paid, Airline Booking Fully Paid, Refunded Airline Booking, and so on. The two diagrams may interact with one another. For example, if the payment is not made, the booking may not be confirmed.

Another example of state changes that can be illustrated as a lifecycle would be the information displayed on the screen. Each display can be in many different states. Figure 7.4 shows a diagram used in some CASE tools that shows the interaction among the different displays. It illustrates the structure, or flow, of the dialog, that is, the dialog transitioning from one state to another.

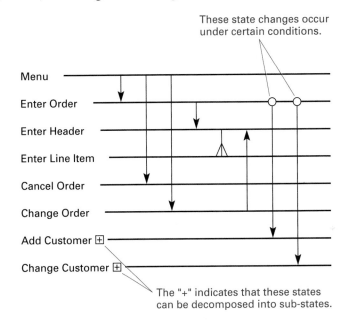

Figure 7.4   A fence diagram indicating that a Screen Dialog object can be in one of many states, each displaying a different panel. The horizontal lines represent states; the vertical lines show transitions between states.

INTERACTIONS BETWEEN TYPES OF OBJECTS

State transition diagrams are useful for expressing a lifecycle of one particular object. However, most processes involve an interaction of many different objects. For example, the OO program implementation in Fig. 7.5 illustrates that a request is made to pay the salary of an Employee object. In order to accomplish this, a request must be sent to compute and return a Tax amount. When this state change has occurred, a request is then made to create a Check object. As a result, the Employee object's state changes to that of a Paid Employee.

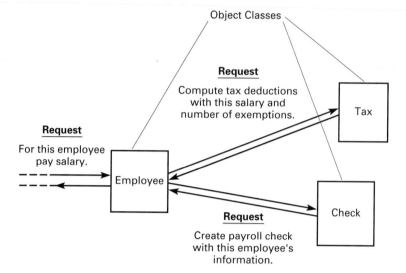

Figure 7.5 A diagram of messages passing among classes.

This brief payroll example requires three different objects—each with its own state change in its own lifecycle. The network diagram illustrates the way in which different types of objects change state and can request other objects to change state in the process. Figure 7.6 extends this diagram to depict the operations that are invoked to support the payroll process.

When diagrams are expressed in this way, it is easy to see how they can be implemented as OO program structures: object types are implemented as classes;

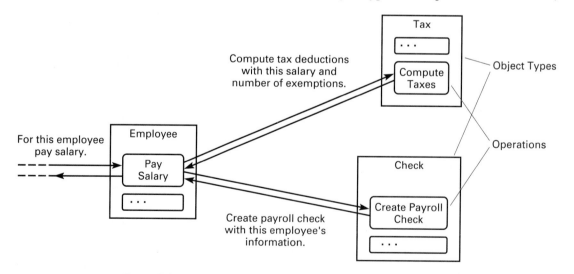

Figure 7.6 An extension of Fig. 7.5 showing the operations invoked.

and operations become OO program operations. If the user can express processing requirements in this fashion during analysis, the job of the OOPL designer is made easier. However, many users do not typically think of their application processing in terms of object types that are populated with operations and make various types of requests. As an alternative form, a script format is often found preferable where events occur that trigger operations that, in turn, result in events that trigger other operations, and so on. In other words, this script format—called an event schema—represents single-object lifecycle changes triggering other object lifecycle changes.

OPERATIONS

In OO analysis, the term *operation* refers to a processing unit that can be requested. The procedure is implemented with a *method. The method* is *the specification of how the operation is carried out. It is the script for the operation.* At the program level, the method is the code that implements the operation.

Operations are *invoked.* An *invoked operation* is an *instance* of an operation. An operation may or may not change the state of an object. If it changes the state of an object, an *event* occurs. Operations are represented as round-cornered boxes. Event types are represented by solid black triangles connected to the box:

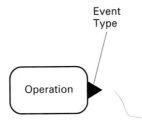

Figure 7.7 shows an *event schema* drawn in this way.

EXTERNAL SOURCES OF EVENTS

Events are state changes that a system must know about and react to in some way. Often, many of the operations that cause these events are *external* to the system. In these circumstances, the operation symbol is drawn as a shadowed box with round corners as illustrated in Fig. 7.8(a).

An *external clock* is a special form of external source. It indicates that an external process will emit clock ticks at some previously specified frequency, such as every second, the end of the every day, the beginning of every month, or April 15th of every year. The event, then, is when the external clock tick occurs. External clocks are represented as clock faces.

Figure 7.7 contains two external events resulting from an external operation.

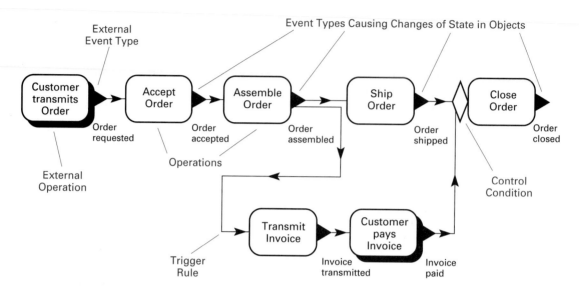

Figure 7.7 Event schema showing a sequence of events that trigger operations. An event schema relates to a corresponding object schema and state-transition diagram.

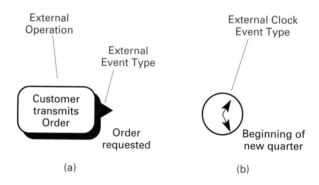

Figure 7.8 External operations are represented as round-cornered boxes with a shadow. When the event type is caused by an external clock, a clock face is used.

TRIGGER RULES   When an event occurs, the state change usually triggers the invocation of one or more operations. For example, if goods are withdrawn from a warehouse taking the quantity held below a certain level, this may trigger a reorder operation. In Fig. 7.7, an Order assembled event triggers two operations: Ship Order and Transmit Invoice.

    Trigger rules, then, define the link between cause and effect. Whenever an event of one type occurs, the trigger rule invokes a predefined operation. The event type Order assembled has two trigger rules that react to each event occurrence and trigger their associated operations. An event type may have many trigger rules—each invoking its own operation *in parallel.* Parallel operations can result simultaneously in different state changes.

In addition, an operation may be invoked by multiple triggers. For example, in Fig. 7.9 the Produce Check operation is triggered whenever a Check requested or an End-of-month event occurs. In other words, *either* trigger results in the operation being executed.

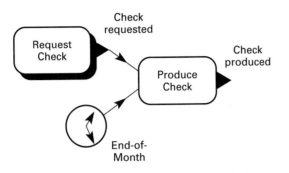

Figure 7.9   The produce Check operation is triggered whenever *either* a Check requested or an End-of-month event occurs.

CONTROL CONDITIONS

As depicted above, an operation may be invoked by one or more triggers. For example, in Fig. 7.7 the Close Order operation is triggered whenever an Order shipped or Invoice transmitted event occurs. However, before the operation is actually invoked, its *control condition* is checked. If the results of evaluating the condition are true, its operation is invoked. If false, the operation is not invoked.

Whenever a control condition must be checked prior to invoking an operation, it should be represented with a diamond-shaped symbol preceding the operation:

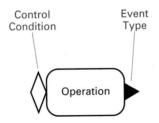

Control conditions can also act as synchronization points for parallel processing. In other words, control conditions can ensure that a set of events is complete before proceeding with an operation. The control condition in Fig. 7.7, for instance, might state that an Order object cannot be classified as a Closed Order unless it has been shipped and its invoice paid.

EVENT SUBTYPES AND SUPERTYPES   In Fig. 7.10(a), the Review Task operation results in two events: Task accepted and Task rejected. Yet, only one of these event types can occur when a Task is reviewed. Disjoint types are expressed in this book using type partitions. For example, in a separate window Fig. 7.10(b) indicates that these two event types are mutually exclusive, because Task accepted and Task rejected are contained within the same partition box.

The word partition implies that something is being divided into disjoint subsets. In OO techniques, this "something" is called a supertype. Task reviewed, then, is an event supertype partitioned into two disjoint types of events. Therefore, the method defined within Review Task has, as a goal, that a Task is reviewed. Furthermore, to achieve this goal, one of two subgoals is necessary—either to accept or reject the Task being reviewed. In other words, event partitions are *not* separate operations that coordinate branching conditions for disjoint triggers. Instead, they *indicate* the goals and disjoint subgoals of the operations

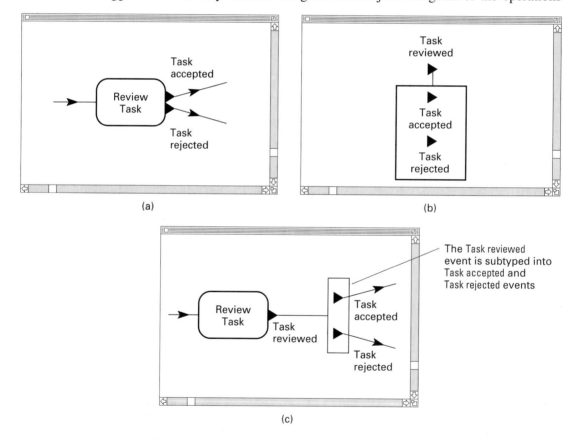

Figure 7.10   Events can be subtyped by using two separate diagrams (a) and (b); or the same information can be expressed on one expanded diagram (c).

with which they are associated. Figure 7.10(c) combines both notions in the same window by expanding the diagram depicted in Fig. 7.10(a).

HIERARCHICAL SCHEMAS

The operation that causes an event to happen may be complex. The operation that rewinds a VCR tape appears simple. The VCR user presses one button.

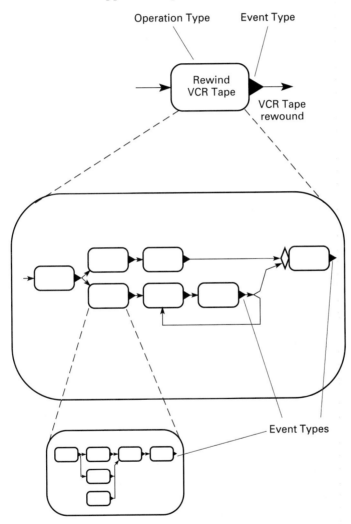

Figure 7.11 Rewinding a VCR tape is a simple operation for the VCR user. However, a complex set of operations and events have to occur inside the VCR in order for it to perform the rewind operation. They define the *method* for the rewind *operation*. Event schemas may be decomposed hierarchically, like this, making a high-level operation appear simple.

When the Tape rewound event occurs, the user receives a simple message when the rewind is complete. However, internally, the rewind operation involves a whole set of operations and events, as illustrated in Fig. 7.11.

Figure 7.11 illustrates a hierarchical decomposition of event schemas. Boundaries can be placed around a complex event schema and treated as one high-level operation. The lower-level event schema, then, becomes the *method for the operation it decomposes.*

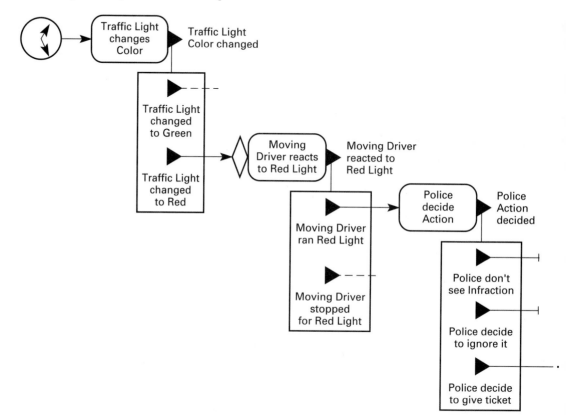

Figure 7.12   An event schema for a car chase with event and control conditi symbols, and expanded event subtypes.

CAUSE-AND-EFFECT ISOLATION   Each operation carries out its task, regardless of what happens elsewhere. An operation is invoked by one or more triggers, executes its method, and is expected to change the state of one object. The operation has no knowledge of what event triggered it and why. Additionally, it does not know what operations are triggered from its event. In short, it does not recognize its cause and effect— only that it is invoked to produce a state change of a given object. This isolation from cause-and-effect considerations is necessary for the operation to be reusable in many different applications.

In Object Structure Analysis, we draw diagrams to represent the structure of object types. In behavior analysis, we draw diagrams to show the dynamic interaction of events—types and states and the sequence of events. These diagrams are referred to as *schemas*. An *object schema* expresses the type of objects and their associations for a given system. An *event schema* expresses processing scripts that change the states of objects. Event schemas, then, must be expressed in terms of object schemas, because events are expressed in changing the state of given types of objects. Therefore, a CASE tool for object-oriented analysis should enable its users to build object schemas and event schemas, and maintain the close relationship that exists between these two types of representation.

CLEAR MODULARIZATION

OO techniques provide two important ways to divide complex software into simple procedures. First, methods should result in a state change in one object. This state change, by itself, is usually simple and easy to program. Second, each operation is isolated from cause and effect. The operation can be reused on different software and on multiple interacting processors.

OO techniques thus provide clear modularization that is simpler and more precise than that of conventional structured techniques. Objects of great complexity may be used with relatively simple requests, such as the use of a VCR. Complex objects may interact in one piece of software or on machines scattered across a network. Maintenance of software designed with OO techniques is easier than conventional software maintenance.

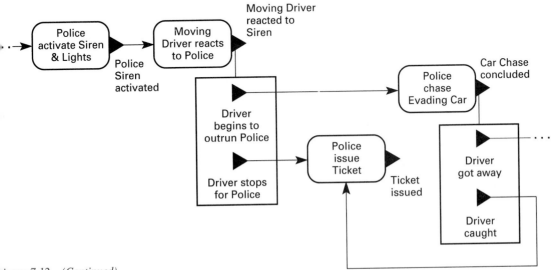

igure 7.12   (Continued)

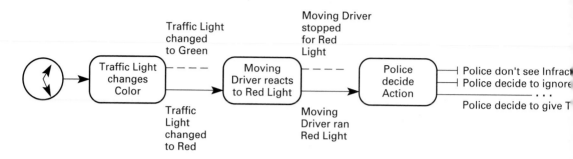

Figure 7.13 An event schema for a car chase with all symbols and event type representation contracted.

A world of difference exists between this clear modularization and the amorphous jelly-like nature of most non-OO software.

THE SIMILARITY OF ANALYSIS AND DESIGN

Analysts, designers, and implementors should all possess the same systems model. As the model progresses from analysis to implementation, more detail is added, but it remains essentially the same.

As illustrated in Fig. 5.3, this is not the case with conventional structured techniques. Analysts think with data-flow diagrams, designers think with structure charts, and programmers think with COBOL and SQL. With OO techniques, the same paradigm is used for analysis, design, and implementation. The analyst identifies object types and inheritance, and thinks about events that change the state of objects. The designer adds detail to this model, perhaps designing screens, user interaction, and client-server interaction. With a powerful CASE tool, code is generated from the design.

The thought process flows so naturally from analysis to design that it may be difficult to tell where analysis ends and design begins. Communications between the analyst and designer will be better, especially if both use the same repository-based CASE toolset.

End users should also think in terms of object types, events, changes to the state of the objects, and business rules that trigger and control events. They often think intuitively in such terms before being exposed to the OO vocabulary and its schemas. We should make sure that the schemas we draw help the users to think in these terms. The diagrams for analysis must avoid constructs that bewilder the users.

Analysts and users, working together, should create a model of the enterprise, showing how the business people want to run the enterprise, and helping them to reinvent its procedures. The enterprise model should be translated as directly as possible into system designs.

OBJECT-FLOW DIAGRAMS

Event schemas are appropriate for describing processes in terms of events, triggers, conditions, and operations. However, expressing large complicated

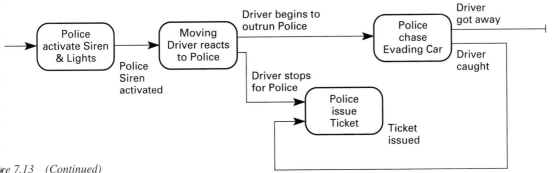

re 7.13   (Continued)

processes in this way may not be appropriate. Often a system area is too vast or intricate to express the dynamics of events and triggers. Perhaps, in addition, only a high level of understanding is necessary. This is particularly true of strategic-level planning. In situations such as these, an *object-flow diagram* is useful.

Object-flow diagrams (OFDs) are similar to data-flow diagrams (DFDs), because they depict activities interfacing with other activities. In DFDs, the interface passes data. In OO techniques, we do not want to be limited to data passing. Instead, the diagram should represent any kind of thing that passes from one activity to another: whether it be orders, parts, finished goods, designs, services, hardware, software—or data. In short, the OFD indicates the *objects* that are produced and the activities that produce and exchange them. Figure 7.14 is an example of an object-flow diagram.

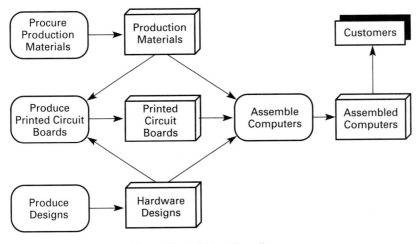

Figure 7.14   Object-flow diagram.

A person familiar with data-flow diagrams will readily recognize the round-cornered activity boxes, the shadowed, external-agent box, and the direction of the flow lines. Absent here, however, is the data-store symbol. In its place, a three-dimensional box is used. The three-dimensionality of the symbol indicates that the OFD represents that real-life objects flow between activities.

OFDs describe objects and the way in which they are produced and consumed:

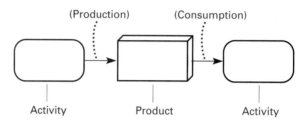

The *product* is the end result that fulfills the purpose of the activity. However, products are not just produced for production's sake. They are produced for consumption by other activities that add value to the consumed product—to produce yet another more complex product. At every step, new, more complex, and subtle qualities are created. In this way, the OFD can be used for strategic business planning as well as strategic information planning.

Object-flow diagrams, then, can represent either top-down or bottom-up modeling. In particular, object-flow diagrams are very useful in modeling organizations in a top-down fashion at the strategic level. Activities can be decomposed into OFDs. However, at a more detailed level in behavior analysis, expressing the dynamic aspects of event schemas is also appropriate. An activity can be expressed in terms of an OFD, an event schema, or both, as shown in Fig. 7.15.

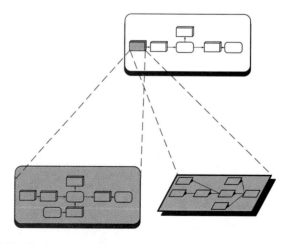

Figure 7.15 Each activity can be expressed as an object-flow diagram, an event schema, or both.

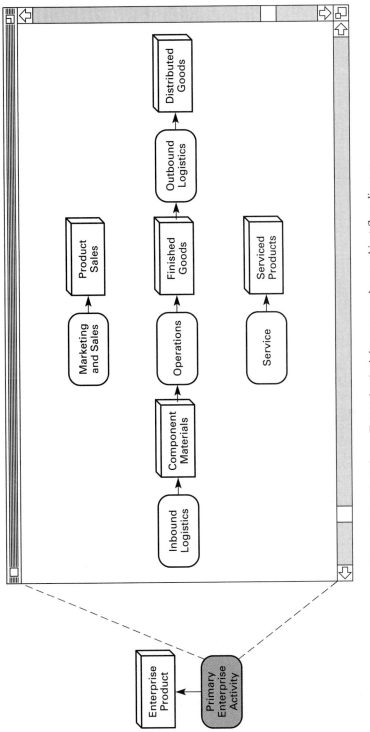

Figure 7.16 The Primary Enterprise Activity expressed as an object-flow diagram.

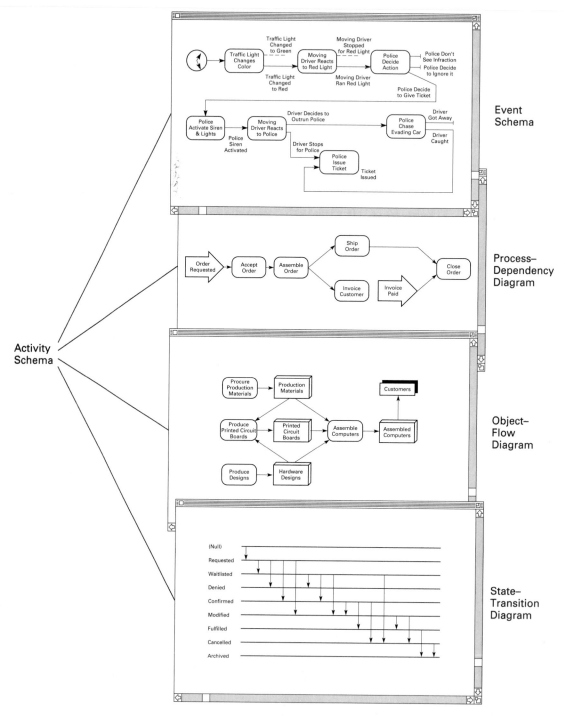

Activity
Schema

Event
Schema

Process–
Dependency
Diagram

Object–
Flow
Diagram

State–
Transition
Diagram

Figure 7.17

Each activity can be expressed in more detail. For example, the high-level primary activity of a manufacturing company could be represented in more detail as shown in Fig. 7.16.

To express a process in a rigorous fashion that can generate code, an event schema is appropriate. To represent basic control structures and processing flow, and when the dynamics of events and triggers are not yet comprehensible, the object-flow diagram is useful.

In summary, Object Behavior Analysis can use a variety of diagramming approaches, shown in Fig. 7.17.

8 OBJECT STRUCTURE AND BEHAVIOR DESIGN

Object-oriented analysis has two aspects: Object Structure Analysis (OSA) and Object Behavior Analysis (OBA). In object-oriented design, the same division can also be described: Object Structure Design (OSD) and Object Behavior Design (OBD). OO programming languages have data structures and methods—both subject to inheritance and combined into units called *classes*. Because of this, both OSD and OBD are intertwined and will be described together.

Box 8.1 lists the information identified in Object Structure and Behavior Design.

BOX 8.1

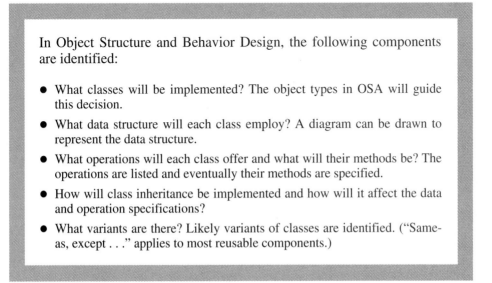

In Object Structure and Behavior Design, the following components are identified:

- What classes will be implemented? The object types in OSA will guide this decision.
- What data structure will each class employ? A diagram can be drawn to represent the data structure.
- What operations will each class offer and what will their methods be? The operations are listed and eventually their methods are specified.
- How will class inheritance be implemented and how will it affect the data and operation specifications?
- What variants are there? Likely variants of classes are identified. ("Same-as, except . . ." applies to most reusable components.)

CLASS

In Object Structure Analysis, we identify object types. In Object Structure Design, our concern focuses on the implementation of these object types.

> A *class* is an implementation of an object type. It specifies the data structure and permissible operational methods that apply to each of its objects.

Figure 8.1 illustrates a class. The class specifies the *data structure* for each of its objects and the *operations* that are used when accessing the objects. The specification of the way in which a class's operations are carried out is called the *method.* Objects can be used *only* with specific *methods.*

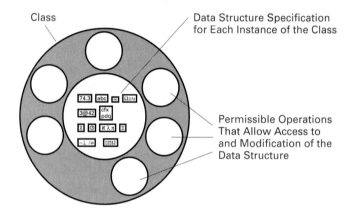

Class

Data Structure Specification for Each Instance of the Class

Permissible Operations That Allow Access to and Modification of the Data Structure

Figure 8.1　Each class specifies a data structure, permissible operations, and methods of operation.

Figure 8.2 illustrates an object that is an instance of the class in Fig. 8.1. The data and operations it encapsulates are specified by its class. The object's *data* are stored within the object and are accessed and modified only by permissible operations. This restriction to access is due to *encapsulation.* Encapsulation protects the data from arbitrary and unintended use. Direct user access or update of an object's data would violate encapsulation.

Users observe object "behavior" in terms of the operations that may be applied to objects and the results of such operations. These operations comprise an object's *interface* with its users.

WHAT IS THE DIFFERENCE BETWEEN AN OPERATION AND A METHOD?

Operations are processes that can be requested as units. *Methods* are procedural specifications of an operation within a class. In other words, the operation is the kind of service requested, and the method is the programming code for it.

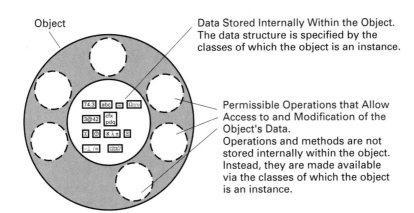

Object

Data Stored Internally Within the Object.
The data structure is specified by the
classes of which the object is an instance.

Permissible Operations that Allow
Access to and Modification of the
Object's Data.
Operations and methods are not
stored internally within the object.
Instead, they are made available
via the classes of which the object
is an instance.

Figure 8.2   Encapsulation hides the implementation of each object's data
structure and methods. Only the object's permissible operations, or *interface,*
are known to its users.

> An *operation* is a process that can be requested as a unit.
>
> A *method* is the specification of an operation.

For example, an operation associated with the class **Purchase Order** might
be one that computes the total of the **Purchase Order**. The method would specify
the way of computing the total. In doing so, the method might acquire the price
of each item on the order by sending a request to its associated **Item** objects.
Each **Item** object, in turn, would return its price to the **Purchase Order** method
using a method in the **Item** class.

The methods in a class manipulate *only* the objects of that class. They cannot directly access the data structures of an object in a different class. To use the
data structures of a different class of object, they must send a request to that
object.

As described in Chapter 2 and illustrated again in Fig. 8.2, *encapsulation*
means that the methods of a class protect all of the objects that are in that class.

CLASS
INHERITANCE

Generalization is a conceptual notion. *Class inheritance* (usually referred to simply as *inheritance*) is an
implementation of generalization. Generalization
states that the properties of a type *apply* to its subtypes. Class inheritance makes
the data structure and operations of a class *physically available for reuse* by its
subclasses. Inheriting the operations from a superclass enables code sharing—
rather than code redefinition—among classes. Inheriting the data structure
enables structure reuse.

For example, in Fig. 8.3 Customer Account inherits operations 1 and 2 from Account. In addition to these, it has operations of its own—3 and 4. Overdue Customer Account also inherits operations 1, 2, 3, and 4 from Customer Account, as well as having 6 as its own.

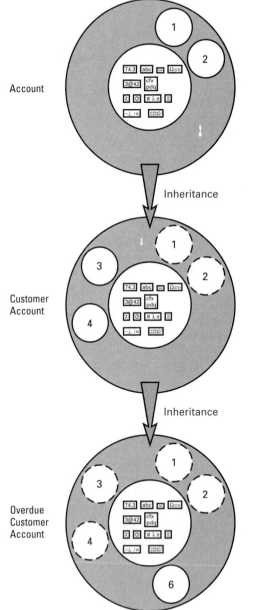

Figure 8.3   Inheritance. The class Customer Account inherits methods 1 and 2 from the class Account. Customer Account has two methods of its own—3 and 4. The class Overdue Customer Account inherits methods 1, 2, 3, and 4 from the class Customer Account—while having its own method 6.

Multiple Inheritance

In *multiple inheritance,* a class may inherit data structures and operations from more than one superclass. Figure 8.3 shows *single inheritance,* while Fig. 8.4 shows *multiple inheritance.*

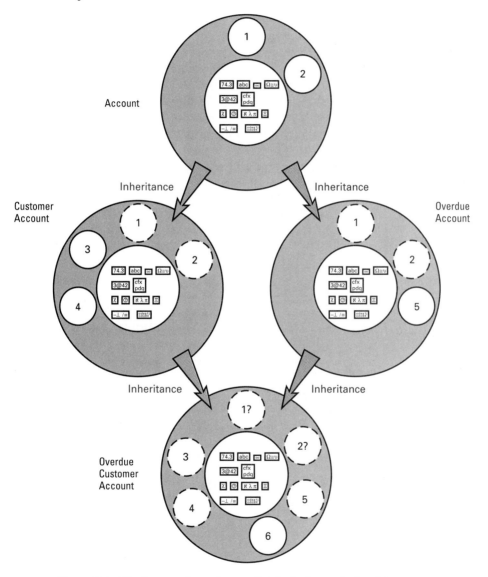

Figure 8.4   The bottom three classes all inherit the methods of Account. Overdue Customer Account inherits methods from both Customer Account and Overdue Account. (When operations with identical names are inherited from multiple superclasses, problems can arise.)

In Object Structure Analysis, the analyst would indicate that Overdue Customer Account has two supertypes—sharing a common Account supertype. In OO design, this generalization hierarchy is implemented using inheritance. Overdue Customer Account inherits the features from classes Customer Account and Overdue Account. Therefore, Overdue Customer Account has the following operations physically available for reuse—1, 2, 3, 4, 5, and 6.

> *Class inheritance* implements the generalization hierarchy by making it possible for one class to share the data structure and operations of another class.
>
> *Single inheritance* is where a class may inherit the data structure and operations of one superclass.
>
> *Multiple inheritance* is where a class may inherit the data structure and operations of more than one superclass.

Fern diagrams are used for showing multiple inheritance paths among classes. Figure 8.5 is such a diagram that shows some of the classes in the ProKappa OO-CASE tool. At the top of Fig. 8.5, for example, a CoerceToSlotProbeHook inherits the properties of SelfCoercingProbeHooks, SelfCoercingProbeHooks inherit the properties of CoercingProbeHooks, and CoercingProbeHooks inherit the properties of ProbeHooks.

SELECTING
A METHOD

When a request is sent to an object, the software selects the methods that will be used. We commented earlier that the method is not stored "in the object," because this would cause multiple replication. Instead, the method is associated with the *class*. The method can not be in the class of which the object is an instance—but in a superclass. Figure 8.6 illustrates one way of thinking about this.

Here, a request is sent to an Executive object named Betty to change her phone extension to x6667. The list of permissible operations within the Executive class is checked, and "change phone extension" is not there. The OO implementation would then automatically check the superclass of Employee. In this example, the "change phone extension" operation is found in Employee and is selected to carry out the request. Should the operation not be found in that superclass, the inheritance selection mechanism would continue its search through all the object's superclasses, level-by-level. If found, the operation is selected. If the operation is not found at any level of superclass, the source of the request is regarded invalid. OO programming languages, such as Smalltalk, detect these invalid requests at runtime. OO programming languages, such as C++ or Objective C, resolve these requests at compile-time so that no invalid requests can occur.

Inheritance, then, allows a class to reuse the features of its superclasses. In this way, users need only specify what should be done—leaving the *selection mechanism* to determine how the operation is located and executed. The selection mechanism shifts the burden of locating the correct operation from the source of the request to the OO application.

POLYMORPHISM   One of the major goals of OO techniques is the reuse of code. However, some operations may require customization to meet a particular need. For example, in Fig. 8.7 the **Employee** class defines a retire operation. In OO implementations, this operation is automatically inherited by all the subclasses of **Employee**. However, an organization may have different methods for retiring an **Executive** than for retiring an **Employee**. In this situation, the method for retiring executives *overrides* the method for retiring employees in general. Yet, even though these methods differ, they accomplish the same operational purpose. This phenomenon is known as *polymorphism.* The word polymorphism is chosen for an operation that takes on many forms of implementation depending on the type of object. The example is polymorphic, because the retire operation has a different method of implementation depending on whether an object is an **Employee** or an **Executive**.

One strength of polymorphism is that a request for an operation can be made without knowing which method should be invoked. These implementation details are hidden from the user. Instead, the responsibility rests with the selection mechanism of the OO implementation.

"SAME AS,   Most reusability in practice requires the implementor
EXCEPT . . ."   to modify the reusable component. A house architect takes a standard bathroom design and modifies it to include pink marble and a larger tub. A lawyer takes a prenuptial agreement from a repository and customizes it. (The lawyer charges 50 hours for only 2 hours of actual work.) The phrase "same as, except . . ." describes most reusability.

Object-oriented techniques should allow customization of classes. You should be able to take a class from a repository and customize it to your needs.

We do not want implementors to change the code of a class any more than we want you to change the circuit boards of your VCR. Classes become highly complex. Therefore, the class should be designed so that it can be customized easily on a CASE-tool screen. Good CASE tools that enable you to use OO designs from a repository allow you to customize those designs.

Figures 8.8 and 8.9 give a simple illustration of customization. A class stored in the CASE repository is **Field**. **Screens** are built from **Fields** and **Field Groups**, **Dialogs** are built from **Screens**.

ProbeHooks — CoercingProbeHooks < SelfCoercingProbeHook
                                    TargetCoercingProbeHooks < CoerceToSlotProbeHook
FindObjectDialogBox
EditMixin — MotifEditMixin
Coordinators — BrowserCoordinators < ProbeCoordinators
                                      StandardObjectBrowserCoordinators
            TouchHandle
CoordinationEvents < SimpleCoordinate
            OpenSet
            ChgOverallObjectSet
                        SlotFacetValueReferences
SlotPartReferences < SlotFacetReferences
                     SlotValueReferences
                     SlotReferences
References < GenericSlotNameReferences
            ObjectReferences
DialogBoxMixin — MotifDialogBoxMixin — MotifSlotPropertiesMixin — MotifSlotPropertiesDisplayer

MotifProbeFrameMixin

CompositeMixin — MotifCompositeMixin — MotifBrowserMixin

MotifProtalkStepperMixin — MotifProtalkSteppers
MotifSlotFacetBrowserMixin — MotifSlotFacetBrowser
MotifStandardObjectBrowserMixin — MotifStandardObjectBrowsers
MotifProtalkStatementTraceMixin — MotifProtalkStatementTraceDisplayers

WSysSpecifxMx — TextDisplayerMixin — MotifTextMixin — MotifProtalkTextMixin — MotifProtalkTextDisplayers
                                                       MotifTextDisplayers

MotifProtalkLogMixin — MotifProtalkLogDisplayers
MotifProtalkBindingsTableMixin — MotifProtalkBindingsTableDisplayers
TableDisplayerMixin — MotifTableMixin < MotifFacetTableMixin — MotifFacetTableDisplayer
                                        MotifObjectSlotTableMixin — MotifObjectSlotTableDisplayers
                                        MotifMvListMixin
                                        MotifAppListMixin

GraphDisplayerMixin — MotifGraphMixin — MotifObjectGraphMixin — MotifObjectGraphDisplayers
MotifMixin — MotifSelectorMixin — MotifSlotSelectorMixin

                        FacetTableProbeFrames
                        MvListProbeFrames
ProbeFrames < SlotTableProbeFrames
              ObjectGraphProbeFrames

CompositeDisplayers — BrowserDisplayers < ProbeFrames
                                          ProtalkSteppers
                                          SlotFacetBrowser
                                          StandardObjectBrowsers

TextDisplayers — ProtalkTextDisplayers
DialogBoxDisplayer — SlotPropertiesDisplayers

MotifFacetTableProbeFrameMixin — MotifFacetTableProbeFrames
MotifMvListProbeFrameMixin — MotifMvListProbeFrames
MotifSlotTableProbeFrameMixin — MotifSlotTableProbeFrames
MotifObjectGraphProbeFrameMixin — MotifObjectGraphProbeFrames

ProtalkStatementTraceDisplayers

Displayers

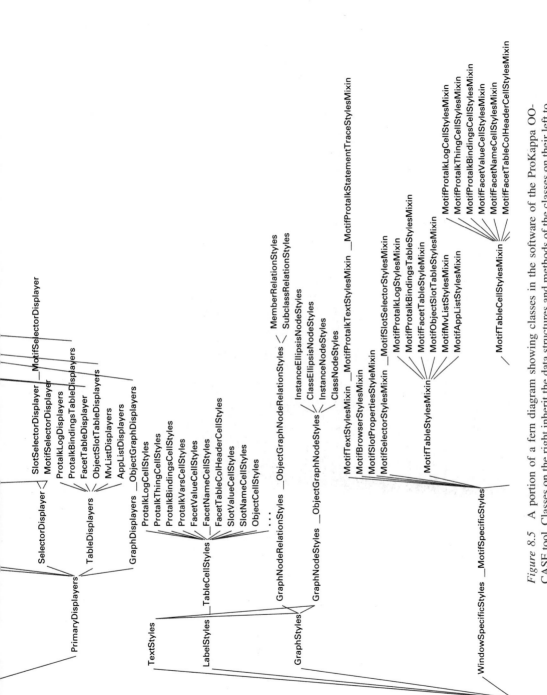

Figure 8.5 A portion of a fern diagram showing classes in the software of the ProKappa OO-CASE tool. Classes on the right inherit the data structures and methods of the classes on their left to which they are connected. (Courtesy of IntelliCorp, Inc.)

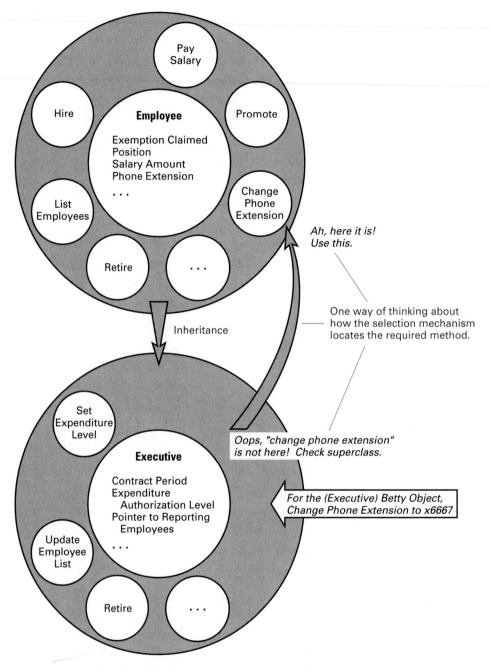

Figure 8.6 The OO *selection mechanism* locates the appropriate method for the requested operation.

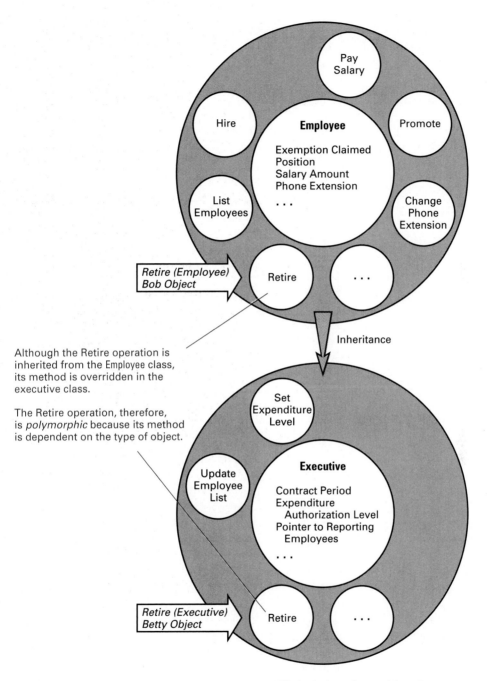

Although the Retire operation is inherited from the Employee class, its method is overridden in the executive class.

The Retire operation, therefore, is *polymorphic* because its method is dependent on the type of object.

Figure 8.7 A method may be implemented differently in a class and its subclass. Subclasses may implement the same operation with different methods. This is called *polymorphism*.

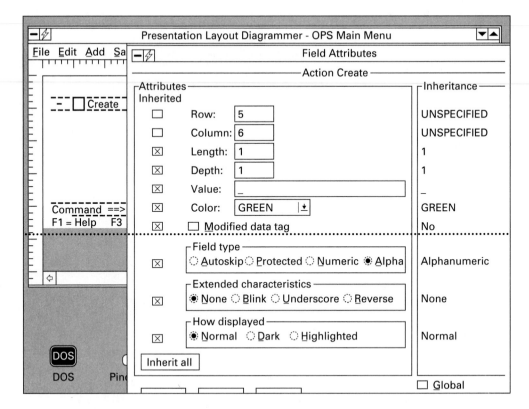

Figure 8.8   A window from an I-CASE tool that allows the designer to override inherited properties of the object class Field. (Courtesy of KnowledgeWare, Inc., Atlanta, GA)

The class Field has several attributes—row, column, color, and so on. The default value for color is "Green." This means that every instance of the class Field will be created with a color value of "Green"—unless the value is specifically changed by the user. This is a form of inheritance called class-instance inheritance.

Figure 8.8 shows various subclasses of Field that inherit the values of their parent unless the designer overrides a value. The designer makes the Color of input fields "White." Customer Number and Customer Name are both input fields, so they appear white on the screen.

Figure 8.9 shows a type CASE-tool window that allows the designer to override inherited properties of an object.

This type of customization is simple for the user. Customized applications can be built quickly without tampering with the code of a class. Designers should anticipate what aspects of a design users will want to modify and provide them with easy-to-use means of customization. This is an essential aspect of OO

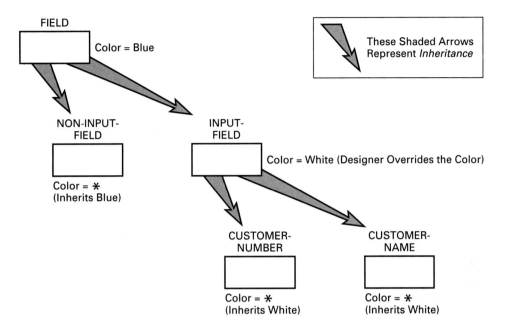

Figure 8.9   Subclasses of Field inherit the color of their parents, but the designer can override the color.

CASE tools. It is also an essential part of the *methodologies* for systems development that use OO techniques to achieve high reusability.

The analyst or designer who creates a class should be asking the question, "How will this class be used in the future?" He should create the class in a way that can be easily adapted for future needs. In a well-managed OO environment, everything is either built out of existing classes or it creates new classes that will be reused in the future. Everything relates to reusability from the past or reusability in the future.

Some corporations have achieved a high degree of reuse. Noma Industries, a large Canadian manufacturer, emphasized reusability across its 14 divisions. It succeeded in achieving such a level of reusability that only 3.8 percent of the code is custom built. Because of the high level of reuse, the code added or replaced per developer person-day averages about 1000 source lines of COBOL.

As OO CASE tools spread, managing software development will provide challenges. The highest level of automation will be achieved by assembling applications from object classes and easily adapting the objects in a *same-as, except* fashion.

9 RECOMMENDED DIAGRAMMING STANDARDS

Object-oriented analysis and design require precise diagrams. The diagrams should appear on the screen of OO CASE tools. These tools should collect enough information to drive a code generator producing code that is free from syntax errors. The diagrams, therefore, must have an engineering-like precision.

The set of diagramming standards described in this chapter are employed throughout the book. Most I.S. professionals learning OO techniques are likely to have existing knowledge of conventional techniques. Diagrams for conventional techniques are widely used on CASE tools. As far as possible, the diagrams for OO techniques should incorporate those for conventional techniques.

Many widely used CASE tools employ the diagrams described in James Martin's book written at the start of the CASE era: *Recommended Diagramming Standards for Analysts and Programmers* [1]. This book has been a "bible" for many CASE vendors. The OO diagrams used in the current book are an extension of the diagrams in the earlier book. We recommend that builders of OO CASE tools use diagrams that are already widely understood and avoid inventing incompatible diagrams. These would cause confusion and make the techniques difficult to learn. (OO CASE tools using strange diagrams are best avoided.)

A FORM OF LANGUAGE   Philosophers have described how our thinking depends upon the language we use. When mankind used only Roman numerals, ordinary people could not multiply or divide. Multiplication and division spread when we had Arabic numerals. The diagrams we draw of complex processes are a form of language. With computers, we create processes more complex than those we perform manually. Appropriate diagrams help us to visualize and invent those processes.

If only one person is developing a system design or program, the diagrams that person uses are an aid to clear thinking. A poor choice of diagramming technique can inhibit thinking. A good choice can speed up work and improve the results.

When several people work on a system or program, the diagrams are an essential communications tool. A formal diagramming technique enables the developers to interchange ideas and make their separate components fit together precisely.

When systems are modified, clear diagrams simplify maintenance. With them, a new team can understand how the programs work and can design changes. Such changes often affect other parts of the program. However, clear diagrams of the program structure enable maintenance programmers to understand the consequences of their changes. In debugging, clear diagrams are a valuable tool for understanding how the programs ought to work and for tracking down what might be wrong.

Diagramming, then, is a language essential both for clear thinking and for human communication. An enterprise needs standards for I.S. diagrams, just as it has standards for engineering drawings.

We have emphasized that OO techniques give us a more natural way to think about our complex world than the techniques used for conventional programming and analysis. Business people can easily visualize the procedures that need automating in terms of objects, events, event rules, and triggers, whereas they find it more difficult to relate to structure charts and data-flow diagrams. A vital challenge in I.S. today is improved communications for I.S. professionals and business people. I.S. professionals must understand the business and invent how it should change. Business people must think more clearly about systems and automation.

We ought to be building a generation of CASE tools that represent systems in a form that business people relate to easily and drive this representation into code. OO techniques are desirable for this.

When a CASE tool is used, the computer deciphers the *meaning* of the diagrams. The computer should help the designer to think clearly and help represent the procedures and generate code automatically.

The diagrams and their manipulation by computer are a form of *thought* processing. The analyst, designer, programmer, user, and executive need a family of diagram types that help them to think clearly. These diagram types should be as clear and simple as possible. Although there are many types of diagrams, the number of icons should be limited and their meaning should be relatively obvious.

The diagrams must be sufficiently complete and rigorous to serve as a basis for code generation and for automatic conversion from one type of diagram into another. The diagrams become the documentation for systems (along with a *repository* that stores the meaning of the diagrams and additional information collected when they were drawn). When changes are made to a system, the diagrams will be changed on the screen and the code regenerated. The design documentation does not slip out of date as changes are made.

The diagrams for designing systems are a language of communication. Good CASE tools enforce precision in this language. As with other languages, *standards* must apply to it so that diverse parties can communicate. Developers should be prevented from inventing their own forms of diagramming. Researchers should use existing diagramming techniques where they are applicable. Incompatible diagramming is a barrier to communication.

Above all, the diagrams need to be standardized throughout the corporation so that all persons involved with computers have a common powerful language and can discuss one another's plans, specifications, designs, and programs.

CONVENTIONAL DIAGRAMS

Figure 9.1 summarizes the symbols commonly used on diagrams with CASE tools employing conventional techniques. These symbols are used in many different types of diagrams, including entity-relationship diagrams, decomposition diagrams, dependency diagrams, data-flow diagrams, decision trees, state-transition diagrams, dialog-design diagrams, data-analysis diagrams, and action diagrams.

OBJECT-ORIENTED DIAGRAMS

Figure 9.2 summarizes the symbols used for OO analysis and design, extending the set of symbols in Fig. 9.1.

SQUARE-CORNERED AND ROUND-CORNERED BOXES

Recommended Diagramming Standards suggests that nodes representing data be drawn with square-cornered rectangles (fields, record layouts, entity types, and so on) and boxes representing activities be drawn with round corners (procedures, processes, program modules, and so on). This is a widely accepted convention.

Similarly, we recommend that object types and classes be drawn with square-cornered boxes and activities with round-cornered boxes. This makes some of the complex schemas, described later in the book, more easily interpretable.

An entity type is drawn as a rectangle:

An object, like an entity, is a thing, real or abstract. We, therefore, use a rectangle for drawing object types:

DATA
Square-cornered
boxes represent
data (entity types,
entity subtypes,
records, datasets)

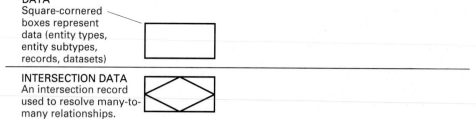

INTERSECTION DATA
An intersection record
used to resolve many-to-
many relationships.

CARDINALITY
This is often drawn as a single bar

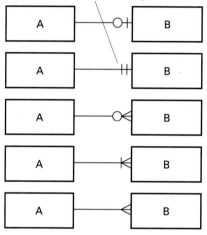

MUTUAL EXCLUSIVITY
One and only one of the
branches is taken:

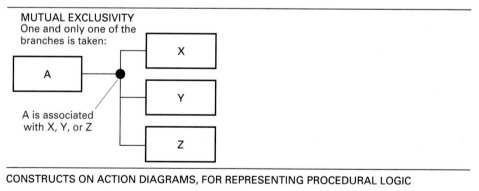

A is associated
with X, Y, or Z

CONSTRUCTS ON ACTION DIAGRAMS, FOR REPRESENTING PROCEDURAL LOGIC

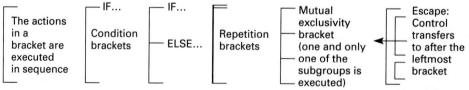

The actions in a bracket are executed in sequence

IF... Condition brackets

IF... ELSE...

Repetition brackets

Mutual exclusivity bracket (one and only one of the subgroups is executed)

Escape: Control transfers to after the leftmost bracket

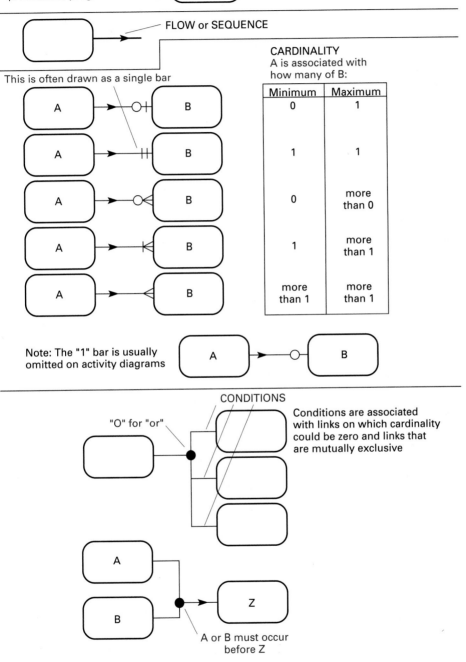

ACTIVITIES
Round-cornered
boxes represent
activities (functions, processes,
procedures, program modules)

FLOW or SEQUENCE

This is often drawn as a single bar

CARDINALITY
A is associated with
how many of B:

Minimum	Maximum
0	1
1	1
0	more than 0
1	more than 1
more than 1	more than 1

Note: The "1" bar is usually
omitted on activity diagrams

CONDITIONS

"O" for "or"

Conditions are associated
with links on which cardinality
could be zero and links that
are mutually exclusive

A or B must occur
before Z

Figure 9.1 Symbols commonly used on diagrams with CASE tools employing conventional techniques.

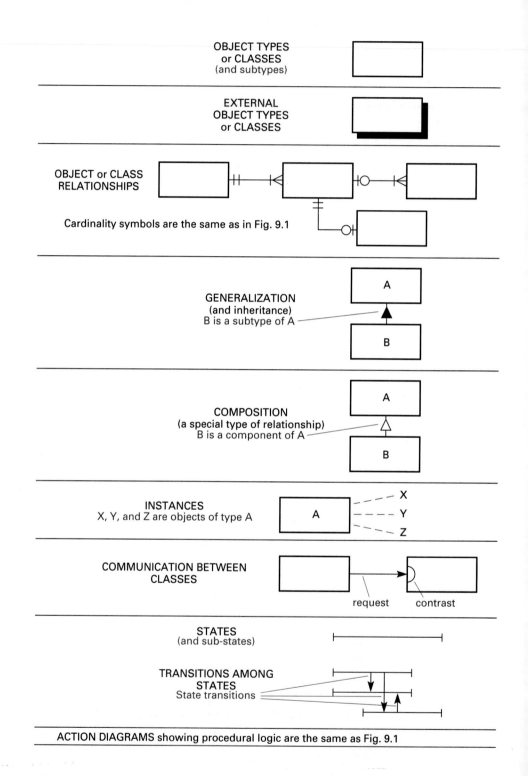

OBJECT TYPES or CLASSES (and subtypes)	
EXTERNAL OBJECT TYPES or CLASSES	
OBJECT or CLASS RELATIONSHIPS Cardinality symbols are the same as in Fig. 9.1	
GENERALIZATION (and inheritance) B is a subtype of A	A B
COMPOSITION (a special type of relationship) B is a component of A	A B
INSTANCES X, Y, and Z are objects of type A	A X Y Z
COMMUNICATION BETWEEN CLASSES	request contrast
STATES (and sub-states)	
TRANSITIONS AMONG STATES State transitions	

ACTION DIAGRAMS showing procedural logic are the same as Fig. 9.1

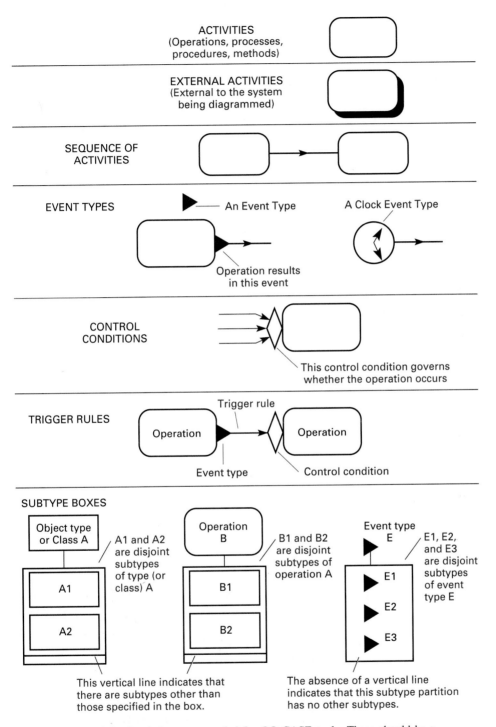

Figure 9.2 Symbols recommended for OO CASE tools. These should be a natural extension of the symbols in widespread use for conventional techniques (shown in Fig. 9.1).

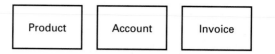

An object may be an instance of an entity type, but often object types incorporate *many* entity types.

Activities such as processes or operations are drawn with round-cornered boxes (sometimes called soft boxes):

REALITY AND INFORMATION ABOUT REALITY

Most of the blocks on CASE diagrams represent how the computer reflects reality. These are drawn with two-dimensional boxes or symbols. However, some blocks on the CASE diagrams represent reality itself. They might, for example, represent a physical object moving from one process to another. These are drawn with three-dimensional boxes or other three-dimensional pictures.

An object type, or an instance of an object type stored in the computer, is drawn with a rectangle. However, on *object-flow diagrams*, shown in Chapter 7, the object is a physical thing, like a product, rather than a symbolic representation in a computer. The physical object may be drawn as a three-dimensional box:

Other three-dimensional pictures of objects are sometimes used:

EXTERNAL OBJECTS AND OPERATIONS

The diagrams represent mostly what goes on in a system or collection of systems. Sometimes, an object or an operation is external to the system but affects the system.

External objects and operations are drawn as boxes with shadows:

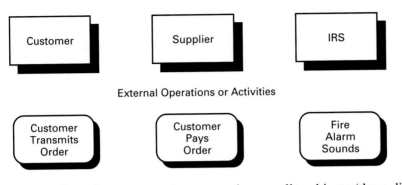

An object-flow diagram can show operations, reality objects (three-dimensional), and external objects on the same diagram:

LINES AND ARROWS
Most diagrams have lines interconnecting the nodes. The line can represent such notions as associations, decomposition, flow, time dependencies, and trigger rules.

Sometimes, the lines connecting nodes have arrows on them to indicate processing direction. For example, an event schema indicates that one operation must occur *before* another. A trigger-rule line indicates that the occurrence of an event comes before an operation and *causes* the invocation of an operation. Depending on the context, one indicates precedence only, the other causality:

Precedence   Causality

Sometimes the end of a line has cardinality symbols. In this case, the arrow should be placed in the middle of the line (or some distance from the ends).

MUTUAL EXCLUSIVITY
Sometimes a node is associated with *one and only one* of a group of nodes. They are mutually exclusive. For example, a **Product** is *either* **Goods** or a **Service**. The process **Prepare Material** may be followed by *either* **Operation 1** or **Operation 2** or **Operation 3**.

Mutual exclusivity can be represented by a branching line with a filled-in circle at the branch (see Fig. 9.3). The circle looks like an "o" for "or" and means

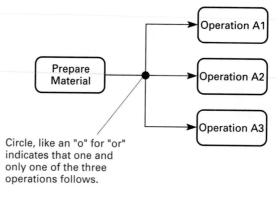

Figure 9.3

that the branches are mutually exclusive. Mutual exclusivity can also be represented with a partitioned box, as shown in Fig. 9.4. Here, **Operation A1** or **Operation A2** or **Operation A3** are all mutually exclusive subtypes of **Operation A**.

While the mutual exclusivity (or) circle is handy to use, using partitions to represent exclusive associations encourages the analyst to capitalize on a major feature in the OO approach—generalization. Without generalization, there would be no class inheritance. In the example, placing **Goods** and **Service** in a partition indicates that they both can have common attributes and operations. For instance, all **Products** have a unique **Product ID** and participate in order-processing operations. By not identifying a common supertype, the analyst runs the risk of defining redundant attributes and operations.

Figure 9.5 shows alternate ways of showing a mutually exclusive association among object types.

CARDINALITY CONSTRAINTS　　　　The term *cardinality constraint* refers to the restriction of how many of one item can be associated with another. For instance, a cardinality can be constrained

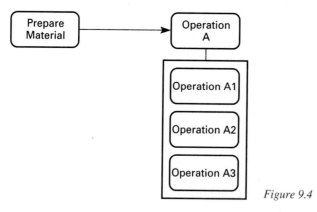

Figure 9.4

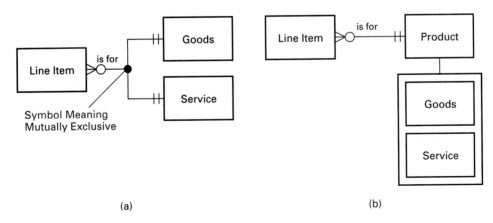

(a)   (b)

Figure 9.5 Two alternate ways of showing that Line Items are for Goods or Services. The example in 9.5(b) is better, because it encourages thinking about generalization and inheritance.

as one-with-one or one-with-many cardinality. Sometimes, numbers can be used to designate the upper and lower limits on cardinality.

Crow's Feet

A crow's foot connector from a line to a node is drawn like this:

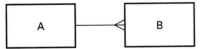

It means that one or more instances of B can be associated with one instance of A. It is called a *one-with-many association.*

One-With-One Cardinality Constraints

On diagrams using cardinality constraints, one-with-one cardinality is drawn with a small bar across the line (looking like a "1" symbol):

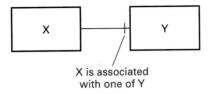

Zero Cardinality Constraints

A zero as part of the cardinality-constraint symbol means that an instance of one object type is not associated with any instances of another. In other words, an object of one type can have zero associations with the objects of another type:

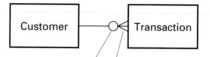

Customer has zero, one, or many Transactions

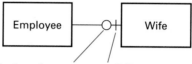

Employee has zero or one Wife

On object schemas, however, a line representing an association between object types should *always* have a cardinality-constraint symbol on both ends. It is sloppy analysis to draw a line connecting an object-type rectangle with no cardinality-constraint symbol.

Minimum and Maximum Constraints

The cardinality symbols express a maximum and minimum constraint:

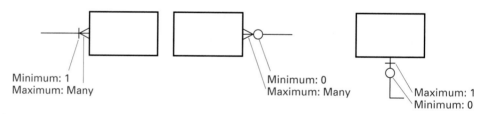

Minimum: 1
Maximum: Many

Minimum: 0
Maximum: Many

Maximum: 1
Minimum: 0

The maximum is always placed next to the box it refers to. Where minimum and maximum are both 1, two 1 bars are placed on the line. The two bars mean "one and only one":

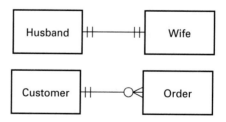

Figure 9.6 summarizes the representation of minimum and maximum cardinality constraints.

Figure 9.7 depicts four object types with associations between the types. It is expressed in the same way as an entity-relationship diagram.

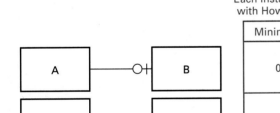

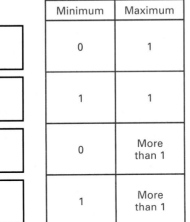

	Each Instance of A Is Associated with How Many Instances of B:	
	Minimum	Maximum
	0	1
	1	1
	0	More than 1
	1	More than 1

Figure 9.6   Cardinality-constraint symbols indicate minimum and maximum cardinality constraints.

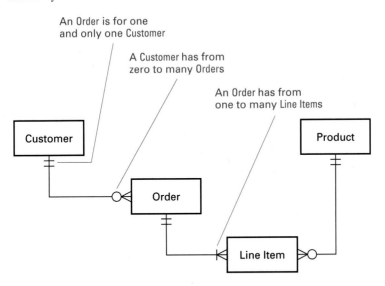

An Order is for one
and only one Customer

A Customer has from
zero to many Orders

An Order has from
one to many Line Items

Figure 9.7   Four object classes with cardinality symbols.

Sometimes cardinality cannot be expressed in terms of zero, one, or many. For example, a **Meeting** requires at least two **Persons**. Here, the minimum cardinality is two. In addition, an organization can place a restriction that a meeting can have no more than 20 people attending it. This is expressed by enumerating the cardinality constraint:

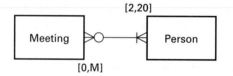

Labeling of Lines

On some types of diagrams, the lines connecting nodes should be labeled. Lines between event types and operations are unidirectional. Lines between object-type boxes, on the other hand, are usually bidirectional. The line can be read in either direction:

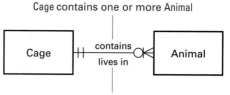

Only labeling lines in one direction is necessary, though labeling all associations between object types is recommended.

A label *above* a horizontal line is the name of the association when read from left to right. A label *below* a horizontal line is the name when read from right to left. As the line is rotated, the label remains on the same side of the line:

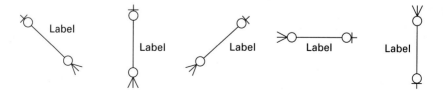

Thus, the label to the right of the vertical line is read when going *down* the line. The label on the left of a vertical line is read going *up* the line.

Reading Associations Like Sentences

Lines between object types give information about the association between the objects. This information ought to read like a sentence, for example

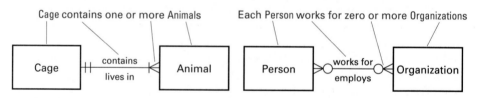

EXPANSION AND CONTRACTION   Some CASE diagrams can become very complex—having hundreds of blocks in one diagram. To avoid this, the diagrams are *nested.* Many adjacent blocks or lines can shrink into one block or line, where they can be expanded when required with a mouse-click.

To indicate that a line or block can be expanded to show more detail, the symbol "..." or "⊞" is used. Sometimes, the symbol "⊟" is used to indicate that a portion of the diagram can be contracted into one block or line. Figures 9.21 and 9.23 show this.

USING WINDOWS TO ACHIEVE CLARITY   Diagrams can be confusing if different types of ideas or types of representations are shown on the same diagram. To avoid this, the different types of representations should be separated into different windows. The user of a computerized tool can point to a node or line and indicate SHOW DETAIL. A pop-on window will display the detail stored about the node or line. A window can be a diagram of a different type. Figures 9.25 and 9.26 illustrate this.

SUBTYPES AND SUPERTYPES   As described earlier, object types can have more specialized types called *subtypes* and more general types called *supertypes.* For instance, Animal is a supertype of Mammal, which is a supertype of Person. Person, in turn, has its own subtypes, where a Person can be an Employee, and either a Female Person or a Male Person. Generalization hierarchies can be expressed as boxes within boxes:

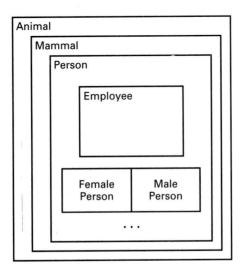

A subtype partition can be a *complete partition* because it contains all possible subtypes, or an *incomplete partition* because other subtypes are possible. An empty area at the bottom of the partition box indicates an incomplete subtype partition, as shown in Fig. 9.8.

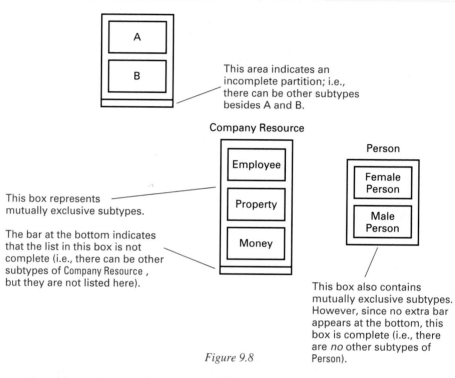

This area indicates an incomplete partition; i.e., there can be other subtypes besides A and B.

This box represents mutually exclusive subtypes.

The bar at the bottom indicates that the list in this box is not complete (i.e., there can be other subtypes of Company Resource , but they are not listed here).

This box also contains mutually exclusive subtypes. However, since no extra bar appears at the bottom, this box is complete (i.e., there are *no* other subtypes of Person).

Figure 9.8

An object type may have many different subtypes. For example, a **Person** might be a **Male** or **Female**, **Civilian** or **Military**, and various subtypes of **Military**. These different subtypes might be drawn as shown in Fig. 9.9.

In a generalization diagram, large filled arrows are sometimes used to indicate the direction of generalization:

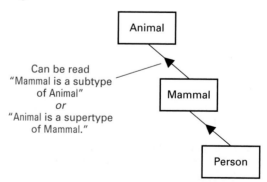

Can be read "Mammal is a subtype of Animal" *or* "Animal is a supertype of Mammal."

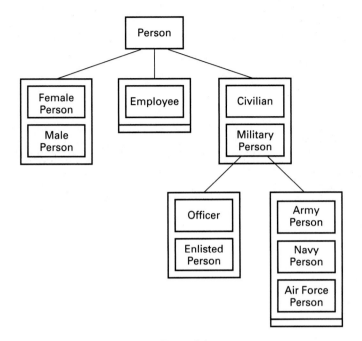

Figure 9.9

Arrows are not necessary when a generalization is represented from top to bottom, or from left to right.

FERN DIAGRAMS

Generalization is commonly represented with a fern diagram as in Fig. 9.10. The fern diagram progresses from left to right and usually has no arrows on it. Since inheritance is based on

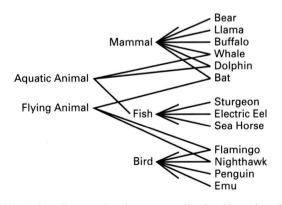

Figure 9.10   A fern diagram showing a generalization hierarchy where types can have multiple supertypes. The properties of more than one supertype can apply to any one object type.

generalization, diagrams are useful because they indicate the *direction* of inheritance. They do not, however, depict what is being inherited or how the inheritance mechanism will work within a given OO programming language. Therefore, diagrams depicting type/subtype hierarchies are called *generalization hierarchies* rather than inheritance hierarchies.

TYPES AND INSTANCES

A fern diagram sometimes shows instances of objects. Instances are connected to their object type with dotted lines. For example, Bear in Fig. 9.10 is a subtype of Mammal, while Wilber, Edward, and Yogi are instances of Bears—that is, they are specific bears:

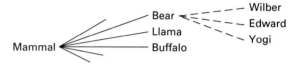

Fern diagrams sometimes become large. A CASE tool should be able to show a portion of the diagram when required, for example

Bear ⤐⊏‒ ‒ ‒ Wilber
         ‒ ‒ Edward

SUBSETS OF ASSOCIATIONS

The solid-arrow symbol is used when specifying that one *association* is a subtype of another. For example, the set of applied skills associated with an employee is a subset of those actually attained by the employee.

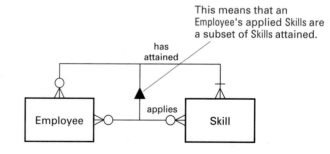

COMPOSED-OF DIAGRAMS

Tree and network structures can show more than just generalization or inheritance. They are also used for indicating that one object is composed of other objects. The composed-of diagram should be drawn so that it is immediately distinguished from a generalization diagram. This is done by putting large hollow arrows on the composed-of diagram and solid arrows on the generalization diagrams. (Although in directional representations such as the fern diagram, no arrow is required.) A comparison of a generalization diagram and a composed-of diagram is made in Fig. 9.11.

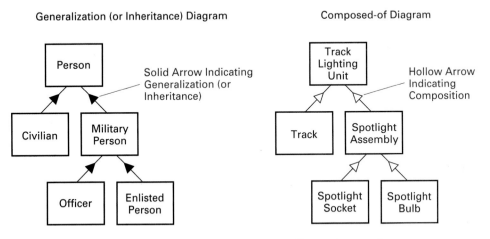

Figure 9.11   Solid arrows (or no arrows on fern diagrams) are used on generalization diagrams. Hollow arrows are used on composed-of diagrams.

Expressing cardinality constraints on composition associations is important, because a composite object can consist of zero, one, or many objects of different types. For instance, in Fig. 9.12, while each Track Lighting Unit will always have

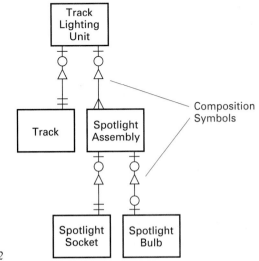

Figure 9.12

one **Track**, it will also have one or more **Spotlight Assembly** objects. In addition, while each **Spotlight Assembly** always has a **Spotlight Socket**, it may or may not have a **Spotlight Bulb** in it.

Cardinality-constraint symbols distinguish composed-of diagrams from generalization diagrams.

Sometimes generalization and composition are shown on the same diagram (see Fig. 9.13).

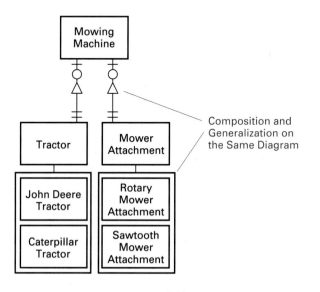

Figure 9.13

Elaborate diagrams can be drawn with both inheritance and composition. Many of the currently published approaches to OO analysis mix different types of information on one diagram—although the symbols representing them vary. This can be confusing, especially to beginners. To reduce this confusion, it is often useful to have the different types of information appear in different windows.

DERIVED OBJECT TYPES

Instances of an object type are often determined by somebody asserting the fact. For example, a manufacturer might point to an object and say, "That thing over there is one of my **Products**." When a person is hired, a personnel recruiter can say, "That person is now an **Employee**." However, the set of instances for many object types can be derived. For instance, the collection of all **Adult Persons** can be derived from the set of all **Persons** who have attained the age of 18. The collection can also be derived by subtracting all the **Child** objects from

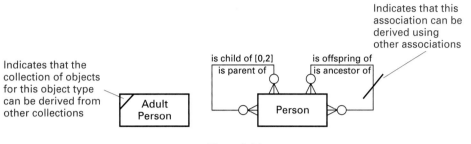

Indicates that this association can be derived using other associations

is child of [0,2]
is parent of

is offspring of
is ancestor of

Indicates that the collection of objects for this object type can be derived from other collections

Adult Person

Person

Figure 9.14

the set. Associations can also be derived. For example, in Fig. 9.14 all of a Person's ancestors can be computed by iteratively following a parents-of-parents association chain.

OBJECT-RELATIONSHIP DIAGRAMS

Entity-relationship diagrams are in common use in non-OO analysis. As discussed in Chapter 6, object-relationship diagrams are similar. They show that one object type is associated with other object types. For example, in Fig. 9.15 an **Employee** works at a location; a **Customer** places **Orders**; an **Order** is for certain **Products**.

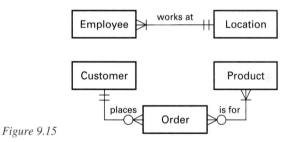

Employee — works at — Location

Customer

Product

places — Order — is for

Figure 9.15

Cardinality-constraint symbols are used on object-relationship diagrams. Diagrams associating object types can thus show three types of information:

- Generalization
- Composition
- Relationships

It is possible to put all three types of information on one diagram. Again, if this is confusing at first, represent the different types of information on different diagrams. All diagrams should be clearly understood.

EVENTS

Operations are processes that can be requested as units. When operations are successful, events occur. Operations and events are thus closely connected. An event type may be represented with a solid triangle at the start of a line leaving the process box. A triangle is chosen, because it "points" to the moment when an object-state change occurs as a result of the preceding operation.

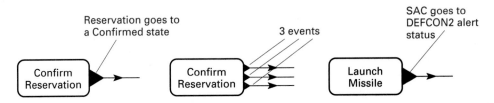

The line leaving the operation box can serve as a combined representation of the event type and the trigger. Putting a small solid triangle at the start of the line provides a place at which a mouse-click may be made to look at detail of the event type or the postconditions of the operation.

CLOCK EVENTS

A special type of event is a clock time being reached that triggers some operation. This type of event is drawn like a clock face:

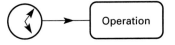

ACTIVITY SCHEMAS

An activity schema shows a sequence of operations. There are several different ways to express activity, as shown in Fig. 9.16. The Event Schema is one type of activity schema. Figure 9.17 is an example of an Event Schema.

CONTROL CONDITIONS

Some operations can only take place when certain conditions apply. These are called *control conditions.* Control conditions are shown with a small diamond at the front of an operation box:

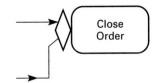

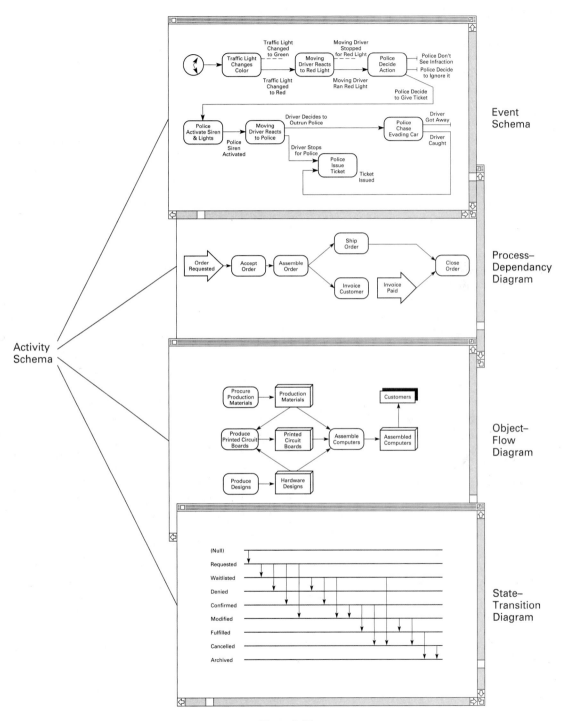

Activity
Schema

Event
Schema

Process–
Dependancy
Diagram

Object–
Flow
Diagram

State–
Transition
Diagram

Figure 9.16

143

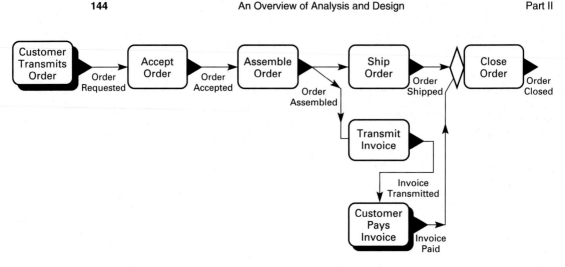

Figure 9.17

The diamond shape is similar to the decision symbol used in flow charting.

The control-condition diamond can define a single condition or a complex collection of Boolean conditions. The CASE-tool user should be able to mouse-click on the control-condition diamond and display a window showing the conditions.

OMITTING EVENTS AND CONTROL CONDITIONS

The lines between the operations on an event schema indicate that operations result in events that trigger other operations. Because this is always the case, the event triangle is often omitted. Similarly, the control-

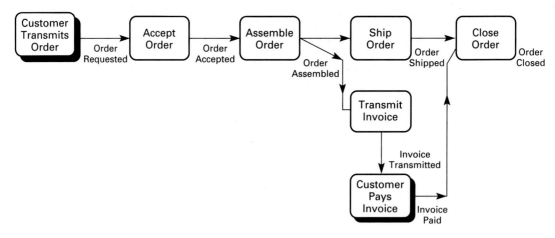

Figure 9.18

condition diamond is often omitted, because all operations have these conditions (even if they are trivial). The CASE-tool user should be able to display the event or the control conditions with a mouse-click. All operations boxes have a set of control conditions and event types. Figure 9.18 shows an event schema with the triangles and diamonds omitted. In this book, we draw them to increase clarity and to remind the reader of their existence and fundamental importance.

TRIGGER RULES   An arrowed line going to an operation box indicates that the operation is triggered by the occurrence of a preceding event. The trigger-rule line indicates the association of an event type to the operation invoked. Additionally, it can indicate the way in which the necessary objects are supplied to the operation it invokes. In this way, the trigger rule defines a causal relation between event and operation—as well as a form of "data flow."

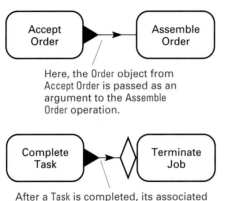

Here, the Order object from Accept Order is passed as an argument to the Assemble Order operation.

After a Task is completed, its associated Job object must be determined by the trigger for invocation of the Terminate Job operation.

    Trigger lines, then, indicate two things. First, they link cause (the event) and effect (the operation). In other words, when an event occurs, a trigger invokes an operation. Second, they determine the objects required as arguments for the operation that the trigger invokes. These lines, therefore, define the rules for triggering an operation when a particular kind of event occurs. In this way, they are called *trigger rules*.

    Operations may be triggered by one of many events occurring (see Fig. 9.19). This diagram indicates that only one of the three events must occur to trigger the **Estimate Modified Revenue** operation. In other words, the operation is triggered each time one of the three indicated events occurs. However, if a combination of conditions is necessary, a control condition is necessary. *Each* time a control condition is triggered, it checks whether a given condition is true or not. If true, its

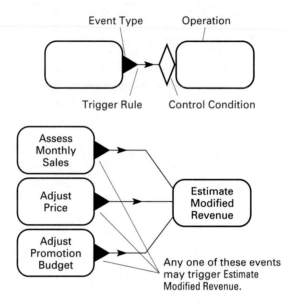

Figure 9.19

event occurs. Control conditions are not necessarily just "and" conditions. They can involve elaborate conditions with "ands" and "ors" as shown in Fig. 9.20.

Operations, once triggered, are always expected to complete an event. When control conditions are specified, the operation may not be invoked unless its control conditions are true.

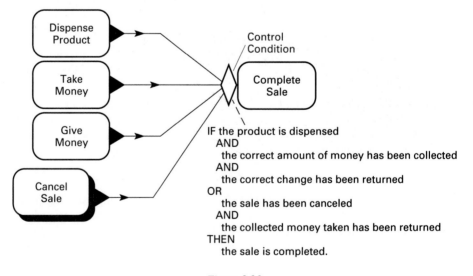

Figure 9.20

**PARALLEL
PROCESSING**
Specifying parallel processing requirements is important in those environments having distributed processing requirements or using massively parallel computers. Event schemas can indicate when processing can occur in parallel:

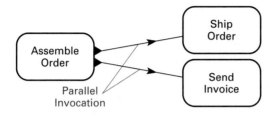

GUARDS
Sometimes a line going to an operation box indicates that the operation cannot take place until some other event has occurred. In this case, the international "DON'T DO IT" symbol may be placed on the line: ⊘. This is referred to as a *guard*. The lines connecting to an operation box may include triggers and guards.

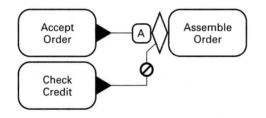

LEVELING
An activity schema often has many activities. It may be drawn more clearly by *leveling* it, that is, putting a box around a collection of activities and showing them as one activity. Activities with a "..." or "+" symbol next to them indicate they can be expanded in this way. In Fig. 9.21, the operation **Person has Breakfast** is expanded into component operations.

STATES
An object can be in many states. A state is drawn with the following symbol:

|———————— Confirmed ————————|

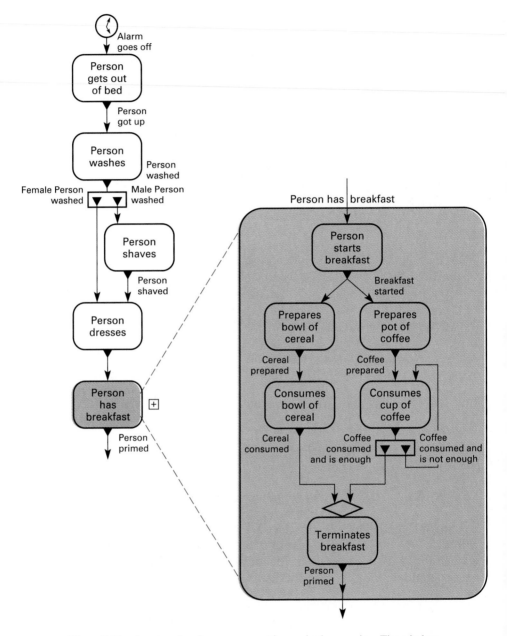

Figure 9.21 An operation for a person getting up in the morning. The window on the bottom shows the detail of the Person has Breakfast operation.

States are most commonly represented on state-transition diagrams. The transitions are represented as vertical lines connecting the states, as shown in Fig. 9.22.

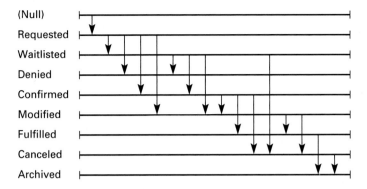

Figure 9.22   A fence diagram expressing some possible states of an Airline Booking object.

SUBSTATES

An object can have many permissible states. These may be drawn more closely by representing them as states and substates. When the substates of a particular state are not shown on a diagram, a "..." or "⊞" symbol is displayed next to the state. Clicking on this symbol causes its substates to be displayed as represented in Fig. 9.23.

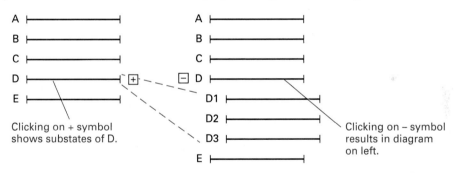

Figure 9.23   There may be multiple levels of substates.

Permissible states differ slightly, depending on the attributes of the object. For example, Fig. 9.24 shows five states that relate to objects of the type **Person** getting up in the morning. The state transitions are slightly different for a male person than for a female person.

In object-oriented analysis, recognizing opportunities for reusability is important. When diagramming object behavior, the analyst must consider which operations and object types can be reused and which cannot. For example, is the operation that makes a **Male Person** ambulatory the same as that for a **Female Person**? If so, the same behavior should be specified for both. Without this understanding, uncontrolled redundancy will run rampant. For instance, an order-

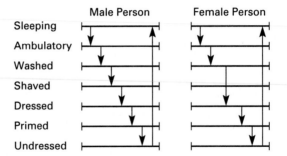

Figure 9.24   Personal-grooming related state changes can be slightly different for a male and female person.

processing system may have over a hundred different kinds of orders—each with its own lifecycle. By blindly analyzing each lifecycle separately, no opportunity for reusability will be discovered. A notation combining the generalizations and specializations on the same diagram can help remedy this.

LINKING ACTIVITIES AND STATE CHANGES

An *event* is a change in state of an object. A mouse-click on the event triangle can show the change on a state-transition diagram corresponding to that event. Figure 9.25 depicts an event schema for a person starting the day. The two windows show state-transition diagrams, with color showing the state of the **Person** object type. Conversely, Fig. 9.26 shows a state-transition diagram and a window containing an activity schema corresponding to one state transition.

Operations could be represented on state-transition diagrams, as shown in Fig. 9.27. Conversely, states may be represented on event schemas, as shown in Fig 9.28.

Tying the behavioral aspects of modeling to the structural aspects is very important, as illustrated in Fig. 9.29. The resulting state of a **Person** object must have a corresponding object subtype in the object schema. For instance, the result of a **Person dressed** event is a **Person** object that is an instance of **Dressed Person**. Without this modeling integration, object-oriented implementation would not be possible. Figure 9.28 represents the states from the state-transition diagram in Figs. 9.27 and 9.28 next to their corresponding object types.

REFERENCE

1. Martin, James, *Recommended Diagramming Standards for Analysts and Programmers: A Basis for Automation,* Prentice-Hall, Englewood Cliffs, NJ, 1987.

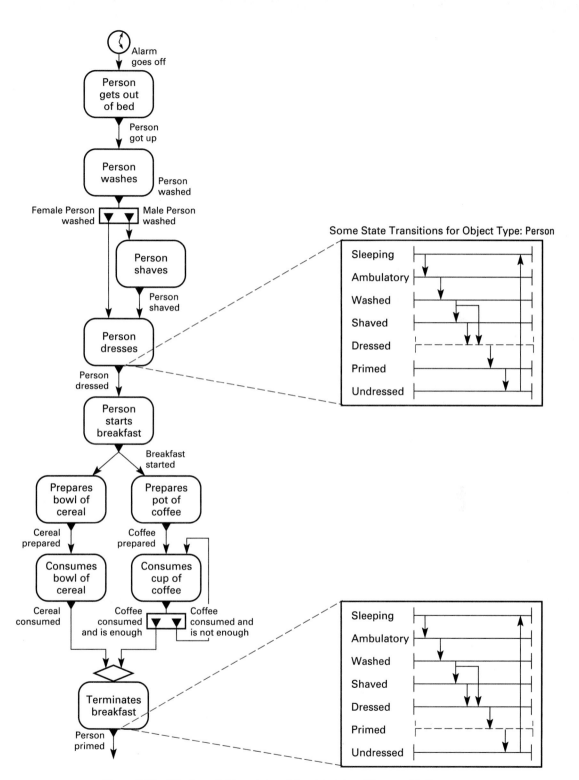

Figure 9.25 Windows linking *states* of the object type **Person** with the operation of getting up in the morning.

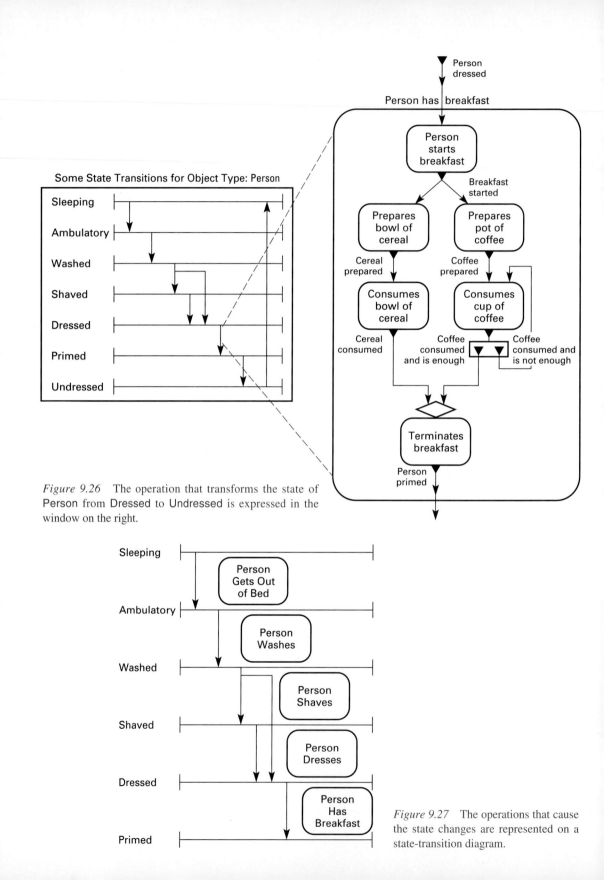

Figure 9.26 The operation that transforms the state of Person from Dressed to Undressed is expressed in the window on the right.

Figure 9.27 The operations that cause the state changes are represented on a state-transition diagram.

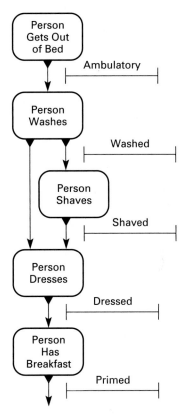

Figure 9.28 On an event schema, the resulting state of the object Person can be depicted after each event type.

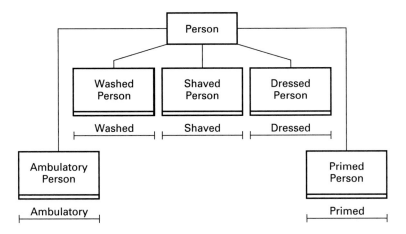

Figure 9.29 Tying the behavioral aspects of modeling to the structural aspects is very important. Without this modeling integration, object-oriented implementation would not be possible.

10 OBJECT-ORIENTED PROGRAMMING LANGUAGES

THE GENESIS OF OO TECHNOLOGY The genesis of the technology now called *object-oriented* dates back to the early 1960s. It arose from the need to describe and simulate a variety of phenomena such as nerve networks, communications systems, traffic flow, production systems, administrative systems, and even social systems. In the spring of 1961, Kristen Nygaard originated the ideas for a language that would serve the dual purpose of system description and simulation programming. Together with Ole-Johan Dahl, Nygaard developed the simulation language now known as Simula I. The first Simula-based application package was implemented for the simulation of logic circuits. However, operations research applications were the most popular usage. For example, in 1965 a large and complex job shop simulation was programmed in less than four weeks—with an execution efficiency at least four times higher than that of available technology.

Simula was intended to be a system description and simulation programming language. However, its users quickly discovered that Simula also provided new and powerful facilities when used for purposes *other than* simulation, such as prototyping and application development. In September 1965, the possibilities of a "new, improved Simula" as a general purpose language were being planned. By December 1966, the necessary foundation for the new, general programming language, called Simula 67, was defined.

Smalltalk

In the late 1960s, another development of OO technology was under way, guided by research at the University of Utah and by the central ideas of Simula. Alan Kay envisioned that by the 1980s

> Both adults and children will be able to have as a personal possession a computer about the size of a notebook with the power to handle virtually all their

information-related needs. . . . Ideally the personal computer will be designed in such a way that all ages and walks of life can mold and channel its power to their own needs [7].

Early in the 1970s, Alan Kay went to Xerox and formed the Learning Research Group (LRG). Xerox was responsible for producing the interim model for the personal computer, called Dynabook. The LRG was engaged to produce the software, called Smalltalk. After observing the project, they quickly realized that one of the major design problems involved expressive communication—particularly when children were seriously considered as users. For this reason, the LRG invited some 250 children (aged six to fifteen) and 50 adults to try versions of Smalltalk and suggest ways of improving it. In order to test the usability of Smalltalk, they started with simple situations that embodied a concept and gradually increased the complexity of the examples. A major goal of Smalltalk was providing a single name (or symbol) for a complex collection of ideas. Later, these ideas could be invoked and manipulated through the name. They found that children by the age of six were able to do this.

While the Dynabook project did not realize its goal, the concept remains a kind of Holy Grail for computer manufacturers. However, the Smalltalk language is alive and well today. Alan Kay foresaw the need to characterize and communicate application concepts in developing computer programs. Smalltalk provides the means to write programs in a style that brings our concepts to life.

Alan Kay expected the personal computer to be a human medium of communication. The actual term *object-oriented* originated during the development of Smalltalk.

THE EVOLUTION FROM UNTYPED TO TYPED LANGUAGES

The so-called object-oriented approach introduced by Simula and Smalltalk was not a totally new idea. It resulted from an evolutionary momentum. Object orientation grew out of the need to organize the kinds, or *types,* of data on which a program could operate. Initially, only one data type described the universe of bit strings in a computer memory—the data type Word. Words are bit strings of fixed size that can be used as units of information.

However, when developers design their systems, they organize their universe of data in different ways for different purposes. The need for data types arises whenever data must be categorized for a particular usage. As early as 1954, Fortran distinguished between Integer and Floating-point types of data. Later, Algol 60 incorporated data types for Integer, Real, and Boolean. Still later, languages included additional data types, such as the Character, String, Bit, Byte, Array, Pointer, Record, File, and Procedure.

A *data type* describes a certain kind of data—its representation and the set of valid operations that access and maintain that data. In this way, each data type is a known commodity, protected from unintended use. For example, the data type Character describes the kind of data that is displayable by a program. Furthermore, a set of operations is provided for creating, destroying, examining, and manipulating Character data. Since arithmetic operations such as add and subtract are not defined for Character data, computational requests are not permitted.

User-Defined Types (UDTs)

Prior to the early 1970s, a programmer could reference only those data types built into a programming language compiler. As a result, even often-used types like Month, Date, Time, Coefficient, Tree, and Stack were not explicitly accessible. These ideas had to be implicitly embedded somewhere in the programmer's code. An additional limiting characteristic of built-in types was their definition by the way in which the information was physically stored. They had little useful relationship to the real-world objects that the application was trying to implement. Programmers spent more time thinking about whether or not a number should be an Integer than about Customer Orders and Part Requisitions.

Eventually, the computer industry felt pressured to provide programmers with a facility for expressing their own typing needs. The first languages to offer *user-defined types* (UDTs) were Pascal and Algol 68. In Pascal, for example, a programmer could write

    TYPE MONTH = (JANUARY, FEBRUARY, MARCH, APRIL, MAY, JUNE,
        JULY, AUGUST, SEPTEMBER, OCTOBER, NOVEMBER, DECEMBER);

This expression would then define the UDT Month as being the set of twelve literals. At this point, the developer could define relational operations to compare two given Month variables for less than, equal to, and so on. Other operations could include computing the preceding or succeeding month when supplied with a Month variable.

The *types* of Pascal and the *nodes* of Algol 68 were an important step forward. They permitted the programmer to go from manufacturer-imposed types to user-imposed types. UDTs raised the expressive power of programming languages. More importantly, they encouraged systems developers to translate the real-world types of the system application into coded data types.

ABSTRACT DATA TYPES (ADTs)   The *abstract data type* (ADT) extends the notion of the *user-defined type* (UDT) by adding encapsulation.

The ADT contains the representation and the operations of a data type. The *encapsulation* feature of the ADT not only hides the data type's implementation but provides a protective wall that shields its objects from improper use. All interface occurs through named *operations* defined within the ADT. The operations, then, provide a well-defined means for accessing the objects of a data type. In short, ADTs give objects a *public* interface through its permitted operations. However, the representations and executable code, or *method,* for each operation are *private.*

The ADT facility first appeared in Simula 67. Its implementation is called a *class.* Modula refers to its ADT implementation as a *module,* while Ada uses the word *package.* In all cases, the ADT provides a way for the systems developer to identify real-world data types and package them in a more convenient and compact form. In this way, ADTs can be defined for things such as Dates, Screen Panels, Customer Orders, and Part Requisitions. Once defined, the developer can address the ADTs directly in future operations.

Figure 10.1 illustrates an example of the ADT named Employee. At its heart, the ADT is defined by its data structure representation. For Employee, this includes data about exemptions, position, salary amount, phone extension, and so on. The ADT is also defined by a set of permissible operations. These operations, such as hire, promote, and change phone extension, provide a suit of armor that protects the underlying Employee structure from arbitrary and unintended use. In

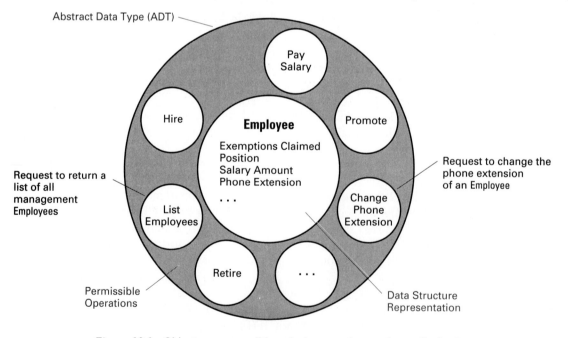

Figure 10.1   Objects are accessible only by named operations; all else is hidden.

other words, the Employee operations provide the *only* method of accessing and maintaining the data of an Employee.

Additionally, each *method* or processing algorithm, employed to carry out an operation, is hidden from its users. What the user must provide is an appropriate object to invoke, or *request,* the operation along with any applicable supporting parameters. For example, Fig. 10.2 depicts three instances, or *objects,* of Employee. In order to give Bob a promotion, the request must specify Bob, the promote operation, and the salary grade of his promotion. In its abbreviated form, this request could be written: Bob, promote, director.

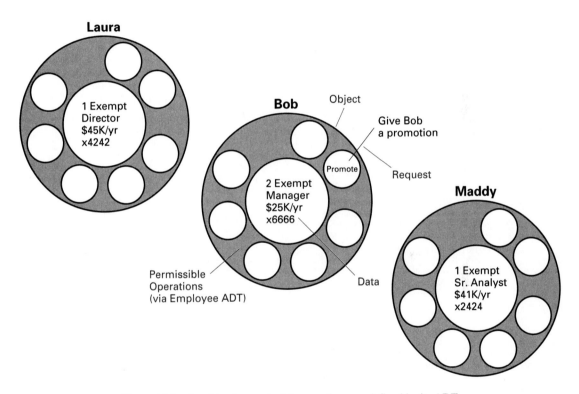

Figure 10.2   An object's permissible operations are defined by its ADT.

Objects as Encapsulations

Figure 10.2 depicts three Employee objects as miniature representations of the Employee ADT. In this way, an object can be regarded as any instance of an abstract data type—each encapsulating its own private data and its own permissible operations. Each object can be considered as a thing in its own right, with its own behavior. While each object should encapsulate a physical record of its own data, encapsulating a physical copy of each operational method is unnecessary and wasteful. Since the same coding is contained within each ADT, an ADT's operations need only be *virtually* available to an object. In other words, all operations that apply to a particular ADT also apply to the instances of that ADT. As illustrated in Fig. 10.3, since Bob is an instance of the **Employee** ADT, all **Employee** operations (such as promote) also apply to Bob—without the object having to contain them physically. When an object is an instance of an ADT, this linkage is established. Most ADT-oriented languages accomplish this with a physical pointer mechanism.

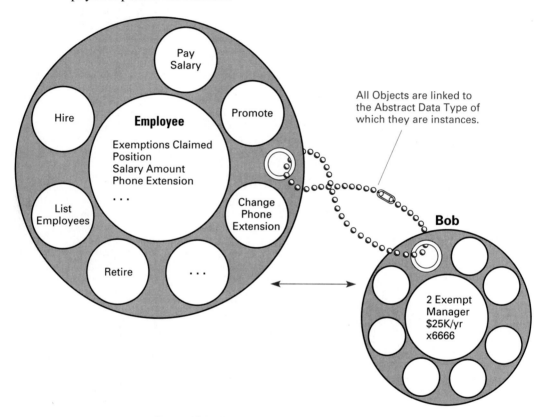

Figure 10.3   Every ADT is linked to its instances.

Objects and Requests

With encapsulation, each object need only know *what* it can request of another object, because operations are the "public" interface for all objects. All the specifics of *how* its structure is stored and *how* its operations are coded are tucked neatly out of sight. This not only protects each object, it simplifies the interactions between them. Most OO languages call these interactions *messages*.

For instance, a Customer object can send a message to an Order object to add a product to its already existing line items. The Order object, in turn, may send a message to a Customer Account object with a request to update the amount due for the customer.

While the word *message* is a useful metaphor in some contexts, the idea of inanimate objects sending messages to one another can cause conceptual difficulties. (An example is the interaction of Orders and Customer Accounts.) Figure 10.4 depicts several objects sending messages. To say that object A is sending a message to object B means that one of the encapsulated operations of object A has been invoked. This operation requires—and therefore *requests*—the invocation of an operation on object B. This operation results in a change to the encapsulated data for object B.

For clarity, then, the standard term emerging for a message is the *request*. In addition, request is a more general notion, because more than one object can participate in a request. For instance, to which object is a message sent so that a Part can be placed in a Bin—the Part or the Bin? A request involves both by specifying the Part and Bin objects as parameters along with the operation name. It then lets the method selection mechanism locate the appropriate method for placing

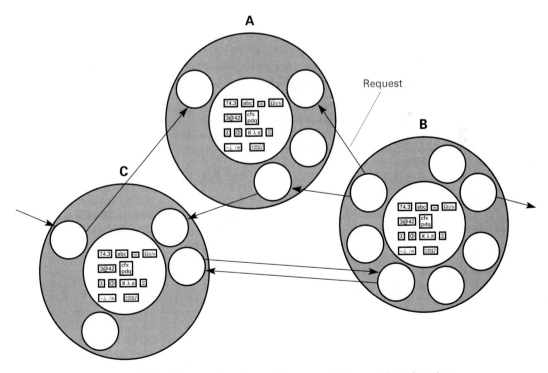

Figure 10.4   The operation of one object *requests* the operation of another.

inventory. In short, requests expand the notion of message by saying "With *these* objects, do this."

The ADT is a conceptual notion that describes a way of organizing data and process by type of data. When the programming language is ADT-oriented, the conceptual notions of abstract data types directly correspond to physical units of code. In this way, Fig. 10.4 also indicates what the code structure would be like if the ADTs were implemented.

Objects Relating to Other Objects

While an ADT's operations act as a gateway for object access, its data structure describes the data attributes that each object possesses. This structure allows objects to be considered as records. Their *fields* may contain values or pointers to other objects. For example, Fig. 10.5(a) depicts two **Musical Composition** objects. Each contains a musical catalog identifier, a composition name, and a pointer to a **Composer** object. The **Composer** object's structure contains the name of the composer, the year of the composer's birth, and the year of the composer's death.

Object Identification

As Fig. 10.5(b) suggests, objects of various types can contain various kinds of data and can point to and be pointed to by other objects. However, in order to point to an object, every object must be uniquely identifiable.

Each object is created by an explicit action. Therefore, it is distinct from those objects created previously or those to be created in the future. It has a unique identity. Even if two objects have identical characteristics, they are not the same object—just as identical twins are not the same person. If we *know* that two objects exist, they are not the same object. In order for an OOPL to provide this knowledge, a good object-identification mechanism is required. These are typically implemented using memory references, user-supplied names, and identifier keys [8].

Inheritance and Polymorphism

Inheritance, as described in Chapter 8, is an important feature of OO design. While different OOPLs have different inheritance mechanisms, we can think about them in the following way. When a request for an operation goes to a subclass, that class's list of permissible operations is checked. If the operation is found on the list, it is invoked; if not, the parent classes are examined to locate the operation as illustrated in Fig. 10.6.

An important feature of inheritance is the ability of an ADT to *override* inherited features. Here, the processing algorithm, or *method,* of an inherited operation can be redefined at the subtype level. The example in Fig. 10.6 illustrates three ADTs. The most general, **Polygon**, contains the data structure and

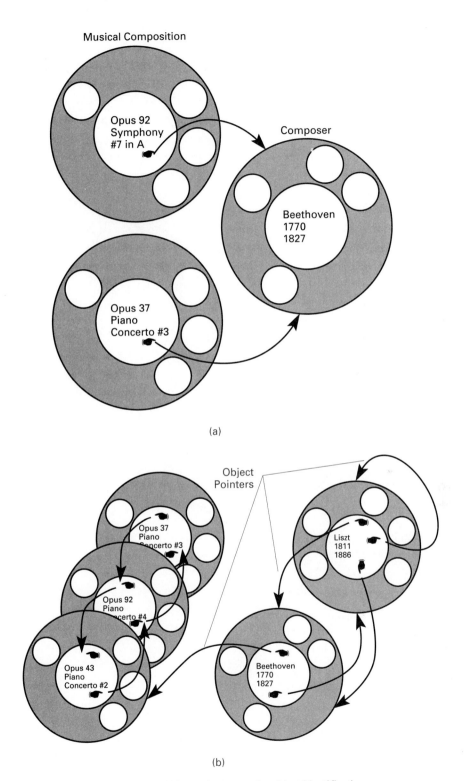

Musical Composition

Opus 92
Symphony
#7 in A

Composer

Beethoven
1770
1827

Opus 37
Piano
Concerto #3

(a)

Object
Pointers

Opus 37
Piano
Concerto #3

Opus 92
Piano
Concerto #4

Opus 43
Piano
Concerto #2

Liszt
1811
1886

Beethoven
1770
1827

(b)

Figure 10.5   Object pointers require object identification.

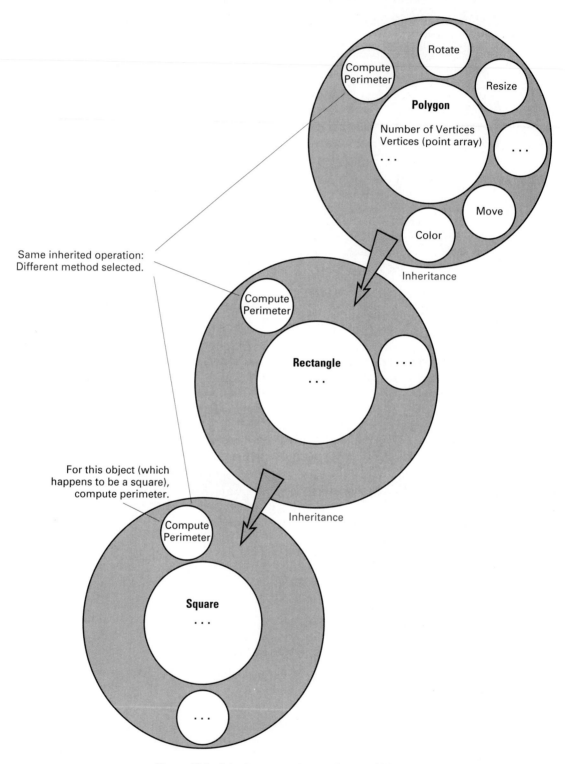

Same inherited operation:
Different method selected.

For this object (which
happens to be a square),
compute perimeter.

Figure 10.6 Inheritance searches can be overridden.

permissible operations for polygons. Because every instance of a Rectangle is also an instance of a Polygon, the Rectangle subtype need not repeat those features it inherits from Polygon. However, while all Polygon operations apply to subtypes, the *method* of operation may be different. For example, the method of rotating a Polygon is the same as rotating a Rectangle. However, the method of computing perimeters may differ. The perimeter of a Polygon is the sum of all its sides; the perimeter of a Rectangle is the sum of two of its adjacent sides multiplied by two. The Square perimeter differs again as the product of multiplying four times the length of any one side.

Whenever a request is made for an operation on an object, the method selected depends on whether or not the inheritance hierarchy has been overridden. The method for moving a Square three centimeters to the right is selected from Polygon. However, even though the *operation* for compute perimeter is inherited from the Polygon, the *method* selected for a Square is located in the Square ADT.* An *operation,* then, is the kind of process being requested. Its *method* is the specification of how to carry out the operation.

Cancelling Inherited Features

Some expert systems in AI allow some inherited features to be cancelled. For example, one of the features of Birds includes flying. However, this same feature does not apply to Penguins and Ostriches. Therefore, this feature can be cancelled. The arbitrary overriding and cancelling of inherited features is a questionable practice. Logically it is incorrect, because, by definition, all features of a type apply to its subtypes. Therefore, to rectify the problem of Birds flying and Penguins not, the subtyping hierarchy needs to be changed. To solve this, Bird can be specialized into two subtypes: Flying Bird and Nonflying Bird. Following this, all the data structures and operations relating to flying should be shifted from Bird to Flying Bird. Types such as Penguin and Ostrich should then be realigned as subtypes of Nonflying Bird. This would correct the logical inconsistency. However, *physically* it might create an intolerable system overhead. For this reason, some languages allow the programmer to deviate from what is logically correct—for the sake of performance.

Multiple Inheritance

Allowing a subtype to inherit from more than one immediate supertype is often useful. For example, the type Working Student has the supertypes Employee and Student. A Panda is a Bear, a Herbivore, and Endangered Animal. In Fig. 10.7, the example defines Sales Manager as a subtype of Manager and Salesperson. This means that the features of both Manager *and* Salesperson

---

* This approach to overriding inheritance properties through redefinition is often referred to as a category of *polymorphism* known as *parametric polymorphism* [2]. Here, an operation is considered polymorphic because, given different types of objects, it produces the same kind of results.

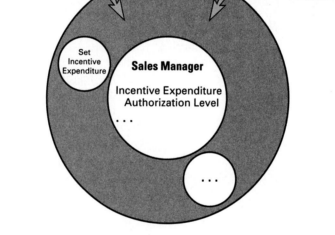

Figure 10.7   Multiple inheritance.

apply to **Sales Manager**. Since every instance of a **Sales Manager** is also an instance of **Manager** and **Salesperson**, both sets of data structures and permissible operations are reusable for a **Sales Manager** object.

Unfortunately, combining the features of supertypes is not straightforward. A conflict arises when data items or operations from different supertypes have the *same name* but have *different meanings*. For instance, in Fig. 10.7, **Manager** and **Salesperson** both have a feature named "skill." In one case, skill reflects the ability to manage people; in the other, the ability to sell. The same situation applies to the two supertype operations named "identify skill"—same name but totally unrelated meanings. What, then, are the ramifications when a subtype inherits both? On the one hand, it is true that all the features of a type are inherited by its subtype. On the other, the ability to request just one of the available operations based on its name presents a problem. Which operation is chosen when requested to "identify skill"? Several strategies exist for resolving conflicts of unrelated features. In one strategy, an algorithm is defined to choose a feature based on placement in the supertype hierarchy. While this hides the conflict resolution from the user, it does not always produce the desired results. Another strategy forbids such conflicts and renames the offending features—removing the problem entirely.

OBJECT-ORIENTED AND OBJECT-BASED IMPLEMENTATIONS

In the preceding sections, two important programming language characteristics were presented. A language is *object-oriented* if, and only if, it satisfies the following requirements.

- *It supports abstract data types (ADTs).* ADTs are based on the kinds of data envisioned by the systems developer. Each ADT protects its data from improper use by offering a number of permissible operations. To accomplish this, both the data representation and its permissible operations are veiled with a protective covering that hides the details of its implementation. If a programming language is ADT-oriented, the types identified for an application system map directly into units of code—the gulf from concept to reality is greatly reduced.

- *Method selection is supported.* With method selection, the user need only specify which operation should be applied to an object (or in more expanded languages, one or more objects). The system will then choose the method appropriate for the specified parameters. In other words, the user only needs to specify *what* is to be done, and the method selector determines *how* it is to be applied. Polymorphism is one of the most common applications of method selection.

- *Type inheritance is supported.* With type inheritance, systems are extended and refined using existing type components. Type inheritance allows systems to be constructed from existing type hierarchies. It provides mechanisms for both construction and reuse of software. In this way, we do not have to reinvent the wheel—only the portion of it that is different. Inheritance imposes a mechanism on ADTs that greatly reduces the complexity of the resulting systems.

Much debate has focused on which languages are more object-oriented. The requirements for an object-oriented implementation can be summarized in the following way:

OBJECT-ORIENTED IMPLEMENTATION =
ABSTRACT DATA TYPES + METHOD SELECTION + TYPE INHERITANCE

In OOPL terminology, different terms would be used to express this:

    OOPL IMPLEMENTATION =
        CLASSES + METHOD SELECTION + CLASS INHERITANCE

If the language does not satisfy these requirements, it is not object-oriented. However, a few programming languages, including Modula and Ada, do satisfy the first of the three requirements. These languages are called *object-based.*

REFERENCES

1. Budd, Timothy, *A Little Smalltalk,* Addison-Wesley, Reading, MA, 1987.

2. Cardelli, Luca and Peter Wegner, "On Understanding Types, Data Abstraction, and Polymorphism," *ACM Computing Surveys,* 17:4, December 1985, pp. 471–522.

3. Cox, Brad J. and Andrew J. Novobilski, *Object-Oriented Programming: An Evolutionary Approach* (2nd edition), Addison-Wesley, Reading, MA, 1991.

4. Dahl, Ole-Johan and Kristen Nygaard, "SIMULA - An Algol-based Simulation Language," *Communications of the ACM,* 9:9, September 1966, pp. 671–678.

5. Horowitz, Ellis, *Fundamentals of Programming Languages* (2nd edition), W. H. Freeman, NY, 1984.

6. Goldberg, Adele and David Robson, *Smalltalk-80: The Language and its Implementation,* Addison-Wesley, Reading, MA, 1983.

7. Kay, Alan C., "Microelectronics and the Personal Computer," *Scientific American,* September 1977, pp. 231–244.

8. Kent, William, "A Rigorous Model of Object Reference, Identity, and Existence," *Journal of Object-Oriented Programming,* 4:3, June 1991, pp. 28–36.

9. Khoshafian, Setrag and Razmik Abnous, *Object Orientation: Concepts, Languages, Databases, User Interfaces,* John Wiley & Sons, NY, 1990.

10. Liskov, Barbara and John Guttag, *Abstraction and Specification in Program Development,* MIT Press, Cambridge, MA, 1986.

11. Nygaard, Kristen and Ole-Johan Dahl, "The Development of the Simula Language," *History of Programming Languages,* ACM SIGPLAN History of Programming Languages Conference (Los Angeles), Richard L. Wexelblat ed., Academic Press, New York, 1981, pp. 439–493.

12. Soley, Richard Mark, ed., *Object Management Architecture Guide,* Object Management Group, Document 90.10.1, November 1, 1990, Framingham, MA, 1990.

13. Taylor, David A., *Object-Oriented Technology: A Manager's Guide,* Addison-Wesley, Reading, MA, 1991.

11 CASE TOOLS

Object-oriented techniques and CASE technology fit naturally together. While the OO world initially emphasized OO programming, the emphasis, today, should be on repository-based development with integrated CASE tools and a powerful code generator.

Object orientation is much more than a computer language or design technique: it is a way of thinking. CASE tools oriented to this way of thinking will help the I.S. professional, as well as the business person, engineer, or end user, to visualize automation in terms of OO models and specifications.

Several OO analysis methods already exist in the data-processing industry. However, most are based on the structure of object-oriented programming languages—rather than its fundamental principles. They begin by defining classes and superclasses and continue by specifying the data structure of the classes. Next, the operations associated with each class are identified. Since these operations must connect in some way, their interfaces or request structures are defined. Finally, the methods for each operation are specified. Most methodologies do not identify events, triggers, control conditions, and state changes as described in Chapter 7 and Part IV of this book. This Object Behavior Analysis is important and should be an essential part of analysis and design methodologies.

OO analysis methods should not be tied to OO languages and their support facilities. Since technology for development is changing rapidly, we should analyze our systems *independently* of the programming tools used. Programming techniques should not drive the way we understand and communicate about our organizations.

A VARIETY OF TOOLS

Various tools have been created to help make I.S. development faster, cheaper, and higher quality. Some tools are simple, others are complex. Simple tools should be reserved for simple systems, where a complex tool might slow down development. Certain needs require only a report generator or a spreadsheet tool.

In the early 1980s, fourth-generation languages (4GLs) were invented [2]. Some 4GLs use nonprocedural languages that offer ways to express what result is required—not *how* to achieve it. SQL became a standard and provided a nonprocedural way to access relational databases. Other, more user-friendly, query languages and report-generation languages proliferated.

Most fourth-generation languages were invented before object-oriented techniques were well understood. Today, we need better end-user languages that incorporate OO techniques. Objects that have complex behavior may be shown on the screen as an icon. The end user can link many such icons together on a PC screen to build applications. This is done in some process-control software (e.g., from Gensym Inc.) and some decision-support software (e.g., from Metaphor Inc.).

Prototyping tools are important, enabling developers to build prototypes quickly and see how end users react to them. Prototyping languages gave rise to iterative development in which a prototype was successively refined.

CASE (Computer-Aided Systems Engineering) tools provided graphically oriented ways of expressing plans, models, and designs [3]. Code generators were created that could generate COBOL or other languages from high-level constructs [1].

As CASE tools became more powerful, much of the design could be synthesized rather than built from scratch. The design tools were linked to a repository containing information used in building the design. The repository stored the information involved in planning, analysis, design, and code generation. The repository contained templates and reusable constructs that could be customized for the system being built. It might contain specimen applications that could be modified. Particularly important now, the repository should contain reusable OO classes, designed to be incorporated in applications.

The tools really started to look powerful when these facilities were integrated. CASE tools for planning, for data and process modeling, and for creating designs, were integrated with code generators. Prototyping capability was linked into the design tools. Nonprocedural languages, including SQL and report generators, were integrated into the CASE environment. The term I-CASE describes integrated CASE products. Most important in I-CASE is the ability to generate code directly from the CASE design tool. An I-CASE repository contains design components in the form of reusable classes.

**CATEGORIES
OF CASE TOOLS**   CASE tools can be categorized as those built for the OO world and those built for the world of conventional computing. There are some that are half way between these categories. Many of these started life as non-OO tools, and OO

facilities have been added to them—particularly the representation of design objects that can be modified by the user to incorporate into a particular application (as in Figs. 11.7 and 11.8).

CASE tools are also categorized as I-CASE and fragment CASE—that is, supporting the whole lifecycle or only a portion of it, such as front-end analysis or back-end code generation. Some support information engineering (see Figs. 11.5 and 11.6) and help their users to build a model of the enterprise and analyze business areas. We thus have IE-CASE (for complete information engineering), I-CASE (integrated CASE not necessarily information engineering), and fragment CASE.

Figure 11.1 maps together these three categorizations and forms a useful framework for comparing CASE tools.

	Non-OO	Some OO	Fully OO
IE-CASE (complete information engineering)			
I-CASE (integrated CASE but not information engineering)			
Fragment CASE (often called front-end or back-end tools)			

Figure 11.1   Categorization of CASE tools.

INSIGHTFUL MODELS

Figure 11.2 repeats the figure showing how we model and design systems. The capabilities in this figure should be those of a CASE toolset. The methodology supported by the toolset should be such that the modeling leads directly to design as automatically as possible, and code is generated immediately from the design.

The model of reality should be as meaningful as possible to end users. In corporate I.S. we build a model of the enterprise. This should reflect the way the business people want to run the enterprise and facilitate discussion of how the enterprise procedures should be changed.

The early CASE tools modeled the enterprise with functional decomposition, entity-relationship diagrams, and matrices mapping entity types against functions. This modeling did not reflect how the enterprise operates and was not very meaningful to business people. OO modeling is more effective. Here we identify events and the operations triggered by events. Various business rules state how the business should react to events, that is, what to do about late payers, what factors have priority in shop-floor scheduling, and so on. These rules relate to business objects. We identify the business objects, operations that change their states, and the rules that should govern these operations.

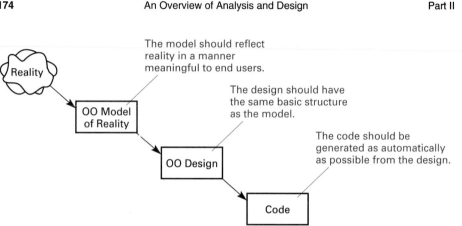

Figure 11.2   CASE tools should enable us to model reality in a manner as insightful as possible to end users and to translate those models as automatically as possible into the systems the users need.

The challenge of CASE tools today is modeling reality in a manner as insightful as possible to end users and to translate the models as automatically as possible into the required systems. OO techniques help us to do that.

DESIGN SYNTHESIS AND CODE GENERATION   The most powerful I-CASE tools allow as much design as possible to be *synthesized* from high-level constructs in the repository. The designer assembles the design and creates its detailed logic. Some design may be generated from high-level behavioral and structural statements such as state-transition diagrams, rules, decision trees, event schemas, and object schemas [3].

The design feeds a code generator that creates 100 percent of the code. Good code generators produce code with zero programming errors. The generated code should never have an ABEND. However, *design* errors are reflected in the code. The testing process is geared more for catching the *design* errors than catching detailed coding bugs.

The combination of *design synthesis* and *code generation,* shown in Fig. 11.3, enables high-quality applications to be built quickly. A world of difference exists between the modern development lifecycle using the tools in Fig. 11.1 and the traditional building of systems with plastic templates and line-by-line COBOL coding.

As far as possible, the design should be synthesized from

- Object-structure diagrams and specifications
- Object-behavior diagrams and specifications
- Rules

- Application-independent classes
- Classes for specific applications
- Entire applications designed for customization
- Designs that can be customized
- Declarative tables (e.g., decision tables, event-condition-action tables)
- A report generator
- A screen painter
- A dialog prototyping tool (GUI)

Like 4GLs, most early CASE tools were built before the ideas of object-oriented analysis and design were widespread. More recently, reusable OOPL classes began to appear in CASE tools. These reusable classes include screens, dialogs, reports, tables, procedures, procedures composed of other procedures, and so on.

Even though many CASE tools now have reusable classes for design, they do not allow the user to build directly the object schemas and event schemas

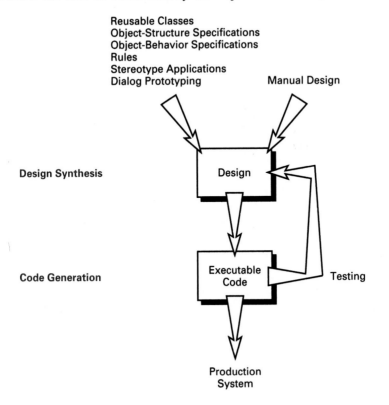

Figure 11.3 Design synthesis and code generation.

described in this book. A major upgrading of the best-selling CASE tools is needed to support OO analysis and design. OO analysis and design have been done with some CASE tools by improvising with facilities intended for conventional design. What we really need are tools that directly support the OO paradigm.

PRECISION IN DIAGRAMMING

In CASE, diagrams are used whenever appropriate as an aid to clear thinking. In the past, systems analysts drew their diagrams with pencils and erasers. These hand-drawn diagrams often became unwieldy, straggling across white boards or pasted on large sheets of paper. Frequently, the diagrams were sloppy and the diagramming technique casual or ill-conceived. Designs often had binders of nested data-flow diagrams and structure charts. These binders contained numerous errors, inconsistencies, and omissions that were overlooked. Today, one finds OO schemas being drawn by hand.

A good CASE tool employs diagram types that are precise and can be checked by computer. Large, complex diagrams can be handled by means of zooming, nesting, windowing, and other computer techniques. The computer quickly catches errors and inconsistencies even in very large sets of diagrams. Business, government, and the military need highly complex, integrated computer applications. The size and complexity of these applications require accurate diagramming using computers.

The *meaning* represented by the diagram is more valuable than its graphic image. A good CASE tool stores that meaning in a computer-processable form. The tool helps build up a design, a data model, or some other deliverable segment of the development process, so that it can be validated and used in a subsequent development stage.

An article in *Fortune* [4] attempts to describe why software is so difficult to create:

> Software is "pure thought stuff," so conceptual that designers cannot draw explicit, detailed diagrams and schematics—as creators of electronic circuits can—to guide programmers in their work. Consequently, routine communication among programmers, managers and the ordinary people who use software is a chore in itself.

This popular wisdom is *wrong* today. With the I-CASE tools, explicit, detailed diagrams and schematics are drawn, analogous to those used by electronic circuit designers, and code is generated from them. Much testing can be done at the diagram level. These diagrams are very effective for routine communications among programmers, analysts, managers, and end users. Just as other engineering disciplines have precision represented in formal diagrams, so computer system developers also need formality and precision—in this case, enforced by the computer.

Given appropriate diagramming techniques, describing complex activities and procedures is easier through diagrams than text. A picture can be much better than a thousand words, because it is concise, precise, and clear. Computerized diagrams do not allow the sloppiness and woolly thinking common in textual specifications. Engineers of different types use formal diagrams that are precise in meaning—mechanical drawings, architectural drawings, circuit diagrams, microelectronics designs, and so on. The diagrams become the documentation for systems (along with the additional information collected in the repository when the diagrams are drawn).

The evolution of CASE technology represents an evolution of application development from being a *craft* to being an *engineering discipline.*

DIAGRAMS FOR OO DEVELOPMENT   For OO analysis and development, CASE tools should enable their users to build the diagram types listed in Box 11.1. Many of these diagrams are the same as those for non-OO development:

- Data structure diagrams (showing records, their fields, keys, and interrelations)
- Action diagrams (showing the structure of procedural code)
- Declarative tables (e.g., decision tables or event-condition-action tables)
- Tools for designing the graphic user interface
- State-change diagrams (showing the state changes of an object)

Some of the diagrams are essentially the same as those used in conventional data-centered development but with an OO flavor:

- Object-inheritance diagrams (which are broadly similar to entity diagrams showing subtypes and supertypes)
- Object-relationship diagrams (similar to entity-relationship diagrams)
- Object composed-of diagrams (similar to diagrams showing hierarchical decomposition)

One important type of diagram is not supported by non-OO tools. This is the event schema shown in Fig. 9.8.

Conventional mass-market CASE tools should be enhanced to make them support OO analysis and design as naturally as possible. Some CASE tools are designed solely for OO development. Some of these are powerful single-user tools but do not support object behavior analysis well or development by teams of developers.

While CASE tools do not now have everything needed for OO work, they are still useful and even essential for OO analysis and design. Some corporations have made very effective use of them.

BOX 11.1

CASE tools for OO analysis and design should enable their users to build the following types of diagrams and generate code from them:

For Object Structures:

- Data-structure diagrams
- Object-generalization hierarchy diagrams
- Object-relationship diagrams
- Object composed-of diagrams

For Object Behavior:

- Representations of methods
  —Action diagrams
  —Structure charts
  —Declarative tables
- State-change diagrams
- Event diagrams
- Tools for designing the graphic user interface

All of these diagram types are supported by mass-market CASE tools except event diagrams. The latter diagram types need to be added to today's CASE tools. OO code generation needs improving on most tools. While today's CASE tools are not perfect, they are usable and valuable for OO analysis and development.

REPOSITORY   A computer can be extremely effective at accumulating and storing in an organized fashion a large amount of knowledge, supplemented at different times, by different people, in different places. An I-CASE repository is designed for this purpose.

The best way we know of organizing the I-CASE repository is using object-oriented techniques. The repository stores and catalogs the reusable OOPL classes.

A repository is the heart of a CASE environment. It stores all the information about systems, designs, and code in a basically nonredundant fashion. It is used by all developers. Using powerful tools, the developers employ the information in the repository and create new information that, in turn, is placed in the repository. The repository and its affiliated system check and correlate all the information stored to ensure its consistency and integrity. The repository should contain reusable classes that enable the developers to build systems quickly.

As the repository is the heart of the CASE environment, it should also be the heart of the methodology employed for building systems. The developers create designs with the help of information from the repository. They progressively build their designs in the repository and generate code from them.

MORE THAN A DICTIONARY

It is important to understand that a CASE repository is more than a dictionary.

A *dictionary* contains names and descriptions of data items, processes, variables, and so on.

A *repository* contains a complete coded representation of the objects used in planning, analysis, design, and code generation. Object-oriented methods are used to ensure consistency and integrity of this knowledge. Many rules are used, with rule-based processing, to help achieve accuracy, integrity, and completeness of the plans, models, and designs. The repository stores the meaning represented in CASE diagrams and enforces consistency within this representation. The repository thus *understands* the design whereas a simple dictionary does not. Particularly important, the repository drives a code generator. The developer should not have to code languages with an arcane syntax, such as COBOL, C, or CH. The best code generators in use today, generating COBOL or C, produce 100 percent of the code for the production system.

The diagrams that appear on the screen of the CASE tools are created in real time from the repository. Different diagram types can be derived from the same information, representing different ways of visualizing the integrated body of knowledge in the repository. As illustrated in Fig. 11.4 the repository stores the meaning represented in the diagrams. Diagrams are generated from the repository. The repository stores more detail than the diagrams contain. Additional detail can be obtained by pointing to an object on the diagram. Details will appear in another window.

The repository views the world as a collection of objects—the objects that appear on the CASE screens as boxes, lines, or other elements of diagrams. Even if the analyst is using conventional techniques rather than OO techniques, the repository should store object types such as

- Object types themselves
- Relationships among object types
- Classes
- Event types
- Trigger rules

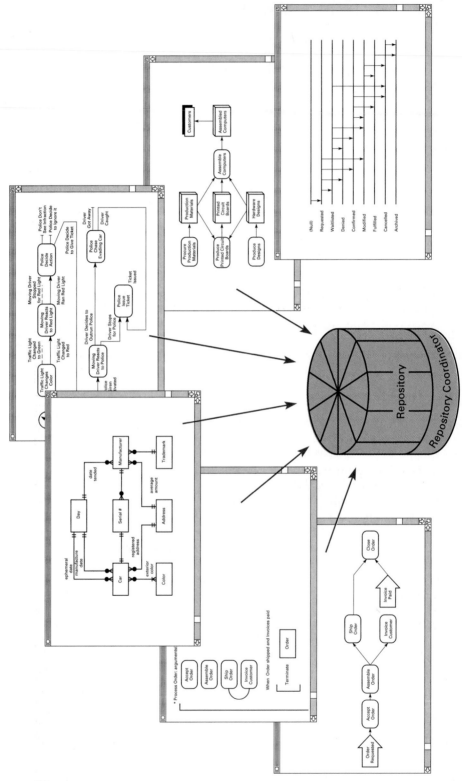

Figure 11.4 CASE diagrams, and windows associated with them, are used to communicate information to the repository. CASE tools use the objects in the repository to help to synthesize designs.

- Control conditions
- Operations
- Action diagram showing method procedures
- Detailed components of action diagrams
- Declarative statements
- Data types
- Records in a database
- Screen designs
- Report designs

In a comprehensive repository, there are hundreds of classes.

INTELLIGENCE IN THE REPOSITORY

The repository stores many types of objects. In order to handle them correctly, the repository requires its own set of classes and associated methods. These methods may be expressed as collections of rules or may be algorithms that process the information stored in the repository. The repository that contains rules can employ rule processing to help achieve accuracy, integrity, and completeness of the plans, models, and designs. Thus, the repository both stores development information and helps control its accuracy and validity.

Any one diagram on a CASE screen is a facet of a broader set of knowledge that may reside in the repository. The repository normally contains far more detail than is contained in the diagram. Any portion of this detail can be displayed in other windows by using a mouse.

The knowledge coming from the CASE diagrams must be coordinated to ensure that it fits together logically and consistently. IBM refers to this capability as *repository services.* KnowledgeWare Inc. calls it the *knowledge coordinator.* We will refer to it as the *repository coordinator.* A good repository coordinator is highly complex—capable of handling repositories with thousands of rules.

OO REPOSITORY FOR NON-OO TECHNIQUES

Currently, most system developers who are using repository-based developments are not using OO analysis and design. A good repository and repository coordinator operates in an OO fashion even though it supports non-OO development, as shown in Fig. 11.5.

Conventional development uses CASE screens with nodes on the screen and lines connecting the nodes. The repository treats the nodes and lines as objects. It collects information about these objects and uses methods to establish integrity. Examples of these objects are

	Analysis	Design	Repository
①	The analyst uses conventional non-OO analysis.	The designer uses conventional non-OO analysis.	The repository stores non-OO CASE information in an OO fashion.
②	The analyst uses conventional non-OO analysis.	The designer uses design objects such as screens, dialogs, fields, reports, templates.	The repository stores CASE information in an OO fashion.
③	Analysis and design are fully OO and use object schemas, event schemas, and design objects.		The repository stores OO CASE information in an OO fashion.

Figure 11.5 The repository uses and operates in an OO fashion even if the analysts or designers do not.

- Nodes
  — an entity type
  — a process
  — a data store
  — a program module
  — a department
  — a business goal
- Lines between nodes
  — a relationship between two entity types
  — a data-flow line on a data-flow schema
  — a parent-child association on a decomposition diagram
  — a line showing how a procedure is dependent on other procedures
  — a line connecting events on a Pert chart

The CASE software asks the user for detailed information about each type of object. This information is entered or displayed in windows. The CASE software uses such windows to collect a complete set of data. It can then check the integrity of models and designs, do design calculations, and accumulate the information it needs for code generation.

Sometimes, the relationships among objects are best displayed with a matrix diagram. Again, details may be entered or displayed using windows. If the user points to a cell in the matrix, a window may appear that shows the details known about that intersection or the details that must be entered.

CONSISTENCY AMONG DIAGRAMS   Different types of diagrams show different manifestations of the same information. These diagrams are logically interlinked in the computer. Data can be entered in one type of diagram and displayed with a different type of diagram. The repository tools ensure that the different diagrams reflect a consistent meaning. If a procedure node is added to a data-flow diagram, that procedure must appear on the equivalent decomposition diagram and vice versa.

Sometimes, analysts have two windows on the screen with different diagram types containing the same information. When they change one diagram, the change needed to ensure consistency should appear automatically on the other diagram. Analysts may add a process node to a decomposition diagram, for example, and the equivalent node appears on a data-flow diagram. Because the software does not know how to link it to the other nodes on the data-flow diagram, it asks for that information. In this way, one type of diagram can be converted into another or used as a component of another diagram.

For example, knowledge X may be best entered into the repository by Mr. Jones via an event schema. Ms. Smith then requests the same information from the repository, reinterpreted automatically, as a state-transition diagram. This logically interconnected family of diagrams constitutes an integrated set of knowledge that the developers can explore via the screens of the I-CASE toolset.

CONSISTENCY AMONG DIFFERENT ANALYSTS

Multiple developers often work on one project. Designs done by different people need to work together with absolute precision—a difficult goal using manual methods. A good repository coordinator tool enforces consistency among the work of different analysts and implementors. One major benefit of using such tools is this computerized enforcement of consistency among the different parts of the evolving design. The larger and more complex a project, the more it needs precise computerized coordination of the work of different implementors.

CONSISTENCY AMONG DIFFERENT PROJECTS

A computerized corporation has many different databases and systems. Consistency among different systems must be achieved, because they interact with one another in complex ways. Systems in different plants and locations transmit information to one another. Data are often extracted from multiple systems and aggregated for business management. Different locations need commonality of management measurements. Sometimes, the term *corporate transparency* is used to mean that detailed information in all locations is accessible in a computerized form by a central management group for decision support and control.

CASE tools make it practical to achieve consistency among multiple projects. Designs for different systems are derived from a common collection of reusable classes—available to implementors from the repository, that is accessible from all locations.

The term *I-CASE* (Integrated CASE) refers to a toolset in which tools for each phase and aspect of the development lifecycle are integrated—utilizing a single logically consistent repository. Complete I-CASE toolsets today have tools for planning, analysis, design, prototyping, full code generation, and testing. Maintenance is done by modifying the design diagrams and regenerating the code. Efficient development employs an I-CASE toolset and an *I-CASE methodology* (sometimes referred to as an ICM). *OO-CASE* refers to an object-oriented CASE toolset that also should be fully integrated. *OOCM* refers to an object-oriented CASE methodology that should take full advantage of an OO-CASE toolset. Figure 11.6 details these integrated and object-oriented CASE methods.

I-CASE (Integrated CASE)

> A CASE toolset that supports all lifecycle stages including complete code generation, with a single logically consistent repository.

ICM (I-CASE Methodology)

> A methodology designed to take full advantage of an I-CASE toolset.

OO-CASE (Object-Oriented CASE)

> An I-CASE toolset that supports object-oriented analysis and design.

OOCM (Object-Oriented CASE Methodology)

> A methodology for object-oriented analysis and design that takes full advantage of an OO-CASE toolset.

Figure 11.6   Integrated and object-oriented CASE methods.

MAXIMUM REUSABILITY

Perhaps the single most important thrust in software development in the years ahead is achieving the highest level of reusability. Software should be built by assembling and customizing existing components with repository-based tools. Today, nearly every programmer is reinventing something that has been built, debugged, and painfully improved—a thousand times before.

Box 11.2 lists a number of desirable properties of reusable components. The best way to achieve a high degree of reusability is with object-oriented techniques. The CASE repository should be populated with a library of reusable classes that enable development to be done rapidly and with high quality. In hardware engineering, the change from transistor-by-transistor design to chip-by-chip design gave orders-of-magnitude improvements in productivity.

BOX 11.2 Desirable properties of reusable components.

I-CASE workbenches should employ the techniques of object-oriented design to maximize reusability.

- *Formal semantic basis.* A formalism should be used that precisely describes the component.
- *Expressiveness.* The formalism should express all possible kinds of components.
- *Easy to understand.*
- *Easy to customize in an unplanned way.* Customizing the components should be easier than rewriting them from scratch.
- *Easy to add or delete details.*
- *Designed for graphics workbench.* In order to satisfy the above three properties, the design should be represented with the graphics capability of an I-CASE toolset that integrates multiple diagrammatic representations.
- *Clear, simple, precise interfaces.* The formalism should precisely define the interfaces between components.
- *Self-contained.* The components should be self-contained and have predictable behavior.
- *Cause-and-effect isolation.* The component should execute its behavior independently of preceding causes or subsequent effects.
- *Self-organizing.* The components should know which other components they need, so that the programmer does not have to remember or search for them.
- *Verifiable.* Techniques for verifying the behavior of components should be used where practical.
- *Flexible without compromising efficiency.* It should be possible to use standard components without suffering performance problems.
- *Independent of programming language.* The formalism should be independent of programming languages.
- *Application standards.* Standards should be used as fully as possible for the interface to networks, interface to database, interface to operating systems, end-user dialog, client-server operation, and so on.
- *Electronic document standards.* Standards for electronically represented documents should be used—for example, the ANSI X.12/ISO, Edifact EDI standards.
- *Defined protocols.* Protocols should exist for the use of components, so that a software builder can employ components licensed from many companies.

Design by a much wider range of people was made practical. The change from line-at-a-time programming to design using software chips will be similarly effective.

If you request an architect to build a house for you, he will usually not design the house from scratch. He may start with a preexisting design and modify it or assemble a design from separate, preexisting drawings. He has reusable plans, configurable in many ways. Details can be pulled from a large number of standard components—doors, windows, plumbing, fittings, electrical components, heating units, lights, and so on. These are listed in numerous catalogs of off-the-shelf components. Most components have standard plugs, sockets, or measurements so that they fit together.

The building of data-processing applications will one day be similar, shown in Fig. 11.7. The designer should start with preexisting plans that can be reconfigured in many ways, use a repository of designs and components, and tools for adapting these to the system in question. There should be catalogs of many reusable OOPL classes that can be purchased and loaded into the repository.

A House Builder Uses:	A Software Builder Should Use:
● Reusable plans that can be configured in many ways	● Reusable plans that can be configured in many ways
● Standard, well-proven designs and components	● Standard, well-proven designs and components
● Off-the-shelf units	● Off-the-shelf classes that are easy to modify
● Catalogs of many components	● Catalogs of many classes
● Good knowledge of what components are available	● Good knowledge of what classes are available
● Standard plugs and sockets	● Standard interfaces

Figure 11.7   Comparison of a house builder and a software builder. The software builder should use many of the techniques of the house builder.

The designer may employ an expert system to help find the most useful classes. The house architect works with standard designs and components in order to minimize the amount of custom work. This reduces the time and cost of the project. Similarly, if the components are accessible, the system designer can minimize the amount of custom work for the same reason.

In the future, a major sector of the software industry will develop that sells reusable designs and classes. These classes will be easily found, understood, modified, and interlinked.

THREE SOURCES OF REUSABLE COMPONENTS

When a developer builds an application from existing classes, these classes come from three different sources, shown in Fig. 11.8:

- tool vendors
- software companies that sell object-oriented applications
- internal development

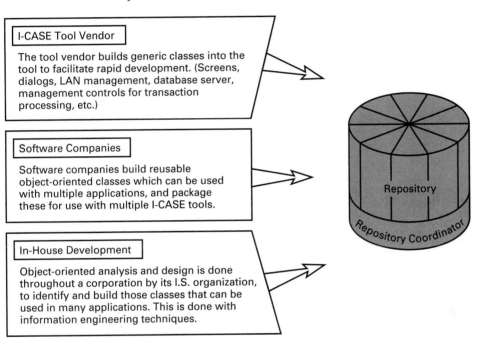

I-CASE Tool Vendor

The tool vendor builds generic classes into the tool to facilitate rapid development. (Screens, dialogs, LAN management, database server, management controls for transaction processing, etc.)

Software Companies

Software companies build reusable object-oriented classes which can be used with multiple applications, and package these for use with multiple I-CASE tools.

In-House Development

Object-oriented analysis and design is done throughout a corporation by its I.S. organization, to identify and build those classes that can be used in many applications. This is done with information engineering techniques.

Repository

Repository Coordinator

Figure 11.8 Three sources of OOPL classes.

To make its tools as useful as possible, a CASE tool vendor should package class libraries with the tools. Some classes are application independent, including screens, dialogs, LAN management, a database server, management controls for transaction processing, and so on. Other classes relate to specific applications. These would include such items as order entry, general accounting, bill of materials, and so on. A successful tool vendor may resell classes developed by customers, consultants, or software entrepreneurs.

Application packages have been sold by software companies since the days of vacuum tubes. Many of these packages are ill-structured and difficult to modify but nevertheless need adapting to their users' procedures.

Some software companies are now selling applications in I-CASE format that are easy to modify with I-CASE tools. Some are selling object-oriented classes that can be used with multiple applications. A software industry will likely grow selling libraries of reusable classes designed for standard repositories. Versions of such libraries may be created for all the leading I-CASE vendors.

It is cheaper to buy reusable classes than to build them (just as most manufacturers buy components). Where appropriate classes do not exist, they are sometimes designed by an I.S. organization for its own use. Some corporations have done top-down analysis and design with information engineering techniques. These organizations have identified and built reusable classes that apply to many applications such as account, customer, part, and so on. This has enabled them to achieve such a level of software reusability that only a small proportion of lines of code for new applications are custom generated. They can quickly create most new applications by reusing available classes. Equally important, it enables them to modify (maintain) applications quickly and easily.

REFERENCES

1. Freeman, Lee, ed., *Computer-Aided Software Engineering (CASE),* James Martin Insight Inc, Naperville, Ill., The Martin Report, Vol. VI, updated quarterly, 1991.

2. Martin, James, *Fourth-Generation Languages,* Vol. I, Prentice-Hall, Englewood Cliffs, NJ, 1985.

3. Martin, James and Carma McClure, *Structured Techniques: A Basis for CASE,* Prentice-Hall, Englewood Cliffs, NJ, 1988.

4. Schlender, Brenton R., "How to Break the Software Logjam," *Fortune,* 120:7, Sept 25, 1989, pp. 100ff.

12 STANDARDS FOR OBJECT INTERACTION

Object-oriented technology cannot begin to reach its potential until there are industry standards that enable classes from one vendor to interact with classes from other vendors. The classes can execute on networked machines from different manufacturers with different operating systems, database systems, and user interfaces. Software vendors creating new classes are likely to do so by employing existing software from other vendors. International standards enabling classes to intercommunicate are as important as international *open* standards for networks.

CASE tools for OO design and code generation should help to enforce the standards, generating requests of standard format and employing standard classes from a repository for object services and common facilities.

THE OBJECT MANAGEMENT GROUP
The organization primarily concerned with establishing industry standards is the Object Management Group (OMG). The OMG is a nonprofit, international, trade association, funded by about 200 computer and software companies. Its mission is stated as follows [1]:

- The Object Management Group is dedicated to maximizing the portability, reusability, and interoperability of software. The OMG is the leading worldwide organization dedicated to producing a framework and specifications for commercially available object-oriented environments.

- The Object Management Group provides a Reference Architecture with terms and definitions upon which all specifications are based. Implementations of these specifications will be made available under fair and equitable terms and conditions. The OMG will create industry standards for commercially available object-oriented systems by focusing on remote object network access, encapsulation of existing applications, and object database interfaces.

- The OMG provides an open forum for industry discussion, education, and promotion of OMG endorsed object technology. The OMG coordinates its activities with related organizations and acts as a technology/marketing center for object-oriented software.

The members of the Object Management Group (OMG) have a shared goal of developing and using integrated software systems. These systems should be built using a methodology that supports modular production of software; encourages reuse of code; allows useful integration across lines of developers, operating systems, and hardware; and enhances long-range maintenance of that code. Members of the OMG believe that the object-oriented approach to software construction best supports their goals.

OBJECT MANAGEMENT ARCHITECTURE

The OMG has a Reference Model for an *Object Management Architecture.* The goal of the architecture is to enable different software from different vendors to work together. It is intended to influence the design of components only to the extent of achieving interoperability. Diverse design solutions can be accommodated.

The Reference Model addresses

- How objects make and receive requests and responses
- The basic operations that must be provided for every object
- Object interfaces that provide common facilities useful in many applications

The Object Management Architecture consists of four major parts as illustrated in Fig. 12.1:

Application Objects (AO)

Application Objects are end-use applications that may be built by diverse vendors or by in-house I.S. organizations.

Common Facilities (CF)

Common Facilities are objects and classes providing general purpose capabilities useful in many applications. Types of facilities that are candidates for CF include

- Cataloging and browsing of classes and objects
- Link management
- Reusable user interfaces (e.g., text editors)

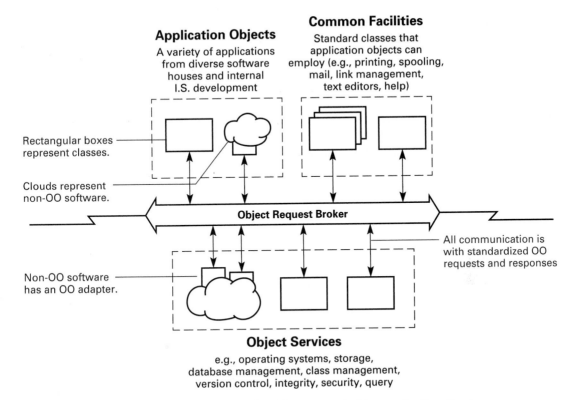

Figure 12.1   The OMG's Object Management Architecture is attempting to achieve industry standardization for OO interoperability.

- Printing and spooling
- Error reporting
- Help facility
- Electronic mail facility
- Tutorials and computer-based training
- Common access to remote information repositories
- Agent (intelligent macro) facilities
- Interfaces to external systems
- Object querying facilities
- User preferences and profiles

Object Services (OS)

Object Services is a collection of services that provides basic functions for realizing and maintaining objects. They include file or database management systems, transaction managers, directory services, and so on. OMG lists examples of the operations that Object Services can provide:

- Class management. The ability to create, modify, delete, copy, distribute, describe, and control the definitions of classes, the interfaces to classes, and the relationships between class definitions.

- Instance management. The ability to create, modify, delete, copy, move, invoke, and control objects and the relationships between objects.

- Storage. The provision of permanent or transient storage for large and small objects, including their state and methods.

- Integrity. The ability to ensure the consistency and integrity of object states both within single objects (e.g., through locks) and among objects (e.g., through transactions).

- Security. The ability to provide (define and enforce) access constraints at an appropriate level of granularity on objects and their components.

- Query. The ability to select objects or classes from implicitly or explicitly identified collections based on a specified predicate.

- Versions. The ability to store, correlate, and manage variants of objects.

Object Request Broker (ORB)

The Object Request Broker is the heart of the Object Management Architecture. It allows objects to communicate independently of specific platforms and techniques. The goal of the Object Request Broker is to guarantee that objects can interoperate with one another, whether they are on the same machines, on machines connected in a client-server fashion, or on diverse networks of heterogeneous systems.

An object makes a request in a standard fashion, and the Object Request Broker arranges for the request to be processed. The Object Request Broker causes some method to be invoked, and conveys the results to the requester. Box 12.1 lists functions that the Object Request Broker must address, at least to some degree.

STANDARD REQUESTS AND RESPONSES To achieve interaction, an object needs to send requests to other objects and receive their responses in a standard fashion. The OMG Architecture defines the requests and responses. A request names an *operation* and includes zero or more parameter values, any of which may be object names, identifying specific objects. This causes some *method* to be invoked that performs the operation using the parameters.

The request may be sent to the Object Request Broker, which arranges for the request to be processed and conveys the results to the requester. This may be

BOX 12.1 Functions of the Object Request Broker.

- **Name Services.** Object name mapping services map object names in the naming domain of the requester into equivalent names in the domain of the method to be executed and vice versa. The OMG Object Model does not require object names to be unique or universal. Object location services use the object names in the request to locate the method to perform the requested operation. Object location services may involve simple attribute lookups on objects. In practice, different object systems or domains will have locally preferred object naming schemes.

- **Request Dispatch.** This function determines which method to invoke. The OMG Object Model does not require a request to be delivered to any particular object. As far as the requester is concerned, it does not matter whether the request first goes to a method that then operates on the state variables of objects passed as parameters or whether it goes to any particular object in the parameter list.

- **Parameter Encoding.** These facilities convey the local representation of parameter values in the requester's environment to equivalent representations in the recipient's environment. To accomplish this, parameter encodings may employ standards or de facto standards.

- **Delivery.** Requests and results must be delivered to the proper location as characterized by a particular node, address, space, thread, or entry point. These facilities may use standard transport protocols.

- **Synchronization.** Synchronization primarily deals with handling the parallelism of the objects making and processing a request and the rendezvous between the requester and the response to the request. Possible synchronization models include asynchronous (request with no response), synchronous (request; await reply), and deferred synchronous (proceed after sending request; claim replay later).

- **Activation.** Activation is the housekeeping processing necessary before a method can be invoked. Activation and deactivation of persistent objects is needed to obtain the object state for use when the object is accessed and save the state when it no longer needs to be accessed. For objects that hold persistent information in nonobject storage facilities (e.g., files and databases), explicit requests can be made to objects to activate and deactivate themselves.

- **Exception Handling.** Various failures in the process of object location and attempted request delivery must be reported to requester and/or recipient in ways that distinguish them from other errors. Actions are needed to

Continued

BOX 12.1   *(Continued)*

> recover session resources and resynchronize requester and recipient. The ORB coordinates recovery housekeeping activities.
>
> - **Security Mechanisms.** The ORB provides security enforcement mechanisms that support high-level security control and policies. These mechanisms ensure the secure conveyance of requests among objects. Authentication mechanisms ensure the identities of requesting and receiving objects, threads, address spaces, nodes, and communication routes. Protection mechanisms assure the integrity of data being conveyed and assure that the data being communicated and the fact of communication are accessible only to authorized parties. Access enforcement mechanisms enforce access and licensing policies.

a simple operation. However, the Object Request Broker sometimes has to contact Object Services in order to find the class and method that is requested. The Object Services may include a class dictionary service or might search run-time method libraries.

OMG gives an example [1]:

> Consider the request "print layout_312 laser_plotter." This could be sent to the object "layout_312" whose "print" method would then print it on "laser_plotter." Or the request could be sent to "laser_plotter" whose "print" method would access "layout_312". Or the request could be sent to the generalized "print" routine that would figure out a good way to arrange the printing, based on some attributes of these two objects. Or, instead of relying on a generalized "print" routine, the Name Service in the ORB could determine an appropriate method jointly owned by the (the classes of) "layout_312" and "laser_plotter".

INTERFACE TO NON-OO SOFTWARE

If OO software is to have widespread use, it must interact with other software that is not OO in nature. A vast amount of non-OO software exists, including basic software such as operating systems, database management systems, network software, and so on. Object-oriented software will ease its way steadily into a world that is largely non-OO. It will be a long time before all of the software that needs to interact is object-oriented.

The *Application Objects* and *Object Services* of Fig. 12.1 will often be non-OO. In order to connect to the Object Management Architecture, they must have an OO interface, sometimes called an *adapter* or *wrapper,* that accepts OO requests in their standard format and translates them to whatever form the non-OO software uses. Similarly, the wrapper translates the responses into standard OO responses.

Figure 12.1 draws non-OO software as clouds and shows it having a square-cornered OO interface. Providing software has an OMA-compliant interface, it can participate in the Object Management Architecture.

The Object Management Architecture does not define the screen interface for the end user. A variety of graphic, or other, user interfaces could be employed. These are the subject of standardization efforts outside the OMG. The user interface must interact with the Object Request Broker using standard requests and responses. Eventually, Common Facilities may provide standard user interface classes.

Basically, the goal of the OMG is providing the *glue* that enables classes from all vendors to interoperate. Standards for this glue are needed quickly and need to have the widest industry support, so that the object-oriented revolution can gain maximum momentum.

REFERENCE

1. Soley, Richard Mark, ed., *Object Management Architecture Guide,* Object Management Group, Document 90.9.1, November 1, 1990.

13 OBJECT-ORIENTED DATABASES*

A traditional database stores just data—with no procedures. It attempts to make the data independent from the procedures. The data are accessible by diverse users for diverse purposes. In contrast, an object-oriented database stores objects. The data are stored along with the *methods* that process those data.

After traditional databases had been in use for some time, a need arose to associate certain procedures with the data and activate them when the data were accessed. Such procedures were used to help control the integrity of the data or their security. Sometimes, a value was computed from fields other than those stored—a procedure referred to as putting *intelligence* in the database. Intelligent database techniques were useful for controlling integrity in a client-server environment, because the identity of a client accessing a database server was never certain.

Object-oriented databases take the idea of intelligent databases to its logical conclusion. *No* data are accessed except with the methods stored in the database. These methods are ready to take action the moment they receive a request. The data of all objects are thus *encapsulated.* The data are generally *active* rather than *passive.*

We described the enterprise of the future as similar to an electronic organism. The corporate functions are carried out with object-oriented processing. Low-level objects, rather like cells in the body, are grouped into higher-level objects that carry out the functions useful to business people. The corporate network plays a role rather like the human nervous system, enabling fast interaction among the active collections of objects. Unlike the human nervous system, the network may be worldwide. The corporation will be like a worldwide electronic creature interacting electronically with other such creatures—its trading partners. The world patterns of commerce will change rapidly as these networked electronic organisms interact with one another using advanced forms of EDI (electronic

*Sometimes referred to as simply object databases

data interchange). Corporations that do not have this fast-reacting electronic infrastructure will be unable to compete effectively.

Object-oriented databases will become a very important corporate technology. There are complex questions about how such databases should be structured. Should they be extensions of today's relational databases, or should they have entirely different structures?

A BRIEF HISTORY OF DATABASE DEVELOPMENT

As Fig. 13.1 illustrates, four generations of systems have managed computer data. In the beginning, languages and the machine instructions were very similar, resulting in a process-oriented programming model. For example, programs for addition were organized around the machine process of addition—loading registers with numbers, executing the add instruction, and dealing with overflow and underflow. Few results were stored for later use. Programs primarily executed tasks and never wrote to a storage device. At this stage, one of the few items stored was the program itself. However, programmers soon realized the value of recording results. Recording program results greatly increased with the advent of rotating magnetic disk storage, which provided random-access capability for large amounts of storage.

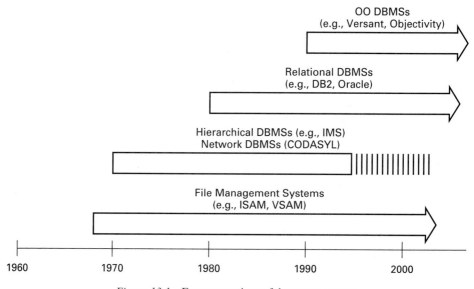

Figure 13.1　Four generations of data management.

File Systems

Eventually most programs made use of this new disk storage. However, the data on rotating media quickly became difficult to organize and manage. This situation led developers to create packages of programs to ease the manipulation of disk storage. File management systems were born.

Many different systems were developed and among the best known were those running on IBM hardware. With them, programmers could create files, store data, and read them back later for analysis or presentation. Programs were still generally organized around the process-oriented model, and availability of higher-level languages, especially COBOL, led to the development of large business programs. These programs viewed the data in files by their business purposes, typically sorted by categories or indexed by some logical key, for example, Order Number. The notion of a record and a file as a group of records was developed. Each record represented an instance of some business concept, such as a Line Item in an Order.

While these early file systems aided the programmer, the data access methods were still primitive. Random access required the application program to know the physical placement of data on the disk. Computing these unique addresses required *hashing* algorithms. Developing hashing algorithms with a good, even distribution was an important skill—especially when different disk drives needed different algorithms. This prompted the first major *implementation independent* aid—the indexed file. Instead of requiring an application to furnish the exact location of a piece of recorded data, only a symbolic key was needed. The index-enhanced file system, then, was necessary in order to compute and assign the data's physical location. Among the most widely used were (and, in many cases, still are) the ISAM (Indexed Sequential Access Method) and VSAM (Virtual Sequential Access Method) systems running on IBM mainframes.

The First DBMSs

The ever increasing demand for more capability from computer applications continued, and researchers realized that even indexed file systems were crude instruments. Order processing applications in particular tended to impose a hierarchical model on their data that corresponded to the hierarchical nature of an Order containing many Line Items and to Products described via hierarchical assembly structures. These pressures prompted the creation of the first systems that were layered on top of the file system and became known as database management systems (DBMSs). The most well known hierarchical DBMS was IMS (Information Management System) from IBM.

The notion of a DBMS combined several ideas into a single system. DBMSs were based on a model of data independent of any particular application. This next step in implementation independence allowed application developers more time to concentrate on their application architecture. It also gave the DBMS a wide range of implementation freedom. With a DBMS, data design became the most important activity, causing a fundamental shift in paradigm to a *data-oriented* model of application development. This shift to a data-oriented model also led to the development of groups of related applications into business systems all running against a common DBMS. From this phenomenon, other needs arose, such as having multiple applications interact simultaneously with the DBMS and creating independent utility applications to manage the DBMS. Thus were born the notions of concurrency control and most of the activities known as database administration—backup, recovery, resource allocation, security, and so on.

The restrictions of the hierarchical data model imposed by IMS soon became apparent. Hierarchies provided a good model for many common business problems. However, developers began to realize that the world was not inherently hierarchical, and that nonhierarchical models were awkward to implement using a system like IMS. For instance, an inventory-control system needs to model the relationship between parts in an inventory and suppliers of those parts. This relationship is a lattice instead of a hierarchy, since most parts can be obtained from more than one supplier and most suppliers handle multiple parts. Lattice relationships were such a common problem that new DBMSs were developed that supported both set-based models and hierarchical models. Eventually, a standard model known as CODASYL was developed with several DBMSs providing implementations. The DBMS came with a data model used to describe the business independent of any particular application. A data definition language (DDL) was developed to describe a particular business model, along with a data manipulation language (DML) that created and processed data in a particular database. The DDL and DML could be used to completely specify and build applications or used in conjunction with other programming languages, such as COBOL. Finally, a set of ancillary functions administered physical storage of the DBMS, security, and other services not covered by the DDL and DML.

As systems built on top of DBMSs grew, so did the problems—centering around reorganization and navigation. Reorganization was the biggest problem, because the conceptual model and the physical implementation were so closely associated. Hierarchical and set-oriented relationships were typically implemented by placing the physical disk address of one record into another. The DML then compiled a data field for this address into an application. Unfortunately, this implied that any change to the DBMS record layout required, at a minimum, recompilation of all programs. Worse yet, if the physical address of a record changed, all references to it had to be found, so that the correct new location could be inserted. As these DBMSs had contributed to the processing and storage of large amounts of data, the physical reorganization could become untenable. During reorganization, large databases were typically unavailable for days at a time.

Navigation, the second problem, refers to the way that applications are bound to the DBMS. Applications use the DML to find a record, then use the DML to find related records. For example, in a hierarchical model one might find an Order and then find all Line Items of that Order stored as *child* records. In this way, applications could navigate between records in the database. This means the application had incorporated within it knowledge of the relationships in the model, which was fine. However, since the logical description of the relationships and their physical implementation were close, the application also contained implicit knowledge of the implementation. This was potentially confusing. Any change or extension to the model invalidated many applications, and recompilation would no longer cure the problem. The application had to be rewritten to accommodate the new model. With the current size of systems and the centrality of the DBMS to the business, change to and evolution of the model were inevitable. Large applications were rewritten many times at ever increasing expense. Maintenance activities began to dominate new development, and the time required to develop new applications became prohibitive. The systems acted like giant beasts struggling in ancient tar pits—each movement mired them further, until they were stuck.

The Relational Database

During this period, E. F. Codd wrote his seminal paper on the relational data model, and several implementations of relational databases (RDBs) began to appear. RDBs had several important characteristics that solved many of the problems discussed above. In brief, the relational model was not based on any particular data structuring paradigm but rather a particular mathematical foundation. The resulting model could express a nonredundant description of data and a set of fixed operators from which the data could be formally derived. In addition, the relational model could be intuitively represented by a simple tabular structure, providing a useful visual format for displaying information contained in the database.

The relational data model moved the focal point of the system development process away from data structures and computer implementations toward modeling the business application realm. This was its most important aspect. The entire process moved to a higher level as the important questions focused on the central tenets of the business model, rather than the most convenient implementation vehicle for a particular application or set of applications. RDBs represented the first systems that provided an application interface for which implementation issues were removed from the process. A major goal of database technology was achieved—the data were independent of the processes.

The relational data model defines three data types: the table (relation), the row (tuple), and the column (attribute). The model specifies three operators on tables: select, project, and join. *Select* applies a Boolean operator to each row of a table and returns a new table containing only those rows for which the Boolean operator returns true. *Project* specifies a subset of the columns defined in a table. It returns a new table containing all of the original rows along with those rows that correspond to the column values specified by the project. The *join* operator combines the two tables and produces a single table. This table represents the Cartesian product of all the tables from which the join is formed. Then, a Boolean operator compares one column from each original table, and the join result is a new table containing those rows for which the Boolean operator returns true.

The relational data model provides several significant advantages over its predecessors:

- *Data independence.* The data representation on the computer is independent of the interface to the application. The most significant advantage of this over earlier systems is that the physical representation can be modified without affecting applications. The database can be completely reorganized at the physical level without recompiling programs or schema. Performance features such as indexes can be added or removed dynamically, tables can be partitioned across disk drives or compressed to reclaim unused space, and so on. None of this affects the applications developed. Thus, the investment in the application is maintained more easily—a major advantage over prior systems.

- *Declarative manipulation.* By far the most common language used to express the relational model is SQL. SQL is a declarative, nonprocedural language that expresses the kind of data desired—not the way to get it. This use of *queries,* as these declarative statements are called, is generally a simpler mechanism for manipulating a database than using a typical programming language. SQL embodies the philosophy of data independence. It allows the database system to chose from alternative mechanisms and to obtain the desired results from the physical realization of the database. The database management system can dynamically optimize the way queries are executed, freeing the application programmer from this task.

- *Removing redundancy.* When relational data are designed, the process of normalization can be applied. Fully normalizing a data model produces a database in which data redundancy has been eliminated. This has two advantages over prior systems. First, it removes the possibility that portions of the database are out of sync due to redundant storage. This was a problem with both hierarchical and network databases, where redundant data were common. Secondly, it usually minimizes the amount of data stored, reducing the overall size of the database and saving disk space.

- *Simplicity.* The relational model has three basic types and three operations—an improvement over the programming languages that had to be mastered. Whether programmers or not, most people are already familiar with the basic concepts, since they have worked with tables, rows, and columns. The relational model is easier to learn and use.

- *Tables as presentation vehicles.* The result of all relational operators is a table, which often is the required application solution. Previous data models required extracting the appropriate information and then translating it into some desired result format—usually a table. RDBs eliminate this last step since the result is already in table form.

All of the above characteristics enable faster application development and easier application maintenance—hence, the current popularity of RDBs. A further reason is the modern application development environments spawned by RDBs, especially to fourth-generation languages (4GLs). Fourth-generation languages are characterized, in general, by a language with built-in database operators and, perhaps, report formatting. This again simplifies the application development process and reduces the time needed to complete a new application.

Active Databases

The classic relational database was passive. It merely stored data in a data-independent way. The concept of an active database evolved—a database that would take certain actions automatically when an attempt was made to read or update the data. This was referred to as putting *intelligence* into the database. The basic structure of the relational database was the same, but the database management system was changed so that it applied security controls, integrity controls, or automatic computations. This was done in Sybase, for example, and was particularly useful for a database on a client-server system where the clients were unknown.

Knowledgebases

The so-called artificial intelligence world brought another form of active database. It was desirable to store *knowledge.* Knowledge was regarded as being active, whereas data or information were passive. Knowledge was thought to consist of facts and rules that a computer could employ. For example, with expert systems appropriate rules were identified and chained using an inference engine to reason about a problem. The inference engine used forward chaining or backward chaining—or both. This powerful concept was applied successfully to some highly complex problems. This type of computing needed a *knowledgebase* that stored both data and rules, and employed an inference engine to search for rules and perform automatic reasoning. Knowledgebase systems were built by artificial intelligence companies.

Object-Oriented Databases (OODBs)

Object-oriented databases first evolved from a need to support object-oriented programming. Smalltalk and C++ programmers needed a store for what they called *persistent* data, that is, data that remain after a process is terminated. OODBs become important for certain types of applications with complex data, such as CAD (computer-aided design) and CAE (computer-aided engineering). They also became important for handling BLOBs (binary large objects) such as images, sound, video, and unformatted text. Applications, such as newspaper layout and video retrieval in advertising agencies used OODBs with BLOBs. OODBs supported more diverse data types than the simple tables, columns, and rows of relational databases.

Users steadily realized that object-oriented techniques are useful. OO techniques are good for both specialized systems, such as CAD, and for computing in general. An enterprise model should be a model describing business object types, subtypes, their behavior, the relationships among objects, object states, events that are changes in state, business rules, and so on. The enterprise model should be translatable directly in software that makes the enterprise function. This requires databases that store the object and bring the associated methods into operation.

Various needs not met by traditional relational databases converged to form a new generation of database management systems. *Active* databases are best implemented with OO techniques. Knowledgebases became *frame-oriented* where a frame is an object having a collection of rules associated with it. Richly diverse abstract data types (user-defined data types) needed support, including speech, image, and video. Complex data required access techniques that improved performance over relational databases. As shown in Fig. 13.2, these needs converged into OODBs.

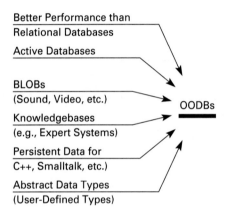

Figure 13.2 A variety of needs converged into OODB technology.

A UNIFIED CONCEPTUAL MODEL

In traditional computing, the conceptual models for analysis, the models for design, and the models for database definition and access are all different. In contrast, OO techniques use the same conceptual models for analysis, design, and construction as described in Chapters 5 to 9 (see Fig. 5.3). OODB technology gives a further stage of unification, illustrated in Fig. 13.3. The OO database conceptual model is the same as the rest of the OO world, rather than separate relational tables and SQL.

Using the same conceptual model for all aspects of development simplifies development, especially with OO CASE tools, improves communication among users, analysts, and programmers, and lessens the likelihood of errors.

Traditional analysis uses entity-relationship models and functional decomposition. Analysts develop matrices mapping functions and entity types. Traditional design uses data-flow diagrams, structure charts, and action diagrams. Programming languages have a different conceptual model of code. Programmers do not think in terms of data-flow diagrams. Relational database technology uses

Traditional development has four conceptual models.

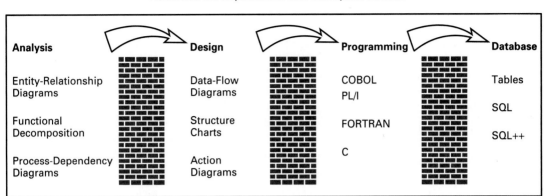

Object-oriented technology uses one consistent model.

Figure 13.3 OODB uses the same conceptual model as OO analysis, design, and programming. OO techniques tear down the conceptual walls between analysis, design, programming (or code generation), and database definition and access.

yet another conceptual model employing tables, with the need to JOIN and PRO-JECT tables. The conceptual model of SQL is quite different from the conceptual models of entity-relationship diagrams, functional decomposition, data-flow diagrams, structure charts, action diagrams, or COBOL.

By contrast, OODBs were designed to be well-integrated with OO programming languages, such as C++ and Smalltalk. They use the same object model. A database language that is different from the programming language is unnecessary. For example, with some OODB products C++ is used for all database definitions and manipulation. The same object model is also used for analysis and design. The analyst may determine high-level objects and high-level behavior. The designer pushes this down to low-level objects that inherit properties and behavior from the higher-level objects. With an OO CASE tool, as soon as the objects are specified on the screen, code can be interpretively generated for them.

Relational database design is quite separate from program design. The database is a separate space from the program space. The programmer has to figure out how to extract data from the tables and push data onto the table. With

OODBs, the programmer deals with transient and persistent objects in a uniform way. The persistent objects are in the OODB, and thus the conceptual walls between programming and database are removed. An OO CASE tool can create code as the analyst or designer thinks. Analysis, design, code generation, and database generation can be done iteratively by one person using the same conceptual model. This can greatly increase the rate at which a creative person invents and refines systems.

As commented earlier, the employment of a unified conceptual model for analysis, design, programming, and database results in

- Higher productivity. The work of translating between paradigms is avoided.
- Fewer errors. Errors occur in translation between the paradigms.
- Better communication among users, analysts, and implementors
- Better quality
- More flexibility
- Greater inventability

The world is not a collection of tables. One common model of the world is the assembly hierarchy found in manufactured items. Here, a **Part** is decomposed into its constituent **Subparts**, that are, in turn, decomposed into additional subparts. These are difficult to represent and manipulate using tables. In fact, by using a standard SQL, all the **Subparts** of given **Part** cannot typically be determined with one query statement. In contrast, an OODB supports both the ability of objects to refer directly to each other and the computational facility of OO languages to process objects.

OO DATABASE ARCHITECTURE

In the late 1980s, the first OODBs appeared. Figure 13.4 lists some of the main OODB products and their vendors. The early ones were designed as an extension of OO programming languages, such as Smalltalk and C++. The DML (data manipulation language) and DDL (data description language) were a common OO language. The design of current OODBs should take full advantage of CASE

Product	Vendor
Gemstone	Servio Corporation, Alameda, CA
Itasca	Itasca Systems Inc., Minneapolis, MN
Objectivity	Objectivity, Menlo Park, CA
Object Store	Object Design Inc., Burlington, MA
Ontos	Ontos Inc., Bellerica, MA
Versant	Versant Object Technology, Menlo Park, CA

Figure 13.4   Six OODB products and their vendors.

and incorporate methods created with any powerful technique, including declarative statements, code generators, and rule-based inferencing.

Many facilities of conventional database management are important in OODBs. These include locking for concurrent update controls, recovery, two-phase commits, security, data integrity, data distribution, and database tools.

Some features are independent of the fundamental architecture of an OODB but are common to most OODBs:

- *Versions.* Most database systems allow only one representation of a database entity to exist in the database. Versions allow alternative representation to exist simultaneously. This is useful in many application areas where a design is evolving and different strategies are being explored concurrently. For example, designers of a circuit may want to try different component layouts to maximize chip density, or software developers may have several versions of a particular subsystem using different algorithms to examine the effect that each has on overall system performance.

- *Shared Transactions.* Transactions typically isolate an individual's actions from the database until the transaction is committed to the database. Only then does it become globally visible. Shared transactions support groups of workstation users who want to coordinate their efforts in real time. In this way, users can share intermediate database results. The shared transaction allows several people to participate in a single transaction. This is useful in such applications as electronic conferences and document editing where several parties work on the document concurrently.

DEVELOPMENT WITH OODB

OODBs are developed by first describing the important object types of the application realm and the behaviors associated with those object types. These object types determine the classes that will form the definition of the OODB. For example, a database designed to store the geometry of mechanical parts would include classes such as, Cylinder, Sphere, and Cube. The behavior of a Cylinder might include information about its dimensions, volume, and surface area:

```
CLASS CYLINDER {
        FLOAT HEIGHT ();
        FLOAT RADIUS ();
        FLOAT VOLUME ();
        FLOAT SURFACEAREA ();
};
```

Similar definitions would be developed for cube and sphere. In the above definition, height (), radius (), volume (), and surfaceArea () represent the messages that can be sent to a Cylinder object. Note the absence of implementation details, including whether the information is stored or computed. The implementation is accomplished in the same language by writing functions corresponding to the OO requests:

CYLINDER::HEIGHT () {RETURN CYLINDER_HEIGHT;}
CYLINDER::VOLUME () {RETURN PI * RADIUS() * RADIUS ()* HEIGHT ();}

In this case, the height of the Cylinder is stored as a data element, while the volume is computed by the appropriate formula. Note that the internal implementation of volume uses requests to get height and radius. However, the most important aspect is the simplicity and uniformity that users of Cylinder experience. They just need to know how to send a request and what requests are available. The entire application can be written in one uniform style. Separating the programming language and DML is no longer necessary.

This approach also gives the OODB flexibility. Since the entire application is written using request sending, implementations can be altered to any degree without affecting applications. Consequently, the application is simpler and much easier to maintain and enhance. In this sense, OODBs provide even greater separation between system specification and its implementation.

THREE APPROACHES TO BUILDING OODBs   OODBs can be built using three approaches. The first uses an existing conventional database management system and adds a layer for processing OO requests and storing methods. This approach has one merit. The highly complex code of today's database management system can be used, so that an OODB can be implemented faster than starting from scratch.

The second approach regards an OODB as an extension of relational database technology. The tools, techniques, and vast experience of relational technology can then be used to build a new DBMS. Pointers may be added to relational tables linking them to large binary objects. Several existing RDB vendors advocate this approach.

The third approach rethinks the architecture of database systems and produces a new architecture optimized to meet the needs of OO technology. The OODB companies listed in Fig. 13.4 have all taken this approach, largely because they can achieve much better performance than with relational technology. Vendors taking this approach claim that relational technology is a subset of a more generalized capability. Relational data structures might be used where appropriate, but other data structures are usually better for complex objects and enable the data for a complex object to be accessed without moving the access mechanism. The OODB vendors claim that nonrelational OODBs are roughly two orders of magnitude faster than relational databases for storing and retrieving complex information [8]. They are therefore essential in applications such as CAD (computer-aided design) and would enable a CASE repository to be a real-time facility rather than a batch facility (as it is with IBM's DB2).

DATA INDEPENDENCE VERSUS ENCAPSULATION

A major goal of traditional database technology is *data independence*. Data structures should be independent of the processes that use data. The data, then, can be employed in any way the user wants.

In contrast, a major goal of object-oriented technology is *encapsulation*. This means that the data can *only* be employed with the methods that are part of a class. Object-oriented classes are intended to be reusable. Therefore, another goal of OO technology is achieving maximum reusability. Because of this, the class should be bug-free and should only be modified if absolutely necessary. Traditional database technology is designed to support processes that are subject to endless modification. Therefore, data independence is necessary. The OODB supports classes, some of which rarely change. Change comes from interlinking classes in diverse ways. The data structures in the OODB should be tightly optimized to support the class in which they are encapsulated. The goals, then, in relational databases and object-oriented databases are fundamentally different.

COMPLEXITY OF DATA STRUCTURE

Objects are composed of objects that in turn are composed of additional objects and so on. Because of this, the class data structure sometimes becomes highly complex. When an object is used, its data should be readable without having to move the disk-access mechanism. The data for each object should be clustered together. This may not be the case if a relational database is used. The object may employ data from multiple relations and hence require multiple movements of the access mechanism.

OODB systems, such as those in Fig. 13.4, have deliberately avoided the relational model in order to improve machine performance. They allow the data for one class to be interlinked efficiently, often resorting to the pointer structure that relational databases tried to avoid.

If a class uses certain methods frequently, it makes sense to optimize the data structure to obtain good machine performance with these methods.

PERFORMANCE

OODBs greatly outperform RDBs in delivering good performance for applications with lots of data connectivity. This is one of the primary reasons that applications sharing this characteristic currently use OODBs. Other reasons are

- OODBs allow objects to refer directly to one another using *soft pointers*. This makes OODBs much faster in getting from object A to object B than RDBs, which must use joins to accomplish this. Even an optimized join is typically much slower than an object traversal. Thus, even without any special tuning, an OODB is typically faster at these pointer-chasing mechanics.

- OODBs make physical clustering more effective. Most database systems allow the developer to place related structures close to each other in disk storage. This dramatically reduces retrieval time for the related data, since all data are read with one, instead of several, disk reads. However, in an RDB, implementation objects get translated into tabular representations and typically get spread out over multiple tables. Thus, in an RDB, these related rows must be clustered together, so that the whole object can be retrieved with one disk read. In an OODB, this is automatic. Furthermore, clustering related objects, such as all subparts of an assembly, can dramatically affect the overall performance of an application. This is relatively straightforward in an OODB, since this represents the first level of clustering. In contrast, physical clustering is typically impossible in an RDB, because it requires a second level of clustering—one level to cluster the rows representing individual objects and a second for the groups of rows that represent related objects.

- OODBs use diverse storage structures. In an RDB, data that cannot be easily expressed in tabular form is difficult to store and access efficiently. For example, multimedia applications require storing large data streams representing digitized video and audio data. CAD applications often require storing large numbers of very small objects, such as the points defining the geometry of a mechanical part. Neither is well-suited to representation in a table. Therefore, RDBs cannot provide efficient storage management for these application areas. The storage model for OODBs is unlimited, since the system is by nature extensible. OODBs can provide different storage mechanisms for different kinds of data. As a result, they have proven very effective in supporting both multimedia and CAD applications.

AVOIDING REDUNDANCY

With RDBs, data are normalized to help avoid redundancy [3, 6] and anomalies caused by data redundancy. This addresses redundancy in data but not redundancy in application code.

OO technology uses *inheritance* to lessen redundant development of *methods*. It also creates classes designed to be reused in many applications. Encapsulation and inheritance thus lower the amount of redundant code, as well as redundant data, in two ways—by inheritance and by reuse of classes. This lowers the cost of development and maintenance.

With traditional database technology, common processing gets replicated across different applications, causing lower productivity and increased maintenance costs. More recently, RDBs have introduced the notion of triggers or procedures that can be executed by the database. Using these capabilities to place common processing into the database is an improvement. However, it still separates the processing from those entities naturally associated with the processing. For instance, one could write a trigger enforcing the behavior that a terminated employee's salary must be $0. However, the termination process cannot be associated with the

Employee table. In an OODB, this process is straightforward, as the Employee class would define the terminate request and enforce the $0 salary constraint.

DIFFERENCES BETWEEN RELATIONAL DATABASES AND OBJECT-ORIENTED DATABASES

Object-oriented and relational databases have some fundamentally different goals and characteristics. In some computing environments, the goals of classic relational databases predominate. Here, RDBs are preferable. In other computing environments, RDBs do not adequately meet the needs and OODBs have major advantages. It is not likely that one database management system will ever meet all types of computing needs.

Insight into the advantages of one database technology over another requires some understanding of the application development process. This development process is not completely general. One database technology cannot satisfy all application domains, and the requirements of applications must be considered when analyzing the advantages of one database technology over another.

Box 13.1 summarizes the differences between RDBs and OODBs. A primary goal of relational databases is *data independence.* Data are separated from processing and normalized. Thus, they can be used for different applications, many of which may be unanticipated when the data are designed.

A primary goal of the OODB is *encapsulation.* The data are associated with a specific class that uses specific methods. The database stores that data plus the methods. The data and methods are inseparable. The data are not designed for any type of use but for use by the class. The class will be used in many different applications, many of which are not yet anticipated. We have *class independence* not merely *data independence.*

With an RDB, the data can be physically reorganized without changing application programs that use the data. With an OODB, the class can be reorganized without disrupting systems that use the class.

OODBs support *active* objects, whereas traditional databases store *passive* data. As the world of computing progresses, more and more systems will be built with *active* objects.

The OODB supports complex data structures and does not break them down into tables. Complex data structures are *encapsulated* in the classes, just as DNA is encapsulated in biological cells. To take highly complex data structures and decompose them into tables every time you store them has been likened to decomposing your car into its components every time you put it in the garage. The more complex the data structure, the greater the advantage of the OODB. A cell would be very inefficient if its DNA was stored in relational form and accessed with SQL.

BOX 13.1   A summary of the differences between relational and object-oriented databases.

Relational Databases	Object-oriented Databases
Primary goal: data independence	Primary goal: encapsulation
Data only. The database generally stores data only.	*Data plus methods.* The database stores data plus methods.
Data sharing. Data can be shared by any processes. Data are designed for any type of use.	*Encapsulation.* Data can be used only by the methods of classes. Data are designed for use by specific methods only.
Passive data. Data are passive. Certain limited operations may be automatically triggered when the data are used.	*Active objects.* Objects are active. Requests cause objects to execute their methods. Some methods may be highly complex, for example those using rules and an inference engine.
Constant change. Processes using data constantly change.	*Classes designed for reuse.* Classes designed for high reusability rarely change.
Data independence. Data can be physically reorganized without affecting how they are used.	*Class independence.* Classes can be reorganized without affecting how they are used.
Simplicity. Users perceive the data as columns, rows, and tables.	*Complexity.* Data structures may be complex. Users are unaware of the complexity because of encapsulation.
Separate tables. Each relation (table) is separate. JOIN commands relate data in separate tables.	*Interlinked data.* Data may be interlinked so that class methods achieve good performance. Tables are one of many data structures that may be used. BLOBs (binary large objects) are used for sound, images, video, and large unstructured bit streams.
Nonredundant data. Normalization of data is done to help eliminate redundancy in data. (It does nothing to help redundancy in application development.)	*Nonredundant methods.* Nonredundant data and methods are achieved with encapsulation and inheritance. Inheritance helps to lower redundancy in methods, and class reuse helps to lower overall redundancy in development.

BOX 13.1 *(Continued)*

SQL. The SQL language is used for the manipulation of tables.

OO requests. Requests cause the execution of methods. Diverse methods can be used.

Performance. Performance is a concern with highly complex data structures.

Class optimization. The data for one object can be interlinked and stored together, so that they can be accessed from one position of the access mechanism. OODBs give much higher performance than relational DBs for certain applications with complex data.

Different conceptual model. The model of data structure and access represented by tables and JOINs is different from that in analysis, design, and programming. Design must be translated into relational tables, and SQL-style access.

Consistent conceptual model. The models used for analysis, design, programming, and database access and structure are similar. Application concepts are directly represented by classes in the OODB. The more complex the application and its data structures the more this saves time and money in application development.

SUMMARY

OODBs represent the next step in database evolution, supporting OO analysis, design, and programming. OODBs allow complex applications to be developed and maintained at significantly lower cost. They enable the same conceptual model to be applied to analysis, design, programming, and database definition and access. This reduces the developer's burden of translating between different models throughout the lifecycle. The conceptual model should be the basis of fully integrated OO CASE tools which help generate the data structures and methods (see Fig. 13.5).

OODBs give much better machine performance than relational databases for applications with complex data structures or classes with complex data structures. However, OODBs will coexist with relational databases for many years to come, because a relational model will often be used as one form of data structure in an OODB.

A corporation tends to become locked into its form of database management system. When many applications share a corporate database, it is difficult and expensive to change it. Future OODBs may have to incorporate the relational

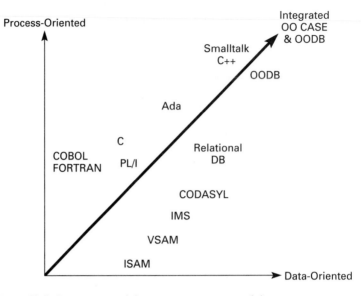

Figure 13.5   Languages and data management are evolving to a common conceptual model with integrated data structures and methods. This requires integrated OO CASE and OODB tools.

model in order to facilitate migration. However, OO systems can be, and are being, built with traditional databases. To do this, though, may preserve existing investments at the expense of efficiency.

Particularly important is that OO databases will be active, rather than passive, collections of data. As we commented earlier, the corporation of the future will be like an electronic organism with objects making requests of other objects, where these objects reside on databases. The OO databases of the future will directly reflect the OO model of the enterprise.

REFERENCES

1. Andrews, Timothy et al., *The ONTOS Object Database,* Ontos, Inc., Technical Report, 1990.

2. Codd, E. F., "A Relational Model of Data for Large Shared Data Banks," *Communications of the ACM,* 13:6, June 1970, pp. 377–387.

3. Codd, E. F., "Further Normalization of the Data Base Relational Model," *Courant Computer Science Symposium 6: Data Base Systems,* Courant Computer Science Symposium 6 (New York), Randall Rustin ed., Prentice-Hall, Englewood Cliffs, NJ, 1972, pp. 33–64.

4. Date, C. J., *An Introduction to Database Systems* (4th edition), Addison-Wesley, Reading, MA, 1986.

5. Loomis, Mary, "Technical Q&A: Ask Mary," *ObjecToday,* 1:4, April 1991, pp. 2–3.

6. Martin, James, *Managing the Data-Base Environment,* Prentice-Hall, Englewood Cliffs, NJ, 1983.

7. Rosen, Steven and Dennis Shasha, "Using a Relational System on Wall Street: The Good, The Bad, The Ugly, and The Ideal," *Communications of the ACM,* 12:4, August 1989, pp. 365–381.

8. Versant, *Product Profile,* Versant Object Technology, Menlo Park, CA, 1991.

9. Wagner, R. E. (1973) "Indexing Design Considerations," *IBM Systems Journal,* 12:4, December 1973, pp. 351–367.

10. Wiederhold, Gio., *Database Design,* McGraw-Hill, New York, 1983.

11. Zdnonik, Stanley B. and David Maier, eds., *Readings on Object-Oriented Database Systems,* Morgan Kaufmann, San Mateo, CA, 1990.

14 OBJECT-ORIENTED INFORMATION ENGINEERING

Building a space shuttle would be unthinkable without an overall plan. Once the overall plan exists, however, separate teams can go to work on the components. Corporate information systems development is scarcely less complex than building a space shuttle. Yet, in most corporations, it is done without an overall plan of sufficient detail to make the components fit together.

The overall architect of the shuttle cannot conceivably specify the detailed design of the rockets, electronics, or other subsystems. These subsystems must be developed by different teams working autonomously. Imagine, however, what would happen if these teams enthusiastically created their own subsystems without any coordination from the top. The data-processing world is full of inspired subsystem builders who want to be left alone. Their numbers are rapidly increasing as small computers proliferate and end users learn to acquire their own facilities. There is all the difference in the world between a corporation with computing that fits into an overall architecture and a corporation with incompatible systems. Systems must be integrated throughout the value chain in an enterprise.

INFORMATION ENGINEERING   Software engineering applies structured techniques to one project. Information engineering applies structured techniques to the enterprise as a whole or to a large sector of the enterprise. The techniques of information engineering encompass those of software engineering in a modified form.

Information engineering (IE) is the application of an interlocking set of formal techniques for the planning, analysis, design, and construction of information systems on a whole enterprise or across a major sector of the enterprise.

Just as different organizations vary their practice of software engineering, so there are variations on the theme of information engineering. Information engineering should not be regarded as one rigid methodology but rather, like software engineering, as a generic class of methodologies. The object-oriented approach described in this book is probably the most effective variant of IE. No matter which variant is chosen, they all have the following characteristics in common:

- IE applies structured techniques on an enterprisewide basis or to a large sector of an enterprise, rather than on a projectwide basis.
- IE progresses in a top-down fashion through the following stages:
  — modeling the enterprise
  — more detailed modeling of business areas
  — individual system planning
  — system design
  — construction
  — cutover
- As it progresses through these stages, IE steadily populates a repository (encyclopedia) with knowledge about the enterprise, its system designs, and their implementation.
- IE creates a framework for developing a computerized enterprise. Separately developed systems fit into this framework. Within the framework, systems can be built and modified quickly.
- The enterprisewide approach makes it possible to achieve coordination among separately built systems and facilitates the maximum use of reusable design and reusable code.
- IE involves end users strongly at each of the stages just mentioned.
- IE facilitates the long-term *evolution* of systems.
- IE identifies how computing can best aid the strategic goals of the enterprise and helps in re-engineering the enterprise.

In traditional data processing, separate systems were built independently. Systems were usually incompatible with one another, had incompatible data, and could be linked together only with difficulty. Some enterprises have hundreds of incompatible computer applications, all difficult and expensive to maintain. These systems are often unnecessarily redundant and expensive, and the information needed for overall management control cannot be extracted from them.

With information engineering, high-level plans and models are created, and separately built systems link into these plans and models. Strategic planning is applied to the enterprise as a whole. More detailed analysis is applied to separate business areas within the enterprise. Design and construction techniques are applied to individual systems.

The same I-CASE (integrated CASE) toolset and repository are used for all of the IE stages. Detailed information is stored in the repository about the enterprise strategy and the business area analysis. The latter uses detailed data models and process models. Different teams of system developers, in different places and at different times, will build systems that link into the computerized framework. Their personal computers and I-CASE tools will be on line to the shared repository, sometimes via telephone lines.

The IE Pyramid

A pyramid, as depicted in Fig. 14.1, is employed to represent information engineering.

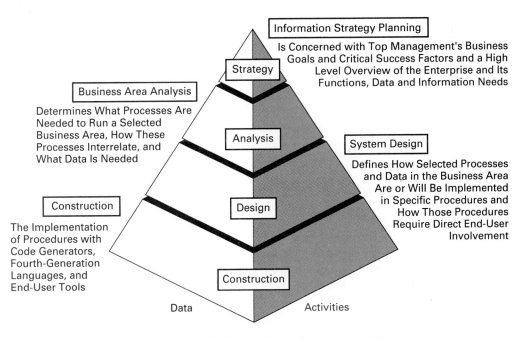

Figure 14.1   The information engineering pyramid.

The *top layer* is information strategy planning. The strategic planning of I.S. (information systems) should relate strongly to the strategic planning of the business. At the top, management must be aware of what strategic opportunities would make the enterprise more competitive. A strategy must be developed relating future technology to its effect on the business, its products or services, or its goals and critical success factors. This is important, because technology is changing so fast. No enterprise is untouched by the growing power of technology; some organizations and industries will be changed drastically by it.

The top-level planning needs to guide and prioritize the expenditures on computing, so that the I.S. department can contribute to the corporate objectives as effectively as possible.

The *second level* relates to a business area. Whereas the top level relates to the enterprise as a whole (or to a major portion of the enterprise), the second level relates to a specific area of the enterprise. A model is built of the fundamental data and processes needed to operate the business area. The need for new or better systems is assessed.

The *third layer* narrows the focus further to a specific system. It defines how a particular portion of the business area analysis (BAA) model will be implemented.

The *bottom layer* includes the implementation of the designed system. This includes both the construction and cutover phases.

Data and Activities

On the left side of the pyramid are data; on the right are activities. Both the data and activities progress from a high-level, management-oriented view at the top to the fully detailed implementation at the bottom.

Information engineering itself needs to fit into a high-level framework that involves the strategic planning for technology networks and how they could affect the business.

Information engineering applies an engineering-like discipline to all facets and levels of the pyramid, resulting in timely implementation of high-quality systems grounded in the business plans of the enterprise. An engineering-like discipline needs formal techniques. These are implemented with computerized tools that guide and help the planners, analysts, and implementors. While the tools impose formality on all stages, they should be designed to maximize the speed with which systems can be built and the ease with which they can be modified.

Divide and Conquer

Rebuilding all of the data-processing resources required by an enterprise is an excessively complex undertaking. An objective of information engineering is to make the separate systems relate to one another in an adequate fashion. This does not happen when the separate development activities are not coordinated. Information engineering, therefore, starts with a top management view of the enterprise and progresses downward into greater detail.

As the progression into detail occurs, selections must be made concerning

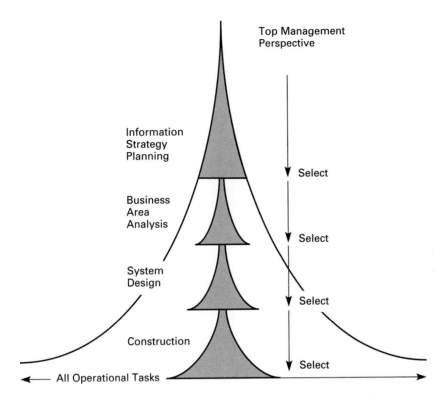

Figure 14.2 Divide-and-conquer approach to manageable system development.

which business areas should be analyzed and which systems should be designed. A divide-and-conquer approach is used, as illustrated in Fig. 14.2.

Information engineering begins at the top of an enterprise by conducting an information strategy plan. From this plan, a business area is selected for analysis. A portion of the business area is selected for detailed system design. If the system is complex, its detailed system design is divided into subsystems, each of which can be built by a construction team.

Top Management

Every top executive today must build a computerized enterprise, and a computerized enterprise cannot be created effectively without information engineering.

To succeed fully, information engineering needs the commitment of top management; it is a corporatewide activity that needs firm direction from the top. The methodology relates to top management planning. When taken to its logical conclusion, it almost always results in the redesign of an enterprise—to streamline it, remove redundancy, enable employees to add more value, and make it most cost competitive.

INFORMATION ENGINEERING USING OO TECHNIQUES

Strategy—Applied to the Enterprise as a Whole

The strategy level takes a corporatewide viewpoint and focuses on how systems will be integrated. For example

- How will they be integrated along the value chain so that information can pass from the sales planning and order-entry systems to the production planning and control systems; to the inventory control and purchasing systems; to the delivery and billing systems; and to the financial control systems?

- How will systems be integrated vertically so that information passes from the low-level operational systems up to the tactical planning systems and up to the executive information systems?

The strategy level is concerned with creating a systems architecture so that changes in procedures can be designed and implemented quickly while preserving the integration along the value chain. In organizations following an object-oriented path, object schemas and object-flow diagrams model this architecture. Additionally, the strategy level is concerned with the ability to seize new business opportunities quickly, even though they need massive computing support. This level focuses on using computing to make the enterprise more competitive.

Top management should be directly interested in and involved with the strategy level. An ISP (information strategy planning) study will have already been conducted. This study takes from three to nine months in most enterprises and is accomplished by a small team that studies the enterprise and interviews its management. Information strategy planning requires commitment from top management. The results are interesting and stimulating to top management, because they are concerned with how technology can be used as a weapon against competition. Diagrammed representations of the enterprise are created that challenge management to think about its structure, its goals, the information needed, and the factors for success. The information strategy planning process, illustrated in Fig. 14.3, often results in identification of organizational and operational problems and solutions.

Analysis—Applied to the Business Area

The analysis level examines a business area, as illustrated in Fig. 14.4. It is done separately for each business area, but the results are integrated into the overall repository, which has knowledge of the ISP and of the analysis done for other business areas. The knowledge coordinator of the I-CASE toolset helps integrate the models created for separate business areas.

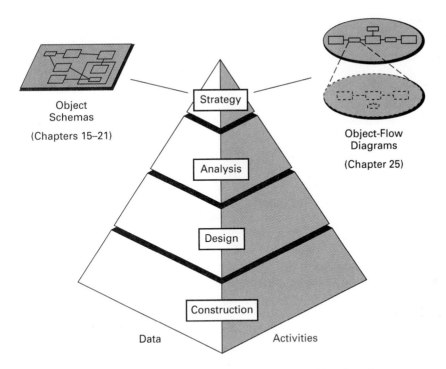

Figure 14.3 Object-oriented ISPs use object schemas and object-flow diagrams.

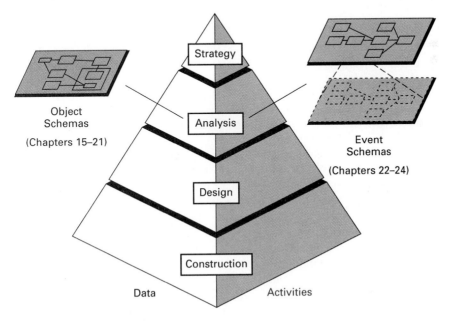

Figure 14.4 Object-oriented BAAs use object schemas and event schemas.

A BAA (business area analysis) study is conducted separately for each business. A typical business area analysis takes from one to six months, depending on the breadth of the area selected and the speed at which the analysts can operate. Several such studies for different business areas may be done by different teams simultaneously.

Business area analysis does not attempt to design systems; it merely attempts to understand and model the processes and objects required to run the business area. In organizations following an object-oriented path, object schemas and event schemas model business areas.

Business area analysis should also be independent of current systems. The old systems in use in an enterprise often constrain it to continue inefficient procedures with batch processing, dumb terminals, unnecessary keypunching, redundancy, too much paperwork, and the bureaucracy that goes with paperwork. Entirely different procedures may be designed if every knowledge-worker's desk can have a personal computer—online to databases anywhere in the enterprise. A fundamental analysis of what processes are needed often causes a fundamental rethinking of the best way to implement them.

Business area analysis (BAA) has particular characteristics:

- It is conducted separately for each business area.
- It creates detailed models of the objects and events in the business area.
- The results are recorded and maintained in the repository.
- It requires intensive user involvement.
- It remains independent of technology.
- It remains independent of current systems and procedures.
- It often causes a rethinking of systems and procedures.
- It identifies areas for system design.

Design—Applied to the Individual System

The design stage is typically divided into two stages. The first stage, called business system design, defines the behavior and structure of the system and produces detailed design specifications for the system. The diagramming techniques used here depend on the target implementation environment for the system. For example, if the system uses a relational database, relational model diagrams should be employed. If object-oriented languages are used, diagrams—such as those in this book—are used. If the I-CASE tool generates code directly from object schemas and event schemas, design-related diagrams are often not necessary.

The second stage, technical system design, defines the system's efficiency, taking into account the available technology and the system's requirements.

Construction—Applied to the Individual System

Construction involves building the designed system and databases and proving that they operate correctly. Correct operation is defined as conforming to the objectives identified during planning, the requirements detailed during analysis, and the behavior specified during design. The object-oriented path does not limit its implementations to object-oriented programming languages. The OO approach in this book can be used for constructing expert systems, simulations, GUIs, or any other approaches that are best described by OO techniques.

ANALYSIS FOR REUSABILITY   We have emphasized that one of the most powerful properties of IE is the construction of systems from components that already exist. A system may be constructed from reusable building blocks, or an existing design may be modified to create a new application.

To maximize the value of reusability, large-scale planning is needed. Reusable design should be a major goal of information engineering. In most large enterprises, many systems exist that do almost the same functions. There are multiple order-entry systems, multiple inventory-control systems, and so on. These systems have been separately designed and separately coded. They also have to be separately maintained—which is expensive.

Analysis for reusability establishes the common procedures and subprocedures that are needed across an enterprise. An attempt is made to create these from a single set of basic designs rather than from multiple sets of designs. The basic designs are kept in an I-CASE repository and can be easily adapted to the needs of separate systems.

Object-Oriented Analysis

Object-oriented analysis identifies the object types in an enterprise, as well as their properties. Object subtypes *inherit* the properties of their parents. Behavior is associated with the object types where the object will exhibit that behavior regardless of the specific application.

Instead of being associated with one object type, some processing routines are associated with a relationship between two or more object types (e.g., when a Customer places an Order, when a Passenger makes or changes a Reservation or when a Warehouse ships a Delivery). Certain reports must be printed, certain information must be filed, or a given user dialog must occur. Particular validation checks must be applied, and an audit trail must be maintained, regardless of the location, department, type of warehouse, or type of application. Procedures should be designed and programmed that are reusable across the enterprise (rather than being designed and programmed uniquely for each project).

> An objective of information engineering is to identify commonality in both data and processes and, consequently, to minimize redundant system-development work.

OO modeling makes it clear that the same object types are used in numerous applications. Whenever they are used, certain routines may be invoked, such as computing derived attributes, applying integrity checks, or creating summary data. A corporation may have many factories that, to a large extent, have the same object types.

Many of the data-processing procedures can be the same from one factory to another; some will be entirely different. The accounting and reporting should be the same in each factory, so that higher-level management can make comparisons. Dialogs programmed for data entry, updating, reporting, and so on should be common across applications and locations. HELP panels should be common. Certain screen designs, user dialogs, validation routines, and so on may be needed whenever an object type is employed.

Often, the processing done on an object or the dialog used is not identical from one process to another but is sufficiently close that the same code or dialog can be used after minor modifications. The end user would like the different application to look similar and have a common dialog style in order to increase familiarity and minimize the training needs. *Similar* processes should be identified in order to minimize the subsequent design, coding, and training requirements.

Modeling must be applied to one business area at a time. Otherwise, models become unwieldy, and the team bogs down. Nevertheless, some object types will be used outside that business area. Associated with these will be operations that are usable outside that business area. The *enterprisewide* object types are discovered (at a summary level) during the ISP study and are recorded in the repository. During business area analysis, the object types and operations having applicability beyond that business area should be marked in the repository. When other business areas are analyzed, the common object types and operations will be identified in detail, so that procedures can be designed to span business areas.

A Large Multinational Bank

The most spectacular examples of reusable design and code are generally found in corporations that have done information engineering with a repository-based I-CASE toolset. A large bank, confronted with new types of competition caused by deregulation, set out to rebuild its collection of core I.S. systems over a five-year period. The bank's business goals were to

- Create an environment that enabled the bank to create new services or respond to new business opportunities significantly faster than its competition.

- Undercut its competition by being able to build new services at a lower cost.
- Streamline the bank's operations making them less expensive.
- Provide better service to customers by, for example, giving customized loans as opposed to off-the-shelf packages.

Top management endorsed these goals fully. To achieve them, more technical goals existed:

- Maximize reusability by fuilding a library of reusable classes.
- Generate code for all new applications using CASE tools.
- Drastically reduce the proliferation of separate applications that need separate, expensive maintenance.

At the ISP (information strategy planning) level, the bank identified the highest-level object types. It identified 19 top-level object types, each at the top of a generalization hierarchy. These were object types such as **Customer**, **Account**, and **Employee**. All lower-level object types were subtypes of these 19.

At the BAA (business area analysis) level, the bank identified 49 business conceptual objects—the next level below the top 19. These were further decomposed into 120 objects that were variants of the 49 business conceptual objects.

Prior to this OO analysis of the corporation, the bank had 1800 transaction codes, each with its own separate program. Maintaining this large collection of programs was expensive. The 1800 programs could be replaced with 49 classes, each with its own methods. The 120 objects were subclasses of the 49, using mostly the same methods. This analysis was done with a CASE toolset which was also used for designing the methods. Code for the methods was generated with a code generator. Neither of these tools was designed for object-oriented development, but both could be adapted to support the OO paradigm. Development would be smoother if an integrated OO toolset were used.

When the bank had established its class library, with many classes developed in-house, and other classes coming from a software vendor, it could assemble new financial applications at high speed.

Human Coordination

As reusability becomes a way of life in an enterprise, the more it spreads, and the more applications can be built from reusable components. A system designer requiring a class must first find out whether a similar class exists that he can use or adapt. If so, he uses it; if not, he creates a class in such a way that it might be reused in the future by some other analyst. All development, thus, relates to reuse of existing classes or class designs with future reuse potential.

After this pattern of development has been in place for some years, a high level of reusability is achieved. One characteristic of reusability is that the facilities for reusability take time to build up, but they eventually enable an enterprise to create most applications rapidly.

Human coordination of the reusable components stored in the repository is necessary. A development team might create new classes or improve upon an existing class. The reusability coordinator must decide whether to make a new class generally available in the repository. It is important that the central repository of reusable classes does not become a mess. The classes should be carefully catalogued. A knowledgeable human decision is needed regarding when to store a new version of a class and whether the old version must be retained.

All Levels of the Pyramid

At all levels of the information-engineering pyramid, there should be a search for commonality. Commonality of object types is usually obvious in building of the object schema. Common functions should be identified at the *planning* level, common processes at the *analysis* level, and common procedures, screens, dialogs, and methods at the *design* level.

In order to find commonality, a central repository is essential. Analysts in different places use a shared repository that steadily accumulates knowledge of the enterprise. When an analyst is planning a procedure that uses an object type, the repository will inform him what other procedures use that object type, so that he can employ common modules where possible. Usually, a central group reporting to a chief information engineer (or equivalent) helps ensure that common modules are used where possible.

Where a code generator is driven from a design workbench, the primary reusability emphasis may be on reusable design. Classes that are reusable are stored in the repository and modified, if necessary, before code is generated.

An advantage of information engineering done with object-oriented techniques is that the conceptual model is the same at each of the four levels of the pyramid. As illustrated in Fig. 12.3, analysis, design, programming, database definition, and access all use essentially the same conceptual model. The enterprise model at the ISP and BAA levels should be as meaningful as possible to business people. They can think of their world in terms of business objects, the events that occur, and the business rules that ought to control those events. The high-level models are expanded into detail as we progress lower in the pyramid but within the same conceptual framework. The high-level analyst establishes an overview with high-level objects, and the lower-level designer adds detail to those objects.

The object types in the enterprise model become active objects when they are implemented. If implemented with OO databases, they retain essentially the same form they have in the model.

REFERENCES

1. Bassett, Paul, Communication from Paul Bassett, Vice President, Netron Inc, Downsview, Ontario, 1990.

2. Martin, James, *Information Engineering,* Prentice-Hall, Englewood Cliffs, NJ, 1990.

3. Martin, James, *Rapid Application Development,* Macmillan, New York, 1991.

PART **III** **FUNDAMENTALS
OF OBJECT STRUCTURE ANALYSIS**

15 CONCEPTS AND OBJECTS

Object-oriented analysis is *not* an approach that models reality. Instead, it models the way *people* understand and process reality—through the concepts they acquire. Understanding the fundamentals of object orientation first requires an understanding of what concepts and objects are and how they are used in object-oriented analysis. This chapter focuses on the nature of concepts and the objects to which they apply.

CONCEPTS Each concept is a particular idea or understanding we have of our world. We know we possess a concept when we can apply it successfully to the things around us. For example, to say that we have the concept of car requires only the ability to identify an instance of a car.

> A *concept* is an idea or notion we share that applies to certain objects in our awareness.

The formation of concepts helps us to order our lives. Psychologists have suggested that when a baby starts out in life, its world is a buzzing confusion. At a very young age, it develops the notion of being fed. Soon after, it learns to differentiate the sounds of its mother and father. Humans seem to possess an innate capacity to perceive regularities and to recognize the many objects our world offers. Eventually, we develop concepts like *blue* and *sky* and then learn to combine concepts to form new ones such as *blue sky*. As we get older still, we construct elaborate conceptual constructs that lead to increased meaning, precision, and subtlety. For example, the sky is blue only on cloudless days, or the sky is not really blue; it only looks blue from our planet Earth because of atmospheric effects.

Concepts Are a Recognition Device

The concepts we form and use can be varied indeed—because *we* choose them. Concepts may be

Concrete	Intangible	Roles	Judgments
person	time	doctor	productive job
pencil	quality	patient	high pay
car	company	owner	good example

Relational	Events	Displayable	Others
marriage	sale	string	image
partnership	purchase	integer	signal
ownership	system crash	icon	gnome

The concepts we acquire supply us with an assortment of mental lenses with which we make sense of and reason about the objects in our world, as illustrated in Fig. 15.1. For example, having the concept of person (written **Person**) allows us to reason about all or part of several billion objects on this earth. Additionally, each new concept permits us to perceive objects in a different way—or even become aware of entirely new objects. For instance, the concept **Atomic Particle** adds new objects to our awareness and enables us to think about matter in a certain way. Without this concept, the physicist's cloud chamber would just hold uninterpreted patterns. The concept of **Particle Spin** will not necessarily introduce any new objects; however, it does allow perceiving and reasoning about an existing **Atomic Particle** in a different manner.

We can possess concepts about things that have existed, do exist, may exist, and probably will not exist. Concepts such as the **Tooth Fairy** and **Santa Claus** have objects for some people; yet, no longer do for others. Concepts like the

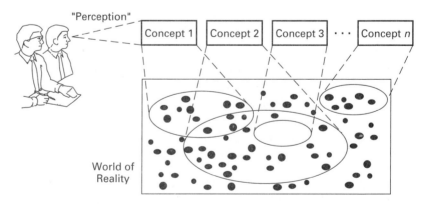

Figure 15.1   Concepts shape our perception of reality.

Fusion-Powered Car and Total World Peace do not apply to any objects we know of now but might in the future. It is highly unlikely, though, that a concept like Perpetual Motion will ever have any instances.

Concepts as Tests for Reality

As already stated, concepts shape our perception of reality. As long as we remain aware beings, we apply concepts to objects in our reality and discard concepts when they no longer apply. When we use a concept, we employ tests that determine whether or not it applies to the objects around us. Each concept, then, is based on tests that determine when it applies. When requested, most people will specify these tests verbally. Programmers state them as program code, logicians employ general propositions.

Figure 15.2 depicts several concepts. By applying the tests associated with each concept, we determine which concepts apply to which objects. For instance, Napoleon passes the conceptual tests of Famous Man and Politician. The concepts of Writer and Perfect Man, however, do not apply. Our reality is based on such tests. Those objects that pass a certain test are *realized* as an instance of a concept. In this way, objects can be perceived in many ways—depending on our conceptual tests.

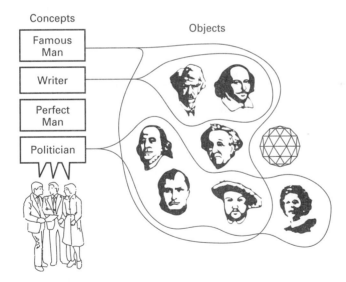

Figure 15.2   People share concepts and apply them to objects.

Concepts without Objects

We can also form concepts for which no object exists. In Fig. 15.2, the people share the same concept of Perfect Man. Yet, no objects have currently passed that concept's test. We may use these concepts to stipulate that certain kinds of objects should *not* exist or to anticipate *future* objects. For example, in the business world, an organization initially forms many such concepts: **Product, Customer, Labor Union, Hostile Competitor,** and even **Industrial Spy.** During the business process, objects for these concepts may or may not be realized. Yet, these concepts are vital to business survival.

Objects without Concepts?

While we can form concepts for which no objects exist, objects cannot exist in a person's awareness without applicable concepts. In other words, a particular object may exist for some people, because they have the conceptual structure necessary to perceive it. However, the same object may simply not exist for others, because it lies outside their set of concepts. For the group in Fig. 15.2, the item outside the loop to the right of Einstein is not an object, and they are, therefore, not aware of it.

Awareness of an object requires applicable concepts. For example, certain rules and regulations may not apply to a particular business. As such, these rules and regulations are not objects as far as this company is concerned—though they can be for other companies. Changes in the business or in legislation might alter this situation. The business would then be prompted to form an immediate and appropriate conceptual understanding of these rules. In this case, the business's realm would be extended accordingly.

Shared Understanding

By convention, privately held ideas or notions are called *conceptions.* When an understanding is shared by others, it becomes a *concept* (see Fig. 15.3). To communicate with others, we must share our individually held conceptions and arrive at agreed concepts. For instance, your conception of **Car** might include only small automobiles that are red. For you, if it's not small and red, it can't be considered a **Car.** However, with the local auto dealer, you may wish to agree upon a

(a)   (b)

Figure 15.3   Conceptions are private; concepts are shared.

common notion, or concept, of **Car** in order to deal effectively. At this point, you might both share the concept that **Car** is not restricted to small and red—as long as *you* don't have to buy one that is not small and red.

Analyzing organizational systems means creating an effective, shared set of concepts. Concepts underlie each and every organizational process. Concepts define a shared organizational reality and form the basis of an organizational language with which to communicate.

CONCEPT INTENSION AND EXTENSION

The previous section established that concepts and their application to objects follow a set of defined tests. For example, forming the concept **Writer** requires a clear definition of what it takes to be a writer. Once this definition is in place, we can then identify objects that are instances of the **Writer** concept. Because we think in this way, concepts are employed as units of knowledge. Adopting this idea has important ramifications. The concept as a unit of knowledge supports discrete definitions of our recognition tests (the *intension**), and identification of those objects a definition applies to or not (the *extension*).

Intension and extension are two sides of the same coin—the notion of concept includes both. The **Musical Instrument** concept in Fig. 15.4 illustrates this. The right of the figure contains a shared definition of the **Musical Instrument** concept. The circle to the left identifies the set of objects qualifying as musical instruments.

Symbols are useful when we wish to refer uniquely to, or denote, objects. They are particularly helpful when we want to communicate about concepts without referring to lengthy definitions. The symbol in Fig. 15.4 for the **Musical**

Figure 15.4   A Musical Instrument concept.

*The word *intension* is used rather than *intention*. Intension reflects more than intent; it implies a thorough and *intensive* definition [4].

Instrument concept is an ellipse containing the string Musical Instrument. However, you may use any symbol to reference the same concept.* Additionally, concepts can exist without any symbolic expression: symbols are merely a practical means of identifying concepts.

Taken in conjunction, the two-sided nature of the concept together with a symbolic representation assist the object-oriented analyst to understand and communicate business concepts. The *concept triad* in Fig. 15.5 graphically illustrates a way of thinking about these three aspects. At the top is the concept's *symbol.* The left side depicts the concept *intension, definition, idea,* or *understanding.* The right side depicts the *extension* or *set of objects* to which the concept applies. The concept in Fig. 15.5 is symbolized by the words Musical Instrument contained within a rectangle. Its intension is expressed as a narrative definition, and its extension is the set of Musical Instrument instances.

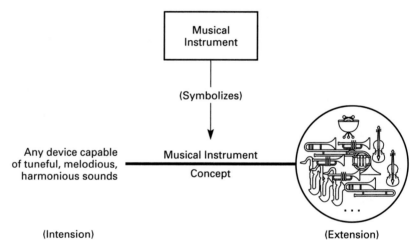

Figure 15.5   Concept triad for Musical Instrument.

Partial Concept Triads

Under some circumstances, one or more aspects of the triad may be missing. For instance, a person may define a concept without symbolizing it with a name. Concepts and their objects have no intrinsic need for names. However, humans communicate more efficiently by using symbols to convey concepts. Referring only to a concept's definition dramatically slows communication. In Fig. 15.6(a) for example, reciting the definition of the concept for what a computer store

---

*As long as a symbol provides a unique reference within a specific scope, or realm, it can be used to denote an object. Multiple symbols for the same object are commonly called synonyms. The same symbol, however, may denote different objects in different realms. These are commonly called homonyms. Homonyms can confound data administrators unless symbol references are qualified by realm.

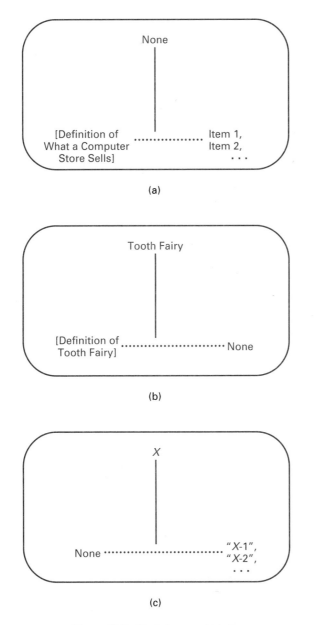

Figure 15.6   Partial concept triads.

sells would be lengthy and tedious. Such a definition would refer to hardware, software, and services. Once a symbol that stands for this concept is adopted, such as **Computer Store Product**, a form of communications shorthand can be developed.

Figure 15.6(b) contains another example of a partial triad that involves a concept symbol and definition. Yet no objects can be found for its set. For example, we may have the concept of **Tooth Fairy**, yet never believe in the existence of a **Tooth Fairy** object. Concepts, like these, that are empty of applicable objects can be useful for modeling businesses. With them we can *expect* that a particular concept will never have any objects. For instance, an organization can expect that no instances of **Corporate Saboteur** will appear. Yet, if and when an instance does appear, having the concept of **Corporate Saboteur** allows the organization to detect the unexpected. Without the concept, detection would not be possible. In short, concepts without instances may or may not be useful to an organization: their usefulness should be examined closely. Concepts that will *never* have instances are probably *not* useful, though concepts that *should* not have instances *could* be useful.

Be wary of situations for which no underlying definition can be established for a concept, yet a set of objects is thought to be identified. For instance, Fig. 15.6(c) depicts a set containing "X-1," "X-2," . . . yet has no documented definition of the concept that applies to these objects. This kind of problem runs rampant in many undocumented system designs. A concept definition existed at one time but disappeared with the original system team. The object-oriented analyst should insist on knowing the definition of each and every concept in a system. A concept without a definition is not a concept; it is meaningless noise.

Coextensive Concepts

Another situation employing the concept triad involves *coextensive* concepts— illustrated in Fig. 15.7. Coextensive concepts are those concepts that share the same extension, yet have different intensions. For example, a Peace Corps volunteer has the concept of **Half-Full Glass of Water**, while a waiter should have the concept of **Half-Empty Glass of Water**. Both concepts have different definitions, yet both will always extend to an identical set of objects, that is, they coextend. The set of planets that can be a morning star and the set of planets that can be an evening star are also coextensive. While these concepts have different definitions, they apply to the same set of planetary objects: Mercury, Venus, Mars, Jupiter, and Saturn.

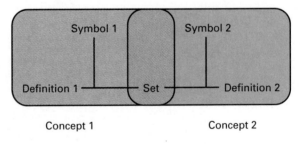

Concept 1   Concept 2

Figure 15.7   Coextensive concepts.

Sharing the same extension requires that the membership of one set is exactly the same as another. However, be careful not to confuse *temporarily* coextensive concepts with *fully* coextensive concepts. For some moment in time, two concepts may apply to an identical set of objects. For example, in the biblical beginning, the concepts **Human**, **Man**, and **Person-Named-Adam** all applied to a single object denoted by the name Adam. Over time, however, this changed. When the Eve object was created, **Human** and **Man** ceased to be coextensive. While every **Man** was still a **Human**, every **Human** was no longer a **Man**. Later, when another person was named Adam, the concepts **Man** and **Person-Named-Adam** no longer applied to identical sets of objects. To be fully coextensive means to share the same extension over *all* moments of time.

OBJECTS

As suggested earlier, our reality consists of those *concepts* that we possess and those *objects* to which the concepts apply.

> An *object* is anything to which a concept applies.

In this way, *any* thing that one can think of, refer to, describe, discuss, or experience is an object. However, as stated earlier, objects cannot exist in our awareness without at least one concept that applies to them. Additionally, one person's object may be perceived differently (or not perceived at all) by another person, because the concepts held by each can differ greatly.

The word *object* is used by OO practitioners in various ways. In this book, objects are *anything* a concept applies to—objects are the instances of concepts. Therefore, the words *objects* and *instances* can be used synonymously. A simple example of an object is the pen on your aunt's table—that specific, individual instance of a pen. Other objects might include the specific city in which you live, you, your job, a certain process in progress, a particular event, a point in time, a record in a database, a piece of data, a sound, an image, an optical signal, the number 42, a magnetic pulse, a document, a vector, a matrix, or my dog Ralph. Please note here that all objects are not data, even though all data are objects. Object-oriented analysis investigates objects without prejudice toward what is going to be data or not. In this way, we analyze human understanding before dealing with bits, bytes, fields, and records.

Object Lifecycles

Most objects have periods of existence. For these objects, the beginning and ending points are reasonably definable. Such objects can include a particular product, an instance of a distribution process, a specific flamingo at the zoo, or your '57 Chevy. However, when does that object you think of as your car cease to be an object? Is it still an object after it enters the junkyard and is squashed into a cube? For you, the object may no longer exist. For the salvager, however, it is an object—though not an instance of the concept Car. What happens when the squashed cube is melted in a pot with 27 other cars? Without doubt the car/cube ceases to be an object then, because we no longer have concepts that apply to it. However, what occurs if you slice it in two? Is it still the same object or two different ones? Objects appear in our awareness when we first apply a concept to them, and objects disappear when concepts no longer apply. In this way, objects can seem to us as having their own lifecycles. *Set membership* is one way we can describe this change.

Concepts as Objects

Can concepts be objects? Take, for example, the concept Macintosh Classic. Macintosh Classic is a concept that applies to many thousands of serial-numbered instances produced by Apple Computer, Inc. However, is the Macintosh Classic concept also an object? For Apple Computer, it is one of the many objects to which the concept Product Type applies. Other Product Type objects include the concepts Macintosh Plus, Macintosh SE, Macintosh IIfx, and so on. What about the concept Product Type? Is it also an object? Ultimately, when something is declared a concept, it is—by definition—an instance of the concept called Concept. Concepts, then, have instances that are concepts—which, in turn, may have instances that are also concepts. (Appendix D discusses how this notion is applied to meta-modeling.)

SETS

While objects are individual, independent instances, a *set* is a particular collection, or class,* of objects. A set's membership is determined solely by its concept's intension. Set, then, is another name for the extension of a concept.

For example, in Fig. 15.8 the concept of Pawn is presented. The intension of the concept is its complete definition of a Pawn. This definition acts as a filter that screens all objects—permitting only those objects into the set that pass the membership test. The set is the resulting collection of objects to which the concept's meaning applies.

> A *set* is the collection of all those objects to which a concept applies. It is the extension of a concept.

Class is—technically—the correct word when referring to the collection of objects to which a concept applies [8], (although some [5] argue that *set* and *class* mean the same thing). Since class has a different meaning in OO programming languages, the word set will be used to avoid confusion. It is worth noting, however, that the inspiration for using the term class in OO originally came from the centuries-old mathematical notion of class.

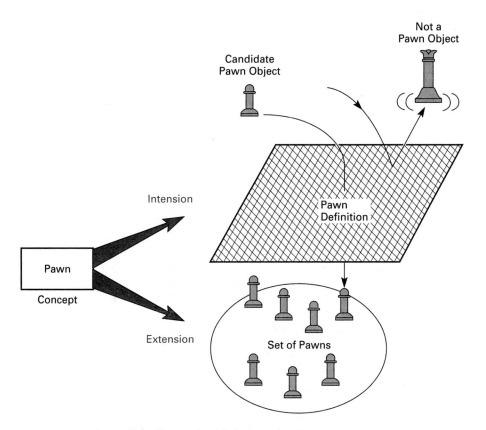

Figure 15.8 Set membership is determined by its intension test.

As stated earlier, concepts define our reality. Yet, at times we think solely in terms of the concept's extension, that is, its set. In Fig. 15.8, we can actually *see* and examine those objects that passed (or did not pass) the concept's test. Ultimately, however, we will need to address sets when we design working systems. Working systems require real processes that add objects to, remove objects from, and query objects in specific sets.

Set Membership

A set can include many objects, and each object can be a member of many sets. In Fig. 15.9, three concepts are displayed—Man, Woman, and Employee. Each set is a collection of objects that complies with the membership requirement of its underlying concept. Of the eight objects in the figure, the two labeled Jane and Paul are members of two sets simultaneously. The Jane object is a member of both the Woman set and the Employee set—and could easily be a member of other sets, such as Wife, Mother, Author, Chief Justice, Fun Person, and Good Friend. Since each object exists only once, there can be only one instance of

Figure 15.9   Sets with many objects; objects in many sets.

Jane. As in life, we can (and usually do) recognize an object in several different ways—at the same time or at different times.

Classification

When we determine that a concept applies to a specific object, the object is *classified* as a member of a specific set. In this case, the set membership is increased by one object. When an object is *declassified,* it is removed from a particular set—thereby decreasing the set size by one.

Figure 15.10 portrays the object Jane classified and declassified in terms of the Employee set. At some point in her life, Jane is first classified as an Employee. Later, through some process, Jane is declassified as an Employee— she becomes unemployed. At another point, Jane may become reemployed, followed again by a period of unemployment. This behavior may continue until a time or decision for retirement is reached, or the process of death takes place. Specifying the method of these classification changes is a technique at the very heart of OO process specification. Part IV suggests ways of specifying this.

Implications of Object Lifecycles

Figure 15.10 depicts an object in terms of only one set membership. However, the Jane object may be classified and declassified in various sets over time. At

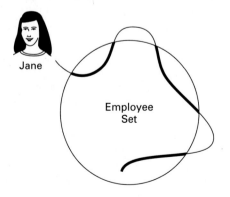

Figure 15.10   Moving in and out of the Employee set over time.

the age of 18, she will change from the set Girl to the set Woman. At some point, she may get married and be added to the sets Married Person and Wife. Quite independently, she may also buy a pet and become a Pet Owner. Later, she may give the pet away and be removed from the Pet Owner set.

In her lifetime, Jane may be a member of several sets and may, on many occasions, change her set membership. This means, first, that an object can have multiple concepts that apply to it at any one moment. Second, it means that the collection of concepts that applies to an object can change over time. Such an approach is alien to the traditional data processing analyst who normally assumes that the data in a record can be obtained *only* by its one record type. Most of the OO programming languages are similarly restrictive—except for their superclasses—requiring an object to be an instance of one OOPL class for life. However, in OO analysis, we are not modeling how computer languages and databases work, we are analyzing our enterprise world as *people* would see it. In this way, we can achieve an understanding that applies to—but is not limited by—data processing.

SUMMARY

Without concepts, mental life would be total chaos. Every item we encountered would be different. The sheer volume of sensory data would be staggering, and communication would be virtually impossible. Concepts determine and shape our reality, and they give us stability. *Reality* for each of us, then, consists of a set of concepts and those things or objects of which we are aware.

In short, a *concept* is what we apply to objects; an *object* is the instance of one or more concepts. Without going into detail, a more precise definition used by logicians and philosophers would be the following—a concept is a shared set of general propositions that can be said to apply to the objects of our awareness.

Concepts are shared by others. If only privately held, they are called *conceptions*. Concepts provide the common vocabulary for communication. In the end, they actually define the organization being analyzed.

Each concept has an intension and an extension. The *intension* is the complete definition of the concept. It is the test that determines whether or not the concept applies to an object. The *extension* is the *set* of all objects to which the concept applies.

This chapter presents foundational notions from which conceptual schemas can be built—concepts (extension and intension) and objects. Subsequent chapters will employ and build upon these ideas to construct representation techniques and methods.

REFERENCES

1. Flew, Anthony, *A Dictionary of Philosophy* (2nd revised edition), Macmillan Press, London, 1984.

2. Langer, Susanne K., *An Introduction to Symbolic Logic* (3rd edition), Dover Publications, New York, 1967.

3. Novak, Joseph D. and D. Bob Gowin, *Learning How to Learn,* Cambridge University Press, Cambridge, 1984.

4. Ogden, C. K. and I. A. Richards, *The Meaning of Meaning* (8th edition 1946), Harcourt, Brace, and World, New York, 1923.

5. Quine, W. V., *Quiddities: An Intermittently Philosophical Dictionary,* Belknap Press, Cambridge, MA, 1987.

6. Smith, Edward E. and Douglas L. Medin, *Categories and Concepts,* Harvard University Press, Cambridge, MA, 1981.

7. Sowa, J. F., *Conceptual Structures,* Addison-Wesley, Reading, MA, 1984.

8. Whitehead, Alfred North and Bertrand Russell, *Principia Mathematica,* Cambridge University Press, Cambridge, 1910.

16 MANAGING OBJECT COMPLEXITY

We live in a complex world. Even the simple tasks of life are confusing without the proper mental tools. One of these tools was discussed in Chapter 15—the acquisition of concepts. Concepts result from our ability to *abstract*. Once these abstractions are formed, we can further organize our world by distinguishing when one abstraction is more general than another. This allows us to build hierarchies of *generalizations*. Finally, we can compose a single object from a configuration of other objects. These three mechanisms are part of our human endowment and give us the ability to grasp and manage the complexity of our world. In object-oriented analysis we can use them to model our enterprise world. This chapter explores abstraction, generalization, and composition.

ABSTRACTION

Each object is unique. However, abstraction removes certain distinctions, so that we can see commonalities between objects. Without abstraction, we would only know that every thing is different. With abstraction, various distinguishing features of one or more objects are selectively omitted, allowing us to concentrate on the features they do share.

> *Abstraction* is the act or result of removing certain distinctions between objects, so that we can see commonalities.

In Fig. 16.1, the man is classifying various objects in his realm. Even though every object is different, the objects on the right share the properties of being narrow containers made of glass. This abstraction is named "bottle."

As indicated in the previous chapter, objects do not form sets by themselves. The process of abstraction does this. Two things having the same abstracted form are analogous. In the previous chapter, these abstracted forms are called

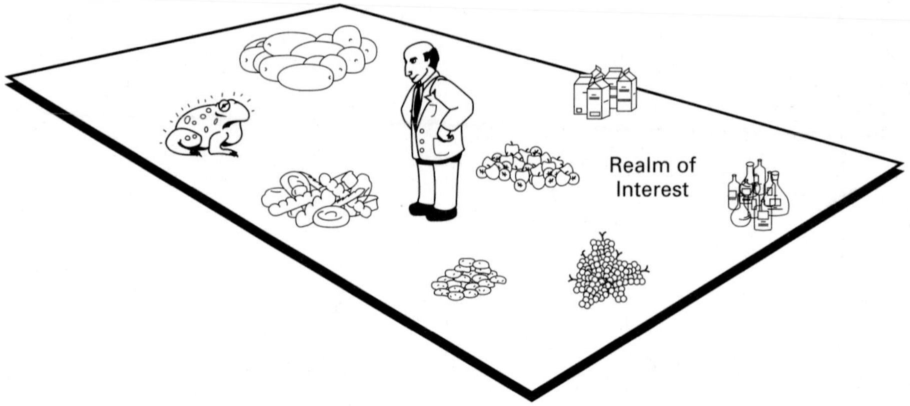

Figure 16.1   Removing certain distinctions to examine commonalities.

concepts. This means that the man's abstraction of bottle objects is another way of saying that he has the concept of Bottle. In short, all objects to which the same concept applies are analogous [6].

Abstraction, then, is one way we manage the complexity of the objects in the world. The results of abstraction are concepts.

GENERALIZATION

When we look in our clothes closet, we recognize the objects we see as slacks, shirts, coats, shoes, roller-skates, squirting bow ties, and so on. Without well-developed generalizing capabilities, we might call this storage area, the shoes-slacks-shirts-coats-roller-skates closet. The more kinds of things we have in the closet, the more cumbersome the name becomes. Generalization enables us to examine whether these concepts have anything in common. Is there a *more general* concept that encompasses concepts like Shoe, Slacks, and Shirt? *In general,* these are known as Clothing. Clothing, in turn, might be incorporated into an even more general category called Merchandise or Household Article—and so on.

> *Generalization* is the act or result of distinguishing a concept that is more general than another.

Generalization enables us to perceive that all instances of a more specific concept are also instances of a general concept—but not necessarily the other way around. For example, all Shoe or Shirt objects are also Clothing objects, however, not all Clothing objects are Shoe or Shirt objects. Therefore, Clothing is a more general concept than Shoe or Shirt. Whatever makes Shoes different from Shirts is not addressed in the definition of Clothing—only their commonality is recognized.

Concepts Hierarchies

With generalization, we can build hierarchies of concepts, forming more and more general concepts. Figure 16.2 demonstrates that a Lifeform is a more general concept (or *superconcept*) of Human, Human is a superconcept of the human Female Human, which is a more general concept of Girl.

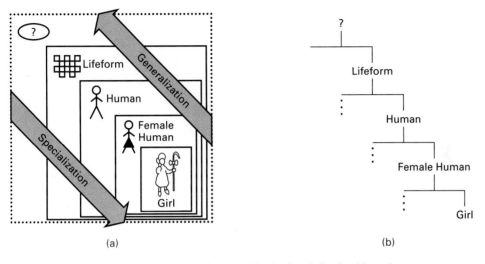

| (a) | (b) |

Figure 16.2   Examples of a generalization/specialization hierarchy.

The opposite of generalization is *specialization*. For example, Human can be *specialized* as Female Human or Male Human; or as Infant, Adolescent, or Adult Humans; and Good, Bad, or Ugly Humans. These specialized concepts are *subconcepts*. In Fig. 16.2, Girl is a subconcept of Female Human, Female Human is a subconcept of Human, and so on.

Hierarchy is not limited to a tree structure.* A *tree* is a special case of a hierarchy with a single root and no shared branch nodes. Generalization is not limited to tree structures, because a concept may have multiple superconcepts. For example, in Fig. 16.3, Female Human is a subconcept of both Female and Human.

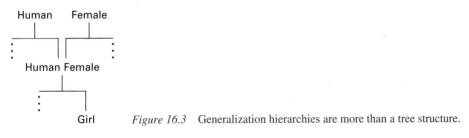

Figure 16.3   Generalization hierarchies are more than a tree structure.

*Hierarchy, here, is used in its mathematical sense as a *directed acyclic graph* or as a *lattice*.

Another way of thinking about generalization is picturing sets of objects within sets of objects. Figure 16.4(a) depicts Jane as an instance of the concepts **Woman** and **Employee**. **Woman** and **Employee**, in turn, are both specializations of the more general **Person** concept. This means that the concept of **Person** applies to Jane, as well.

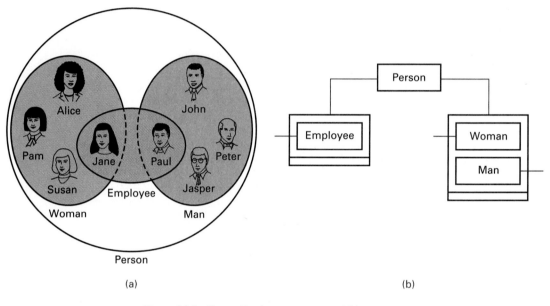

(a)   (b)

Figure 16.4   Generalization as concepts within concepts.

In summary, generalization enables us to define our concepts in even more general terms by using superconcepts. The inverse, specialization, allows us to be more specific about our concepts by using subconcepts. The notation in Fig. 16.4(b) is one way of representing generalization (and specialization). Generalization will be discussed further in Chapter 21.

COMPOSITION

Composition is a mechanism for forming a whole from component parts. For example, composition can configure assembly structures, such as: each **Boat** is made up of its **Hull** and **Motor** (see Fig. 16.5), or each **Hammer** consists of its **Head** and **Handle**. Other groupings of components include compositions such as each **Trade Union** is an association of its **Employee** members, or each **Record** is composed of its **Field Values**.

Additionally, component parts might, in turn, have their own component parts. For example, a particular **Car** could consist of four **Wheels**, its **Chassis**, an **Engine**, a **Radiator**, and so on. Its **Engine** could then consist of various **Pistons**,

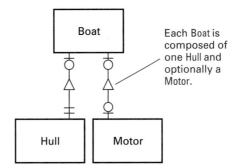

Figure 16.5 Composition can indicate configurations of assembly structures.

Rods, Valves, and an Engine Block.* In this way, composition can define hierarchies of part-whole configurations.

> *Composition* is the act or result of forming an object configured from its component
> parts.

Composition reduces complexity by treating many things as one. For
instance, we treat each Human Body object as one, even though it is a configuration of other objects, such as Arms, Legs, a Head, a Heart, and so on. Some
complex objects, such as a Stock Certificate or a Sales Contract, appear to be
quite stable, while others are not very stable at all. For example, a Human Body
is constantly replacing its Cell components. Yet, when we look at Jane or Jasper,
we still see them as the same object—even though they are not composed of the
same objects from one moment to the next. Similarly, if your Car lost a
Windshield Wiper or one of its Tires was replaced, would it be the same Car
object?

Composition brings up an assortment of questions about how we compose
and recognize the complex objects. We allow certain components of an object to
change over time, yet define other components to remain immutable. For example, a particular married couple consists of the husband and wife. Neither of these
components can be changed without destroying the couple. Each married couple
is an object whose abstraction results in the concept Marriage.

Immutable Composition

An immutable composition is the result of treating one or more related things as
the *immutable components* of a single thing. This invariant form of composition
can define instances such as those of marriages, airline reservations, or desk

---

*Notice that composition is expressed in terms of concepts. This does not mean that con-
cepts are composed of other concepts. It means that *instances* of concepts are composed of
instances of other concepts.

assignments. Each immutably composed object is created solely on the basis of its immutable component parts. Once created, an object cannot change these components. If it did, it would, by definition, become a different object.

The best way to understand immutable composition is by looking at why anyone might want to create a complex object with immutable components. Figure 16.6(a) contains several **Man** and **Woman** objects. During the course of systems analysis, the analyst may wish to refer to certain pairs of people, where each pair must contain one object from each gender. These pairs may be assem-

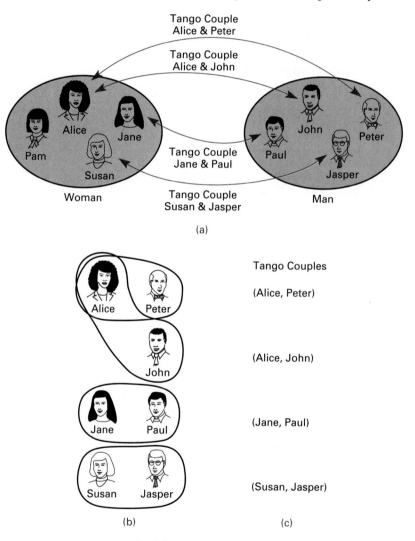

Figure 16.6   Example of different ways of displaying object couples.

bled for a tango competition, for a marriage ceremony, or whatever reality the analyst perceives. The important point is that the analyst wishes to refer to this man-woman object pair as a purposeful unit. For example, Tango Couple Jane and Paul refers to the dancing duo comprising Jane and Paul. Tango Couple Alice and John is a singular collective reference to the dancers Alice and John; and so on. In this way, Alice and John (while free to be components in other compositions) are considered the immutable components of the complex object Tango Couple Alice and John. Immutable components can be thought of *defining* a composition, because if another object were substituted, a *different* tango couple would be defined. If either object were removed, the pairing would cease to exist. Each of these couples, then, is immutably formed on the basis of two specific objects.

Figure 16.6(b) illustrates the tango couples, so that we can visualize the couple-based units. Each encircled composition immutably relates two specific objects—which, in turn, become one object. Instead of referring to the two objects Susan and Jasper who are dancing the tango together, we can refer to them as one named object. In Fig. 16.6(a), the object is named Tango Couple Susan and Jasper.

Figure 16.6(c) contains a third style of expression for the same four tango couples. The area between the parenthesis contains the names of the related objects that define the couple. In this particular situation, the first name in the parenthesis is always the Woman's name; the second, the Man's. By ordering the presentation in a pre-defined manner, the type of object is always understood, and the genders of people named "Pat" and "Bo" are never confused. *Ordered couples,* then, are a useful way of expressing the immutable relationship of objects.

Concepts and Immutable Composition

Each ordered couple is an object in its own right. The set of all tango-couple objects are instances of the concept named Tango Couple. However, Tango Couple is a special kind of concept—the *binary relation*. A binary relation is a concept whose objects are immutably composed of two component objects. Tango Couple, therefore, is a binary relation, because it is an abstraction of all those Woman-Man object pairs forming tango-dancing couples. Figure 16.7 depicts this binary relation in a graphic and notational form.

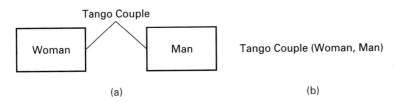

Figure 16.7 Two ways of expressing Tango Couple as a binary relation.

Trinary and *n*-ary Relations

Until this point, the examples have related two objects at a time to form another object. In Fig. 16.8(a), each object is a specific configuration of three objects that defines a different employee/desk/day-of-the-week assignment. One such assignment might be Alice to Desk23 on Monday.

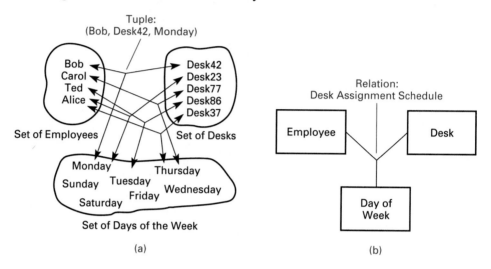

Figure 16.8   Tuples with three components and their trinary relation.

Once this assignment is defined as an object, none of its component parts may change without terminating the assignment and forming a different one. The set of all employee/desk/day-of-the-week assignments is a relation called **Desk Assignment Schedule**. Figure 16.8(b) illustrates a graphic technique for representing this relation. In relational notation, this relation could be generally expressed in the form

Desk Assignment Schedule (Employee, Desk, Day of Week)

Relations can be extended beyond binary and trinary (also called ternary) relations to *n*-ary or *n-place* relations. A complex object can be an immutable composition of any number of objects. Objects defined in this manner are called *n*-tuples or just *tuples*.

A *tuple* is an object that is an immutable composition of other objects.

For instance, an object could be a tuple consisting of a **Vendor** object, a **Customer** object, and one or more contracted **Product** or **Service** objects. The *n*-place relation for this tuple configuration could be called a **Contract**.

SUMMARY   This chapter focuses on a few of the mechanisms analysts may employ to cope with the complexity inherent in our world of objects.

Abstraction removes certain distinctions, so that we can see commonalities between objects. Without abstraction, we would only know that everything is different.

The second mechanism is *generalization*. Generalization distinguishes a concept that is more general than another. It enables us to perceive that all instances of a more specific concept are also instances of a general concept—but not necessarily the other way around. With generalization, we can build hierarchies (lattices) of concepts, forming more and more general concepts. The opposite of generalization is *specialization*.

The last mechanism is *composition*. Abstraction is often described as an *is a* association (That object *is a* Person.), and generalization as *a kind of* association (Man *is a kind of* Person.). Composition, then, could be described as a *has a* association (That Boat object *has a* Hull and a Motor.). *Composition* forms an object configured from its component parts. It reduces complexity by treating many objects as one object. Composition allows certain components of an object to change over time, yet define other components to remain immutable. An *immutable composition* is the result of treating one or more related objects as the immutable components of a single complex object. Concepts based on these immutable complex objects are called *binary relations*.

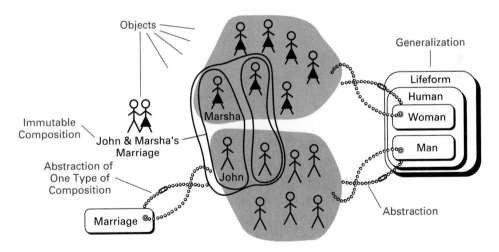

Figure 16.9   Abstraction, generalization, and composition.

As Fig. 16.9 indicates, we can and do employ these mechanisms separately or together. In the coming chapters, we will examine how these constructs can be employed for organizing and representing knowledge.

REFERENCES

1. Abiteboul, Serge and Richard Hull, "IFO: A Formal Semantic Database Model," *ACM Transactions on Database Systems,* 12:4, December 1987, pp. 525–565.

2. Bolton, Neil, *Concept Formation,* Pergamon Press, Oxford, 1977.

3. Borgida, Alexander T. et al., "Generalization/Specialization as a Basis for Software Specification," *On Conceptual Modelling,* Michael L. Brodie *et al.* eds., Springer-Verlag, New York, 1984, pp. 87–117.

4. Brodie, M. L. and D. Ridjanovic, "On the Design and Specification of Database Transactions," *On Conceptual Modelling: Perspectives from Artificial Intelligence, Databases, and Programming Languages,* Michael L. Brodie *et al.* eds., Springer-Verlag, New York, 1984, pp. 277–312.

5. Klausmeier, Herbert J. et al., *Conceptual Learning and Development: A Cognitive View,* Academic Press, New York, 1974.

6. Langer, Susanne K., *An Introduction to Symbolic Logic* (3rd edition), Dover Publications, New York, 1967.

7. Smith, John M. and Diane C. P. Smith, "Database Abstractions: Aggregation and Generalization", *ACM Transactions on Database Systems,* 2:2, June, 1977, pp. 105–133.

8. Smith, John M. and Diane C. P. Smith, "Principles of Database Conceptual Design," *Proceedings of the New York University Symposium on Database Design,* NYU Symposium on Database Design, 1978, pp. 35–49.

17   CONCEPT VERSUS OBJECT TYPE

In the previous two chapters, the term *concept* has been used to mean a shared notion or idea that applies to certain objects in our awareness. In other words, we can say we possess a shared notion or idea that applies to certain objects in our awareness or, we can say we possess a concept. The word "concept," then, is just a symbol we can use in place of repeating its definition. Other words or symbols can be substituted in place of concept while retaining the same definition or intension. Just as "a rose by any other name would smell as sweet," the notion of concept by any other name would have the same intension. The current term for concept in the object-oriented community is *object type*. Therefore, in the remaining chapters of this book, the word object type will be used instead of concept.

> An *object type* is a shared notion or idea that applies to certain objects in our awareness: it is a type of object.

Why Change Terms Now?

The word concept is used initially in this part of the book, because we understand the meaning of concept from an early age. In his early object-oriented research at Xerox, Alan Kay discovered that children as young as seven years could form and manipulate concepts. However, using the term object type is not quite so intuitive. If someone were to ask an end user, "What concepts do you have when performing a sales function?" she would probably understand the question. Yet, the question "What object types do you have?" could cause problems without proper training.

In short, the term concept was used at first, because it is a word we quickly recognize and understand. Now that a basic understanding exists, a change to more standard terminology is possible. (However, some analysts find using the word concept easier to use with end users—avoiding the term object type altogether. Again, since both are just symbols for the same idea, the choice of which to use can be based on expedience.)

The Extension of Concept/Object Type

As mentioned earlier, every concept has an intension and an extension. Since Object Type is synonymous with Concept, it too has an intension and an extension. Its intension is the definition of concept. Its extension is the set of all concepts. In Fig. 17.1, some examples of objects that are instances of Object Type are enclosed in the circle on the right. In other words, objects like Person, Order, and Event Type are themselves Object Types (i.e., Concepts).*

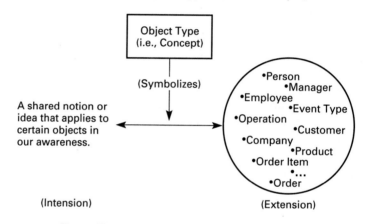

Figure 17.1   A concept triad for concept/object type.

In summary, no matter what you use to name the notion of concept, or whether the name is enclosed in a box, an ellipse, or any other shape, the intension and extension do not change. The primary consideration is clarity for the user.

*Modeling situations like these are called *meta-modeling*. Appendix D discusses this topic in more depth.

18   OBJECT TYPES AND ASSOCIATIONS

Associations define the way objects of various types can be linked or connected—enabling the construction of conceptual networks. Without this associative capability, all objects would seem to stand alone, and our world would not fit together.

This brief chapter introduces ways in which objects, through their object types, can be associated. It is based on the notion of immutable composition discussed in a previous chapter. It examines the representation of stand-alone object types, as well as two different kinds of conceptual associations—relations and functions. In Chapters 19 and 20, relations and functions will be explored in detail.

ASSOCIATIONS

Associations provide a means to link objects in a meaningful way via their object types. Figure 18.1 illustrates an example of an association. The two object types, Organization and Person, are symbolized with rectangular nodes. The line indicates an association between these two object types.

Nodes are often a useful representation device, because they graphically differentiate object types from their linking structures. While a nodal representation is not necessary, it can more clearly differentiate what is being associated from what is doing the associating. For example, Fig. 18.1 depicts the object type Person as having a set membership consisting of objects such as John, Jasper, Jane, and Susan. The object type Organization has instances such as IBM, NEC, and NASA. These set memberships can also be written in the form: Person { John, Jasper, Jane, Susan, . . .} and Organization { IBM, NEC, NASA, . . .}.*

---

*Parentheses in an expression are used to surround the terms of a relation or components of a tuple. Curly brackets, such as these, are used to enumerate the members of a set.

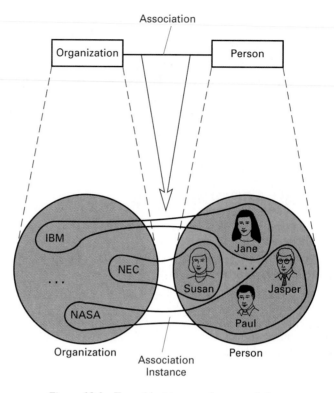

Figure 18.1   Two object types and an association.

Associations, on the other hand, are typically represented as lines. Lines are one intuitive mechanism, because we naturally think of them as linking two or more points. The line in Fig. 18.1 involves an association of objects for two object types. For example, Jane and IBM are two of the objects linked by the Organization-Person association.

While object types involve sets of objects, associations involve connections of objects between sets. As such, this collection of connections forms a special kind of object type.

RELATIONS   The instances of object types are objects by definition. Relations are specialized object types. They are object types whose instances are tuples. As discussed in the previous chapter, each tuple is an invariant composition of other objects. For example, the association instances at the bottom of Fig. 18.1 could be interpreted as invariant pairs of objects. Each composed pair would be an instance of the relation Employment.

Figure 18.2(b) depicts these related instances as object *couples*. As mentioned earlier, IBM and Jane form one such Employment couple. If three objects

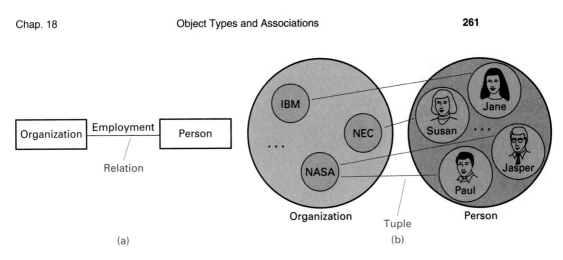

Figure 18.2   Relating two object types.

are related, object *triples* result; four objects result in *quadruples;* and so on. Regardless of the number, these complex objects are called *tuples.* The tuples in Fig. 18.2(b) are all members of the **Employment** set, whose extension can be expressed by enumerating all of the couples: **Employment** { (IBM, Jane), (NEC, Susan), (NASA, Jasper), (NASA, Paul), . . .}.

<table>
<tr><td>A relation is an object type whose extension is a set of tuples.</td></tr>
</table>

In Fig. 18.2(a), **Employment** is the name of the relation between the object types **Organization** and **Person**. This relation has two *places*—one for each of its component object types. The number of object types linked by a relation determines the number of *places* that must be filled in a tuple. For example, a 3-place relation involving **Employee**, **Day of Week**, and **Desk** objects could be presented in tabular forms as follows:

Employs: Person	Is Assigned: Day of Week	Is Assigned: Desk
Bob	Monday	Desk42
Carol	Thursday	Desk77
Ted	Tuesday	Desk86
Alice	Monday	Desk23
Alice	Thursday	Desk37
. . .	. . .	. . .

Here, each object type plays a role by participating as a column in the relational table. In Fig. 18.3(a), this 3-place relation can be expressed as a three-pronged line connecting **Employee, Day of Week,** and **Desk** object types. Furthermore, each row in the relational table is a tuple relating three specific objects as one instance in a **Desk Assignment Schedule.** Figure 18.3(b) is another way of presenting these same rows as separate, yet related, objects.

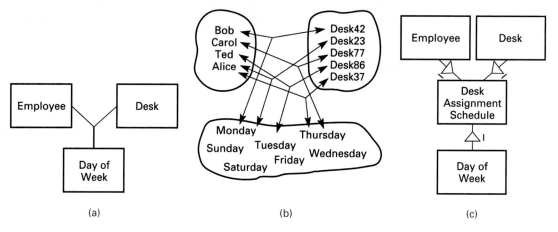

Figure 18.3   A 3-place Desk Assignment Schedule.

Lines are often used to represent relations, particularly 2-place relations. However, representing relations with more than two places as a line can make them difficult to read and understand. Through the mechanism of composition, each tuple is an object in its own right. Therefore, when viewed as a set of objects instead of tuples, the relation can be expressed in its more general form—an object type. The middle object type in Fig. 18.3(c), then, is an object type whose instances are **Desk Assignment Schedule** objects. Furthermore, to preserve the immutable component structure of the original *n*-place relation, the hollow triangle symbol is used to indicate composition. In addition, an "I" is placed next to the composition triangle to indicate the immutable nature of the composition. The three "I" triangled lines emanating from the new node in Fig. 18.3(c) represent the three places originally designated in Fig. 18.3(a). In this way, relations can be represented as lines or in a more general object type form. However, when expressed as an object type, the "I" triangles are necessary to preserve the original relational places. Both representations aid our understanding of the objects in our world and how we link them. Relations, and ways of expressing them, will be discussed in more detail in Chapter 20.

FUNCTIONS

Given the objects of one object type, a function associates them to objects of another object type. Thinking of this as a *mapping* is often useful. In Fig. 18.4, **Organization** objects are

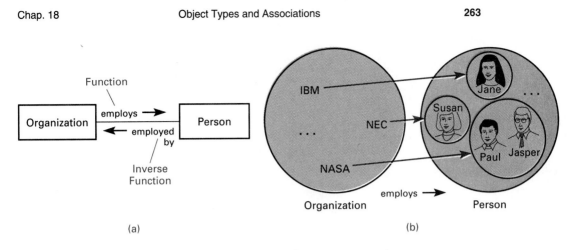

Figure 18.4   Mapping from one set to another.

mapped, via the **employs*** function, to **Person** objects. For example, the IBM **Organization** object links to the Jane **Person** object. NASA links to Paul and Jasper, and so on. In practical terms, the ability to apply such *mappings* in the dynamic world of objects requires a process. A function is a process that—given an object—returns a set containing zero or more objects.

A function that always returns a set containing a single object is called *single-valued*. For example, each **Person** object maps to exactly one **Woman** object that is the person's biological mother. Functions are *multivalued* when they return a set containing an unspecified number of objects, rather than just a single instance. For example, the multivalued **employs** function in Fig. 18.4(a) maps NASA to a set containing Jasper and Paul, and IBM to Jane. A basic, initial definition of function is as follows.

A *function* is a mapping process that—given each object within a set—returns a set of objects of a given type.[†]

Mathematically, a function corresponds to a 2-place relation. In other words, a function can be treated as a relation between two sets. For example, the association in Fig. 18.4(b) can be represented both as a relation and a function as follows.

Functions are directional. The link from IBM to Jane means that the **employs** function in Fig. 18.4(a) maps from an **Organization** object type to a **Person** object type. The reverse direction requires a different function—one that is the *inverse* of **employs**. It is named **employed by**. A more complete explanation of functions will be provided in Chapter 19.

---

*In this book, object type names begin with a capital letter; function names do not.

[†]This function can also be defined as one that maps one set into a power set (or set of all subsets) of another [1].

Relation		Function	
Employed By: Organization	Employs: Person	Argument	Result
IBM	Jane	IBM $\longrightarrow$	{Jane}
NEC	Susan	NEC $\longrightarrow$	{Susan}
NASA	Paul	NASA $\longrightarrow$	{Paul, Jasper}
NASA	Jasper	. . .	. . .
. . .	. . .		

SUMMARY   Associations define the way objects of various types can be linked or connected. Relations and functions are two ways of expressing associations. *Relations* can be used when the analyst wants to consider objects as tuples. For example, **Employment** is a relation that applies to tuples composed of pairs of **Organization** and **Employee** objects. *Functions,* on the other hand, can be used when one object is known, and the analyst wishes to determine the other objects with which it is associated. For example, the **employs** function maps each **Organization** object to its related **Employee** objects. When writing an application system, a relational association could easily be implemented as a record or group item. A functional association could be implemented as a query or pointer. Either way, they both describe associations among objects.

The choice of which way to express an association depends on which is the most useful in describing the problem at hand—without being limited to one or the other. Figure 18.5(a) illustrates both function and relation on the same dia-

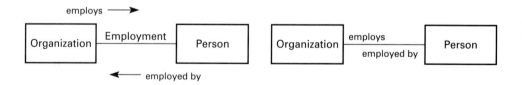

gram. Figure 18.5(b) presents a less cluttered version. Here, the Employment relation is implied rather than stated.

In short, functions exist wherever there are relations. Relations can be defined wherever there are functions. With this basic knowledge, a more detailed presentation is now possible.

REFERENCES

1. Abrial, J. R., "Data Semantics," *Data Base Management,* IFIP Working Conference on Data Base Management (Cargèse, Corsica), J. W. Klimbie *et al.* eds., North-Holland, Amsterdam, 1974, pp. 1–60.

2. Gray, Peter M. D., *Logic, Algebra, and Databases,* John Wiley and Sons, New York, 1984.

19 FUNCTIONS

The previous chapter introduced the notion of associations among types of objects. In particular, it familiarized the reader with the basics of relations and functions. This chapter examines *functions* in greater depth.

FUNCTIONS AND THEIR INVERSE

A function is a process that *maps* each object of one type to a set of objects of another type. In Fig. 19.1(a), the **employs** function maps each **Organiza**tion object to a set of objects within the **Person** set. Each subset represents those **Person**s who are employed by a given **Organization**. In this example, the function maps the **Organization** NASA to the specific set of **Person**s Paul and Jasper. Each arrowed line in this diagram represents one *mapping instance* of the **employs** mapping. An abstract way of representing this mapping is depicted in

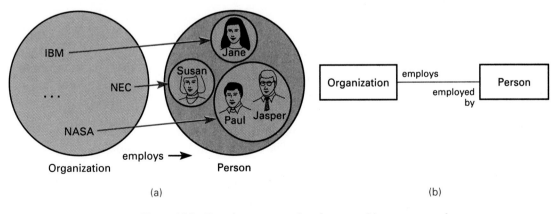

Figure 19.1   Functions are mappings between object types.

Fig. 19.1(b). Here, the **employs** function goes from the **Organization** object type to the **Person** object type.

Inverse Functions

In Fig. 19.1, the **employs** function defines a mapping from **Organization** to **Person**. Many functions, however, have a reverse or *inverse* function. In this example, the inverse function maps employed **Person**s back to each **Organization** where they are employed. In Fig. 19.2(b), for instance, Jane maps back to her employer IBM, Susan to NEC, and so on. The name of this function could be **employed by: Organization** or simply **employed by**. Together, the function and its inverse function comprise all of the *employment* mappings between the two sets. As illustrated in Fig. 19.2(a), having one line labeled with the function names is a way of representing these two mappings more economically.

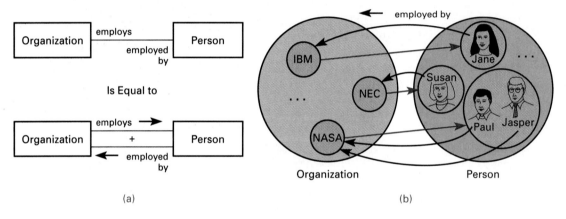

Figure 19.2   Functions and inverse functions.

Function Labels

Labeling functions on an object schema should follow a consistent diagramming notation. The labeling technique used in this book is the following. When representing a function that maps from a node on the left to a node on the right, the label will appear *above* the horizontal line. When reading from right to left, the label appears *below* the line. As the line is rotated, the label remains on the same side of the line, as illustrated in Fig. 19.3.

Thus, the label to the *right* of a vertical line is read when function maps down the line. The label on the *left* of the vertical line is read when mapping up the line [3].

CARDINALITY CONSTRAINTS   Placing constraints on functions is often useful. Limiting the number of objects to which each object maps is called a *cardinality constraint*.

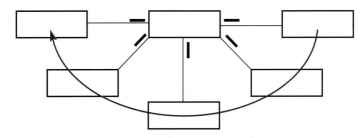

Figure 19.3   A function label during rotation.

Figure 19.4 indicates a mapping that exists between **Employee** objects and **Chair** objects. Yet, it does not indicate how many objects can participate in any one mapping instance. It does not answer such questions as: Can an employee be assigned to more than one office chair? Must an employee be assigned to a chair? Or, does the office have a version of "musical chairs" operating where more than one employee can be assigned to a given chair?

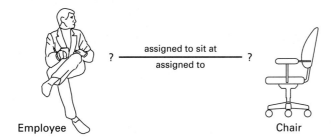

Figure 19.4   How many Chairs can be assigned to an Employee?

This book employs a cardinality constraint notation that indicates the minimum and maximum number of objects that must result from any one mapping instance. The word *cardinality* simply indicates that an integer is used to represent the number of objects. A few cardinality constraint notations commonly employed between nodes are indicated in Fig. 19.5. Alternatively, the analyst may adopt her own brand of notation. The primary consideration here is that the chosen notation provide a clear understanding of minimum and maximum cardinality constraints.

Figure 19.6 applies the standard crow's foot notation [3] to illustrate cardinality constraint. This example indicates that each **Employee** object must map to *at least* one **Desk** object and *at most* one **Desk** object. The cardinality constraint on the inverse function indicates that a **Desk** object need *not* map to any **Employee** objects. However, if it does map, the mapping must be to one object, at most.

An example of mapping to more than one object is represented in Fig. 19.7(a). This diagram can be read: "via the **employs** function, every **Employer**

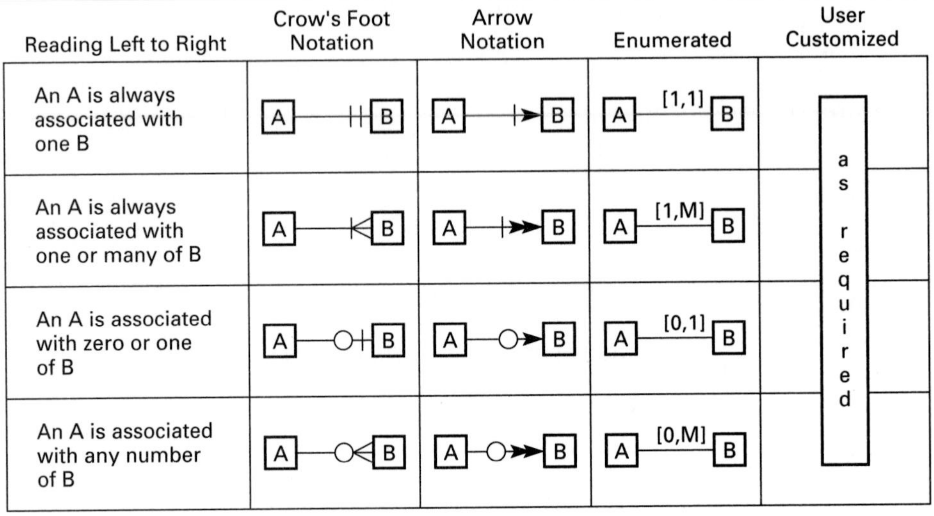

Reading Left to Right	Crow's Foot Notation	Arrow Notation	Enumerated	User Customized
An A is always associated with one B	A ⊢‖ B	A →► B	A [1,1] B	as required
An A is always associated with one or many of B	A ⊣< B	A →►► B	A [1,M] B	
An A is associated with zero or one of B	A ⊸⊢ B	A ⊸► B	A [0,1] B	
An A is associated with any number of B	A ⊸< B	A ⊸►► B	A [0,M] B	

Figure 19.5   Common notations for cardinality.

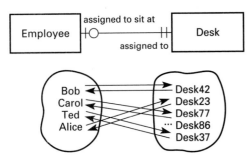

Figure 19.6   Example of a function and its inverse.

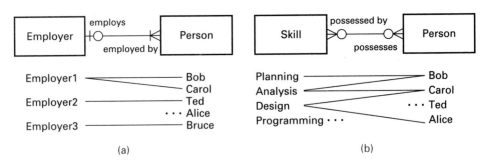

(a)   (b)

Figure 19.7   Examples of functions that map to multiple objects.

object maps to one or more **Person** objects.* Inversely, each **Person** optionally maps to an **Employer**, and if it does, it maps to one **Employer** at most. The cardinality constraints in Fig. 19.7(b) specify that each **Skill** is possessed by any number of **Persons** and that each **Person possesses** zero, one, or many **Skills**.

Beyond Zero, One, and Many Cardinalities

The maximum, or upper bound, cardinality constraint is most often expressed in terms of mapping an object to a set containing at most one or to some undefined many objects. In addition, the minimum, or lower bound, cardinality constraint is most often expressed as zero or one. The zero indicates that each object maps to a set that *may* contain no objects whatsoever. The one indicates that each object maps to a set that *must* contain at least one object. Because of the *may* and *must* aspects of these two minimum constraints, they are sometimes referred to as *optional* or *mandatory* mappings, respectively.

However, in addition to zero, one, and many, cardinality constraints can be enumerated differently for situations requiring options other than these three. For example, in Fig. 19.8, a particular organization has determined that each **Meeting** must have at least 2 **Persons** but cannot exceed 20 **Persons**. (Mappings beyond 20 persons might be considered an **Assembly** instead.) This technique applies to many modeling situations, such as the number of passengers on a flight or episodes in a television series. Whenever cardinality constraints can be stated more precisely than *many,* representing them is important. In fact, constraints on cardinality can be further extended, so that mappings are restricted to an odd or even number of objects; so that only 3, 5, 7, 11, or 13 relatable objects are allowed; or, that the number of permitted objects can even be derived as necessary. Such precise information needs to be formally documented, because it defines and determines the organization.

Figure 19.8 An enumerated cardinality constraint for Meeting attendees.

Ordering Representations

Functions may associate objects of one object type with objects of the *same* object type. These are called *ordering* functions. For example, Fig. 19.9 represents two ways of expressing the ordering of a management hierarchy. Both notations are equivalent.

---

*Implicit in every function is that each maps to a set containing zero, one, or many objects. Therefore, the phrase "to a set containing" may be omitted for easier reading. For additional clarity, mapping instances are not always drawn to sets of objects but directly to the set's underlying objects. For instance, Fig. 19.2(b) depicts its mapping to sets. However, representing the mappings of Fig. 19.7 in this manner would be graphically cumbersome.

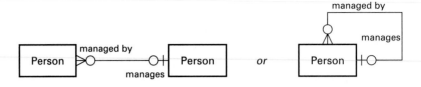

Figure 19.9   Two ordering representations for a management hierarchy.

DOMAIN AND RANGE OF A FUNCTION

Until now, functions have been discussed in terms of mapping *from a set of objects* and *to a set of objects.* The conventional terms for these are *domain* and *range,* respectively. In this way, functions can be described more briefly as mapping from a domain to a range.

The *domain* of a function is the collection of all objects mapped by the function.

The *range* of a function is the collection of all objects to which the function maps.

In Fig. 19.10, several **Organization** objects are mapped by the **employs** function: ACME, IBM, NEC, NASA, XYZ and so on. The **Organization** set, then, is the *domain* of the **employs** function.

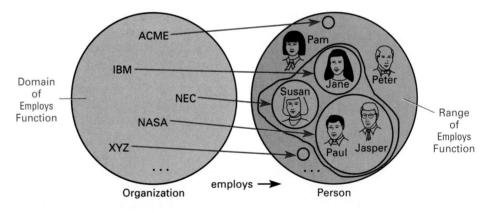

Figure 19.10   Functions map from a domain to a range.

The **employs** function maps to that collection of **Person** objects that an **Organization** employs: Jane, Susan, Paul, and Jasper. This collection of **Person** objects is the *range* of the **employs** function. All other **Person** objects, like Pam and Peter, are currently not employees, and are, therefore, not part of this function's range. In other words, the range of **employs** includes only employed **Persons**.

Specializing Mapped Object Types

Because the range of employs includes only employed Persons, referring to a specialized set of Persons is often useful. This specialization could be called Employed Person, or just Employee. By substituting the Employee object type in place of Person, the function's actual range is also expressed. While this substitution is not necessary, it clarifies the meaning of the employs function and sharpens its cardinality constraint.

In addition, the domain could be examined in a similar manner. ACME and XYZ are currently Organizations without employees. Technically, then, ACME and XYZ are not currently employers. In order to add a degree of precision, the analyst may wish to specialize the domain of employs. Such a specialized object type would include only those organizations having employees and could be called Employing Organization, or simply Employer.

A more succinct depiction of the specialized domain and range object types in Fig. 19.11(a) is illustrated in Fig. 19.11(b). Notice that when object types are specialized in this way, the optional cardinality in Fig. 19.11(a) is removed. This object type specialization technique is important and will be explored more in the chapter on subtypes and supertypes. In this chapter, however, the names of the specialized domain and range object types will provide guidance for naming functions.

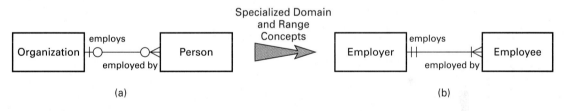

Figure 19.11   Defining object types to fit the specialized domain and range.

Function Naming

A function's label should clearly indicate its meaning. One common technique considers the function's range. In Fig. 19.12 for instance, three functions map to the object type Day. One function maps from Car to Day, designating when the car was manufactured. The range, then, is not all possible Day objects but a subset containing all valid manufacturing days. By naming this function manufactured on: Day (where manufactured on is qualified by its range object type Day for clarity), the purpose and meaning of this mapping is apparent. Another function maps each Car Registration to the Day on which the car is currently registered. Here, registered on: Day might be an appropriate function name.*

*Notice that the Day object type was not depicted as three specialized object types: Car Manufacturing Day, Car Registration Day, Day Founded. Having specialized mapped object types, as described earlier, is an option that can provide greater precision when their intensions differ. However, this precision is not always desirable. In Fig. 19.12, the analyst decided that the extra precision was not appropriate.

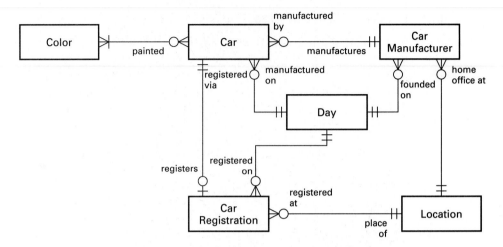

Figure 19.12   Some examples of function names.

In a similar fashion, all of the remaining function names can be assigned. The painted Color function maps each Car to one or more Colors that it has been painted. The manufactured by function maps to the Car Manufacturer that produced the Car. The registered at maps Car Registrations to those Locations that have cars registered, and so on.

Inverse Function Naming

The same guideline that applies to functions, applies to their inverses—except the range and domain are changed. For example, the registered via function maps Cars to Car Registrations. With the inverse, not every Car object actually associates with a Car Registration object—only registered cars. Therefore, the function maps only to those Cars it registers.

Another naming technique for the inverse function adds an inverse symbol to the function name. For example, the inverse of manufactured on of Car can be written manufactured on^{-1}. In this case, manufactured on^{-1} is an inverse function that maps from Day to Car.

The last option omits the inverse name entirely. In Fig. 19.12, the painted mapping from Car to Color might be identified by a business as an essential property of the Car objects. The inverse mapping from Colors to Cars may be deemed totally unnecessary and, therefore, omitted.

Conceptual Attribute Types

A commonly used word in data processing is *attribute* and usually means a particular association of some entity to one of its values. However, in OO analysis, since *entities* and *values* are objects in their own right, the definition of attribute can be generalized as follows.

For example, a **has difference** function requires a number a to be subtracted from a number b. This function can be specified as

DIFFERENCE RESULT = HAS DIFFERENCE (A, B)

A function that locates a point in three-dimensional space can be written as **has point(x,y,z)**.

However, the definition of a function states that, technically, only one object can be mapped at a time. To accommodate this rule, all of the n arguments can be bundled as an n-place relation. This is similar to a program passing a record or an array as a parameter [1]. In this way, each n-tuple can be an object that fills the function's one permitted argument. For instance, the multiargument function, **has difference**, maps ordered pairs of numbers to their respective differences in the following way:

Argument	Result
(1,1)	(0)
(2,1)	(1)
⋮	⋮
(8,3)	(5)
⋮	⋮

In the previous example, the two components in the argument are both from the same object type, **Real Numbers**. However, the components can be drawn from different object types. For example, **has marriage** can be defined as a three-place function. Mapping to a unique **Marriage** object requires a function that can be written in the form, **has marriage (Wife, Husband, Marriage Day)**. Here, each tuple has three components. As a unit, each maps to a specific marriage. For example, (Liz, Richard, 27 May 1946) maps to one particular marriage. (Liz, Richard, 1 April 1980) maps to a second, entirely different marriage even though the same two people are involved.

Since each tuple is an object, the definition of a function given in the previous chapter remains unchanged. However, since tuples can compose multiple objects, in reality, functions do map multiple objects. An extended definition of function is as follows.

A *function* is a process that—given one or more objects in one or more sets—returns a set of objects of a given type.*

---

*This definition of function is closer to that used by programming languages. Functions in programming are processes that—given one or more parameters—return a single value (where the value can be null, a string, a number, an array, and so on).

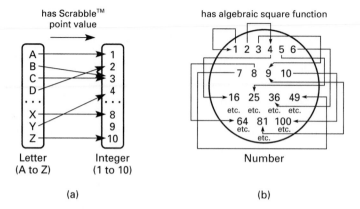

Figure 19.15   Two examples of functional mappings.

BASE AND COMPUTED FUNCTIONS

Many functions involve mappings that are simply asserted to be true. Functions whose mappings are fixed by assertion are called *base functions*. Figure 19.15(a) illustrates a base mapping called the has Scrabble™ point value function. It maps each Scrabble tile containing a letter of the alphabet to a corresponding point value. For instance, "A" in the set of Letter objects is associated to a "1" in the set of Integer objects. This means that the letter A is asserted to be valued as one Scrabble point. The "Z" tile is asserted to be a whopping ten points, and so on.

In contrast to base functions, *computed functions* are those whose mapping results can be derived or computed. For example, Fig. 19.15(b) depicts the has algebraic square function that maps certain number objects to other number objects. The object labeled "4" associates to its square, the object labeled "16;" "5" associates to "25," "6" to "36," and so on. Here, the has algebraic square mapping is defined as an algebraic expression, $y = x^2$.

Expressions of Function

The previous example involved a relatively simple numeric calculation. However, computed functions can involve a much richer set of operations. An expressive functional language must employ numeric functions as well as set functions, filters, and transitive closure. In addition, they may use other user-defined functions as building blocks.

Figure 19.16 represents an object schema with both base and computed functions. The base function indicates that each Person can have two biological parents. This function can be written has parents(x), or x has parents, where x is some Person object.

However, determining one's cousins can require a computation. First, the grandparents must be identified. The parents of the parents of x can be expressed

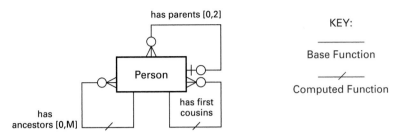

Figure 19.16　Examples of base and computed functions.

as has parents(has parents(x)). Then, the grandparent's children must be computed: has offspring(has parents(has parents(x))). Next, subtract the original has parents(x) from these children, so that x and x's siblings do not compute as cousins. Finally, with the remainder, compute the children. Expressed in terms of other functions, the full version of this computed function can be expressed as

HAS FIRST COUSINS(X) = HAS OFFSPRING(HAS OFFSPRING(HAS PARENTS
(HAS PARENTS(X)))-HAS PARENTS(X))

Deriving all of a person's ancestors is a different function than that for has first cousins. It can be expressed as an iterative search starting with the parents, then computing the parent's parents, and so on, until no more parents can be determined. Such a cyclic process is known as *transitive closure* and is used for many applications, such as bill-of-materials parts explosions. This expression involves a statement (again using the already defined parents function) to satisfy the has ancestors function:

HAS ANCESTORS(X) = TRANSITIVE CLOSURE (HAS PARENTS, PERSON(X))

While the expressions presented here are accurate, they can be difficult to read by an untrained analyst. Their capabilities can be explored further by reading Appendix C. In addition, Appendix C includes a graphic alternative for expressing these functions.

SUMMARY

This chapter proposed a way in which functions are used to make conceptual associations. A *function* is a process that *maps* each given object of one set to a set of objects in another. Each function can have a logical *inverse function*.

Functions map *from* a set *to* a set. The conventional terms for these sets are domain and range, respectively. A function's *domain* is the collection of all objects mapped by the function. A function's *range* is the collection of all objects to which the function maps.

Mappings can be constrained. *Cardinality constraints* restrict the number of objects that may be contained in the set to which a function maps. The *maximum,* or upper bound, cardinality constraint is most often expressed in terms of mapping an object to a set containing at most one or to some undefined, many objects. In addition, the *minimum,* or lower bound, cardinality constraint is most often expressed as zero or one. The zero indicates that each object maps to a set that *may* contain no objects whatsoever. The one indicates that each object maps to a set that *must* contain at least one object. Cardinalities are typically expressed in terms of zero, one, and many. However, they can be enumerated with other positive integers, as well.

The subject or independent variable of a function is called an *argument.* When this argument is *filled,* the function returns a specific set of objects. An *argument-filled function,* then, is an instance of a function mapping. Argument-filled functions are also object types in their own right. Their extension is the set of objects to which the supplied argument maps.

The attributes of an object are the set of all argument-filled functions in which the object is an argument. Functions, then, are the *attribute types* of object types. In this way, the terms *function* and *attribute type* can be used interchangeably.

Functions whose mappings are fixed by assertion are called *base functions. Computed functions,* on the other hand, are computed mappings. Computed functions are explored in more detail in Appendix C.

Object types offer the means to define sets of objects. When viewed in an OO context, functions offer an equally powerful means of associating objects between object types.

REFERENCES

1. Gray, Peter M. D., *Logic, Algebra, and Databases,* John Wiley and Sons, New York, 1984.

2. Hull, Richard and Roger King, "A Tutorial on Semantic Database Modeling," *Research Foundations of Object-Oriented and Semantic Database Systems,* Alfonso F. Cárdenas *et al.* ed., Prentice-Hall, Englewood Cliffs, NJ, 1990, pp. 1–33.

3. Martin, James, *Recommended Diagramming Standards for Analysts and Programmers: A Basis for Automation,* Prentice-Hall, Englewood Cliffs, NJ, 1987.

20 RELATIONS

Object types draw useful distinctions among objects. Without object types, we simply could not think about this or that object. Relations are specialized types of object types that allow us to think about objects that are immutably composed of other objects. This chapter builds on the material in Chapter 18 and describes how relations are used in object schemas.

RELATION CARDINALITY

Chapter 18 characterized a relation as an object type whose instances are immutable compositions of objects. Each immutable composition is known as a *tuple* in relational theory. For example, a tuple that is an instance of the relation Marriage (has wife: Woman, has husband: Man) is any married couple. The marriage of Alice and John is one such instance and can be written, Marriage (has wife: Alice, has husband: John).

Each distinctive feature in a relation is clearly defined by a positional component or *place*. The number of places in a relation is dictated by the number of distinctive features it contains. For instance, the first *place* in the Marriage relation could be occupied by the has wife, the second place by the has husband. The order of relational components is important. Without knowing this order, identifying the has wife in a Marriage tuple, such as Marriage (Kelly, Chris), could be problematic.

The 2-place relation, Marriage, in Fig. 20.1(a) specifies that a given Woman or Man object is not required to be a component of a Marriage tuple. However, if a Woman or Man object is married, it may be a component of only one Marriage tuple. Therefore, the example in Fig. 20.1(b) violates this cardinality constraint, because it reveals that Paul is currently in two Marriages: one with Pam and the other with Jane. In those environments where multiple marriages are permitted, the schema in Fig. 20.1(a) must be changed, so that the maximum cardinality constraint is greater than one.

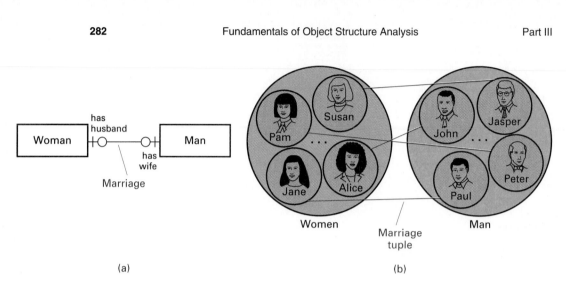

(a)   (b)

Figure 20.1   A Marriage relation and some underlying Marriage tuples.

RELATIONS AS OBJECT TYPES

Figure 20.2 again portrays the marriage example. In this diagram, however, the **Marriage** relation is represented as a set of married couples or 2-tuples. Placing a round-cornered box around these tuples reveals the notion that each tuple is an instance in a collection of tuples. Since each of these tuples is an object in its own right, the **Marriage** relation is an object type whose extension is the set of all married couples.

     Marriage, then, can be represented as a more general object-type node, as well as a relational-line notation. Throughout this chapter, both forms will be

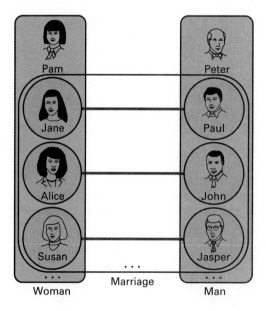

Figure 20.2   A set of Marriage tuples.

exploited along with guidelines for their usage. The example in Fig. 20.3 illustrates representations for both forms.

In Fig. 20.3, the grey line represents the original relation presented in Fig. 20.1(a). It represents Marriage as a 2-place relation. However, as demonstrated above, Marriage can also be regarded, in its more general sense, as an object type. As an object type, Marriage is viewed as a set of objects without regard for its object composition. However, when it is expressed as an object type, the analyst should not lose track of the two places defined by the original relation. One way of handling this is depicted at the bottom of Fig. 20.3. Here, each place in the Marriage is denoted by two composition triangles on the lines pointing to the Marriage object type. Since the composition is immutable, the "I" next to each composition triangle indicates this. (In contrast, the Man and Woman object types have no composition triangles pointing to them and can, therefore, be considered *0-place* relations.)

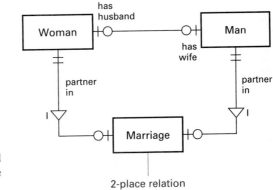

Figure 20.3 Marriage as a relation and as an object type with two immutable attribute types.

In short, when expressing relations as object types, immutable attribute types are necessary to preserve place structure. Relations and object types, then, offer two ways of viewing the same association. Ask a question about instances of relations, get a tuple answer. Ask a question about instances of an object type, get a simple object answer. This is not contradictory—just two sides of the same coin. Guidelines for these choices are presented later in this section.

From Tuples to Objects—and Back Again*

Figure 20.4 presents examples of instances for the schema's relations and object types. Instances of the three object types are simple objects; instances of relations are tuples.

The instances of the Marriage relation are presented as tuples containing immutably composed pairs of Man and Woman objects. The Marriage object type consists of the same Marriage tuples. However, when considered as an

*Material in this subsection is optional.

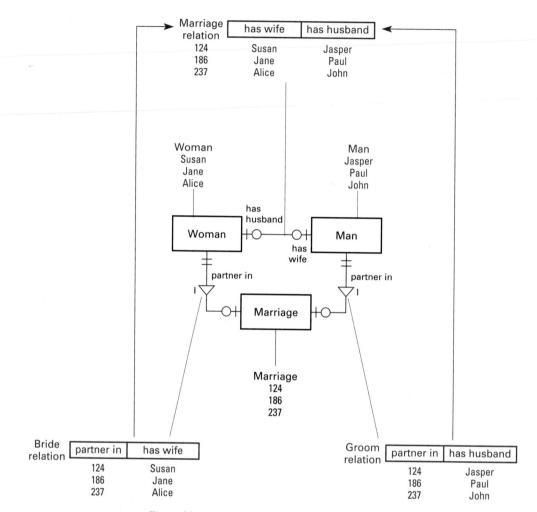

Figure 20.4 Marriage schema with tuple examples.

object type, the instances of **Marriage** can only be referred to as the simple objects 124, 186, and 237.

To this point, going from tuple to simple object is a straightforward procedure, because tuples are objects by definition. For example, the tuple Marriage(Susan,Jasper) is also known as object 124. However, starting with the Marriage object 124, the Marriage(Susan,Jasper) tuple can also be derived. When the object type's immutable attribute types are joined, the relational form can be realized. In Fig. 20.4, when the **Bride** and **Groom** tuples are joined on a common **Marriage** object, a Marriage tuple can be derived. Therefore, the tuples Bride(partner in:124, has wife:Susan) and Groom(partner in:124, has husband:Jasper) can be joined to form the tuple Marriage(has wife:Susan, has husband:Jasper).

Three Ways of Representing Relations

In many situations, the object-type node is used instead of the relational-line notation, because it is clearer. 2-place relations can easily be represented as a line or a node. However, lines depicting other than 2-place relations can be difficult both to represent graphically and to understand conceptually.

　　Figure 20.5(a) depicts a 3-place relation as a line with three end points. Two alternate object-type representations for this relation are displayed in Figs. 20.5(b) and 20.5(c). The first technique is a variant of the *hypergraph* [1]. Hypergraphs allow us to go beyond the requirements of elementary geometry which state that a line segment has only two end points. "Hyper" line segments have many end points. Hypergraph convention involves drawing a box around the things that need to be connected. To think about this in another way, a tiny object-type node can be imagined at the heart of the trinary relationship in Fig. 20.5(a). If this node is stretched outward until it surrounds the object types it relates, it becomes a hypergraph.

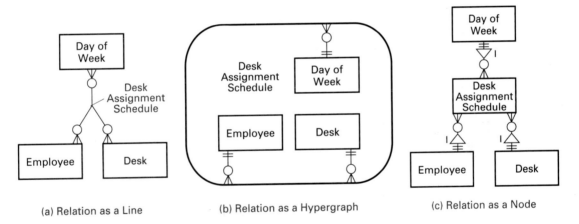

(a) Relation as a Line　　　　　　(b) Relation as a Hypergraph　　　　　　(c) Relation as a Node

Figure 20.5　Three representations of Desk Assignment Schedule relation.

　　The example in Fig. 20.5(c) represents the 3-place relation as a rectangle. The rectangle is a more compact form of the hypergraph. Instead of the object type surrounding its places, it becomes a small hub with radiating place attribute types. Throughout this book, the rectangle will be the symbol chosen for the object-type node.

　　This is no clever trick with mirrors and pencils. The diagrams in Fig. 20.5 represent the same knowledge. According to Bill Kent, portraying an *n*-place relation as an object-type node "acknowledges the existence of a single complex fact, and simply draws a picture connecting the fact with each of its participants" [4]. The analyst must choose the best relational representation for the situation at hand.

Relations with Attribute Types

Declaring attribute types on a relation is another circumstance where a representation by object-type node improves clarity. For example, Fig. 20.6(a) depicts Marriage as a relation between Woman and Man. Associated with the Marriage relation is a Witness attribute. In other words, one or more Witness objects can be associated with each Marriage tuple. Inversely, each Witness can attest zero, one, or many Marriages. However, a construct that relates a relation directly to an object type can be potentially confusing. This is particularly true if further attribute types are added to the Marriage relation—or even worse, to the Marriage-Witness relation line—as depicted in Fig. 20.6(b). Instead, if the Marriage relation is expressed as an object type, the meaning of its attribute types is enhanced. This approach is illustrated in Fig. 20.6(c).

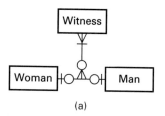

(a)

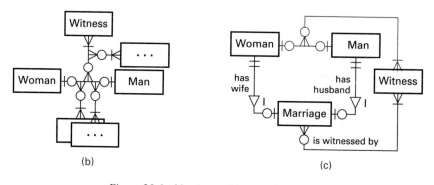

(b)   (c)

Figure 20.6   Marriage with an attribute type.

Mutable and Immutable Attribute Types

Figure 20.7(a) illustrates another example of a Marriage relation expressed as an object type. Although three attribute types emanate from the central object type, it actually represents a 2-place **Marriage** relation. The has husband and has wife attribute types each occupy one of the two places in a **Marriage**. The attribute types with "I" triangles, therefore, reflect the relation's immutable components. However, also emanating from the **Marriage** object-type node is a third attribute type, rated as, that has no "I" triangle. This attribute type is not an immutable component but a changeable attribute on the two-place **Marriage**.

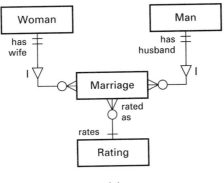

(a)

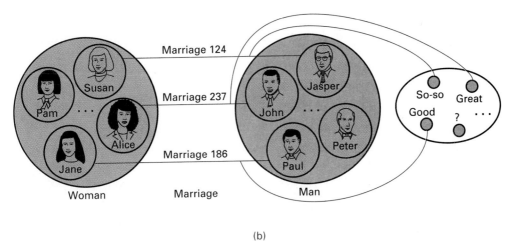

(b)

Figure 20.7   Mutable and immutable relations.

As illustrated in Fig. 20.7(b), each rated as association is an *attribute* of a tuple, not a component in it. In other words, **Marriage** 186 is the couple Jane and Paul, where the couple *as a whole* has an association with a **Rating** object named Good. Therefore, changing the rated as to Great does not in any way change the composition of **Marriage** 186.

As an attribute type of Marriage, rated as is itself a 2-place relation: Marriage Rating(rates, rated as). Its tuples can be written, Marriage Rating { (124, So-so), (186, Good), (237, Great), . . .}. However, if Jane and Paul's marriage becomes a great one, the tuple Marriage Rating(186, Good) will be terminated, and the tuple Marriage Rating(186, Great) will replace it.

Tuples and Change

As already mentioned, a tuple is an immutable composition of objects. For example in Fig. 20.7(b), the set of tuples could be expressed as, Marriage { (Jane, Paul), (Alice, John), (Susan, Jasper), . . .}. These tuples are the Marriage objects "186, 237, and 124, respectively. If one of the spouses leaves a marriage, its tuple is terminated, because the Marriage is terminated. If one person takes a new partner, the Marriage tuple does not change: a totally different Marriage tuple results. For instance, if Susan later marries Peter, the Marriage(Susan, Peter) tuple will be created, and the Marriage(Susan, Jasper) tuple terminated. Jasper cannot be exchanged for Peter in the same tuple, because Marriage 124 is composed on the basis of Marriage(Susan, Jasper), not Marriage(Susan, Peter). Each tuple defines a specific relationship between specific objects. Different related objects require different tuples; different tuples compose different objects.

Immutability also implies that if Susan remarried Jasper, a different couple would be created. The (Susan, Jasper) couple in Fig. 20.7, then, is not the same as the remarried (Susan, Jasper) couple. Even though the same two people are involved, the two couples represent different instances of Marriage. For example, the original Marriage is object 124, the new Marriage would be an entirely different object.

Because this apparent duplication can cause problems for system developers [2], a time stamp can be implied—explicitly or tacitly—for each relation. In this way, each tuple will have its own unique combination of objects. In the Marriage example, Susan and Jasper's first marriage can be represented by the three-tuple (6/6/76@12:37, Susan, Jasper); the second time, (9/9/88@10:21, Susan, Jasper). This relation could then be expressed as, Marriage (⬚, has wife, has husband), where ⬚ is the time-stamp place.

OTHER RELATIONAL ISSUES

Duplicate Function Names

Representing a relation as an object type requires depicting the relational places as immutable attribute types. These immutable attribute types, in turn, imply additional cardinalities and functions. For example, Fig. 20.8 contains six func-

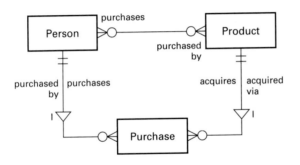

Figure 20.8   Schema with duplicate function names.

tions. Two are functions on the original lined relation. The other four developed, because the Purchase relation was represented as an object type.

Notice that each of the function names in the figure *appears* to be a duplicate. Regardless of the name, these functions are *not* identical. The purchased by function on the Person-Product relation maps instances of Product to instances of Person. The other purchased by function maps from Purchase objects to Person objects. These functions, therefore, define different mappings, because their *domains* are different. In one case, the domain is a subset of Product. In the other, the domain is the entire Purchase set. However, both functions have the same *range:* they map to the identical subset of Person. In this way, the label purchased by is appropriate in both situations—even though they are different functions. Additionally, the two functions labeled purchases are not the same function, yet they both share the same domain.

Using the same name for different functions can cause confusion. This can be remedied by qualifying the functions as they are needed. For example, the above two forms of purchased by may be expressed as, purchased by: Person(Product) and purchased by:Person (Purchase), or more simply, purchased by(Product) and purchased by(Purchase). Here, the domain object type qualifies the function.

Relational Nodes and Cardinality

When Purchase is defined only as a relation, some Purchase-related cardinalities cannot be expressed. For example, without an object type definition, the number of products in any *one* purchase is not known: what is known is that a customer can have purchased many items. In other words, a relation's cardinality constraints are the same as those on its object-type node. For example in Fig. 20.9(a), the zero, one, or many constraints on both ends of the relation line between Person and Product correspond to the same constraints on either side of the Purchase object type.

However, when converting from the line form to the object-type form of Purchase, the number of cardinality constraints doubles. While the cardinality

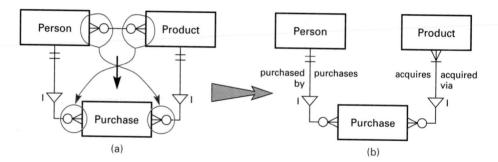

Figure 20.9   Schemas specifying single and multiple Products per Purchase.

on the Purchase object-type portion is known, the other end of the immutable
attribute types is unknown. In Fig. 20.9(a), the cardinality constraint is initially
assumed to be exactly one. While this assumption is often true and can be considered a default technique, it is not always true. In fact, in Fig. 20.9(b), the
acquires: Product cardinality is actually one or more. This means that a customer cannot only have many Purchases, but also that each Purchase acquires
many Products. This change in constraint does not contradict the Purchase rela-
tion-line cardinality in any way. As an object type, however, it does enhance the
meaning of a Purchase.

Relations within Relations

Typically, a relation is expressed as an object type to improve clarity and enhance
meaning. In Fig. 20.9(b), Purchase is expressed as an object type to clarify the
many-to-many relation between Purchase and Product. However, that relation,
in turn, may require more detail. For example, an analyst may wish to specify the
quantity purchased of *each* purchased product. This would require placing an
attribute type on the Purchase-Product relation, also known as the Purchase
Line Item. Figure 20.10 illustrates how this immutable relation can be expressed
as an object type.

Infinite Regress in Relational
Representation*

Representing a relation line as a node requires additional relation lines. In Fig.
20.10 for instance, the Purchase line was expressed as a node with two place
lines. Each of these place relations, in turn, could be represented by a node
accompanied by two more lines, and so on. If allowed, this process would continue forever—a condition known as *infinite regress*.

   The solution to the problem of infinite regress is simple. Each relation line
is automatically expressed by an object-type node and its place attribute types—

*Material in this subsection is optional.

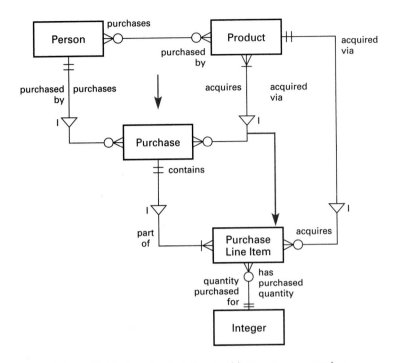

Figure 20.10   Levels of relation-to-object type representation.

unless the relation is immutable. A relation's underlying node and place attribute types, therefore, are not replaced by yet another node-place set. In this way, the underlying node-place structure is always defined to an immutable level without infinite ramifications. For example in Fig. 20.9(a), when the analyst specifies the **Purchase** relation between **Person** and **Product**, the **Purchase** object type and its place attribute types would automatically be implied—and no more. However, if the analyst specified the **Purchase** node and its 2-place line, the process would already have bottomed out because only immutable relations exist. Therefore, the **Purchase Line Item** node-place set would not be automatically generated. It would exist only if the analyst specified it.

To eliminate the problem of relational infinite regress, avoid *continually* making node-place substitutions. The replacement of a relation by an object type with place attribute types should only occur when necessary.

Relations and Relational Databases

Until now, this chapter has adopted the definition of relation as an immutable association of two or more objects. Formally, a 2-place, or binary, relation R on sets X and Y is defined as the set of all ordered couples (x,y)—where x is a member of X, and y is a member of Y—for which the statement x has a relation R to y

is true [3]. (The definition of an *n*-place relation is an expanded version of this two-place definition.) In this way, the 2-place relation Purchase Line Item in Fig. 20.10 can be expressed as

PURCHASE LINE ITEM (PART OF, ACQUIRES)

Or, more fully qualified, it could be expressed as

PURCHASE LINE ITEM (PART OF:PURCHASE, ACQUIRES:PRODUCT)

If a relational database implemented records containing only immutable fields, it would be very cumbersome to use. For example, the item quantity purchased attribute type could not be added to the relation, because quantities are typically allowed to change for a line item. Instead, an additional relation would have to be added, such as

LINE ITEM/QUANTITY PURCHASED (QUANTITY PURCHASED FOR, HAS PURCHASED QUANTITY)

In other words, the attribute type would have to be expressed as a relation immutably associating the object types Purchase Line Item and Integer.

A useful way of representing the object type of Purchase Line Item, then, would be one that expresses all of its attribute types—while preserving the knowledge of its immutability. For example

PURCHASE LINE ITEM (PART OF:PURCHASE, ACQUIRES:PRODUCT, ITEM QUANTITY PURCHASED)

Here, all of the items in the parentheses are attribute types of the object type Purchase Line Item. The two underlined attribute types are constrained to be immutable, the other is changeable. In this way, a relational database actually implements object types, while preserving their relational nature.

Primary Keys Versus Unique Identifiers

Underlining attribute types is customarily used by many relational database designers to indicate two things at the same time. The attribute is immutable and it serves as part of the relation's *primary key*. A primary key comprises a unique value by which a record is identified. However, it is possible for a relation to have more than one potential primary key. For example, Purchase Line Item could also be uniquely identified by a combination of purchase and line item sequence. In this situation, each line item sequence would simply serve as a sequence number for each line item. Furthermore, it would be unique only within a particular Purchase.

　　When two or more choices exist for a primary key, they are often called *candidate keys*. Choosing one of these candidate keys as the primary key is an implementation issue. However, specifying all of the unique identifiers for an object type is an analysis issue and can easily be accomplished by adding an appropriate notation to the object schema illustrated in Fig. 20.11.

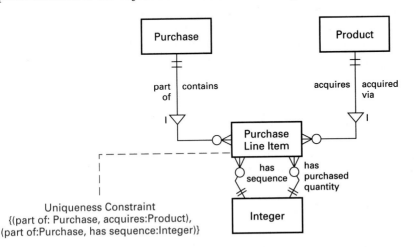

Figure 20.11　　Indicating unique identifiers for the Purchase Line Item object type.

Uniqueness Constraints

The *uniqueness constraint* in Fig. 20.11 can be more formally expressed as

```
UNIQUENESS CONSTRAINT (
OBJECT TYPE  =  { PURCHASE LINE ITEM },
FUNCTIONS    =  { (PART OF:PURCHASE, ACQUIRES:PRODUCT),
                  (PART OF:PURCHASE, HAS SEQUENCE:INTEGER) } )
```

　　This uniqueness constraint expression means that the object type Purchase Line Item is functionally dependent on (part of:Purchase, acquires:Product) and (part of:Purchase, has sequence:Integer) to provide a unique identification for all of its instances. Additionally, it means that if any of the values for these attributes change, the result is still constrained to be unique. While part of:Purchase and acquires:Product attributes cannot change because they are immutable, the sequence of a line item is changeable. Therefore, if a has sequence:Integer does change for a particular Purchase Line Item, the resulting (part of:Purchase, has sequence:Integer) combination is still constrained to identify the same object—and none other. Any changes that do not meet this constraint cannot occur.

The most common uniqueness constraint applies to all objects:

      UNIQUELY CONSTRAINT (
      OBJECT TYPE={OBJECT}, FUNCTIONS ={IDENTIFIED BY:STRING})

This expression means that every object has an identified by consisting of a string of characters that uniquely identifies each object. In object-oriented databases, the identified by is commonly implemented and referred to as the *OID* (object ID). In relational databases, it is the *surrogate key*.

SUMMARY

Object types allow us to distinguish between objects. *Relations* enhance these distinctions by relating objects to form complex or immutably composed objects.

A relation is an object type whose instances are immutable compositions of objects. Each immutable composition is known as a *tuple* in relational theory. For example, a tuple that is an instance of the relation Marriage (has wife, has husband) is any married couple. When a relationship between objects is changed, a different tuple results—because it *is* a different relationship. Formally, tuples are either created or terminated, never modified.

Each distinctive feature in a relation is clearly defined by a positional component or *place*. The number of places in a relation is dictated by the number of distinctive features it contains. When relations are expressed as object types, their place structure must be preserved. Graphically, this book employs attribute types with "I" triangles pointing to a rectangular object-type ellipse to express places.

When representing a relational configuration, the analyst may use the relational line construct, or an object-type node with immutable place attribute types and uniqueness constraint. Relational lines preserve simplicity. However, a node-place substitution may be beneficial in several circumstances:

- when *n*-place relational lines become cumbersome to read and understand
- when representing changeable attribute types on a relation
- when additional meaning should be added that a relational line cannot express

Understanding and representing object-type associations in terms of relations allow us to take advantage of the already well-established relational database. This experience is formally based on relational theory. Object schemas, then, provide the flexibility of representing both functions and relations on the same schema. In this way, we have greater expressiveness and formality.

REFERENCES

1. Berge, C., *Graphs and Hypergraphs,* North-Holland, Amsterdam, 1973.

2. Codd, E. F., *The Relational Model for Database Management: Version 2,* Addison-Wesley, Reading, MA, 1990.

3. Daintith, John and R. D. Nelson eds., *The Penguin Dictionary of Mathematics,* Penguin Books, London, 1989.

4. Kent, William, *Data and Reality,* North-Holland, Amsterdam, 1978.

21 SUPERTYPES AND SUBTYPES

Chapter 16 discussed mechanisms that enable us to grasp and manage complexity. One important mechanism is called *generalization* (and, tacitly, its opposite—*specialization*). Generalization focuses on those object types whose abstractions are more generic than other object types. It presents us with the option of understanding our world from a more general perspective or a more specific one. In other words, it allows us to specify super-object types and sub-object types—also called *supertypes* and *subtypes*.

This chapter provides a practical expression of generalization through the notions of supertypes and subtypes.

SETS THAT INCLUDE SETS

When expressing the fact that one object type is more general than another, the inclusion symbol "<" is typically used. For example, Woman < Person means that the object type Person is more general (or inclusive) than the object type Woman. In addition, the same notation means that the object type Woman is more specific than the object type Person.

The symbol "<" denotes generalization of object types—including their intensions *and* their extensions. When expressing generalization in terms of object-type intension, the definition of one object type is considered to be more generic than another. For instance, Woman < Person means that what is true of being a Person is more general than what is true of being a Woman. As an example, the intension of Woman could be stated as: the notion of Woman is true of any object that is an instance of a Mammal with human characteristics (i.e., a Person) and is an instance of Female. The intension of Person is more general, because being an instance of Female is not part of it. In other words, the abstraction of Person is true of more than the abstraction of Woman, because its intension requires fewer propositions to be true. In a matter of speaking, then, generalization involves subintensions and superintensions.

During systems analysis, however, generalization is frequently used more *in extension* than *in intension*. This is primarily because, as analysts, we tend to refer to sets that include other sets, instead of definitions that are less restrictive than other definitions. Additionally, dealing with sets of objects is often easier and more tangible when working with user experts. Therefore, this book will deal primarily with subsets and supersets, instead of subintensions and superintensions.

Figure 21.1 illustrates an example of considering Woman < Person in terms of sets (also written, has extension(Woman) ⊂ has extension(Person)). In this figure, two sets of objects are represented by the sets labeled Man and Woman. The same eight objects can also be recognized *more generally* as an extension of Person. In this way, the object type Person applies to a set containing Alice, Jasper, and all the other Man or Woman objects without discriminating between them.

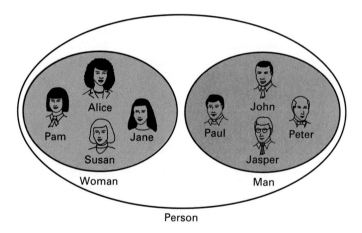

Figure 21.1   A set that includes sets.

Subsets and Supersets

The opposite of generalization is *specialization*. While generalization distinguishes an object type that is more general than another, specialization distinguishes an object type that is more specific and restricted than another. In Fig. 21.1 for example, the eight Person objects are specialized into two separate sets. These are the sets to which the object types Man and Woman apply. The sets Woman and Man, therefore, are *subsets* of Person. The set of Person is the *superset* of Woman and Man. This means that each Woman object is *also* a Person object. However, each Person object is not *necessarily* a Woman object.

Subsets delineate sets within a more general set; supersets delineate sets encompassing more specific sets.

> The term *subset* refers to a set whose members are all included in another set.
>
> The term *superset* refers to a set that includes all the members of one or more sets.

The number of subsets for any one set is limited only by the need to identify more specialized object types. For example, they can be

manager	programmer	key employee	new employee
retiree	good worker	probationer	paid employee

Subtypes and Supertypes

As mentioned earlier, object types are typically applied more in extension than intension. However, analyzing a system only in terms of sets ultimately results in an incomplete understanding of the system's concepts. To know an object type's intension is to know its definition. Application systems implement extensions with databases. The intensions, however, become embedded in coded rules that control the databases. Intelligent databases of the future, then, need both aspects.

In this book, when specializing or generalizing an object type's intension and extension, the terms *subtype* and *supertype* are used.

> The term *subtype* refers to an object type whose
>
> ● set members are all included in another set
> ● definition is more specialized than another
>
> The term *supertype* refers to an object type whose
>
> ● set includes all the members of one or more sets
> ● definition that is more general than another

Generalization Hierarchies

Generalization (and specialization) allow us to understand the same object within the context of a *hierarchy*. Such hierarchies are also called *directed acyclic graphs* (DAGs) or *lattices*. For example, we know that if a particular object is an instance of Man, the same object is an instance of Person. In other words, an object that is a **Man** object implies that the same object is also a **Person** object. Figure 21.2 adds to this by designating that any **Man** object is also a **Mammal**, **Animal**, and **Organism** object.

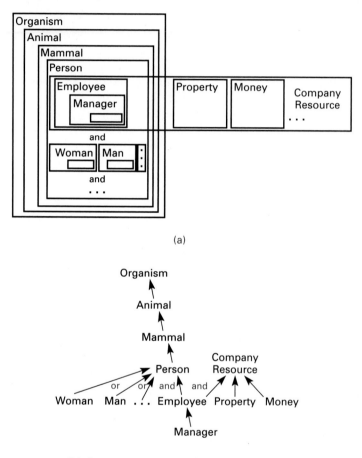

(a)

(b) A neater way to show the same hierarchy

Figure 21.2   A generalization hierarchy.

Figure 21.2 contains two ways of illustrating a generalization hierarchy. Both depict a type/subtype structure in an intuitive fashion—up to a point. A predicament arises when the analyst needs a clearer way of presenting all of the "and" and "or" conditions that arise between the subtypes of an object type. For instance, a **Person** may be subclassified as a **Man** *or* **Woman** *or* something else; *and* a **Person** may be subclassified as an **Employee** *or* something else; *and* so on. One approach to clarifying complex "and" and "or" situations is by using the *type* partition.

TYPE PARTITIONS   *Type partitions* divide a type into disjoint subtypes. For example, one way to partition **Person** is to divide it into the subtypes of **Woman**, **Man**, or other disjoint subtypes that occur along the same age/gender lines as **Girl** and **Boy**. A totally different partitioning of **Person** could be based on whether a **Person** is employed or not. In other words, every object type can be partitioned in more than one way.

Figure 21.3(a) illustrates how a set of **Person** objects can be partitioned into disjoint sets. The word *partition* is chosen, because it readily describes dividing a set into nonoverlapping subsets.

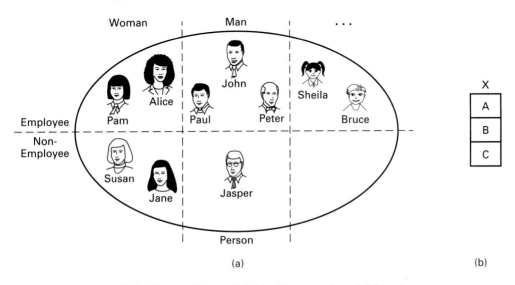

(a)   (b)

Figure 21.3   Type partitions subdivide object types into disjoint subtypes.

Figure 21.3(b) depicts another way of illustrating object-type partitioning without sets. In this figure, the object type **X** is shown as being partitioned into three disjoint subtypes: **A**, **B**, and **C**. In written form, this partition could also be expressed as **X = A + B + C**.

> A *type partition* is a division (or partitioning) of an object type into disjoint subtypes.

Multiple Partitions

As stated above, an object type can be partitioned in more than one way. Sometimes these type partitions (or just *partitions*) have readily identifiable themes. In Fig. 21.4, a **Person** has many such partitions based on employment,

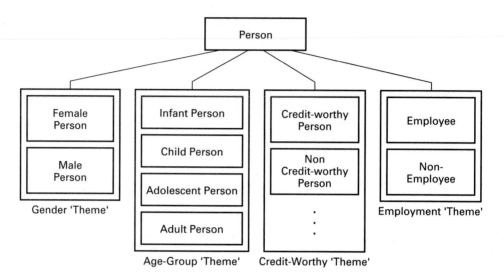

Figure 21.4   Some partitions of Person.

gender, age group, credit-worthiness, and so on. A **Person** object will be involved in each of its partition categories. For instance, a **Person** object can be a **Female Person**, an **Adult Person**, a **Credit-Worthy Person**, *and* an **Employee** object. Multiple partitions, then, allow us to pick one from each column when describing an object. They are the inclusive, overlapping partitions that an object type offers.

However, *within* a partition, the subtypes *must* be exclusive and nonoverlapping. For example, a **Person** can only be an instance of one of the following subtypes: an **Infant Person**, a **Child Person**, an **Adolescent Person**, *or* an **Adult Person**. In other words, while a **Person** can be both a **Female Person** and a **Child Person**, it cannot be both a **Female Person** and a **Male Person**.

Incorrect Partitions

An example of an incorrect partition is represented in Fig. 21.5(a). It indicates that an **Employee** can be either a **Salesperson**, a **Manager**, or a number of other subtypes. If the employee can be both a salesperson and a manager, this representation is incorrect. If the characteristics of **Salesperson** and **Manager** are not disjoint, the example in Fig. 21.5(b) might serve your purpose.

The partition defines those nonoverlapping subtypes appropriate for a particular partitioning criterion. This is called an *exclusive "or" statement.* It means that within a partition you have the choice of one subset or another—but never more than one. The ability to join together several different ideas is accomplished by employing multiple partitions. Each partition, then, represents an "and" condition. In this way, an **Employee** object can be a **Manager** *and* an **Engineer**, yet

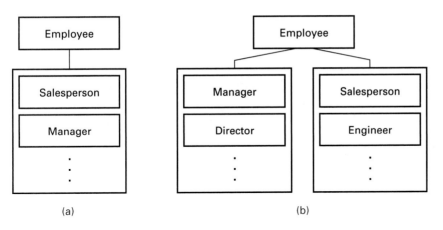

Figure 21.5 Nondisjoint subtypes require different partitions.

cannot be both a **Manager** *and* a **Director**. This technique is called a *conjunctive normal form* in mathematics. For us, it provides a neat and orderly way of untangling a potentially incomprehensible mess of "ands" and "ors" among subsets. When this knowledge is automated, the technique furnishes a well-defined statement of meaning.

COMPLETE VERSUS INCOMPLETE PARTITIONS

Each partition applies to all instances of an object type—and an object-type's instances are subject to all of its partitions. Does this mean that you must anticipate every conceivable subtype required for a particular object type? This would be difficult, even on one very large piece of paper. Such an effort is not only unreasonable but in most cases not feasible. However, we can partition those subtype choices that are useful. These subtypes augment the growing pool of expert knowledge represented in the knowledge base. When identifying type partitions, we need techniques that can completely—as well as incompletely—specify its subtypes.

Complete Partitions

A *complete* partition is applied when all of the subtypes are known for a particular partition. Complete partitions are useful when a full subtype listing is needed by the analyst. They are particularly beneficial when fixing a partition's contents to consist of a certain list of subtypes and only those subtypes.

> A *complete partition* is a partition that contains a full list of subtypes of a specific subtype.

Figure 21.6(a) illustrates one way to represent complete partitions. This diagram reads: For any one instance of Object Type X, it must be either an instance of Object Type 1, or Object Type 2, . . . , or Object Type *n*. It could also indicate: Object Type 1, Object Type 2, . . . , and Object Type *n* are all of the possible [disjoint] subtypes of Object Type X for this particular partition.

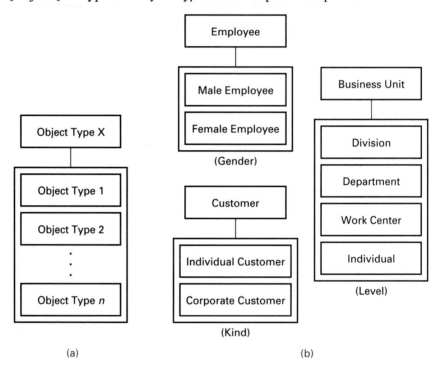

(a) (b)

Figure 21.6 Complete partition representation format and examples.

Sometimes, analysts confuse subtypes with instances of an object type. In this confusion, an analyst might assume that Division, Department, Work Center, and Individual in Fig. 21.6(b) are instances of Business Unit. Partitions do not represent *instances* of its object type; they represent *subtypes*. Therefore, Division is not an instance of Business Unit, it is a *kind* of Business Unit. An instance of an actual Business Unit's Division might be Business Unit #42-The IT Division. When documenting a subtype, always ask if it is a subtype or an instance of the object type.

Incomplete Partitions

Another representation of partitions is the incomplete partition. Incomplete partitions are very useful for those situations where a complete list of subtypes is not appropriate.

> An *incomplete partition* is a partition that contains a partial list of its subtypes.

One way of representing incomplete partitions is illustrated in Fig. 21.7(a). This diagram reads: For any one instance of Object Type X, it must be either an instance of Object Type 1, or Object Type 2, . . . , or Object Type *n* or *something else*. It could also indicate: Object Type 1, Object Type 2, . . . , and Object Type *n* are *some* of the possible [disjoint] subtypes of Object Type X for this particular partition.

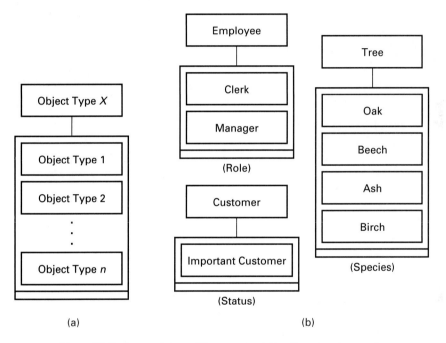

Figure 21.7   Incomplete partition representation format and examples.

In the example, a more specialized form of Customer might be an Important Customer—or something else not specified. Why not specify *all* the possible subtypes? What are the appropriate subtypes that belong here? There are probably a few more such as a Somewhat Important Customer or a Totally Unimportant Customer. We cannot think of everything at once, *and* we do not want to produce a large, unmanageable diagram. The answer lies in how we obtain expert knowledge. In working with users, we should analyze the knowledge they hold of their particular function and expertise to learn what object types have proven effective. The incomplete partition is useful for representing *only* what is necessary and sufficient for a user's realm.

Multiple Superclassification

As discussed earlier, generalization hierarchies are more than tree structures, because an object type may have not only multiple subtypes, but multiple supertypes as well. Figure 21.8(a) depicts two sets, **Employee** and **Vital Resource**, and within each set are various subsets. In particular, **Executive**, **Security Member**, and a portion of **Manager** are contained by *both* sets. Here, **Executives** are not only a subset of **Employee** but are also a subset of **Vital Resource**.

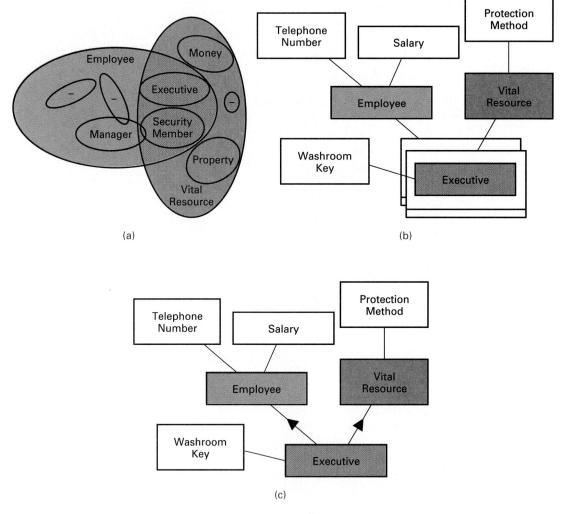

Figure 21.8 Multiple supertypes representing common subtypes.

By translating this sharing of a set by two supersets, Fig. 21.8(b) represents the Executive object type in two different partitions. In doing so, it is easy to see how the properties of multiple object types apply to all their common subtypes as well. For instance, in addition to its own properties, attribute types involving Telephone Number, Salary, *and* Protection Method can apply to every Executive object also. Therefore, these attribute types do not need to be restated for Executive, because they are implied. In this way, generalization hierarchies eliminate the need to specify redundant conceptual attribute types. Instead, they can be conceptually reused via hierarchical implication.

An alternative supertype representation is depicted in Fig. 21.8(c). The two lines with large filled arrows are equivalent to the two partitions shown in Fig. 21.8(b). In the absence of complicated "and" and "or" conditions, the filled-arrowed line provides a simpler alternative to partitions. Each expresses a sub-type relation. Since each is a one-object-type partition, the filled-arrowed lines are not required to be disjoint.

LEVELS OF PARTITIONING

Generalization hierarchies are discussed in the previous sections. Figure 21.2 illustrates an example of a multilevel subset scheme. Now that the means for a more formal representation has been developed, the figure can be reexpressed as Fig. 21.9 below.

The ability to define multiple partitions for a set provides *width* to our generalization/specialization ability. The hierarchy enables *depth*. In this way, we can express high-level generalities and detailed specializations—plus everything in between. However, these various levels are not (and typically should not be) defined all at once. For example, a biologist might fill in the top level, a zoologist the next level, and so forth.

Figure 21.10 presents two very different points of view. The object types involved are similar to those of a chairperson-of-the-board's point of view and those of a payroll clerk's. Even though the two are worlds apart, the added parti-tions in Fig. 21.10 exhibit the way in which these two worlds are bridged. This subtype bridge permits us to express very detail-level generalities without speci-fying every associated supertype, and vice versa.

Sharpening Meaning

Adding levels of partitions also sharpens meaning. In Fig. 21.11, an association is specified between Person and Employer. However, if the association is more accurately expressed between Employee and Employer, then a Person-related partition could be introduced.

This addition accomplishes two important things. First, it improves our understanding of the association's underlying meaning, because we can actually

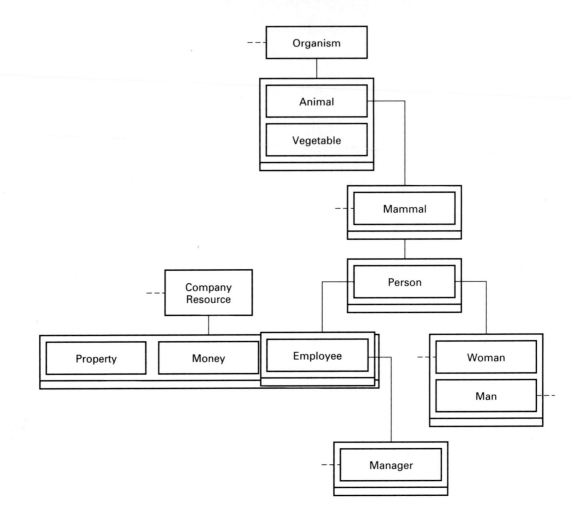

Figure 21.9   Generalization hierarchy using partitions.

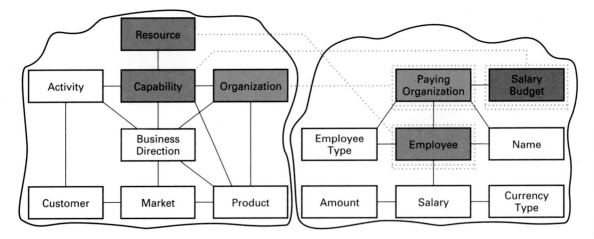

Figure 21.10   Generalization used between different points of view.

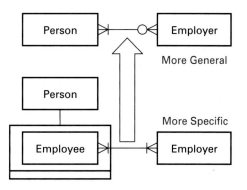

Figure 21.11   Adding a subtyped level can sharpen meaning.

see the knowledge being communicated. Second, we reduce the ambiguity of an *optional* constraint on the association. Now, we know more clearly how the objects of different types *must* relate. By adding this one, we can know more about association meaning, as well as clarify our knowledge of its cardinality constraints.

Transformations, such as those in Fig. 21.11, improve our ability to understand and communicate. However, the change in the relationship between **Person** and **Employer** is very important. Some methods call this process of change *strengthening* [1], *restricting* [2], or *sharpening*. It can also be called *relation subtypes.*

RELATION   Subtypes can be thought of as sets of objects within
SUBTYPES   larger sets. Since relations also have sets of objects—
called tuples—relations can be subtyped, as well.

Figure 21.12(a) exhibits a set of tuples between two object types: **Employee** and **Skill**. All of the tuples displayed are instances of a relation called

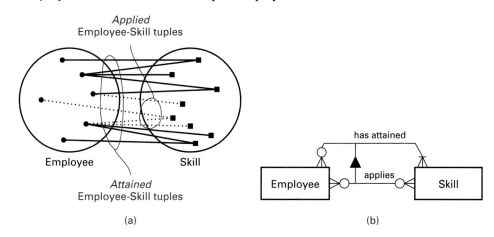

Figure 21.12   Relational subtypes.

Attained Employee Skill. However, only *some* of these Attained Employee Skills are actually being applied on the job. This subset can be called Applied Employee Skill. Since every Applied Employee Skill tuple is also an Attained Employee Skill tuple, the Applied Employee Skill relation is a subtype of Attained Employee Skill. Figure 21.12(b) depicts this generalization as an object schema.

Specialization by Subset

Two situations can result in specialized relations. Limiting the tuples involved in a relation is one. For example, Fig. 21.13 indicates that Messages are sent from one Person to one or more other Persons. The diagram is further specialized to indicate that, while anybody can send an Officer Message, only Officer(s) may receive them. In this case, the sent to:Person remains the same and, therefore, applies to the subtypes as well. However, the received by: Person tuples have been subtyped. The subtyped form, received by: Officer, relates only to Officer objects. Here, the original set of associations has been restricted to those that exist between Officer Message and Officer objects.

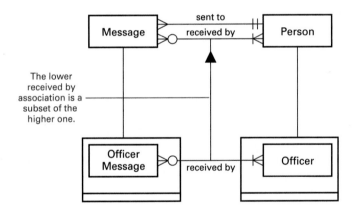

Figure 21.13   Relation subsets define subsets of associations.

Specialization by Cardinality Constraint

Another situation leading to relation subtypes is by limiting the cardinality constraint. For example, Fig. 21.14(a) contains an example of cardinality limitation. The association from Message and Person normally maps to one or more received by: Person objects. However, in the case of sending a Private Message, the cardinality constraint is reduced to permit only one recipient. A Private Message received by: Person, then, is a subtype of a Message Distribution received by: Person based on cardinality constraints. Limiting a cardinality constraint means that the mapping subset must be less than or equal to the maximum cardinality, and greater than or equal to the minimum cardinality.

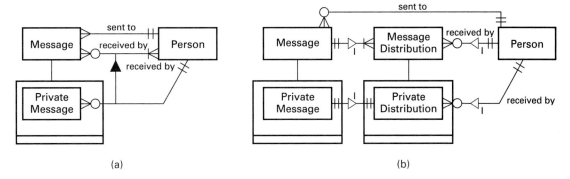

Figure 21.14   Relation subtypes define further limits on cardinality constraints.

The example in Fig. 21.14(b) expresses the same generalization as Fig. 21.14(a) in a different form. Here, the same relation is expressed as a **Message Distribution** object type, and then subtyped as a **Private Distribution** object type. In other words, instead of expressing the subtype between two relation lines, it is expressed between two object-type nodes. The analyst can choose which expression provides the greatest clarity.

Relation subtypes, then, can result from a subset of related objects, from cardinality limitations, or from a combination of both. The principle to remember is that whenever an original set of associations is reduced—not changed—its relation has been subtyped.

SUMMARY

Generalization focuses on those object types whose abstractions are more generic than other object types. It presents us with the option of understanding our world from a more general perspective, or a more specific perspective. It enables us to choose our own emphasis for understanding the world and allows us to think of the forest as well as the trees.

Generalization applies to both an object type's intensions and extensions. When expressing generalization in terms of object-type intension, the definition of one object type is considered to be more generic than another. When expressing generalization in terms of object-type extension, the set of one object type includes the set of another.

Generalization Provides Clarification

Generalization aids us in two major ways. First, it clarifies our representation of object types. For example, Fig. 21.15(a) indicates that a **Person** reports to only one other **Person**. While this is not an error, *per se,* Fig. 21.15(b) shows a clearer and more accurate statement. By allowing us to divide a set into disjoint subtypes, *partitions* are an important tool that can clarify vague situations.

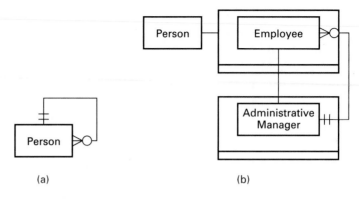

Figure 21.15   Vagueness clarified by specialization.

Figure 21.15(b) contains two *incomplete partitions*. They are called this because they contain only a partial list of object types. A *complete partition,* however, is a partition that contains the full list.

Generalization Provides a Fundamental Object-type Structure

The second way generalization aids us is by providing a conceptual framework. For example, Fig. 21.16(a) contains five unrelated, yet somehow similar, object types. Without generalization, they remain islands of knowledge. Figure 21.16(b) introduces a higher level of meaning and commonality among the object types.

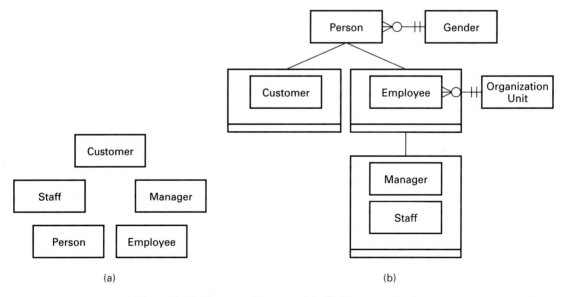

Figure 21.16   Separate object types clarified by generalization.

Previously disparate knowledge converges through the clarification offered by generalization.

REFERENCES

1. Borgida, Alexander T., "Generalization/Specialization as a Basis for Software Specification," *On Conceptual Modelling,* Michael L. Brodie *et al.* eds., Springer-Verlag, New York, 1984, pp. 87–1121.

2. Brachman, Ronald L. and James G. Schmolze, "An Overview of the KL-ONE Knowledge Representation System," *Cognitive Science,* 9:2, 1985, pp. 171–212.

PART **IV** **FUNDAMENTALS
OF OBJECT BEHAVIOR ANALYSIS**

22 ASPECTS OF BEHAVIOR

Part III of this book presented fundamentals of object schemas. Object schemas represent *structure* knowledge, because they focus on static conceptual configurations that are applied to objects. On the other hand, *behavior* knowledge describes how *structure* applies to objects over time. This chapter presents the various components of object-oriented behavior.

OBJECT STRUCTURE AND BEHAVIOR

Object orientation is often described in terms of structure and behavior as illustrated in Fig. 22.1(a). The word structure is a visual, spatial metaphor that refers to a static vision of how objects are laid out in space [5]. Structure can specify various object configurations, such as employees, documents, and engineering designs. In contrast, behavior refers to the way objects

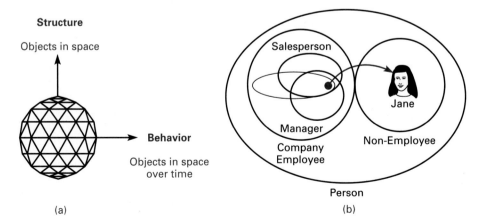

Figure 22.1 Objects have both a structural and behavioral aspect.

change over time within their defined structures. Behavioral aspects include events, operations, and triggers. For instance, behavior can specify how to hire employees, connect circuits, or add diagrams to a document.

In short, the structural aspect describes the way we recognize objects and their associations. The behavioral aspect describes how this recognition changes over time. If the analyst's job involves describing an unchanging world, the task would be limited to producing specifications that are structural in nature. For instance, if an application's data are already defined and in place before processes like a query program or file conversion occur, a structural description would probably suffice. However, if data that affect the application's outcome continue to arrive and change during processing, a behavioral specification would be necessary. The world most analysts seek to understand is not static; it changes over time.

Changes Over Time

For an object, what changes over time are the object types that apply to it. The expression, *an object changes* actually means that the collection of object types that is true for an object changes. This collection of object types defines the object's state.

An *object state* (or a *state*) is the collection of all object types that apply to an object.*

Figure 22.1(b) depicts a change in state for the object Jane. When Jane retired from the managing salesperson position at her company, she was reclassified from a Company Employee to a Non-Employee. In other words, while remaining a Person and becoming a Non-Employee, her state no longer includes the object types of Salesperson, Manager, and Company Employee.

Sequences of State Changes Over Time

System process, then, can be described in terms of object behavior—as an orderly sequence of state changes over time. As depicted in Fig. 22.2, an object's behavior is played out over time as a network of cause-and-effect state changes. If this were an invocation of order processing, it would begin with a Requested Order object. With this object, a Fill Order operation would be invoked resulting in the object being further classified as a Filled Order. This would lead to another state change where the object would be classified as a Shipped Order. It would continue until the order was considered complete and the object terminated. The state change of one object can also lead to a state change in a different object. For instance, once an object's state is changed to Shipped Order, the creation of an

---

*Often state is defined as the set of attributes for an object. Both definitions can be used interchangeably with the same effect. See Appendix E for a more detailed discussion.

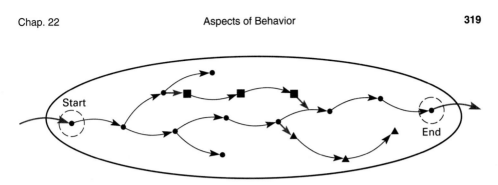

Figure 22.2   Behavior: object state changes over time.

Invoice object might be required. The appearance of an Invoice object would then be followed by a state change that classified the new Invoice object as a Sent Invoice.

Object as Process, Process as Object

In principle, no difference exists between objects and processes. Each running process is an object in its own right. For example, the process of reading this paragraph is an instance of Reading, or a human-life process can be a Patient in a health clinic. In contrast, each object can be considered a process that consists of all the object's state changes—from creation to termination. For example, instances of Shipment, Payment, Performance, or Order are active and have complex processing aspects. Instances of Rock are also processes, albeit, less obviously dynamic ones. Persons are dramatic processes—and usually unstable objects. Contract or Financial Security objects are intangible and highly abstract processes.

Combined Representation

Changing the state of an object means changing the collection of object types that apply to that object. Therefore, to change an object's state, the applicable object types must be identified. Object *behavior,* therefore, is defined by its state-changing process—with respect to its *structure.*

One natural way to represent this is by augmenting an object schema, so that structure and behavior can be represented on one schema. Figure 22.3 depicts an object schema, annotated with state changes, for a person getting up in the morning. Once a Person object is classified as an Ambulatory Person, a process to wash the object is triggered. The result of this process is another change in state. The object is, now, additionally classified as a Washed Person. If the person is a female, the object is also a Washed Female Person object (a result of being both a Washed Person and a Female Person). When an object becomes a Washed Female Person, the process of getting dressed is triggered—resulting in a Dressed Person. If the object is a Washed Male Person, the object must first be in a Shaved Person state before the object can be a Dressed Person.

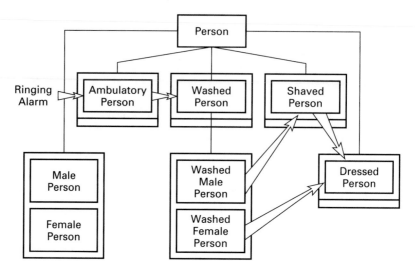

Figure 22.3   A simple example of structure and behavior on the same diagram.

FINITE-STATE MACHINES

One popular technique adopted for OO specification is the finite-state machine. A *finite-state machine* (FSM) is a hypothetical machine that can exist in only one of a finite number of states at any given moment. As Fig. 22.4(a) depicts, each machine—in response to a stimulus from the external environment— changes its state and produces output. The reason for the popularity of FSMs in OO analysis is that its machine metaphor is easily interpreted to include transitions of object state. To accomplish this, each machine describes the behavior of a single set of objects. In short, each machine is a limited context that specifies how an object should behave. For example, the FSM notation in Fig. 22.4(b) (called a state transition diagram or STD) specifies that a Clock object must be in either an Enabled Clock Alarm or a Disabled Clock Alarm state. External stimuli are responsible for triggering the state change. In turn, responses are returned to the invoking external environment.

FSM States

Each machine proceeds in clearly discrete steps from one of a finite number of configurations, or states, to another [10]. As defined earlier, a *state* is the collection of *all* object types that apply to an object. However, having an FSM reflect a complete collection is usually too unwieldy. Accommodating all object types that apply to an object in any given moment would require identifying all possible object-type combinations. This might involve as many as 2^n discrete states, where "n" is the number of possible object types. This means that if a dozen object types applied to an object at any one time, the machine could require as

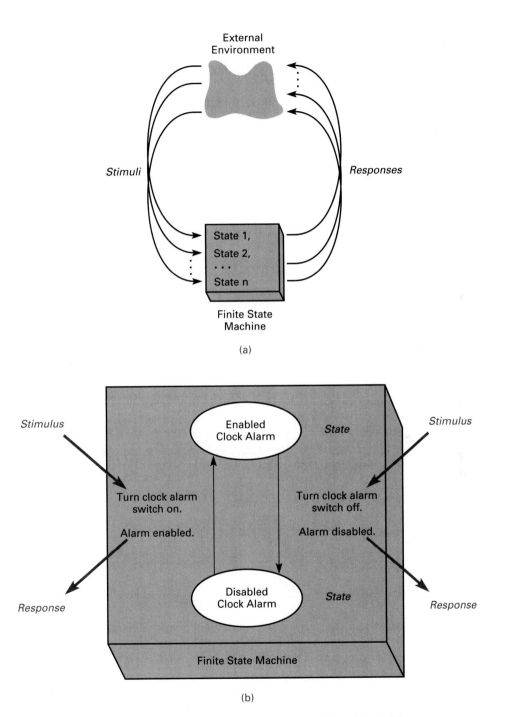

External
Environment

Stimuli

Responses

State 1,

State 2,

...

State n

Finite State
Machine

(a)

Stimulus

Enabled
Clock Alarm

State

Stimulus

Turn clock alarm
switch on.

Turn clock alarm
switch off.

Alarm enabled.

Alarm disabled.

Response

Disabled
Clock Alarm

State

Response

Finite State Machine

(b)

Figure 22.4 A finite-state machine from the outside and the inside.

many as 4096 possible states—each representing a different combination of object types. Therefore, to reduce the complexity of a machine specification, each *machine state* is usually limited to include a *subset* of the object-type collection that can apply to an object. In Fig. 22.4(b), the FSM specifies that the set of all possible states of an object is either an Enabled Clock Alarm or a Disabled Clock Alarm state. However, in a different FSM, the same object can be in a Clock Alarm that Beeps, a Clock Alarm that Buzzes, or a Clock Alarm that Bongs state; in another, a Loud Clock Alarm, or a Soft Clock Alarm; and so on. When all the FSMs are considered together, the *complete* state of the object can be determined.

FSM Stimuli

Each finite-state machine has a finite set of stimuli or *input types* that can reach it and trigger a state change. For example in Fig. 22.4(b), "turn clock alarm switch on" is a stimulus to change the state of a Disabled Clock Alarm object to an Enabled Clock Alarm object. On the other hand, "turn clock alarm switch off" triggers a change from Enabled Clock Alarm to Disabled Clock Alarm.

An FSM state change is a function of its current state and a given stimulus. In other words, a specific state and input type describe the conditions that cause one state to change to another. For example, the state transition diagram illustrated in Fig. 22.5 indicates that I_3 is a stimulus for one of two possible state changes. If the FSM is in the state, $State_2$, a machine "action" changes the state to $State_3$. If the FSM is in $State_3$, the change is to $State_4$. In this way, both the stimulus and current state must be known before any state change, or transition, occurs.

Adaptations of FSMs suggest that elaborate condition-checking can take place before a state-changing action is invoked. In other words, before a stimulus invokes its action, a condition is evaluated that "guards" the transition from

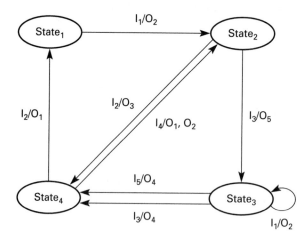

Figure 22.5   State changes depend on both the trigger and prestate.

occuring. If the control condition is true when the stimulus occurs, the state-changing action is invoked [4].

FSM Responses

In addition to a finite set of stimuli and possible states, each FSM has a finite set of responses or *output types* that can be produced. When a machine action is completed successfully, two things occur: a change of object state and the generation of one or more responses. The state change is internal to the machine; the response or output goes to the external environment. For instance in Fig. 22.5, if the machine is in $State_4$, the action triggered by I_4 results in a transition to $State_2$, and the two responses, O_1 and O_2, ensue. Notice also that a particular output type can be a result of more than one kind of transition. For instance, while O_2 is a response by the FSM to stimulus I_4 while in $State_4$, it is also a response to I_1 while in $State_1$. An FSM response, then, is also a function of its current state and a given stimulus.

FSM Notations

Several notations are commonly used to define finite-state machines. Figure 22.6 illustrates two representations of state-transition diagrams for seminar registration. Other adaptations of finite-state machine notations can be found in Martin [8], Davis [2], and Rumbaugh [11].

FSM Foundation Components

As stated earlier, finite-state machines are a way of clearly describing discrete changes of state. Figure 22.7 depicts the primary components of the finite-state machine and its interface with the external environment. Its primary components are:

1. An *event* in the external environment stimulates or *triggers* an *operation* within a machine.

2. Each *operation* is invoked to change the state of exactly one object.

3. Furthermore, each operation is specified in terms of those object types that must apply to an object before the operation, and those that apply after. These *prestates* and *poststates* are guaranteed by each operation.

4. Within each FSM, a specific operation is selected on the basis of trigger and state preconditions.

5. Before the operation is invoked, some adaptations of FSMs require that a *control condition* be evaluated. Only if the condition is true will the operation actually be invoked.

6. When the *invoked operation* is successfully completed (i.e., there is a state change), an *event* occurs.

7. The occurrence of an event is an indication that a response should be sent to the external environment. Since the external environment acts on the machine's results (other-

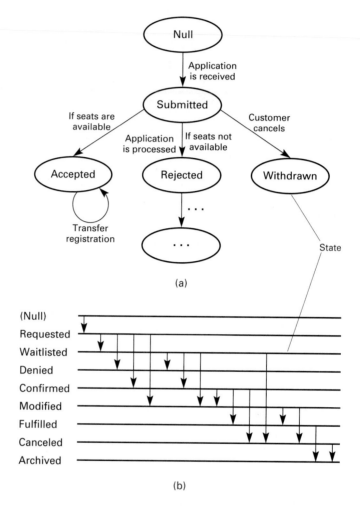

Figure 22.6   Two examples of state-transition diagrams for seminar registration.

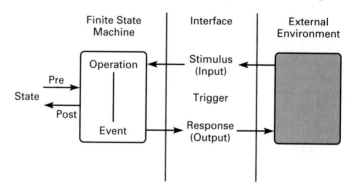

Figure 22.7   Primary components of the finite-state machine.

wise the machine has no purpose), this response is really a *trigger* for yet another machine operation, albeit external. The external environment, then, is just another machine. Its specification, though, is unknown to us. It could be a person, some software, or an automated machine—just as the FSM being specified.

Four important notions of behavior in finite-state machines, then, can be defined.

An *invoked operation** is a processing unit actively engaged in changing the state of an object.

An *event* is the successful completion of an invoked operation—a noteworthy change in state.

A *trigger* links cause and effect. It responds to events and determines the objects necessary as arguments for the operation it invokes.

A *control-condition evaluation* ensures that certain conditions are true. If true, the process that follows is begun.

Furthermore, *operations, event types, trigger rules,* and *control conditions* are object types whose instances are invoked operations, events, triggers, and control-condition evaluations, respectively. *Event prestate* and *event poststate* will be discussed in the next chapter.

EVENT SCHEMAS

As stated above, FSMs are a fundamentally useful approach to describing object behavior. In order to apply this approach when analyzing large and complex systems, additional features are useful:

- Operation scripting. One useful way of expressing how an object's state changes over time is with a step-by-step script. This approach aids experts who are accustomed to stating their problems in a "do this, then do this, then this" manner. The script, then, would entail an orderly sequence of finite-state machines as a method for carrying out a given operation.

- Specification *leveling.* It should be possible to compose or decompose each script using levels of process specification. In this way, analysis can proceed from high levels of generality to more detailed ones—and vice versa—depending on need and available knowledge.

- Operation reusability. In order for a process to be reusable, it must be defined as a processing unit. The kind of inputs and outputs it requires must also be defined. In this form, the same operation can be included within any number of

---

*Technically, an operation is any process that can be requested as a unit and performed as a single step in a series of steps. Operations may or may not have state changes, or side effects. FSMs, however, only involve those operations that cause changes in state. For brevity, these state-change operations will always be referred to as operations in an FSM context.

operation scripts. In other words, each operation is an object type whose instances are its various invocations.

- Processing concurrency. In the real world, processes occur simultaneously. Events can trigger multiple, parallel operations. Parallel operations can simultaneously result in different state changes. Concurrently produced results may require synchronization before invoking further operations. A scripting technique that specifies behavior should be able to express all of these situations.

- Manual and automated mechanisms as processes. An FSM operation can be implemented by a person or on an automated mechanism. Analysis is responsible for identifying which operations are being performed—not the way in which they are being implemented. Therefore, operations by people or by automated mechanisms should not be treated as *external* to a process specification unless they are truly external to the process as a whole. In other words, the jobs performed by people and by automated mechanisms are *part of* a larger process, and the behavior specification technique should not exclude them.

Figure 22.8 is an example of a representation method that can support all of the above requirements. (The example will be discussed in more detail later in this chapter.)

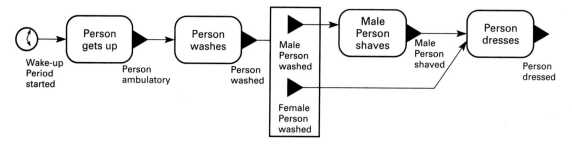

Figure 22.8   Specification for Getting up in the morning.

Fundamental Constructs of OO Processing Revisited

Fundamentally, every OO process includes events, triggers, control-condition evaluations, and invoked operations. Events, triggers, control-condition evaluations, and invoked operations are instances of the **Event Type**, **Trigger Rule**, **Control Condition**, and **Operation**, respectively. Examples of these four object types are illustrated in Fig. 22.9 using an adaptation of the finite-state machine called an *event schema*.

Each time the operation called **Ship Order** is invoked, it is expected to result in an **Order shipped** event. When this event occurs, a trigger invokes the **Close Order** operation. However, before the actual invocation of the operation, its control condition is checked. In this example, the control-condition evaluation ensures that a particular order has been both shipped to and paid for by the cus-

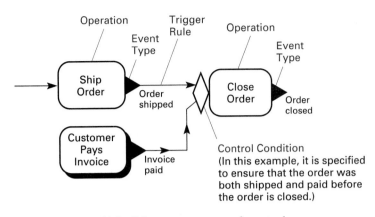

Figure 22.9   Primary components of event schemas.

tomer. Only then can the **Close Order** operation be executed. If no control condition is expressed for the **Close Order** operation, the operation would be executed
straightaway when triggered by *any* event.

The **Customer pays Invoice** operation symbol is shadowed to indicate that
the operation is external to the figure's processing specification. In other words,
the way in which a customer pays (or doesn't pay) a bill is *outside* the scope of
the specification. The operation appears here to indicate that its **Invoice paid**
event is a stimulus for operations *within* the processing scope.

The extension of the event type, **Order shipped**, is the set of all the events
in which a particular order was shipped. The order you shipped at 9:23 this morning would be one such event; the one at 11:21 would be another. The operation
Ship Order is the set of all instances of order shipping processes. The invoked
operation that resulted in the 9:23 A.M. shipment is one such instance; the one
that resulted in the 11:21 order shipment is another. In this way, each event and
invoked operation is an object in its own right.

Event Schema and Object Schema
Connection

While the event schema represents object behavior, it should not be viewed as a
representation constructed separately from object schemas, and then fitted together. Instead, they offer a seamless unification. Figure 22.10 illustrates how event
schemas represent the state changes that occur within the structure of object
schemas. For example, when an instance of **Ambulatory Person** occurs in the
object schema, a state change to **Washed Person** should occur. This same state
change is encircled in the event schema below and is labeled **Person washed**. In
this way, event schema components do not *fit with* object schemas—they are a
different representation of the same thing. The large grey arrow indicating the
state change from **Washed Male Person** to **Shaved Person** *is* the triggered
operation resulting in a **Male Person shaved** event—only the style and order of

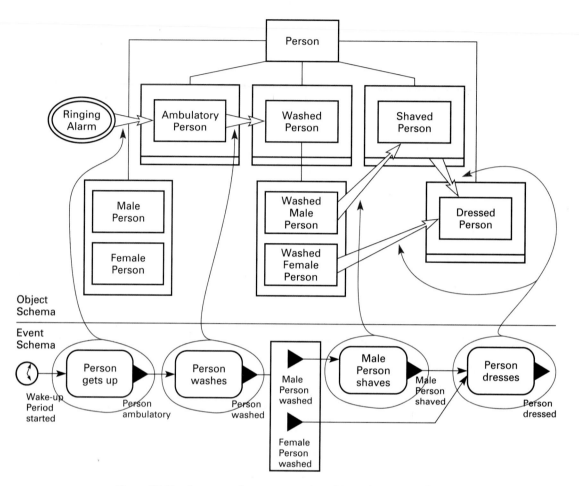

Figure 22.10   An event schema representing object schema state changes.

presentation is different. The two schemas do not represent a jigsaw puzzle, but rather one piece of cloth.

Event schemas represent the behavioral aspects of an object. They specify process by expressing procedural cause and effect in terms of the object schema's structural specification. A formal, step-by-step method for constructing event schemas is presented in Chapter 24.

Leveling Behavior Specification

An important feature of any behavior-specification method must be that it supports a structured *leveling* of complex processes. At the top of Fig. 22.11(a), an operation is depicted with its intended net state change. This change can be expressed in terms of a script that achieves the intended event. Operations at this

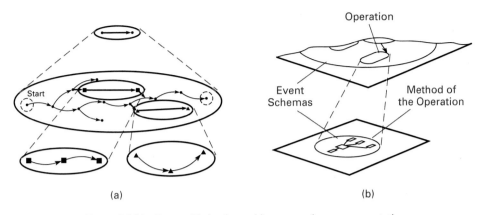

Figure 22.11   Layered behavior and its event schema representation.

level can, in turn, be expressed as scripts at subsequent levels. In OO, these scripts are called methods.

> A *method* is a script of how an operation will be carried out.

In this way, behavioral specifications can be constructed by leveling down or leveling up. For example, Fig. 22.11(b) illustrates an operation in one event schema, whose method can be expressed as another event schema in a layered structure "below" the operation.

Another important feature of methods is that each will affect multiple state changes via its own operations (where each operation, in turn, can have its own methods). For example, the operation at the top of Fig. 22.11(b) results in one state change—its event. However, in order to achieve this state change, other state changes are required. The operation's method, depicted at the bottom of Fig. 22.11(b), is the script for these required state changes.

Methods are Isolated from Cause-and-Effect Considerations

In order for an operation to be reusable, its method must be isolated from cause-and-effect considerations. First, this means that every operation must be *completely* unaware of what events might have triggered it. For example, in Fig. 22.12 the operation resulting in a **Person washed** event can be invoked under many different processing applications: whether getting washed is the first thing done after getting up in the morning, something performed soon after falling in the mud, or something done because mother says so. In each case, the same operation carries out the same person-washing method, and yet, the cause is completely unknown.

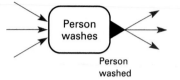

Person
washed

Figure 22.12   Operations have no knowledge of cause and effect.

The second implication of cause-and-effect isolation is that every operation must be *completely* unaware of what operations will be triggered by its completion event. In other words, each operation must carry out its method without any influence from what follows. In the example above, this means that a **Person** can be washed without any knowledge of what its completion event triggers. Only the processing application (i.e., the method to which the operation is a part) defines the cause and effect—not the operation itself.

Being isolated from cause-and-effect considerations does not mean that operations are totally independent of triggers. To the contrary, trigger rules are the mechanism that supplies an operation with those objects serving as arguments. However, this *isolation* does mean that trigger rules can be added or removed without affecting the method of operation in any way. For example, an operation that washes people *does* require a **Person** object as an argument when triggered. Yet, the cause and effect of the operation's triggering is completely unknown to its method. Thus, each operation is a processing unit reusable by any event schema that requires it. Operation reusability is a key factor in OO specification and implementation.

SUMMARY

Object orientation is often described in terms of structure and behavior. The word *structure* is a visual, spatial metaphor that refers to a static vision of how objects are laid out in space. *Behavior,* in contrast, refers to the way object states change over time within a defined *structure.* An *object state* (or *state*) is the collection of all object types that apply to an object.

Finite-state machines (FSMs) offer a useful way of describing discrete state changes. The primary components of FSM specification include *event types, trigger rules, control conditions,* and (state-changing) *operations.* Instances of these are *events, triggers, control-condition evaluations,* and *invoked operations,* respectively. *Events* are changes in object state. *Triggers* respond to events by invoking operations with the required objects as arguments. *Control-condition evaluations* act as guards that ensure an operation is executed only when its condition test proves true. Each *invoked operation* is a process actively engaged in changing the state of an object by implementing a specific *method.* A *method* is a script of operation. This distinction between invoked operation and event is the distinction between *potential* and *actual* change in object state; triggers link actual changes to new potential changes.

The *event schema* is a formal approach to expressing *behavior* and is based on the foundations of the FSM. It incorporates the notions of operation scripting, specification *leveling,* operation reusability, processing concurrency, and implementation-mechanism independence. Event schemas intimately incorporate *structure* expressed by object schemas.

Chapter 23 describes the event schema notation in more detail. Chapter 24 presents an analysis method for constructing event schemas.

REFERENCES

1. Brodie, M. L. and D. Ridjanovic, "On the Design and Specification of Database Transactions," *On Conceptual Modelling: Perspectives from Artificial Intelligence, Databases, and Programming Languages,* Michael L. Brodie *et al.* eds., Springer-Verlag, New York, 1984, pp. 277–312.

2. Davis, Alan M., *Software Requirements: Analysis and Specification,* Prentice-Hall, Englewood Cliffs, NJ, 1990.

3. Dayal, U., "The HiPAC Project: Combining Active Databases and Timing Constraints," *SIGMOD Record,* 17:1, March 1988, pp. 51–70.

4. Harel, D., "Statemate: A Working Environment for the Development of Complex Reactive Systems," *IEEE 10th Conf on Software Engineering,* 1988, pp. 396–406.

5. Kent, William, *A Framework for Object Concepts,* Hewlett-Packard, Report HPL-90-30, April 1990.

6. Lindgren, Paul, *A Framework of Information Systems Concepts,* IFIP WG 8.1 Task Group FRISCO, interim report, May 14, 1990.

7. Manola, Frank, *PDM: An Object-Oriented Data Model for PROBE,* Computer Corporation of America, Technical CCA-87-03, September 1987.

8. Martin, James, *Diagramming Techniques for Analysts and Programmers,* Prentice-Hall, Englewood Cliffs, NJ, 1985.

9. Mills, Harlan D., *Principles of Information Systems Analysis and Design,* Academic Press, Orlando, FL, 1986.

10. Minsky, Marvin L., *Computation: Finite and Infinite Machines,* Prentice-Hall, Englewood Cliffs, NJ, 1967.

11. Rumbaugh, James, *Object-Oriented Modeling and Design,* Prentice-Hall, Englewood Cliffs, NJ, 1991.

12. Shannon, Claude and J. McCarthy eds., *Automata Studies,* Princeton University Press, Princeton, NJ, 1956.

23 EVENT TYPES, TRIGGER RULES, CONTROL CONDITIONS, AND OPERATIONS

Object-oriented behavior is expressed in terms of object-state changes that can invoke operations that, in turn, result in state changes—and so on. The previous chapter introduced four major types of components in this specification: event types, trigger rules, control conditions, and operations. This chapter explores these in more depth.

EVENT TYPES

Changes in state can be important to us, because they often signal the need for a response. Each event indicates that something has happened and that we may be interested in responding to it. As such, events are the very heart of behavior specification. This section elaborates on the nature of events and describes how to specify their state changes.

Internal and External Events

Events always result from the completion of an operation. An *internal event* occurs as a result of an operation that is within the analyst's scope. For example, the event depicted in Fig. 23.1(a) specifies a Book transferred event that occurs as a result of a Transfer Book operation. The word *internal* is usually omitted when referring to events of this kind.

(a) Internal Operation and Event Type   (b) External Operation and Event Type

Figure 23.1   Expressing internal and external events.

An *external event* is the result of an operation that is external to the analyst's scope. Even though the operation is considered external, external events are identified when they have an impact on the analyst's system. For example, the external event in Fig. 23.1(b) indicates that requests to check out a library book occur. For the borrower with a term paper to write, the event would actually be internal, because requesting books is something that borrowers do. For a library, however, the event is external, because the processes leading up to the event belong to the borrower—not the library. Yet, even though the operation is external to the library, its Book Checkout requested events are events to which a library should respond. Other library-related external events may include Checked-Out Book returned, Checked-Out Book advised Lost, and Overdue Book Fine received.

In this book, event types are represented by solid triangles. The notion of whether an event type is internal or external is indicated by the operation. Operations that are internal to the analyst's scope are represented by rounded rectangles; operations considered to be external are represented as rectangles that are shadowed and rounded as illustrated in Fig. 23.1.

Basic Event Types

An event is the net effect of an operation—a change in object state. Two primitive state changes occur: add or remove. An *add* state change increases the number of object types that apply to an object. A *remove* state change decreases the number of object types that apply to an object. From an extensional perspective, an add increases the number of objects in a set by one, and a remove decreases the number by one.

State changes can be specified with more precision. For example, prior to an add operation, a state change requires that its object be an instance of some specific object type—or not exist at all. These and other specifications are addressed by several basic kinds of state changes. In particular, this book discusses how objects can be created, terminated, classified, declassified, reclassified, coalesced and decoalesced; and tuples substituted. Every event can be classified as one of these kinds of state changes.

Object-Creation Event

In an *object-creation* event, an entirely new object appears. For example, the event type Breakfast started occurs when an object is created and becomes a member of the Breakfast set in Fig. 23.2(a). Shipment initiated indicates that an object is created as an instance of the object type Shipment. As mentioned in Chapter 15, an object cannot exist without being an instance of at least one object type. Without an appropriate object type, the object cannot be recognized. Therefore, each time an object is created, it must become a member of some object type's set. In this way, an object creation event is the change from not being an object at all, to that of being an object of a specific type.

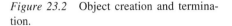

Figure 23.2   Object creation and termination.

(a) Breakfast Started   (b) Breakfast Completed

Object-Termination Event

In an *object-termination* event, the existing object is removed from our awareness. For example, the event type **Breakfast completed**, in Fig. 23.2(b), occurs when a **Breakfast** object no longer exists. **Shipment terminated** indicates that an instance of **Shipment** is terminated from existence.

The state change is from the state of being an object of various types, to not being an object at all. For example, the **Breakfast** object in Fig. 23.2(b) may have been a member of the **Artform** and **Food Fight Object** sets as well. However, after termination, the object is no longer a member of any set. As long as even one object type applies, the object still exists in some way. When no object types apply, the object cannot exist.

Object-Classification Event

An *object-classification* event is the classification of an existing object. For example, the event type **Employee classified Manager**, in Fig. 23.3(a), occurs when an **Employee** object *also* becomes a member of the **Manager** set. **Order shipped** occurs when an **Order** object is also classified as an instance of **Shipped Order**. The state change is from being a member of some set, to that of being a member of an *additional* set. In other words, a specific set is extended by one previously existing object.

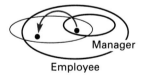

(a) Employee classified Manager   (b) Employee declassified Manager

Figure 23.3   Object classification and declassification.

Object-Declassification Event

An *object-declassification* event is the declassification of an existing object. In Fig. 23.3(b), the event type **Employee declassified Manager** occurs when an **Employee** object is removed as a member of the **Manager** set—after which the object remains an **Employee** but is no longer a **Manager**. **Account declassified Overdue Account** indicates that the **Overdue Account** object type no longer applies to a specific **Account** object. The state change is from being a member of one or more sets, to that of being a member of one less set. (A declassification event that results in no object types applying to a particular object is equivalent to a termination event.)

Compound Events

Create, terminate, classify, and declassify are event types that either add or remove an object from a set. However, some basic event types are more transactional in nature, because they require simultaneous adds and removes. This is particularly true of object reclassification and tuple substitution events.

Object-Reclassification Event

An *object-reclassification* event is the simultaneous declassification of an object as one object type and classification of it as another object type. In Fig. 23.4(a), a marriage event type occurs when an object is removed from the **Unmarried Person** set and is added to the set **Married Person**. The state change was from the state of being an object in one set, to that of being an object in a different set. Put another way, one specific set is reduced by one object and another specific set is extended by one object.

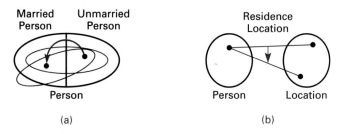

Figure 23.4   Object reclassification and tuple substitution.

Object reclassification is a compound event, because it consists of an object-declassification event and an object-classification event. It is useful when these two events cannot occur separately. For example, a **Person** object must either be married or unmarried. Declassifying an **Unmarried Person** object without *simultaneously* classifying it as a **Married Person** would create an illogical void. Object reclassification eliminates the difficulties of this operation by performing both operations at once.

Tuple-Substitution Event

A *tuple-substitution* event is the simultaneous termination of one tuple and creation of another of the same type—while keeping one of its component objects consistent throughout.

The association of one object with another determines a composite object known as a tuple. For example, in Fig 23.4(b) each tuple in a **Residence Location** relation is a composite object that relates a **Person** object with a **Location** object. Adding a tuple, then, is an object-creation event; removing a tuple is an object-termination event. However, due to cardinality constraints, a relational connection may be required at all times. For instance, assume that the **Residence Location** relation requires that each **Person** object relate to *exactly* one **Location** object at all times. To remove a tuple—even for a moment—violates the **Residence Location** cardinality constraint. Such a situation makes changing a person's residence impossible unless **Residence Location** tuples can be terminated and created simultaneously. The tuple substitution event eliminates the difficulty of this operation by performing both operations at the same time.

Other Compound Events

Object reclassification and tuple substitution are two common compound event types. In addition to these, many analysts suggest the need for others, the most popular of which are component termination and object coalesce and decoalesce.

Component termination is an event that not only terminates an object but all of its components as well. For example, the component termination of a **Boat** object means that when the **Boat** object is terminated, its **Hull** and **Motor** component objects are terminated at the same time. Component termination is appropriate only when the components of an object are terminated along with the object itself. If they are not, component termination is inappropriate. For instance, if a **Motor** object survives the termination of its **Boat**, component termination is not applicable here—only object termination.

In an *object coalesce* event, a set of objects—previously recognized as distinct—become the same object. For example, many mystery stories have one **Murderer** object and another of the set **Butler**. Following the event called **The Butler did It**, these two objects are perceived as one and the same object. As indicated in Fig. 23.5(a), all object types that applied to each object separately now apply to the coalesced object. The previous two objects are henceforth recognized as the same thing. The *object decoalesce* has the opposite effect.

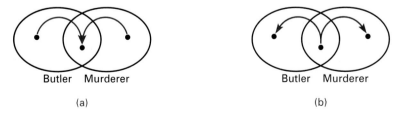

Butler   Murderer   Butler   Murderer

(a)   (b)

Figure 23.5   Object coalesce and decoalesce.

Event Prestates and Poststates

As indicated earlier, each event is a change in the state of one object. This change implies that each event has a collection of object types that apply to an object before an event, and a different collection after. Those object types that must apply before and must apply after an event are defined in event prestate and poststate specifications.

> An *event prestate* specifies those object types that *must* apply to an object *before* the event occurs.
>
> An *event poststate* specifies those object types that *must* apply to an object *after* the event occurs.

Figure 23.6(a) specifies the event prestates and poststates required for each of the six most common basic event types. In addition, Fig. 23.6(b) provides examples of each of these event types.

Event Partitions

As discussed in Chapter 21, object types can have subtypes and supertypes. Event types are no exception, because they, too, are object types. The example in

Event Type	Event Prestate	Event Poststate	Event Example	Event Prestate	Event Poststate
X created	not Object	X	**Breakfast created**	not Object	Breakfast
X terminated	X	not Object	**Breakfast terminated**	Breakfast	not Object
X classified C	X, but not C	X and C	**Person classified Employee**	Person, but not Employee	Person and Employee
X declassified C	X and C	X, but not C	**Person declassified Employee**	Person and Employee	Person, but not Employee
X reclassified from C1 to C2	X and C1, but not C2	X and C2, but not C1	**Person married**	Unmarried Person	Married Person
R substituted	R	R	**Residence changed**	Residence	Residence (different tuple)

(a)   (b)

Figure 23.6   Event prestates and poststates for common basic event types.

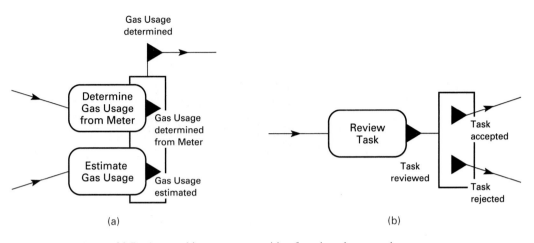

Figure 23.7   Approaching an event partition from its subtypes or its supertype.

Fig. 23.7(a) depicts a Gas Usage determined* event type. Its partition contains two mutually exclusive event types: Gas Usage determined from Meter and Gas Usage estimated. In other words, an event of the type Gas Usage determined from Meter or of the type Gas Usage estimated is also an event of the type Gas Usage determined. This figure indicates that if *either* event subtype occurs, a Gas Usage determined event also occurs. Gas Usage determined is *implied*— not caused—by Gas Usage determined from Meter or Gas Usage estimated.

Figure 23.7(b) expresses the Task reviewed event supertype as being triggered directly. Here, a decision mechanism (within the operation's method) decides whether a Task is accepted or rejected. In other words, an occurrence of a Task reviewed event might also be an occurrence of a Task accepted event, resulting in a specific trigger. However, when the Task reviewed event is a Task rejected, an entirely different trigger results. In this way, event partitions provide a way of representing mutually exclusive processing decisions—decisions made within the operation.

Another example of using the event partition as a decision point is illustrated in Fig. 23.8. Here, Male Person washed triggers an entirely different operation than Female Person washed. In both cases, a person is washed. However, depending on gender, processing differences can be expressed.

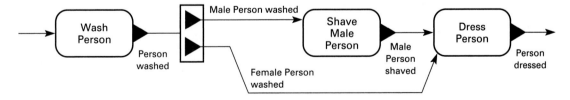

Figure 23.8   Event subtypes express processing decisions.

*For readability, event types are typically named in the past tense.

OPERATIONS While events are changes in state, operations are the processing units that make the change. In Fig. 23.9 for example, each Person employed event is a change resulting from the Employ Person operation. When invoked, this operation changes the state of an object from an Unemployed Person to an Employed Person. In other words, the invoked operation is a process that employs a Person according to a specified method; its event indicates the point in time when the operation is completed.

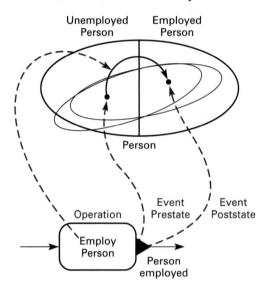

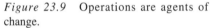

Figure 23.9 Operations are agents of change.

Because of the differences in meaning between operation and event type, two separate symbols connote them. They are paired to acknowledge that, in principle, they are two different views of the same thing. When the OO analyst wishes to focus on the potential for change, she uses the operation view. When focusing on its effect, she uses the event type view. In this way, operations and event types may be defined in pairs.

> An *operation* is a process that can be requested as a unit. In event schemas, they change the states of objects.

Operation Arguments

Each operation requires one or more objects on which to operate. For example, the Wash Person operation requires a Person object to wash. Without an object to wash, the operation has no purpose. The operation resulting in an Employee Classified Manager event requires an Employee object to classify. Add or subtract operations require a pair of Number objects as arguments with which to carry out their computation. In cases such as these, an operation requires one or more objects as independent variables or *arguments*. These arguments are supplied by the invoking trigger. Triggers are described later in this chapter.

Basic Operations

The section on event types in this chapter describes several basic kinds of state changes. Operations are the agents for these changes. These basic operations, therefore, are assertions of object creation, termination, classification, declassification, reclassification, reconnection, and so on.

Operations as Transactions

In event schemas, each operation can be considered a transaction. A transaction is a process or a series of processes acting as one to change the state of an object [4]. Operations are the processing units that carry out some distinct transaction within the context of a larger process. Once invoked, operations are expected to complete their processing—even if it takes seconds, days, or years.

Operations are considered *basic* when their application is limited to one of the basic operations defined above. However, their application can be scripted in terms of cause-and-effect linked operations. This script is known as the *method* of the operation. For example, the operation at the top of Fig. 23.10 is not basic, because its method is composed of a network of operations—culminating in the same event. Moreover, each of the operations in the method could—in turn— have its own method. In this way, operations can be thought of as nested, or tree, transactions.

Operations as Clocks

In event schemas, two forms of time exist—process time and clock time. *Process time* is defined by the relative occurrence of events within a method. The fact that one event occurs before or after another is the primary application of time in an event schema. Each event marks a moment in time relative to another event.

Clock time, on the other hand, reflects the measured time of the world outside the application. Clock time can be incorporated in an application by defining an operation that emits a specified pattern of clock-tick events. This specialization of the operation is usually the *clock operation* and is reusable.

A *clock operation* is an operation that emits a specified pattern of clock-tick events.

An end-of-month clock operation would tick and result in an event at the end of each month. A daily clock operation would tick an event every 24 hours, a

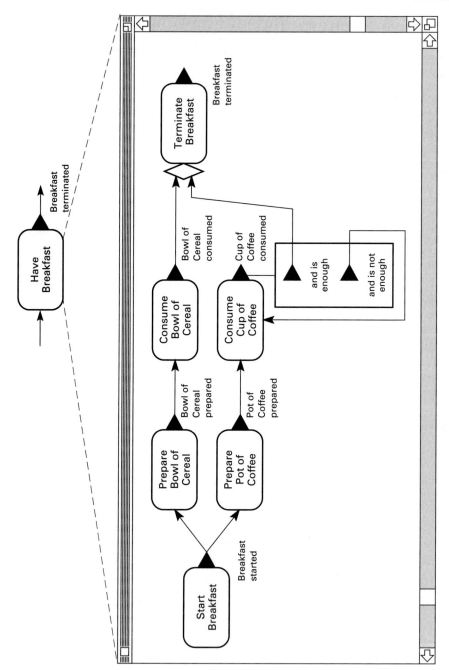

Figure 23.10 Methods describe how operations are carried out.

millisecond clock every thousandth of a second, and so on. A clock can run indefinitely (until terminated) or tick an exact number of times as requested at invocation. In this way, a clock may be invoked to emit a tick indefinitely every 15 days or invoked to tick just once after 15 seconds.

Clock operations can be symbolized like any operation. However, by placing clock hands within the rounded rectangle, the meaning is enhanced (see Fig. 23.11(a)). In addition, clock operations and their events can be considered external to the area being modeled. This book will represent external clocks as illustrated in Fig. 23.11(b).

(a) Clock Operation with Event Type   (b) External Clock Operation and Event Type

Figure 23.11   Internal versus external clock operations.

In Fig. 23.12, one of the events that triggers a customer's gas-billing process is an external clock. **Gas Bill Cycle reached** may occur, for example, on the same day each month. At this time, the **Determine Gas Usage from Meter** operation is invoked to read a gas meter to determine a customer's gas usage. By itself, if this action does not occur in a timely manner, other operations (like sending out the bills) could be unacceptably delayed. Therefore, other contingent operations must be defined. For example, perhaps an operation to estimate gas usage could be invoked if the meter reading operation has not been completed within a certain number of days. In order to trigger the estimating operation, an internal clock operation is invoked to tick once after an alloted number of days

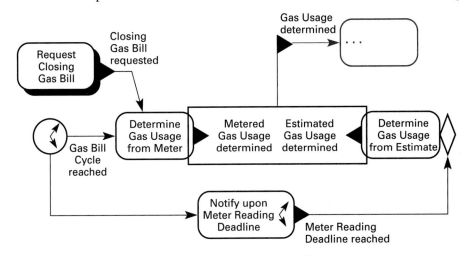

Figure 23.12   Clock operations in a gas-billing example.

elapsed. When the Meter Reading Deadline reached event occurs, a control condition will determine whether a meter reading has already been obtained. If no reading has yet been received, the Determine Gas Usage from Estimate operation estimates the customer's gas usage. Since both Gas Usage from Estimate determined and Gas Usage from Meter determined are event subtypes, the occurrence of *either* is also an occurrence of Gas Usage determined. In other words, if either gas usage operation completes, the Gas Usage determined event occurs and processing proceeds.

CONTROL CONDITIONS

Operations—once invoked—are expected to complete their processing. However, certain conditions may have to exist before an operation is allowed to begin. For example, in Fig. 23.10 before the terminate breakfast operation can begin, certain guarding conditions must exist. In this particular case, the *control condition* requires that *both* Bowl of Cereal consumed and Cup of Coffee consumed and is enough events have occurred. When the control condition is true, the Terminate Breakfast operation can begin; when false, the operation cannot begin.

Control conditions have an "if . . . then" character. When invoked, they determine if certain preexisting conditions are true. In the above example, the control condition could be verbally expressed as If (Bowl of Cereal consumed) and (Cup of Coffee consumed and is enough), then begin the Terminate Breakfast operation.

A *control condition* is a process that evaluates a certain set of conditions to be true or false. Processing continues beyond this point only when the result is true.

Conditional statements can be simple or can consist of a very complex set of "ands" and "ors." For example, a conditional statement could read If (A or B) and (C) and (not D or E) and so on. Such conditions are called Boolean because they result in either a true or a false condition. Ways of expressing Boolean conditions are presented in the next chapter.

Figure 23.13 depicts another example of a control condition. Its conditional statement is defined as follows: If the correct amount of money has been taken, and a product has been dispensed, and any change that is due has been given, then the Complete Sale operation can begin. In this example, at least the Product dispensed and Money taken events must occur to fulfill the conditional statement. The Change given event will only occur when the vending machine has been overpaid for the sale. For instance, if a customer inserts 75¢ and a 60¢ item is dispensed, 15¢ in change is due. In this case, the sale is not complete when the Product dispensed and Money taken events occur, because one condition (any change that is due has been given) in the conditional statement has yet

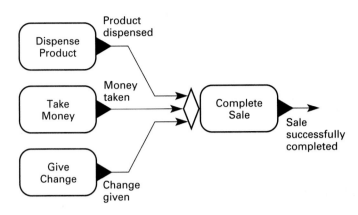

Figure 23.13   Whether or not a vending machine sale can be completed
depends on its control condition.

to be fulfilled. When the **Change given** event finally does occur, the control condition will be retriggered and the entire conditional statement will be reevaluated—this time resulting in a **Sale successfully completed** event. If the customer
inserts the exact amount (i.e., no change is due), only the **Product dispensed** and
Money taken events are necessary for the conditional statement to be true.

Using Control Conditions for Synchronization

A common application for control conditions is synchronizing a series of operations. For example, the control condition in Fig. 23.14(a) synchronizes sending a
Job Bill only after all of the **Tasks** for a particular **Job** are complete. In this
example, each instance of the **Perform Task** operation on the left completes one
Task. After each **Task** is completed, the **Send Job Bill** control condition is evaluated. The control condition—using the object schema information in Fig.
23.14(b)—determines whether any **Tasks** remain uncompleted for the **Job**. If *any*
of the associated **Tasks** are not **Completed Tasks**, the **Send Job Bill** operation
cannot begin. In other words, only when *all* of the **Tasks** for a **Job** are
Completed Tasks does the operation begin.

Control conditions, then, can act as synchronization points within an event
schema. In the example above, various **Tasks** are running to completion (either in
serial or in parallel fashion). The control condition for **Send Job Bill** synchronizes its billing application by not allowing any subsequent processing to occur
until all **Job Tasks** are completed.

Reusing Control Conditions

Each operation can have its own preconditions expressed as a control condition.
Sometimes, however, the control condition specified for one operation will be

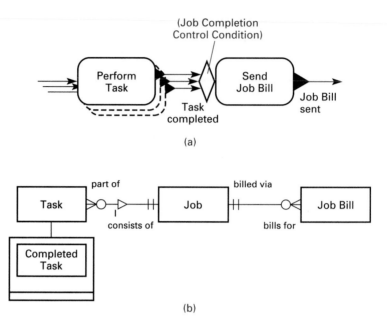

Figure 23.14 A control condition that synchronizes processing and its corresponding object schema.

identical to that of another. For example in Fig. 23.15(a), **Send Job Bill** and **Deliver Product** are both triggered by the same event and have the same control condition. In other words, neither operation can begin until all of the tasks for a job are completed.

When separately-specified control conditions are the same, creating one *reusable* control condition is useful. One mechanism for accomplishing this is by defining an operation specifically for the control condition. For example, the two control conditions in Fig. 23.15(a) are expressed as one in Fig. 23.15(b). In doing so, a **Complete Job** operation is defined. When true, then, the control condition results in an event that can trigger any number of operations—including **Send Job Bill** and **Deliver Product**. In other words, if all of the tasks are completed for a given job, then a **Job completed** event occurs. This change in the state of a **Job** object to being a **Completed Job** object is what triggers the other operations instead of multiple, identical control conditions. In this way, any control condition can be made reusable as a precondition for multiple operations.

Multiple Control Conditions

Sometimes operations can be thought of as having multiple control conditions. For example in Fig. 23.16(a), one control condition evaluates whether conditions A and B are true when invoked by one set of triggers. Another control condition evaluates whether conditions B and C are true when invoked by another set of

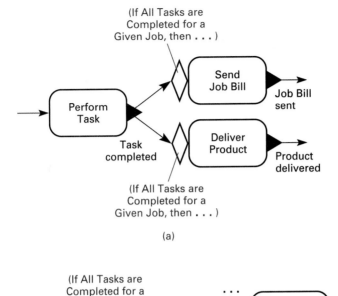

(a)

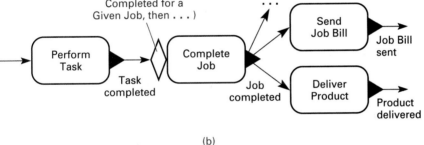

(b)

Figure 23.15   The same condition can be expressed for two operations either by expressing it as two control conditions or as one with its own operation.

triggers. In contrast, some analysts prefer to combine the two conditions into one clause by defining only one control condition as illustrated in Fig. 23.16(b). While this combined form may execute correctly, its efficiency and modularity are compromised.

Another way of expressing Fig. 23.16(a) is by defining separate operations for each control condition, shown in Fig. 23.16(c). Operation Z remains the same. Operations X and Y are additions—just as the Complete Job operation, above, was added. (Here, however, the motivation is not necessarily reusability.) The difference between the approach represented in Figs. 23.16(a) and 23.16(c) is as follows. In Fig. 23.16(a), when the control condition is true, Operation Z begins. In Fig. 23.16(c), when the control condition is true, an event occurs that triggers Operation Z. The ends are the same, the means are different. In one, when the condition tests as "true," an event occurs as illustrated in Fig. 23.16(c).

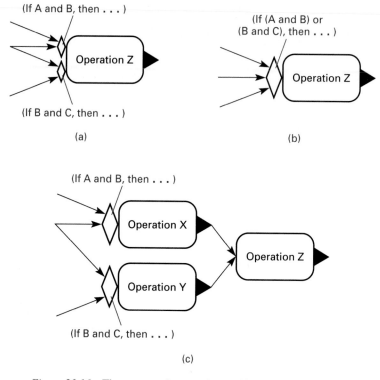

Figure 23.16   Three ways of expressing multiple control conditions.

In the other, an event does not occur. The choice of which representation is best is based on reusability and clarity. The next chapter explores these multiple control conditions further.

TRIGGER RULES   Events trigger operations. *Triggers,* then, are cause-and-effect links. In addition, they take the underlying object of an event and determine those object(s) required to invoke an operation.

As illustrated in Fig. 23.17, each trigger rule has three basic components: an event type (the cause), an operation (the effect), and a function. The function takes the causal event's underlying object and maps it to those objects being passed as arguments to the operation it invokes.

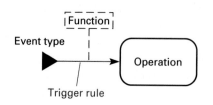

Figure 23.17   The three basic components of a trigger rule.

> A *trigger rule* is a process that invokes a specific operation when a specific type of event occurs. It also specifies the way in which objects are filled as arguments to the operation.

Trivial Functions

In many cases, a trigger passes an event's underlying object directly to a subsequent operation. Functions of this kind can be thought of as *trivial*. Figure 23.18 illustrates two such examples.

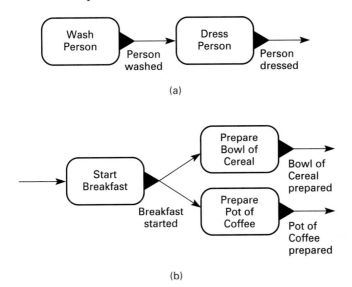

Figure 23.18   Examples of trivial functions in trigger rules.

In Fig. 23.18(a), the underlying object from a **Person washed** event is a specific **Person** object. The trigger rule expresses the following: When a **Person washed** event occurs, use the same **Person** object as the argument to invoke the **Dress Person** operation.

In Fig. 23.18(b), the underlying object is a **Breakfast** object. The two trigger lines indicate that the two related operations can be performed in parallel, because no sequence is specified. In both cases, the same **Breakfast** object is passed simultaneously to both operations as arguments. In other words, a **Breakfast** object is an argument for preparing a **Bowl of Cereal** as well as preparing a **Pot of Coffee**. These operations use this argument to create a **Bowl of Cereal** and **Pot of Coffee** and associate them to a specific **Breakfast**. (If only one **Breakfast** object existed at one time, this association would not be necessary. However, in a coffee shop for instance, keeping track of which cereal and pot of coffee goes with which breakfast is important to the process.) The object schema in Fig. 23.19(b) depicts these object types and their associations.

Trigger Rules with Specified Functions

Often, an event has a different underlying object than needed by one of its triggered operations. For example, the Terminate Breakfast operation in Fig. 23.19(a) requires a Breakfast object. However, the two invoking events do not

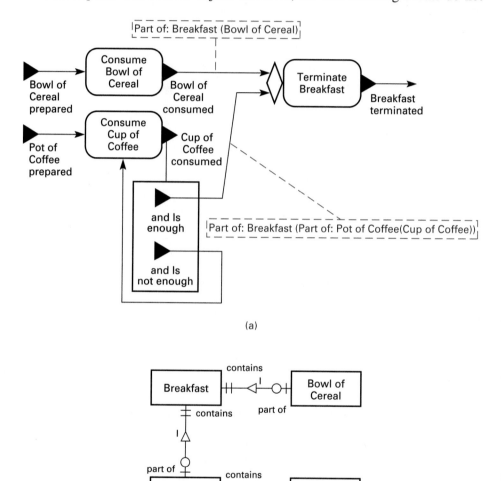

(a)

(b)

Figure 23.19   Example of triggers with specified functions.

have a **Breakfast** object as their underlying object. Figure 23.19(b) illustrates an object schema containing four object types and their functions. The function that maps each **Bowl of Cereal** object to a **Breakfast** object is the very same function specified on the top trigger line in Fig. 23.19(a). The function that maps each **Cup of Coffee** object to a **Breakfast** object is the function specified on the bottom trigger line. These two functions can be expressed as, part of:Breakfast(Bowl of Cereal) and part of:Breakfast(pot of coffee(Cup of Coffee)). In other words, these functions specify the **Breakfast** that a given **Bowl of Cereal** is part of and the **Breakfast** that a given **Pot of Coffee's Cup of Coffee** is part of, respectively.

Figure 23.20(a) depicts another example of a trigger with a specified function. The event on the left indicates when a particular passenger's journey has been fully routed. Its underlying object is a **Journey** object. For each invocation of the operation on the right, a **Journey Segment** will be booked. The object schema in Fig. 23.20(b) indicates that the function from **Journey** to **Journey Segment** is a one-to-many association. The contains:Journey Segment is the function required for the trigger in Fig. 23.20(a). However, this function can yield many **Journey Segment** objects, while its triggered operation can process only one object at a time. The net effect defined for this trigger rule is that multiple invocations of the operation will occur—one for each **Journey Segment** object. If a particular journey has three segments, one such trigger will invoke three operations in parallel—one for each segment. (Note: the extra **Book Journey Segment** operation symbols are here for illustration purpose only.)

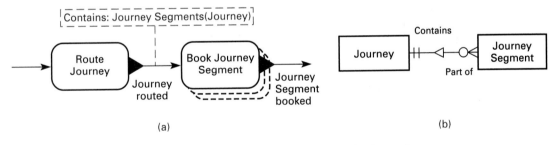

(a)   (b)

Figure 23.20   One trigger with parallel operation invocations.

Operation invocations are not restricted to requiring only one object as an argument. Figure 23.21(a) illustrates one such example. The event's underlying object is a **Marriage License** object. However, the marriage-performance operation requires two arguments: a bride and a groom. This trigger line, therefore, specifies two functions, has groom(Marriage License) and has bride(Marriage License). In other words, a given **Marriage License** object has an association with both bride and groom object via its has bride and has groom functions. The trigger rule uses these functions to obtain the two objects required by the Perform Marriage Ceremony operation.

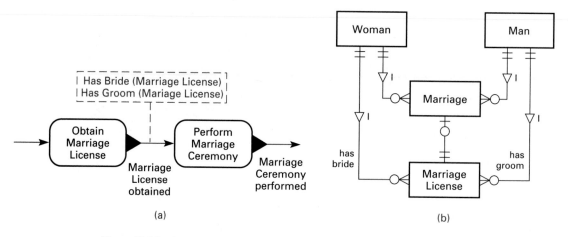

Figure 23.21　An operation that has multiple arguments and its object schema.

Arguments and Dataflows

The way in which arguments are supplied to operations gives trigger rules the appearance of dataflows. They act like dataflows, because objects do seem to *flow* from an event to an operation. However, not every object required to carry out an operation flows through its trigger—only those required to invoke the operation. The additional objects required to carry out an operation will be filled by the operation's method. For example, in Fig. 23.21(b) a specific Marriage requires only two objects as operational components, a groom and a bride. In other words, given groom and bride objects, a Marriage object can be created. However, within the wedding operation, many other objects may be required such as an Officiator, Witnesses, Bridesmaids, and so on. These objects, as needed, will be arguments for other operations specified within the wedding method.

Arguments, then, are the subject or independent variables of an operation. They define the basic components required for the operation's underlying object. In this way, when an argument is filled, the operation can be invoked with a specific result in mind. Only components of the operation's underlying object (or the object itself) should *flow* on a trigger line—and none other. All supporting objects will flow on the appropriate triggers within the method.

SUMMARY

This chapter presented object-oriented behavior specification in terms of events, triggers, control-condition evaluations, and operation invocations.

An *event* results from the successful application of an operation. It is a change in object state. When several basic kinds of object state changes occur, objects can be *created, terminated, classified, declassified, reclassified, coalesced* and *decoalesced, components terminated;* and *tuples substituted.* Events can be classified as one of these common kinds of changes.

State change means that one state changes to another. Therefore, every change has a prestate and a poststate for its underlying object. An *event prestate* specifies those object types that must apply to the underlying object *before* the event has occurred. An *event poststate* specifies those object types that must apply to the underlying object *after* the event has occurred. Every event type is expressed in terms of these prestates and poststates.

While events are changes in object state, *operations* are the agents of that change. Operations are completely unaware of the events that trigger them, and they have no knowledge of what will be triggered by their completion.

A *clock operation* is a special kind of operation that emits specific clock-tick events. Without clocks, processes operate in their own relative time; with clocks, a defined unit of time measurement is introduced.

A *control condition* is a process that recognizes when a condition is true or not. If it is true, processing continues beyond the control condition; otherwise it does not.

Triggers are cause-and-effect links. In addition, they take the underlying object of an event and determine those object(s) required to invoke an operation. In this way, triggers create a cause-and-effect chain between event/operation pairs. Triggers pass objects as arguments to operations they invoke. Functions are *trivial* when the event's underlying object is mapped directly to the invoked operation. Triggers with specified functions can pass different objects to their operations than are received from events.

This chapter discusses four behavioral components: event types, trigger rules, control conditions, and operations. The next chapter presents a way of assembling these components to define an operation's method.

REFERENCES

1. Dayal, U., "The HiPAC Project: Combining Active Databases and Timing Constraints," *SIGMOD Record,* 17:1 (March 1988), 51–70.

2. Mills, Harlan D., *Principles of Information Systems Analysis and Design,* Academic Press, Orlando, FL, 1986.

3. Sakai, Hirotaka, "A Method for Entity-Relationship Behavior Modeling," *Entity-Relationship Approach to Software Engineering,* 3rd International Conference on Entity-Relationship Approach (Anaheim, CA), C. G. Davis et al. eds., Elsevier Science, Amsterdam, 1983, pp. 111–129.

4. Tsichritzis, Dionysios C. and Frederick H. Lochovsky, *Data Models,* Prentice-Hall, Englewood Cliffs, NJ, 1982.

24 OBJECT BEHAVIOR ANALYSIS

Analysis has elements of both art and science. While its art is not easily taught, its science can be studied and learned. This chapter attempts to impart some science to object-oriented behavior analysis by presenting a step-by-step analysis method. While many other methods are possible, this was chosen because of its rigorous and formal approach to capturing expert knowledge.

OBJECT BEHAVIOR ANALYSIS USING EVENT SCHEMAS

The previous two chapters presented elements of event schemas. The step-by-step method for constructing them is summarized in Fig. 24.1.

Step 0. Define Analysis Focus

When constructing an event schema, the analysis effort must begin by examining what to model—and what not to model. In short, the analyst and expert must define the focus of the schema.

Step 0a. Identify the Realm

Object-oriented analysis specifies the object structure and behavior that is relevant to a *realm* of interest. Each realm defines a particular *universe* of objects that we wish to model. It provides a frame of reference. (Realms are also called domains, universes, and spaces in other methodologies.) By considering each realm as a method of operation, the analyst and expert can focus on a targeted area of analysis. In this way, the realm could be management payroll, product manufacturing, or vending-machine operation.

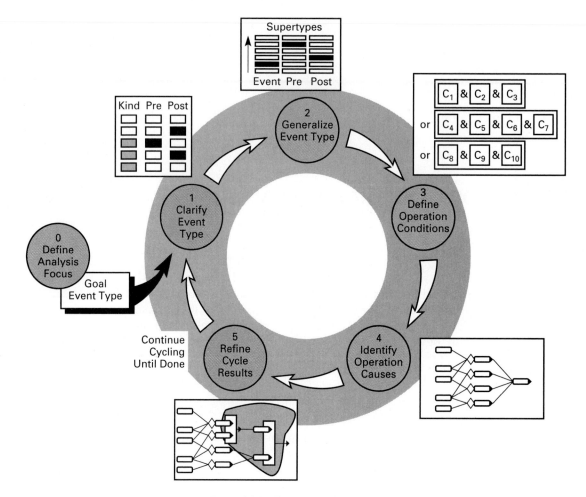

Figure 24.1   Event analysis method.

Additionally, by having the specification confined to a particular realm, both the analyst and the expert will have a manageable area in which they can focus their analysis efforts. While a picture may be worth a thousand words, a picture with a thousand object types is not a good analysis tool. Therefore, each realm must provide a tangible platform for a topic. With it, the analyst is saying "let's discuss a specification at this level of detail."

Step 0b. Identify the Goal Event Type

Once the realm has been identified, its purpose or goal must be expressed. For instance, some realms and their goal event types might be

realm	goal event types
Recruitment	Employee added
Accounts Payable	Payment created
Order Administration	Order terminated
Vending-Machine Operation	Sale completed
Battle Management	Threat removed

Identifying the goal event types is crucial to the method. Without a goal, the selected realm has no clearly understood purpose. (Object-flow diagrams described in the next chapter, can help in such situations.)

The starting event type is also important (see Fig. 24.2). Identifying when a realm begins its processing provides another analysis boundary. By knowing the start and end of a realm, its specification has borders, so that the analyst and end user can "bracket" their work.

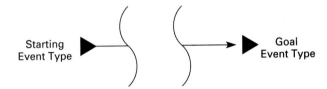

Figure 24.2 While the goal event type is mandatory, the starting point is also important.

After Step 0, the next step in this analysis begins by clarifying the goal event type.

Step 1. Clarify Event Type

This step enables the analyst to define the underlying meaning of the chosen event type and provide its label.

Step 1a. Identify the Basic Kind of Event

As discussed in the previous chapter, several basic kinds of events are create, terminate, classify, declassify, reclassify, tuple substitution, and so on. In this step, the analyst identifies the kind of event to which the chosen event type conforms.

Associated with each basic kind of event are event prestate and poststate object types. The event prestate specifies those object types that must apply to the underlying object before the event takes place. The event poststate specifies those object types that must apply to the underlying object after the event takes place. In addition to indicating the basic kind of event, then, this step also identifies their associated event prestates and poststates. Examples of these are illustrated in Fig. 24.3.

Naming event types
provides understanding
when reading event
schemas.

Event Type	Example Event	Event Prestate	Event Poststate
Create	**Breakfast started**	not Object	Breakfast
Terminate	**Breakfast completed**	Breakfast	not Object
Classify	**Person classified Employee**	Person, but not Employee	Person and Employee
Declassify	**Person declassified Employee**	Person and Employee	Person, but not Employee
Reclassify	**Person married**	Unmarried Person	Married Person
Tuple substitution	**Residence changed**	Residence	Residence (different tuple)

Formalizing the event
type's actual state change
provides exactness.

Figure 24.3   Examples of event prestates and poststates.

The purpose of this step is to formalize the meaning of the event type. The event-type name (defined in the next step) provides us with a way of referencing the event type. However, by explicitly stating the kind of state change and the actual object types involved, the meaning of the event is rigorously expressed.

Step 1b. Name the Event Type

Event-type names convey meaning effectively if they incorporate two characteristics. First, the name should document one or both of the prestate and post-state object-type names. For example, Account opened indicates an operation on the object type Account. Staff Employee promoted Manager indicates a reclassification from Staff Employee to Manager. Account reclassified from Major to

Key refers to three object types: Account, Major Account, and Key Account. Second, the name should convey some indication of the process it represents. Since an event is the successful completion of an operation, naming the event type in the past tense is appropriate. The process of changing one's residence might be successfully completed with a Residence changed event.

Some deviations to this can occur for the sake of clarity. For example, consuming a Breakfast results in its termination. Placing this in the past tense yields Breakfast terminated. However, the name Breakfast completed may be more user-friendly. In another example, the Pay Employee operation may have an event type named Employee paid. However, this event's underlying object type may not be Employee; instead, it may be Employee Payment. Here, the event name would be Employee Payment created—if standards were strictly enforced. In short, names need not be precisely standard. However, the underlying meaning should be. This is why the formality of Step 1a, above, is vital.

Step 2. Generalize Event Type

Once the underlying meaning is clarified, the chosen event type should be examined for more general event types. The purpose here is twofold. First, it helps the analyst determine whether the analysis is being performed at the appropriate level of abstraction or scope. Second, it encourages integration with other more general analysis efforts.

Step 2a. Generalize Event Type and Choose Level

Generalizing an event requires the analyst to rise above the immediate details of a system and momentarily explore a broader scope. For instance, an analyst may be specifying a management payroll system. A key event in that system will be Manager Paid. As depicted in Fig. 24.4(a), a more general form of this is Employee paid. By considering Payment creations in a yet more general form, the Payment made event type may describe the next level of abstraction. The ultimate generality, however, is Object created.

Once the possible levels of abstraction have been explored, the analyst should choose which level is appropriate for the system at hand—and change the chosen event type, if necessary. For example, the Employee paid abstraction is perhaps a better level than Manager paid. In this situation, the scope of the system may change to a more general payroll system. Without the generalization step, the analyst may never have considered the possibility.

A useful technique for identifying possible generalizations is illustrated in Fig. 24.4(b). Here, the event type is expressed along with its prestates and poststates. By generalizing these, the event type is also generalized. As indicated, prestate and poststate can be generalized separately. For example, since a Library Item is a more general form of Book, Audio Tape, Disk-based Work, and so on,

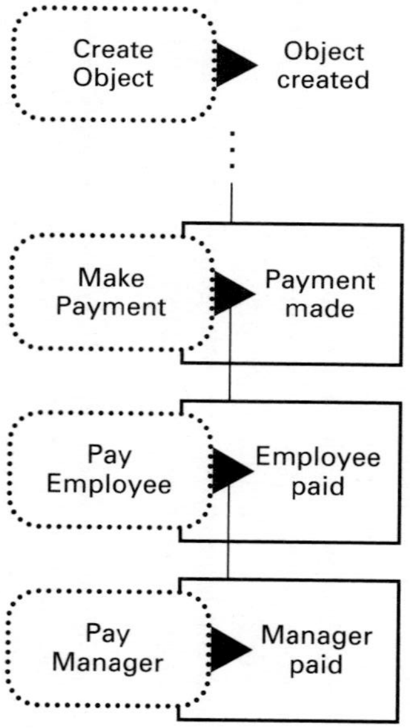

Event Type Name	Event Prestate	Event Poststate
Object Reclassified	Concept	Concept
...		
Item checked out	Available Item	Checked-Out Item
Library Item checked out	Available Library Item	Checked-Out Library Item
Book checked out	Available Book	Checked-Out Book

(b)

Level of Abstraction ←

Object created — Create Object

Payment made — Make Payment

Employee paid — Pay Employee

Manager paid — Pay Manager

(a)

Figure 24.4 Generalizing event types.

the poststate of checking out an **Available Book** is also a **Checked-Out Library Item**. Additionally, the **Available Book** object type can itself be generalized to Available Library Item, resulting in a more general **Library Item checked out** event. Abstractions such as these encourage the analyst to ponder more general systems—in this case a library system that administers more than just collections of books.

Step 2b. Integrate the Event Type

The results of generalization also aid system integration. After generalizing the event type, look to see if it has already been specified. If so, the generalized event may already be part of a system that is in progress or one that is already completed. In this case, an integration point has been identified and can be administered accordingly.

Step 3. Define Operation Conditions

By this point, the event type should be reasonably well understood. Now, the operation and its triggering conditions need to be considered.

Step 3a. Identify the Operation

In order to produce the change in state specified in Step 2, above, an operation is required. This step identifies the operation that, when applied, will result in the specified type of event. For example, an **Order shipped** event occurs as a result of a **Ship Order** operation. Events **Part stored in Bin** and **Bin contents increased** may both have the same operation: **Store Part in Bin.**

Step 3b. Determine Whether Operation is Internal or External

As presented in the previous chapter, operations can be internal or external. In this step, the analyst chooses one of the forms illustrated in Fig. 24.5. An internal operation is an operation whose processing occurs within the realm (as defined in Step 0a). In addition, since its process is internal, its method can be expressed as another event schema.

An external operation is an operation whose processing occurs outside the realm being analyzed. Since its processing method and causes are not addressed

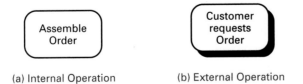

(a) Internal Operation   (b) External Operation

Figure 24.5   Symbolizing internal and external operations.

with this schema, no further analysis steps are performed for this operation. To indicate this, a different symbol is used as illustrated in Fig. 24.5(b).

Step 3c. Identify Control Conditions

An operation is invoked by one or more triggers. However, certain preexisting conditions, called *control conditions,* may be necessary before an operation can actually begin its process (see Fig. 24.6). Take, for example, the Terminate Order operation. The analyst must first ask the user expert, "Under what conditions is the Terminate Order operation permitted to begin?"

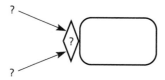

Figure 24.6   Determining control conditions.

The expert should respond, then, with the required conditions. A control condition that proves "true" implies that the proper circumstances exist for the operation to begin. A "false" condition makes no such implication.

An expert's response to the question of "Under what conditions . . . ?" will be an expert's statement in an expert's own language. For example, the question "Under what conditions is the Complete Sale operation in a vending machine permitted to begin?" may lead to an answer like the one that follows:

> Well, let me see. Ummm. The machine can definitely complete a sale when the product the person selected is dispensed. Oh, and also when the machine has taken the right amount of money and given the correct change. And that's it, I think. No, there's one other situation: when the customer hits the "cancel" button. When that button is hit, all the money is returned and the sale is considered "complete" even though it was canceled.

Expert statements in expert language, such as the one above, should be encouraged. The analyst needs to glean as much expert knowledge as possible. Therefore, the user should be allowed to speak in an unrestricted manner using familiar terms. The user should be encouraged (and even prompted) to provide as much detail as necessary. This will increase the probability that the knowledge transfer is complete and accurate.

Step 3d. Normalize Control Conditions

While expert statements of the control condition are vital to systems analysis, they need to be transformed into a simple and standard arrangement of conditional statements. One way of expressing these is called the *disjunctive normal form* (DNF). DNF is often a convenient form in which to write Boolean expressions for switching circuits or conditions for something to happen. In DNF, the conditions that must all occur at the same time are grouped and tested separately. If any *one* group is true, the entire *conditional clause* is true—justifying the change in state. If *none* of the condition groups in the clause holds true, the operation is not justified.

For example in Fig. 24.7, condition-1, *and* condition-2, *and* condition-3 must be true for the entire condition *group* to be true. If the condition group is true, processing can proceed as specified. If one condition group is not true, other groups may be. This is why each group is connected by the word "or." In the example, this means the operation can also be warranted if condition-3 is true and condition-4 is not true. Additionally, if condition-5 is true, the processing can proceed as specified.

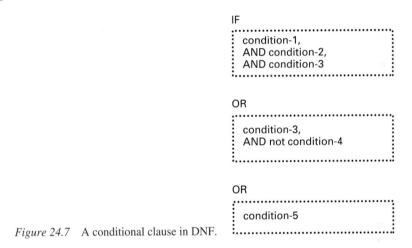

IF

> condition-1,
> AND condition-2,
> AND condition-3

OR

> condition-3,
> AND not condition-4

OR

> condition-5

Figure 24.7   A conditional clause in DNF.

Figure 24.8 illustrates taking the expert knowledge from the above question "Under what conditions is the **Complete Sale** operation in a vending machine permitted to begin" and transforming it to DNF. (The conditional statements assume that all values relate to a particular sale-in-progress. If this were not the case, the terms in the conditions would require qualification.) At the bottom of the example, the initial DNF expression is refined even further. Notice that this more formal refinement has reduced the number of conditions.

Step 4. Identify Operation Causes

In the previous step, the control conditions for processing were defined. Now, the analyst should determine *when* a control condition should be evaluated, so that the associated change in state can occur. In other words, the analyst should establish what events must occur for one or more of the conditions to be true— so that another event can occur. The analyst should also establish the nature of their triggers.

"Well, let me see. Ummmm. The machine can definitely complete a sale when the product the person selected is dispensed. . . . Oh, and also when the machine has taken the right amount of money and given the correct change. And that's it, I think. . . . No, there's one other situation, and that's when the customer hits the 'cancel' button. When that button is hit, all the money is returned and the sale is considered 'complete' even though it was canceled."

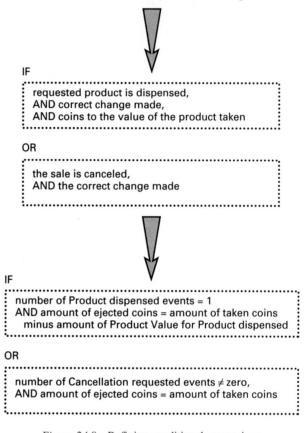

IF

> requested product is dispensed,
> AND correct change made,
> AND coins to the value of the product taken

OR

> the sale is canceled,
> AND the correct change made

IF

> number of Product dispensed events = 1
> AND amount of ejected coins = amount of taken coins
>   minus amount of Product Value for Product dispensed

OR

> number of Cancellation requested events ≠ zero,
> AND amount of ejected coins = amount of taken coins

Figure 24.8   Refining conditional expressions.

Step 4a. Identify Triggering Event Types

Often the condition for processing is simple. For example, in Fig. 24.9 the Consume Bowl of Cereal operation requires only one condition that must be true—a Bowl of Cereal object has been created to consume. In order to make this condition true, a Bowl of Cereal object must be created. Therefore, a preceding Bowl of Cereal prepared event must occur to satisfy the processing preconditions of the Consume Bowl of Cereal operation.

When the conditional clause is more complex, several events may be required for a control condition to be evaluated as "true." The example in Fig. 24.10 requires four event types. Notice that each condition and each term within

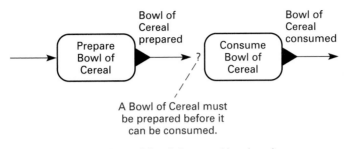

Figure 24.9   A simple conditional clause and its triggering event type.

a condition needs to be examined. For the "number of Product dispensed events" for this Sale to be equal to 1, a **Product dispensed** event must occur. (Yes, events *are* objects.) To compute the "amount of **Given Coins**," coins must be ejected. To compute the "amount of **Taken Coins**," Coin objects must be taken. To examine the "amount of **Product Value**," a Product must have a value.

All of these events must take place prior to a **Sale completed** event. However, not all of them should trigger a sale-completion operation. For instance, a **Product dispensed** event must occur before a sale can be completed. Each time **Product dispensed** occurs, the sale-completion control condition should be checked to see if it proves true. The same rule applies to **Coin ejected** and **Coin taken**. Anytime they occur, the control condition should be checked straightaway. However, a **Product valued** event is *not* an immediate cause for checking the condition, because **Product valued** events do not trigger sale-completion operations. A change in **Product** value should by no means trigger a vending-machine **Complete Sale** operation.

In summary, this step first asks which events must occur to cause a control condition to evaluate as "true." Then, it determines which of these events *should actually* trigger the operation.

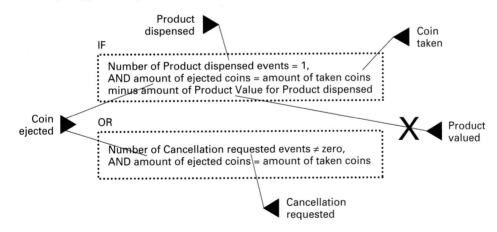

Figure 24.10   Events must occur for the conditions to evaluate as "true."

Step 4b. Indicate Complex Control Conditions

Often, a control condition is limited to only requiring that one event or another must occur before a process can begin. For instance, a Consume Bowl of Cereal operation should begin whenever a Bowl of Cereal prepared event has occurred. In another example, a Determine Gas Usage From Meter operation can begin whenever either a Closing Gas Bill Request or a Gas Bill Cycle Request event occurs. When diagramming situations such as these, the control-condition diamond should not be displayed. The diamond is reserved for those operations that may *not* begin immediately when triggered. The diamond indicates that the operation must *first* evaluate its control condition. In Fig. 24.11, both operations begin whenever they are triggered by *any* event. In other words, the control conditions are when a Bowl of Cereal prepared event has occurred or when a Closing Gas Bill Request *or* a Gas Bill Cycle Request event occurs, respectively.

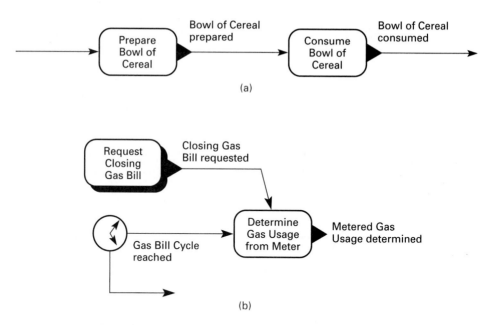

Figure 24.11 Triggering without depicting a control condition.

However, the condition clause specified in Fig. 24.10, requires more than simple WHEN conditions to begin. Instead, a complex IF . . . AND . . . OR requirement exists. Since a Complete Sale operation has such a requirement, a control-condition diamond is required. The resulting event schema is depicted in Fig. 24.12.

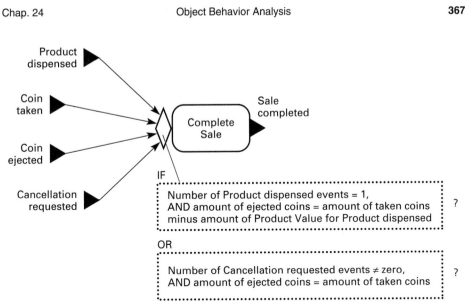

Figure 24.12   The triggering event types and control-condition statement for the Complete Sale operation.

Step 4c. Normalize Triggering Event Types

In Step 3d, above, conditions were arranged in disjunctive normal form (DNF) so that if any one group is true, the entire condition clause is true. The diagram in Fig. 24.12 depicts a control condition whose condition clause is expressed in DNF. If every event in this figure required evaluation of the entire control condition, Fig. 24.12 would remain as illustrated. However, as indicated in Fig. 24.10, the first condition group should be evaluated only when three types of events occur; the second, only when two types of events occur. For example, the Product dispensed event relates to the first condition group and not to the second. Therefore, the control condition should be expressed as two control conditions—each with a different condition group (see Fig. 24.13). In this way, each control condition is triggered only by those events appropriate to the condition group.

Some analysts, however, find that the notation in Fig. 24.13 is either cumbersome or requires special treatment. One way to accommodate this is by representing each control condition with its own operation. Expressed in this way, each new operation would result in an event that only occurs when its control condition is true. In other words, the event would simply indicate that a "true" evaluation had occurred. For example, a successful evaluation of the control condition at the top of the figure results in a state change named Sale successfully completed. The state change might classify a Sale object as a Completed Sale object or terminate it altogether. Or, perhaps the evaluation result itself is classified as True. In either case, the Completed Sale operation is triggered.

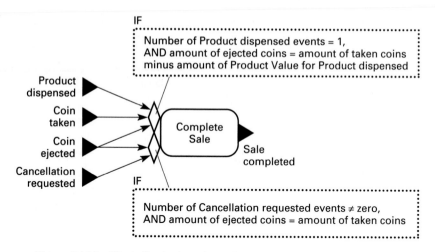

IF

Number of Product dispensed events = 1,
AND amount of ejected coins = amount of taken coins
minus amount of Product Value for Product dispensed

Product dispensed

Coin taken

Coin ejected

Cancellation requested

Complete Sale

Sale completed

IF

Number of Cancellation requested events ≠ zero,
AND amount of ejected coins = amount of taken coins

Figure 24.13 Normalized triggering using multiple control-condition diamonds on an operation.

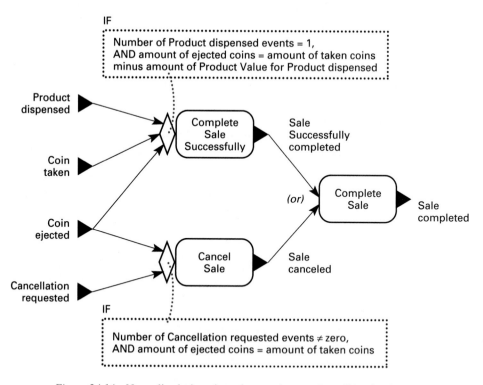

IF

Number of Product dispensed events = 1,
AND amount of ejected coins = amount of taken coins
minus amount of Product Value for Product dispensed

Product dispensed

Coin taken

Complete Sale Successfully

Sale Successfully completed

(or)

Complete Sale

Sale completed

Coin ejected

Cancel Sale

Sale canceled

Cancellation requested

IF

Number of Cancellation requested events ≠ zero,
AND amount of ejected coins = amount of taken coins

Figure 24.14 Normalized triggering where each control condition has its own specialized operation.

In summary, to be in DNF, trigger rules may need regrouping, because certain events apply only to certain condition groups. When this occurs, the original control condition needs to be divided accordingly. The division can be represented as multiple control-condition diamonds on the same operation as illustrated in Fig. 24.14. Or, each control condition can be expressed with its own specialized operation—whose event triggers the original operation.

Step 4d. Specify Trigger Rules

Now that normalized triggering events are in place, the analyst needs to complete the specification of operational causes by identifying exactly what objects are needed to invoke the operation. In other words, the analyst must determine which arguments are needed to trigger the operation, and what functions are required to do the appropriate mapping.

For instance, the argument needed for a sale completion operation is a **Sale** object. Since this is the same underlying object resulting from the **Sale Successfully completed** or **Sale canceled** events, the function is a *trivial* mapping. However, the trigger rules required for the operations in Fig. 24.15 involve a little more thought. In order to perform a wedding, two objects are necessary. The trigger rule in Fig. 24.15(a), then, consists of two functions.

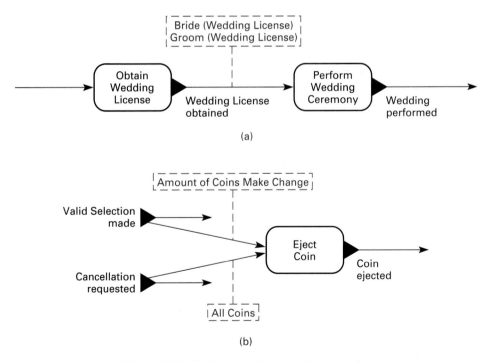

Figure 24.15   Defining the functions of trigger rules.

The coin-ejection operation in Fig. 24.15(b) requires a currency value to eject the appropriate coins. The amount of coins to make change function computes the amount of required change by subtracting the value of the selected product from the amount of money inserted into the machine. The result of the mapping is a currency value—a value from which the coin-ejection operation can determine which coins will be ejected. The all coins function simply computes the value of all the money put into the machine during this sale and passes it to the coin-ejection operation.

Step 5. Refine Cycle Results

Steps 1 through 4 guide the analyst in working with a given event, formalizing it, and determining what leads up to it. Basically, this cycle is now complete. However, before proceeding through the next cycle, a few refinements are useful.

Step 5a. Generalize Triggering Event Type

Triggering event types can often be defined in terms of a more general event type. For example, Fig. 24.16(a) depicts three events triggering the goal event A. Examining B, C, and D more closely, the analyst can determine that B and D are really special cases of one general event, E. This means that whenever B and D occur, it is also an occurrence of E. The event type E, therefore, has two event subtypes.

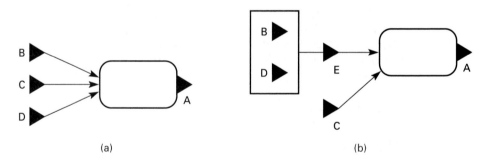

(a)   (b)

Figure 24.16   Generalizing triggering event types.

In the example of Fig. 24.14, two of the triggering event types can be generalized, Sale successfully completed and Sale canceled. In Fig. 24.17, the event supertype is named Sale Finalized. This is another way of saying that a Sale finalized event is a mutually exclusive occurrence of either a Sale successfully completed or a Sale canceled. Generality provides the convenience of homogeneity. Simplifications of this sort clarify the way we think.

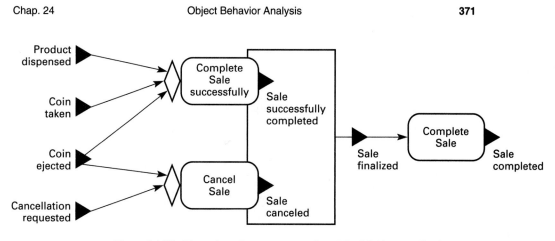

Figure 24.17   Two triggering event types from Fig. 24.14 generalized.

Step 5b. Specialize Goal Event Type

In contrast to Step 5a, operations are sometimes specified too abstractly. For example in Fig. 24.18(a), the goal event A is triggered by three events. Perhaps, the B, C, and D events trigger specialized applications within the operation resulting in A. If this is the case, the specialization can be expressed as event subtypes of A. In Fig. 24.18(b), A' and A" are the specializations of A, triggered by B, C, and D.

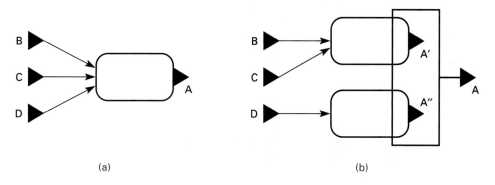

(a)   (b)

Figure 24.18   Specializing goal event types.

Figure 24.19 illustrates an example of how a goal event might be specialized. In the example, the goal event type **Coin ejected** may be applied in two ways. First, a currency value is supplied by the trigger from the events **Valid Selection made** and **Cancellation requested**. Here, the coin-ejection operation determines which coins must be ejected, based on their value. Second, specific **Coin** objects must be ejected. In this scenario, when an improper coin is inserted by a customer or a coin is inserted into a busy vending machine, that *same* coin must be rejected. The notion of value does not apply to these coins at all.

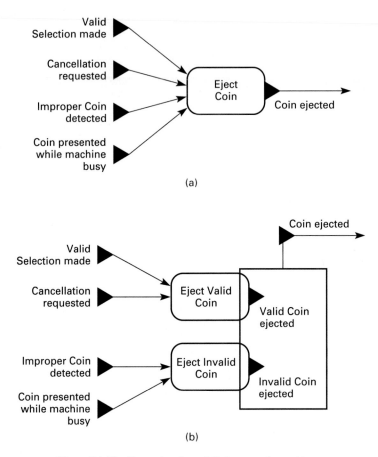

Figure 24.19   Example of specializing a goal event type.

Therefore, the object passed by the trigger is not a currency value, but a coin. In this way, Coin ejected can be specialized as two different methods of it: Valid Coin ejected and Invalid Coin ejected.

Specializing goal event types often clarifies the meaning, though it is not always necessary. For example, if Coin ejected was not expressed as two subevent types, the method selection mechanism would need to be defined *within the method* of the coin-ejection operation. One way or another, then, the specialization will be expressed. The choice of level is determined by the analyst and expert.

Step 5c. Check for Duplicate Events

Another situation to look for is a triggering event type that is either the same as or a subclassification of the goal event type. For instance in Fig. 24.20(a), the expert may determine that event type B and A are really the same

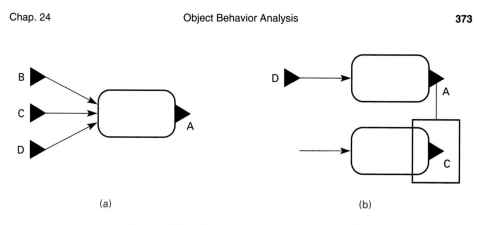

(a)   (b)

Figure 24.20   Removing duplicate event types.

event type, except they have two different names. In other words, the occurrence of **B** is no different than the occurrence of **A**. **B** does not trigger **A** to do anything different than what **B** has already done. **B** and **A** should, therefore, be combined. This is why **B** no longer appears in Fig. 24.20(b).

Event type **C**, on the other hand, is not *exactly* the same as event type **A**. It is, however, a specialized form of **A**. In this way, **C** does not trigger an operation resulting in **A**. An occurrence of **C** is *already* an occurrence of **A**. There is no intervening operation, because a **C** event *is* an **A** event.

As a result of Step 5c, the event schema in Fig. 24.17 is modified as indicated in Fig. 24.21. The reason for removing the **Sale finalized** event type is that its occurrence is exactly the same as **Sale completed**. Therefore, a **Sale finalized** does not trigger an operation to complete a sale: it *is* a **Sale completed**.

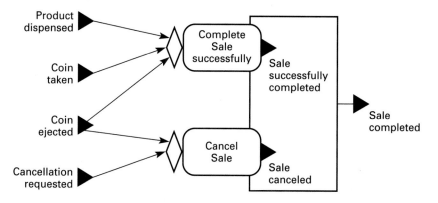

Figure 24.21   Results of checking for duplicate event types from Fig. 24.17.

Next Step

Starting with a goal event, Steps 1 through 5 guide the analyst in formalizing the event, specifying its causes, and making refinements to the resulting schema. In the next step, take the newly identified triggering event types, and—treating each as a goal event type—continue again with Step 1. As long as internal events exist, this "spin-until-dry" cycle continues. It stops when only external operations remain and the starting event type has been reached. For example, in Fig. 24.21 the event types **Product dispensed, Coin taken,** and **Coin ejected** should each be treated as goal event types in their own Step 1-5 cycle. **Cancellation requested,** however, does not become a goal event. Its operation is defined by the customer—not the machine—and is, therefore, outside the focus of the diagramming realm.

Looking at the Results

In order to be useful as a visual communication device, any diagram must be aesthetically pleasing as well as correct. As such, analysts should judge their schemas by the following rules:

- If it looks messy, it's probably wrong.
- If it's too complex, it's probably wrong.
- If it's too big, it's probably wrong.
- If people don't like it, it's probably wrong.
- If it doesn't work, it *is* wrong.

Leveling the Results

What happens when the event schema is completed? Is the analysis complete, or should it be taken to the next level of detail? The answer depends on the nature of each event schema operation, the scope of the analysis project, and the expertise available:

- For those operations that are at the *basic* level, no *next level* of modeling detail exists. This applies to those operations where the *only* task is to create, terminate, classify, declassify, reclassify, and so on.
- However, when an operation is not at the *basic* level, it can be specified at the next level of detail. For instance, the operation resulting in a **Coin ejected** is one such operation that could be expressed in more detail. This more detailed specification is called the *method* specification, as illustrated in Fig. 24.22.
- The choice to express operations at the next level of detail belongs to the analyst, the expert, and the manager. The manager may determine that pursuing more detail in a particular area is outside the project's scope at that time. The analyst may determine that the next level cannot be diagrammed without making implementation decisions. In this situation, further work will be continued by a design team, instead. On the other hand, the expert and analyst may decide that the extra detail is required to clarify their modeling effort. Either way, if it's going to be automated, somebody will define the method eventually.

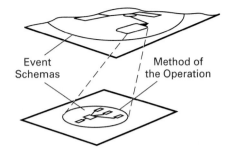

Figure 24.22 Leveling event schemas.

The bulleted items above provide a rationale for *decomposing* operations in a top-down fashion. However, the event schema produced with the steps above also defines a subrealm for a higher level event schema. In other words, the event schema can be used for bottom-up analysis as well. An approach of this kind is very practical at the beginning of an analysis project when a high-level of understanding is lacking. Analysis should always begin at the level of the expert's ability. Rising above the expert's level of competency jeopardizes the accuracy of the analysis project. Practicing top-down analysis in a top-down manner is not the *only* way to analyze a process: in fact, it is usually a downright dangerous way of conducting an analysis effort.

EVENT AND OBJECT ANALYSIS Object-oriented specification is often divided into *structural* and *behavioral* approaches. The structural approach is a visual, spatial metaphor that provides a static vision of how things are laid out in space. In contrast, the behavioral approach describes what a thing does. While this dichotomy is a handy slogan, it can cause the OO analyst to miss the point. The important distinction concerns who defines the process. The structures of the structural approach are primarily defined by and for the builders of databases. Processes, however, are defined by application developers and are intended to be universal. The structures defined by the processes, then, are real and important ones. Therefore, a useful OO analysis method should rest on a behavioral foundation [1]. The diagram in Fig. 24.23 illustrates a goal-directed, behavior-driven method that intimately incorporates structural definitions.

The diagram in the center depicts the major components of object schemas. By using the event analysis steps described in the beginning of this chapter, the analyst is presented with a very good way of finding and identifying the object types. In fact, by using this method, *all* the necessary object types will be identified—and not more.

Below are the steps indicated in Fig. 24.23. The description of each step is specified in detail within this chapter. They are reiterated here to add the structural portion of this method.

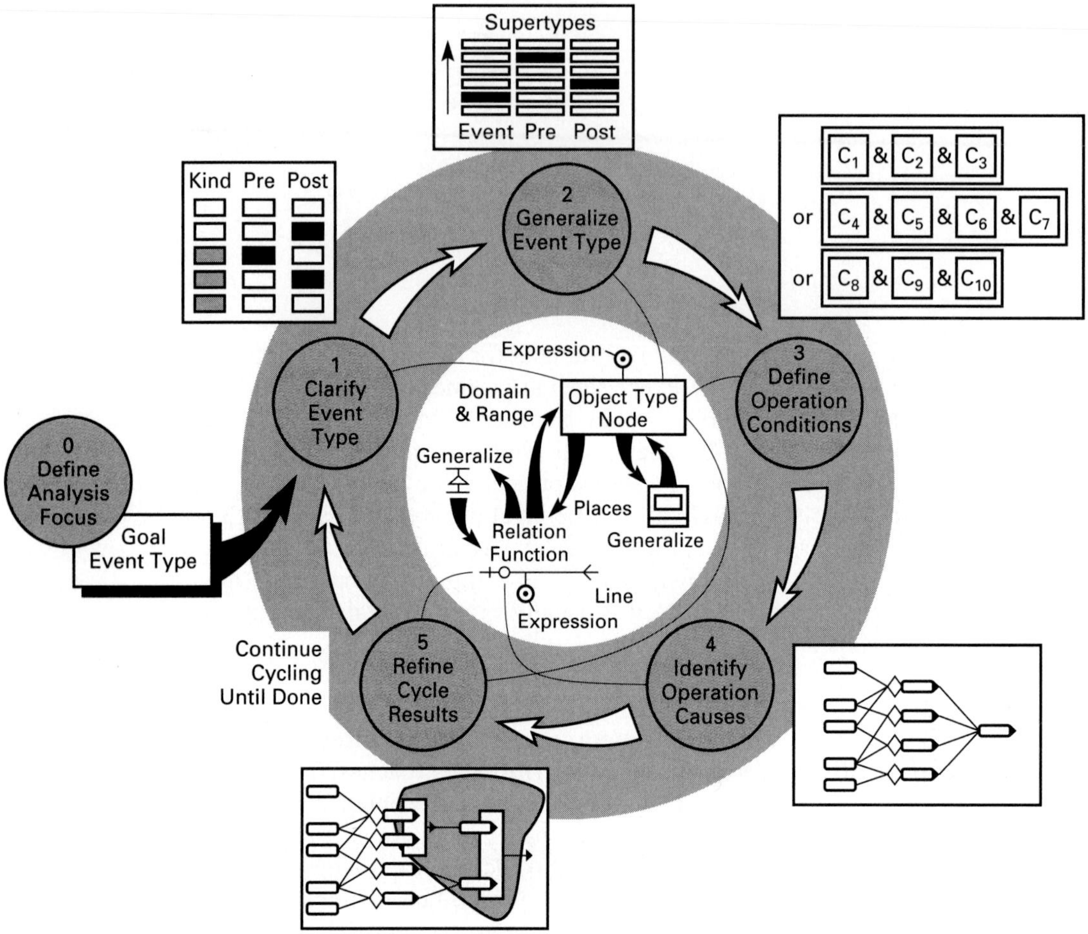

Figure 24.23 Event-driven event and object analysis method.

Step 1. Clarify Event Type

In Step 1a, the event prestates and poststates are specified in terms of object types. For example, a **Person classified Employee** event identifies two object types that must be present in the object schema: **Person** and **Employee**.

Step 2. Generalize Event Type

If a more general event type is identified to become part of this event schema, new event prestates and poststates must be identified as in Step 1, above—yielding more general object types.

Step 3. Define Operation Conditions

The conditions defined in this step contain terms. Each term requires a valid object type that must be expressed in the object schema. For example, the condition that a Bowl of Cereal object must be available for consumption requires a Bowl of Cereal object type in order to execute the condition check.

Step 4. Identify Operation Causes

Step 4d specifies the trigger rules for the event schema. Each contains a function that maps from an object of one object type to an object of another object type. For instance, to trigger a wedding operation, a function maps a given Wedding License object to bride and groom objects. In this way, the Wedding object type and its bride and groom functions must also be present in the object schema.

Step 5. Refine Cycle Results

During the refinement, both object types and functions can be generalized, specialized, or even removed. These changes, too, must be reflected in the object schema.

SUMMARY   This chapter attempts to impart some science to the process of object-oriented behavior analysis. It does so by describing a step-by-step goal-driven analysis technique for constructing event schemas.

The division between the object schemas and event schemas corresponds to the dichotomy of the *structural* and *behavioral* approaches. While this dichotomy is popular, it can cause the OO analyst to miss the point. Instead, a useful OO analysis method should rest on a behavioral foundation that incorporates the structural. This chapter, then, concludes by intimately integrating object structure analysis techniques with the object behavior analysis techniques described in the first part of the chapter.

REFERENCE

1. Kent, William, *A Framework for Object Concepts,* Hewlett-Packard, Report HPL-90-30, April 1990.

25 OBJECT-FLOW DIAGRAMS

Behavioral modeling methods, like event analysis, are appropriate for describing processes in terms of triggers, events, control conditions, and operations. However, for complicated processes like companies and large organizations, specifying the dynamics of events, triggers, and control conditions is not always possible or appropriate. Under these circumstances, a different representation method should be employed.

    This chapter presents a strategic-level approach to modeling processes. In particular, it describes an approach that is compatible with both event diagramming and strategic planning. The models built with this approach are called object-flow diagrams.

A HIGH-LEVEL FUNCTIONAL VIEW   A method that clarifies complicated processes is very important. An approach producing a coherent overview of a process landscape is preferable to an ad hoc approach which produces isolated islands of information. Specifically, this high-level perspective is very useful in the following scenarios:

- When an organization is analyzed, the problem domain is often too vast or intricate to understand using behavioral techniques (at least initially). Dividing complicated processes into manageable chunks is critical for understanding complex situations.

- The high-level understanding gained above is immediately helpful to the knowledge administrator. Those object types and processes identified form the beginnings of an enterprise model that will provide the standards for further analysis work. In this way, these reusable components support a cut-and-paste environment in which domain experts can evolve their schemas. Additionally, the simplifications inherent in this high-level orientation often provide insights into more generally useful components than originally recognized. Just how much depends on the level of abstraction. Scheduling, Allocation, and Transaction Accounting are examples of high-level processes, because they apply to many types of enterprise objects: People, Money, Goods, and so on. Reusability is actually amplified through abstractions like these.

- Existing process schemas can be expressed in terms of more general processing notions. By eliminating the details of event/trigger/condition dynamics, the analyst can concentrate on representing activity control flows and protocols. Identification of more generally useful components is now possible as described above.

- Strategic planning requires a general view of how an organization functions. Without this perspective, planning and plan execution lacks coherence. For strategic-level models, the dynamics of a behavioral model are neither necessary nor helpful. Here, a firm's collection of activities and their interactions are the important focus. The series of corporate *functions* define a baseline business model.

The Function of a Process

As already stated, the OO analyst requires a method for analyzing complicated processes such as companies and large organizations in terms of the way it functions. Here, an enterprise *function* refers to the purpose of a process. This function or purpose, then, determines the essential activities that manage the operations and resources of an organization. As such, strategic-level models do not specify dynamics. They do not indicate when activities will be activated, nor whether they will terminate on their own. Strategic-level models describe interactions among processes. The activities depicted can exist in parallel, can occur at different places, and are not synchronized with one another [1].

Data-Flow Diagrams

One way of modeling at the strategic-level is with data-flow diagrams (DFDs) as illustrated in Fig. 25.1. DFDs readily depict the strategic-level model's sense of decomposition and information flow. For example, the data can flow without necessarily defining whether or when it will flow, how often it will flow, and whether the flow will be initiated by the former activity or requested by the latter.

In other words, the strategic-level approach describes the possible flow of information and the decomposition of activities. However, it indicates nothing about how these activities and their inputs and outputs are controlled [1].

Object-Flow Diagrams

Instead of being limited to just data that flow, OO strategic-level models indicate *any* kind of object that flows between activities. In this way, this approach is relevant to the object-oriented analysis. The strategic-level model presented in this book is called an object-flow diagram. Object-flow diagrams employ a strategic-

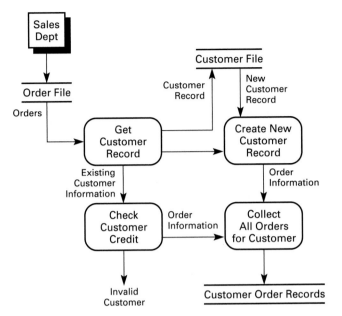

Figure 25.1   Example of a data-flow diagram.

level approach that is object-oriented. Additionally, they represent processing requirements in a way that business planners can understand and apply to strategic planning projects—not just IT projects.

Object-flow diagrams represent key enterprise activities linked by the products that activities produce and exchange.

As illustrated in Fig. 25.2(a), object-flow diagrams have two primary elements—*activities* and *products.* An activity will *produce* a product, and its product is *consumed* by one or more activities. For example, in Fig. 25.2(b), the Produce Printed Circuit Board activity produces its product, Printed Circuit Boards. This product is, in turn, consumed by the Assemble Computers activity—along with two other products—to produce yet another product, Assembled Computers. Products are considered *consumed,* because they become an integral part of the end product in some way. For instance, the Production Materials and Printed Circuit Boards become actual components in the Assemble Computers. The Hardware Designs knowledge is also an essential part of the final product— even though the knowledge is not used up in the process as are physical components. All three of these products, then, are considered consumed, because they are present—in some form—within the end product.

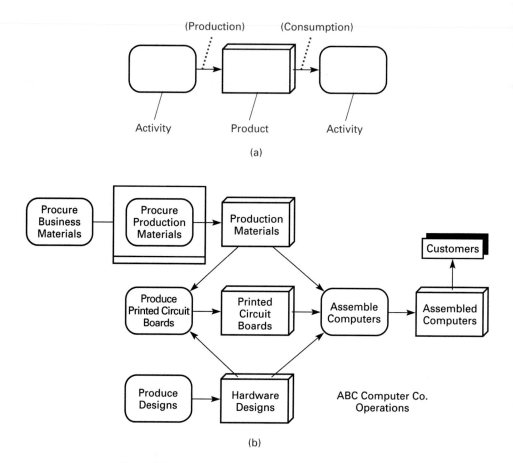

Figure 25.2   Object-flow diagram elements and example.

PRODUCTS

Products reflect the purpose of the activities that the analyst expects to understand and model. Linking back to the purpose is a sound technique in business modeling. Products are the manifestation of that purpose. When seeking productivity improvements or cost reductions, the business analyst should first identify the products. Products justify process. When designing data-processing systems, these products will guide the database structure.

> A *product* is the end result that fulfills the purpose of an activity.

Correct product identification is vital to company direction. For example, one national railway company defined its product as Running Railways, when in fact their real product was Transportation. Lacking this knowledge, they failed to realize that they were competing with other transportation vendors, such as airlines and buses. Consequently, the railway company's business and system planning went down the wrong track.

Products, therefore, should satisfy two criteria: they should be saleable and have a measurable quantity and quality.

Product Saleability

An activity can have many *outputs* such as sweat and paperwork. However, by ensuring that products are actually or potentially saleable, the modeling effort acquires a business-driven perspective.

While every product is not necessarily for sale, it should at least be potentially saleable. For example, in Fig. 25.2(b) Assembled Computers is obviously a product, because external Customers are purchasing them. While Printed Circuit Boards, Hardware Designs, and Production Materials are not currently being sold by ABC Computers, they could be sold to external customers. Additionally, if the three producing activities were external to the company or a strict accounting existed between departments, the Assemble Computers activity would be the paying customer.

While value is an important criteria for products, ownership is also important. For instance, the presence of Disneyland in Southern California dramatically boosted land values in parts of Orange County. However, Higher Land Value was not a product as far as the amusement park was concerned. Since Disneyland did not own the surrounding land, it could not sell it. Only landowners could claim this product.

Product Measureability

In addition to its value, a product should be quantifiable and its quality measureable. Unless the product can be counted and graded, the reason for producing and consuming it is questionable. For example, if a marketing firm promises to bring a company potential customers, the company should want to know how many, of what kind or quality, and when. If the marketing firm cannot provide answers, there is no way of knowing whether or not they have a product.

Worthless Products

Rigidly requiring that a product be saleable is not always appropriate. While a worthy goal of any activity, it is not always practical. For example, the Time Reports and Invoices produced by accounting and billing functions are not products that can be *sold* to accounts-payable activities. Nevertheless, they are consumed in the paying process—along with Available Money—and Payments are produced. Can this be considered value-added? Certainly, the end product of the payable function is better and more useful to some consuming activity—otherwise, the payables process would not be needed.

The point is that not every product can be sold. However, every product must be, at least, a *useful* commodity. It must be valuable enough to be consumed by another activity—one that produces something more important and useful out of something that is less so. Therefore, object-flow diagrams do not *always* represent measurable, saleable products. They do, however, model how new, more complex and subtle qualities are created at every step in an enterprise.

Products and Goals

Products and goals are often confused because both are produced by an activity. For example, in response to the analyst's question, "What is the product of this organization?" a familiar answer is, "Good profit." However, companies do not sell **Good Profit**. While a good profit is an important selling point, it is not a product. It is, however, a goal. In short, activities *produce* products and *support* goals. The solid, arrowed line leaving an activity represents production; the rectangle, its product. A different technique would have to be devised for representing goal support (such as presented in Fig. 25.3).

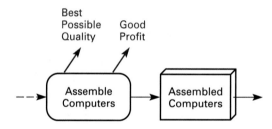

Figure 25.3   Products and goals should be modeled differently.

Another common mistake is including goal statements as part of the product name. One such example states that the product of **Assemble Computers** is "The Best Possible Quality of Assembled Computers at a Good Profit." Again, this name confuses *what* is produced with *why* it is produced. Products determine what business the activity is in; goals determine why the activity is in business. While both are immensely important for strategic planning, both have different meanings and uses. Products and goals, therefore, require separate representation.

Producer/Consumer Relationships

Each product is produced with the assumption of having at least one consumer. (Otherwise, the product has no real purpose.) Each product exchanged between a producer activity and a consumer activity establishes a relationship. Such a relationship only occurs when two activities come to an agreement on an exchanged product. Products, then, are what producers and consumers discuss.

For example, Fig. 25.4 depicts a relationship between the activity of **Telephone Operations** and the external activity of **Telephone Customers**. This relationship is based on the **Communications Channel**. The agreement is a

Figure 25.4   A telephone producer/consumer relationship.

strictly defined dialing sequence that is understood and adhered to by both parties. In this way, the caller does not need to know about the internal operations of the telephone company, as long as it responds correctly to a dialing sequence. The telephone company does not need to know what is being communicated, as long as the caller initiates a call with the correct sequence of pulses or tones. Moreover, either party is free to evolve and change the internals of its activities— as long as the interface is unaffected. If the interface is changed, it must do so with the agreement of both parties.

Two producer/consumer relationships are depicted at the top of Fig. 25.5. (These are extracted from the ABC Computer Co. Operations schema presented earlier.) The single shared subject between Produce Printed Circuit Boards and Assemble Computers is Printed Circuit Boards. Between Assemble Computers and Customers, it is Assembled Computers. These products might actually involve orders placed by the consumer, responses to these orders, product specifications, exception problems, product returns, and so on. A language should be used to express products in a clear and formal fashion. In Fig. 25.5, the Assembled Computers product is expressed with an object schema.

Handoff Versus Final Product

Sometimes an activity's product is used by another activity to produce another product. Products passed from one activity to another are called *handoffs*. Products passed to external consumers are called *final products*. In either case, a product is being produced by one activity and *bought* by another. For handoffs, the *buy-in* is internal to the analysis; for final products it is external. Qualifying products in this manner may (or may not) improve communications between analysts and experts but in no way restricts a product's usage. In other words, a product may be a handoff, a final product, or both. For example, in Fig. 25.6 Printed Circuit Boards is a handoff from Produce Printed Circuit Boards and Assemble Computers. However, if the ABC Computer Co. decided to sell its PC boards to Customers as well, Printed Circuit Boards would also be a final product.

Products as Object Types

As indicated in Fig. 25.7(a), each product is an object type in its own right. The objects to which a product applies reflect the purpose (or function) of a specific activity. As such, products can be modeled as any object type. For example, products can define product subtypes or product supertypes. In Fig. 25.7(b),

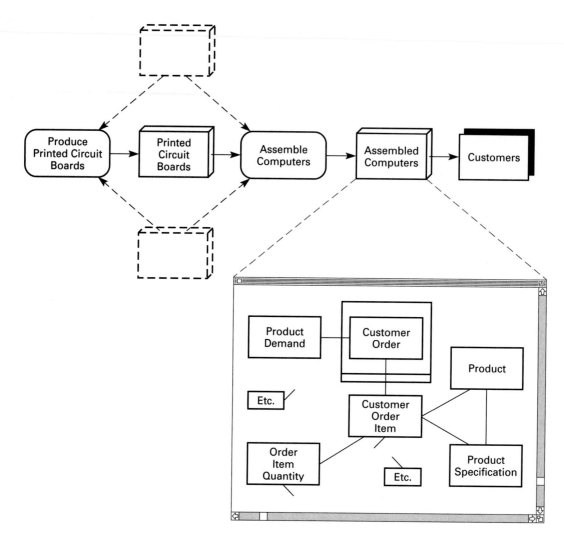

Figure 25.5 A product expressed as an object schema.

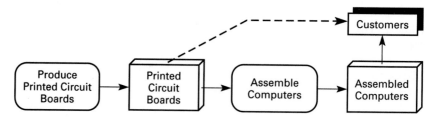

Figure 25.6 Handoffs and final products.

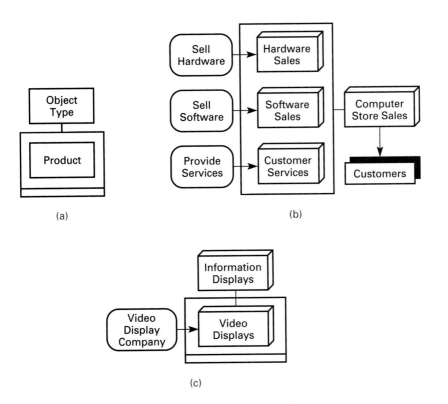

Figure 25.7   Employing products as object types.

Hardware Sales, Software Sales, and **Customer Services** are subtypes of the **Computer Store Sales** product.

Another example involves a video display company. In Fig. 25.7(c), its product is indicated as **Video Displays.** However, in order for the company executives to illustrate the type of business they were in, a product supertype is depicted. **Information Displays,** then, is a more general business segment into which the video display company fits.

ACTIVITIES

Each activity fulfills a function, namely to produce a certain product. In the process of creating its products, an activity usually consumes products created by other activities.

> An *activity* is a process whose production and consumption are specified.

In other words, activities are just processes whose dynamics are not specified. If the dynamics of events, triggers, and control conditions are known and useful, the process can be represented using an event schema.

Activity Persistence

Due to their high-level nature, activities are typically regarded as continuous processes. Because of this, each activity can be viewed as a small business in its own right. They maintain their own internal *black box* world with no indication of when they are activated and when they are terminated. We only know that they consume and emit product.

For example, Fig. 25.8 illustrates a **Flower Sales** activity. In the process, it consumes two products, **Available Flower Stock** and **Flower Requests**, and emits **Delivered Flowers**. It would seem that when **Flower Sales** receives an instance of **Flower Requests**, the activity is activated. However, this would probably not be true unless business was incredibly slow or a new shop had just received its first order. While the activity is usually not activated by flower requests, it does react to them. Additionally, the product is not necessarily emitted immediately—perhaps stock of the requested flowers has to be ordered from a supplier. Once the flower stock has arrived and been packaged for the customer, the product may then be emitted. At that point, the activity is not necessarily terminated, because other orders may also be in the works. In fact, there may be standing orders to deliver fresh bouquets periodically to various locations. In this way, activities can be processing continuously, while the external world knows nothing of how the processing occurs. While activities must react and emit, their

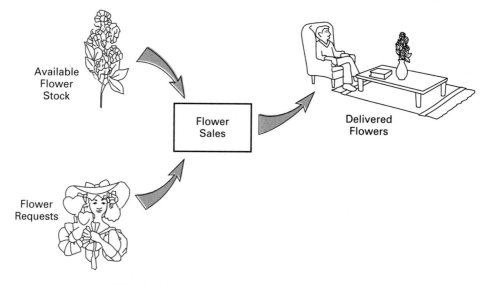

Available
Flower
Stock

Flower
Sales

Delivered
Flowers

Flower
Requests

Figure 25.8   Activities are typically continuous processes in a black box.

processes are unknown—thus the term *black box*. Such process boxes remain opaque unless an analyst *chooses* to examine their contents.

Activities Add Value

In most data-processing methods, activities transform data. An activity takes data produced by other activities and increases its value by transforming it. The transformed data then becomes a product used by other activities. In object-oriented analysis, this transformation can occur on any enterprise object—not just data objects. As indicated in Fig. 25.8, the **Flower Sales** activity takes two externally provided products of some value. The activity transforms these products in a way that adds value, since a new product must be more valuable than its components in order to be marketable.

Value Chains

These value-added transformations form *value chains*. Value chains both help analysts to think about activity analysis and are a useful technique for business planning. Value-chain analysis, as illustrated in Fig. 25.9, examines the value of the products consumed, the cost of their transformation, and the value of the produced product.

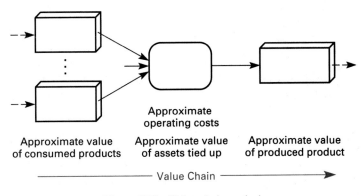

Figure 25.9   Value-chain analysis.

In particular, each activity can be analyzed to obtain the cost of carrying out the activity and the value of assets that will be tied up. Additionally, both the value of its product and the products it consumes can also be determined. In this way, value-chain analysis offers a sound financial basis for further business planning [2].

Activity-Product Pairs

As stated earlier, each product results from some purpose, and one activity fulfills that purpose. In short, each activity produces exactly one product, and each product is produced by exactly one activity. This not only keeps object-flow diagrams product oriented, it encourages clear and straightforward business modeling. In addition, this product orientation leads to object orientation.

The activity in Fig. 25.10(a) creates two products, **Access to Buying Public** and **Magazine**. To clarify the underlying complexity, breaking down such activities into two or more activities is necessary. Each activity will produce just one discrete product. Figure 25.10(b) depicts one solution to decomposing the activity in Fig. 25.10(a).

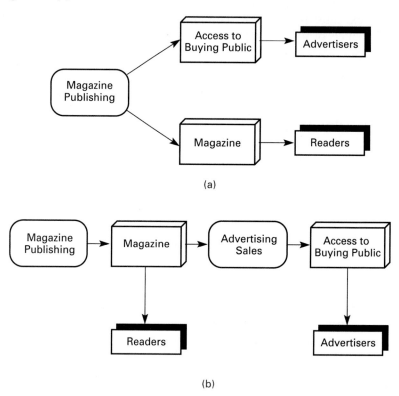

(a)

(b)

Figure 25.10   Splitting the activity to express one product for one activity.

Figure 25.11(a) illustrates a different situation where one product results from more than one activity. Here, the extent to which **Magazine Products** is produced separately by each activity is unclear. An accurate value-chain analysis is not possible. Additionally, the portion of the consolidated end-product going to **Advertisers** and the part going to **Readers** is unknowable. Without a precise idea of who produces what for whom, the analysis result will be, at best, fuzzy. Figure 25.11(b) provides greater clarity. Each activity has one product, while both products can be represented as subproducts of a more encompassing **Magazine**

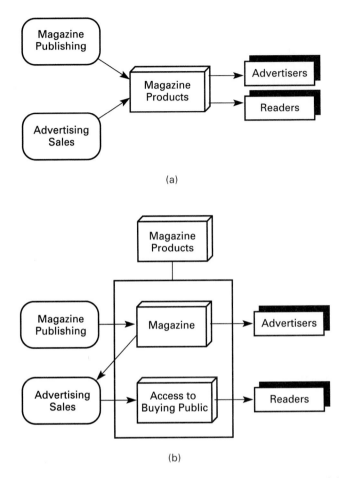

(a)

(b)

Figure 25.11   Splitting the product to express one product for one activity.

Products. Both production and consumption lines are now clear and understandable; the notion of **Magazine Products** is preserved.

Products and By-Products

Associating one activity with one product is a sound analysis guideline. The only exception is when the product is a natural by-product. *By-products* emerge as an inherent addition to an activity's primary product. By-products are often produced by an indivisible process within an activity. For example, when metal is melted, dross appears on the surface. Figure 25.12 depicts the product and a by-product of the **Car Servicing** activity. The by-product, **Scrap Metal**, is indicated with a dashed line.

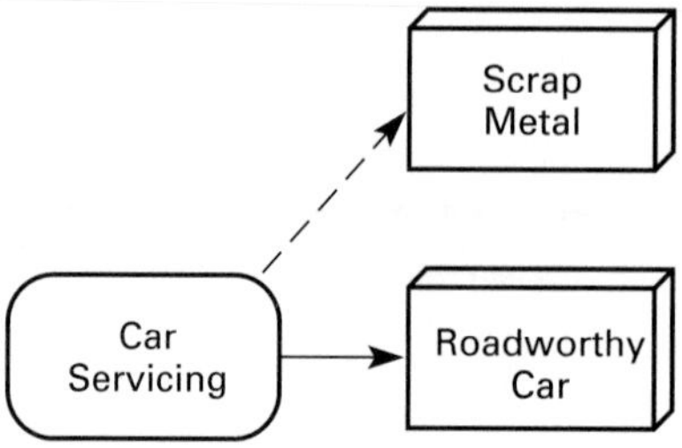

Figure 25.12   Activity product and by-product.

Consumed Products

Object-flow diagrams depict only those items that are consumed to add value—not just any kind of object flowing into an activity. This approach to object-flow representation is not so much restrictive as it is more appropriately focused. In this way, flow is addressed at its relevant level of abstraction—not earlier or later than is useful. For example, Fig. 25.13(a) represents only two valid products for **Flower Sales** consumption. The remaining products are not appropriate at this level of abstraction. Resources, such as **Working Capital** and **Order Filling Personnel**, are important to any organization. Yet, they are not consumed in order to increase value. Their consumption does not produce **Delivered Flowers**. Instead, they may be consumed by other activities such as those that are *internal* to **Flower Sales**.

Activity Leveling

Until now, activities have been presented as black boxes. This method furnishes a tangible approach for humans, while it promotes reusable, modular thinking. At some point, however, the analyst may wish to examine the inner workings of an activity. As illustrated in Fig. 25.13(b) and Fig. 25.14, activities are composed of process clusters. By *leveling down,* an activity can be functionally decomposed into its appropriate process components. In contrast, by *leveling up,* a group of interrelated processes can be defined as a higher level activity.

Each level in a hierarchy establishes its own separate process space or *realm.* Each process realm is subject to its own object schema, with its own nested behavior. An activity's process realm is not visible to its superrealm until a product is emitted or consumed products are injected. This modularity greatly simplifies large processes. Some objects may be known only within a realm, while others may be known externally as well. As long as the external products have been agreed on, each process realm can have an internal reality that is quite different from any of the others.

Figure 25.15 illustrates an example of activity leveling. On the left, a **Primary Enterprise Activity** produces an **Enterprise Product**. (Nonprimary or supporting activities are presented following this subsection.) *Primary activities* involve product creation, its sale and distribution, and any subsequent servicing.

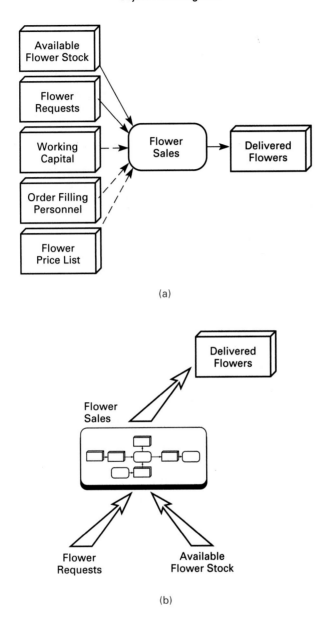

(a)

(b)

Figure 25.13   Not all resources are consumed products.

These activities are diagrammed within the shaded realm. While each of them has its own specialized purpose, together they fulfill the function specified for the Primary Enterprise Activity.

    These five activities are generic to most organizations. Each activity is

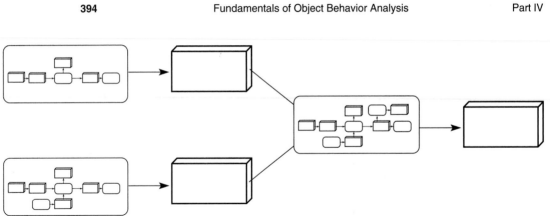

Figure 25.14   Each realm is a nested activity space.

decomposable into even more distinct activities depending on the particular industry. Inbound Logistics involves materials handling, storage, inventory control, and returns to suppliers. If it were tied to another general enterprise activity, Inbound Logistics would be declared a subtype of Procurement. Operations includes such activities as machining, assembly, testing, packaging, and facility operations. Outbound Logistics are associated with warehousing finished goods, material handling, and delivery operations. Marketing and Sales includes everything from advertising and promotion, to pricing and order processing. Finally, a Service activity provides the service to enhance or maintain the value of a product, such as installation, training, and repair [2].

The Primary Enterprise Activity, described above, is one example of activity leveling. When doing top-down leveling, activity analysis is not completely accurate, because not enough is known about the detail it comprises. However, even having a high level, strategic view that is approximately correct gives a vantage point for planning and coordinating the enterprise process.

Object-Flow Diagrams and Event Schema Leveling

The object-flow diagrams in Fig. 25.16 are depicted as decomposing to further levels of object-flow diagrams. However, since activities represent processes, each can also be decomposed into an event schema representation. In top-down analysis, object-flow diagrams are commonly decomposed to object-flow diagrams until enough is known to represent a process as an event schema. However, this is not necessarily the case. Object-flow diagrams are one way of describing processes, event schemas are another. Therefore, an object-flow diagram can be decomposed into either or both descriptions—depending on the analyst's need.

Additionally, object-flow diagrams are not necessarily for top-down analysis. They can also be employed to compose bottom-up descriptions. In many

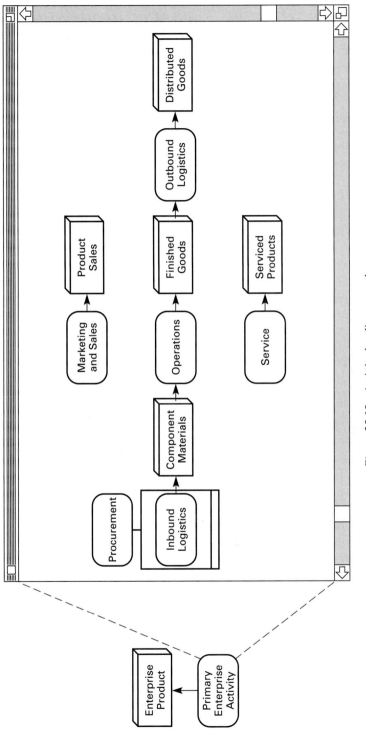

Figure 25.15 Activity leveling example.

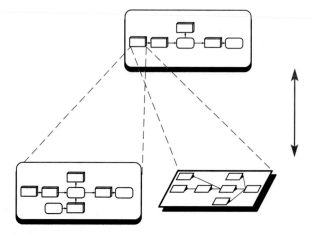

Figure 25.16 Leveling with object-flow diagrams and/or event schemas.

cases an analyst may wish to do both. For example, one analysis approach might begin with top-down approach and followed by a bottom-up refinement once the details are better understood.

Activities as Object Types

Like the product, activities are also types of objects (see Fig. 25.17). Each activity object is an executing process realm. This realm consumes objects from specific product(s) and produces objects for a specific product. As such, activities can be modeled as an object type. For example, Fig. 25.17(b) represents

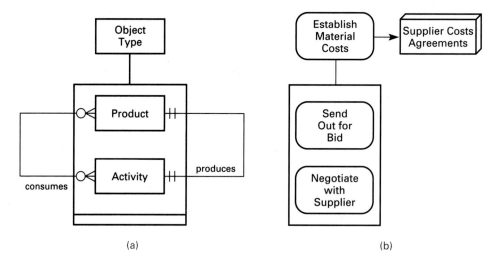

Figure 25.17 Activity is an object type and can, therefore, be partitioned.

Establish Material Costs partitioned into two more specific activities. In this case, an execution of either **Send Out for Bid** or **Negotiate with Supplier** activities is also an execution of **Establish Material Costs**.

Figure 25.18 depicts an example of partitioned activities at the highest level of modeling. As with the example in Fig 25.15, these activities are generic examples of those found in any competing industry. Government services and nonprofit organizations may differ, but only slightly. The **Enterprise Activity** is initially partitioned into two activities, a **Primary Enterprise Activity** (presented earlier) and a **Supporting Enterprise Activity**. Support activities are separated, because they service the primary activities and each other through various company-wide functions.

The **Supporting Enterprise Activity** is further partitioned into four more activities. **Enterprise Infrastructure Management** consists of activities including

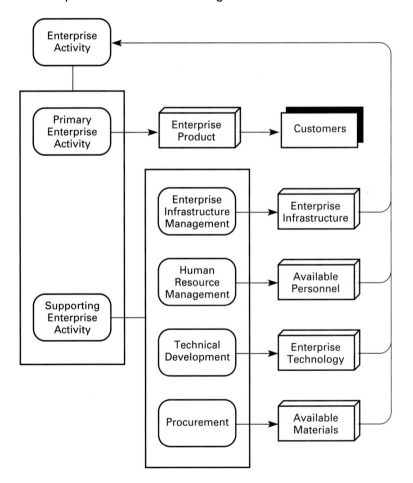

Figure 25.18 Activity subtypes.

general management, planning, finance, accounting, legal, government affairs, and so on. Human Resource Management entails all personnel related issues from recruiting, hiring, and contracting through training, development, and compensation. Technical Development is involved in improving the product and the process and takes many forms. It embodies the know-how and procedures for product design, product servicing, and equipment design—as well as, all supporting services. Last, Procurement refers to the function of purchasing products to be consumed by all of the firm's activities. It deals with suppliers, orders, and goods, and tracks them to their final distribution point [2].

Activity subtypes, then, provide a hierarchy of activity generalization and specialization that can be reused during activity analysis. In Fig. 25.15, every instance of Inbound Logistics is an instance of Procurement. With Fig. 25.17, this same instance is also an instance of Supporting Enterprise Activity, which is also an instance of Enterprise Activity.

SUMMARY

Object-flow diagrams provide an architecture of self-contained components and strictly defined interfaces. By dividing complicated processes into manageable chunks, they enable an understanding that is critical in complex situations.

Object-flow diagrams represent the *function* or purpose of a process instead of the dynamics of its triggers, events, and control conditions. They describe interactions among processes, yet do not indicate when or how its processes will be activated or terminated. Their processes can exist in parallel, can occur at different places, and are not synchronized with one another. Object-flow diagrams employ a strategic-level approach in an OO manner. Additionally, they represent processing requirements in a way that business planners can understand and apply to strategic planning exercises.

Each *activity* is a process that is performed to achieve a specific purpose. A *product* is the end result of that purpose. Each product is potentially saleable. Activities consume these saleable objects, add value to the objects, and produce a new product.

Object-flow diagrams indicate chains of producer/consumer relationships by depicting them as a series of activities and exchanged products. Such a relationship only occurs when two activities come to an agreement on an exchanged product. The product, then, is the subject matter of their communications.

In terms of systems construction, object-flow diagrams offer additional benefits in the following areas:

- Concurrent Engineering—Object-flow diagrams clearly show those sets of activities that exhibit sequence independence. They are, therefore, considered to be acting in parallel. For example in Fig. 25.18, Technical Development and Procurement, though they may interface in some manner, operate in parallel. In this way, object-flow diagrams can support the concurrent engineering of application systems—as well as develop distributed processing or parallel computing applications.

- Systems Integration—The history of systems development has taught us that independent development of component activities is no great trick. The real skill is ensuring that independently developed activities are integrated. This can be achieved by locking down their interfaces. Object-flow diagrams aid integration by precisely defining the products exchanged and the communications specification for this exchange. Once these are defined, the analyst can evolve the implementation rules for interface communication.

REFERENCES

1. Harel, D., "Statemate: A Working Environment for the Development of Complex Reactive Systems," *IEEE 10th Conference on Software Engineering,* 1988, pp. 396–406.

2. Porter, Michael E., *Competitive Advantage,* The Free Press, New York, 1985.

3. Tsichritzis, Dionysios C. and Frederick H. Lochovsky, *Data Models,* Prentice-Hall, Englewood Cliffs, NJ, 1982.

PART **V** DESIGN

26 OBJECT-ORIENTED DESIGN: MAPPING TO OOPL STRUCTURES

The particular approach to object-oriented analysis presented in this book models the way people understand and process reality—through the concepts they acquire. These concepts can be implemented in a variety of ways, including machines, computers, and people. Implementation, then, can involve valves, pipes, measurement devices, circuitry, gates, controllers, material flow, management rules, and so on. However, in this book, the design scope is restricted to software applications. This chapter applies the knowledge gained from object schemas and maps them into the *structural* aspects of object-oriented programming languages. The next chapter presents ways of mapping event schemas for designing the *behavioral* aspects of an OOPL. Chapter 28 will explore a few considerations for implementing OO analysis schemas with traditional languages and relational databases.

MAPPING FROM SCHEMAS TO OO CODE

Producing OOPL designs with the OO analysis schemas presented in this book is very straightforward. OO programming languages are structured similarly to the way we conceptualize. This is one of the benefits of OOPLs.

The conversion from OOA terms to OOPL constructs can be described in a basic way using the table that follows:

Object-schema term	OOPL mapping
object type	*class*
object	*object*
function, base (or base attribute)	*field*
generalization hierarchy	*class/subclass hierarchy with inheritance*
function, computed* (or computed attribute)	*operation*
computed object-type*	*operation*

*Described in detail in Appendix C.

Event-schema term	OOPL mapping
operation	*operation*
trigger rule	*request type* supported by an event scheduler
event type	no equivalent; supported by an event scheduler
event schema	*method* or event scheduler

MAPPING FROM OBJECT TYPES

As defined in Chapter 15, concepts are shared notions that we apply to the objects around us. In OO programming languages, concepts, also called object types, can be implemented as OOPL *classes.*

When implementing object types as OOPL classes, the designer must also ensure that two basic kinds of fundamental operations are provided for each class: operations that construct instances of classes and operations that destruct instances of classes.

Object Construction

When a class constructs its instances, it allocates storage and sets up the initial values of the object's attributes or *fields.* In doing so, it not only brings the object into existence but ensures that all constraints are met. For example, to construct an Employee object, an Employee class operation must first allocate storage for the object. If the Employee class is implemented as indicated in Fig. 26.1, a class operation must—in addition—ensure that each Employee object have an association with exactly one Organization object. Without an actual employed by association, the Employee object cannot exist. However, according to this diagram, an Employee object can exist without a works for or supervised by association. Therefore, the only other constraint that needs checking is that the Employee object is created with no more than one works for: Employee association.

Every OOPL class has an operation to allocate storage for its new instances. However in several OOPLs, the operation is awkward to supplement or cannot be supplemented at all—making it difficult or impossible to embed constraint checking code. Thus, it is advisable to design object construction as two separate operations for each class: Create and Initialize. The Create operation allocates the storage for the class's object. The Initialize operation builds the object according to the class's specifications and constraints.

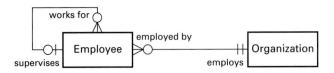

Figure 26.1   Cardinality constraints are observed when creating and terminating objects.

In practice, the Create operation in a C++ class is called the *constructor* and always has the same name as its class. A separate Initialize operation can then be invoked when the execution of the constructor is complete. While some designers may wish to combine the Create and Initialize operations, in Object Pascal the developer must provide an Initialize operation. This is because the Object Pascal creation operation cannot be overridden. On the other hand, OOCobol already incorporates both Create and Initialize as predefined operations.

Object Destruction

The destruction of an object must also adhere to the constraints defined in the object schema. For example, in Fig. 26.1 each Employee object has a mandatory association with an Organization object. By removing an Organization object to which an Employee is linked, the employed by cardinality constraint is violated. This can be resolved in two ways. One is by preventing the company's termination until all the employees are terminated. The other involves rippling the effect of terminating the company by terminating all linked employees. Thus, the termination of one instance of a class can have far-reaching consequences across many objects.

As with object construction, object destruction also suggests separate operations for each class: Finalize and Terminate. The Finalize operation detaches the object from its class-related associations while ensuring the integrity of the database. The Terminate operation deallocates any class-related storage occupied by the object. All OOPLs have a Terminate equivalent; only OOCobol has both Finalize and Terminate as predefined operations.

MAPPING FROM OBJECTS

In analysis, objects are instances of object types. In an OOPL, objects are instances of classes. The physical implementation, then, of an OOA object is also called an *object*.

In OO programs, objects are often thought of as records—records whose access is permitted via the operations of its class. In conventional languages, a record can only be accessed by the *file* to which it belongs. This record cannot be readily used by different types of files—only by the file description that created it. The same limitation is true of most OOPLs: an object is an instance of its creating class for the life of the object.

Dynamic Classification

Changing an object from being an instance of one class to an instance of another is called *dynamic classification*. For example, in Fig. 26.2 the Sigourney object can be reclassified from being an Unemployed Person to being an Employed Person. In an OODBMS such as Iris, dynamic classification is supported. In OOPLs such as Smalltalk and CLOS, the ability to change the class of an object

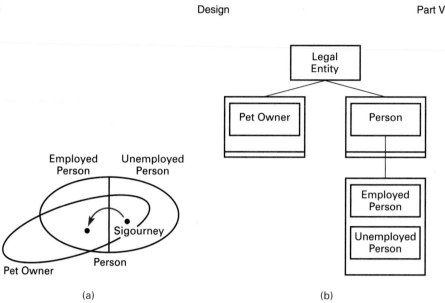

Figure 26.2   Few OOPLs directly support dynamic and multiple classification.

is limited. In general, it is not directly supported by most OOPLs and is therefore cumbersome to implement. Typically, dynamic classification is implemented by explicitly creating a new object, copying the attributes of the old object to the new object, and then deleting the old object.

When a developer wishes to implement dynamic classification, the same functionality of the Initialize and Finalize must be present. Before an existing object can become an instance of a different class, the class's Initialize operation must be invoked. Before an object is declassified from a class, the class's Finalize operation must be invoked. These operations ensure that the class changes result in structures that are consistent with the object schema.

Multiple Classification

Classifying an object as an instance of several OOPL classes at the same time is called *multiple classification*. The class/subclass hierarchy is one way of classifying an object in multiple ways. For example, if Sigourney is an instance of the Employed Person class, she is also an instance of Person and Legal Entity* as shown in Fig. 26.2(b). In other words, when Sigourney is classified as an Employed Person, the Person and Legal Entity classifications are implied by the superclass hierarchy.

However, an object can also be an instance of multiple classes that are not implied using a superclass hierarchy. For example, multiple classification makes

---

*A Legal Entity can be a Person or an Organization. Therefore, either can be a Pet Owner. In this way, Sigourney and the Evanston Emus Bugle Corps can each have an Emu as a pet.

it possible for the Sigourney object in Fig. 26.2 to be an instance of both the Person and Pet Owner classes. The class of Pet Owner is not a superclass of Employed Person. Therefore, if Sigourney is an instance of Employed Person, she is not necessarily an instance of Pet Owner. In order for Sigourney to be a Pet Owner, Sigourney must—in addition—be explicitly classified as a Pet Owner. Over time, this change in classification could look something like the graph in Fig. 26.3(a).

Multiple classification, based on a class/subclass hierarchy, is supported and is one of the benefits of OOPLs. However, multiple classifications that are *not* part of an object's inheritance hierarchy are not supported by OOPLs. Typically, if a developer wishes to get around this limitation, additional classes are specified. These additional classes define the necessary multiple classification combinations. For instance, to support the Sigourney object as a Pet Owner being reclassified from an Unemployed Person to an Employed Person, two additional subclasses are defined: Unemployed Pet Owner and Employed Pet Owner as illustrated in Fig 26.3(b). The Unemployed Pet Owner class will be a subclass of both Unemployed Person and Pet Owner; the Employed Pet Owner class will be a subclass of both Employed Person and Pet Owner. In this way, multiple classification could be handled via the inheritance mechanisms when using multiple inheritance OOPLs. This approach has two drawbacks: a class is needed for every combination, and not all OOPLs support multiple inheritance.

Object Slicing

In order to support the dynamic and multiple classification requirements of a system, one recommended technique is called *object slicing*. In object slicing, an object with multiple classifications can be thought of as being sliced into multiple pieces. Each piece is then distributed to one of the object's various classes. For example in Fig. 26.2, the Sigourney object is depicted as an instance of the Employed Person and Pet Owner classes. To record these two facts in a typical OOPL, one piece of the Sigourney object must become an instance of Employed Person, and the other an instance of Pet Owner.

Obviously, objects cannot be sliced and made into instances of classes: it is a metaphor. These slices, however, can be implemented by surrogate objects. In addition, an unsliced version of the object must also be recorded to serve—physically and conceptually—as a unification point for its surrogates. The slices, then, become the various recorded aspects of one unsliced object. One way to accomplish this is by adding two new classes: Implementation Object and Conceptual Object. The instances of Implementation Object are the object slices, where each is an instance of a different class. The instances of Conceptual Object are the unsliced objects, where each maintains pointers to its various slices.

An example of how object slicing can be applied is illustrated in Fig. 26.4. In this figure, the unsliced Sigourney object is represented as an instance of the Conceptual Object class. This one object representing Sigourney as a whole

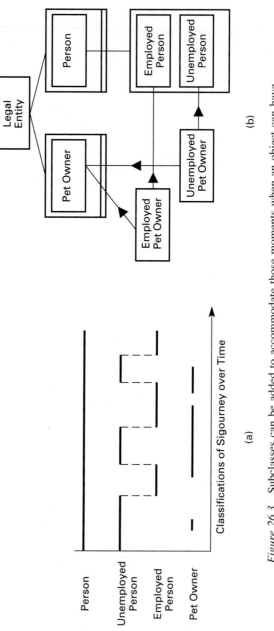

(b)

Classifications of Sigourney over Time

(a)

Figure 26.3 Subclasses can be added to accommodate those moments when an object can have multiple classifications.

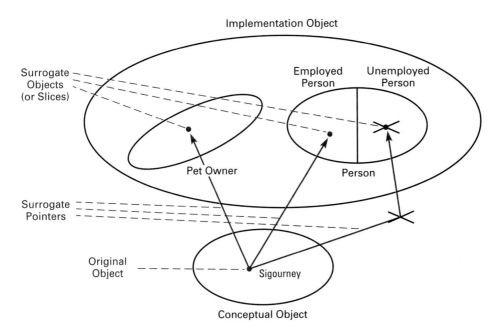

Figure 26.4   Object slicing supports dynamic and multiple classification.

points to multiple Sigourney object slices. Since these slices represent different class implementations of the conceptual Sigourney object, they are instances of the **Implementation Object** class. The instances in the **Pet Owner** and **Employed Person** classes are slices of the Sigourney object. In other words, object slices of the whole Sigourney object are also Sigourney objects. However, the slices comply with the conventional OOPL requirement that each is an instance of only one class.

Changes in state can be accomplished by adding or removing the surrogates and their pointers. For instance, when Sigourney was classified as **Unemployed Person**, there was a pointer from the **Conceptual Object** Sigourney to the **Unemployed Person** Sigourney surrogate. When Sigourney became employed, the surrogate **Unemployed Person** object and its pointer were removed, and replaced by a surrogate **Employed Person** Sigourney object and its pointer.

As each object is added or removed from the various classes, the **Create**, **Initialize**, **Finalize**, and **Terminate** operations would still apply. However, the object-slicing mechanism must add to these class-level operations by ensuring that objects do not have conflicting multiple states. For instance, an object can simultaneously be an instance of the **Pet Owner** and **Employed Person** classes. However, it cannot simultaneously be an instance of both the **Unemployed Person** and **Employed Person** classes: it must be an instance of one or the other. In other words, an object cannot be classified as an **Employed Person** without first removing the object from the **Unemployed Person** class.

Object slicing is a reasonably elegant solution to a problem not yet well-supported by OOPLs. However, in addition to the programming overhead mentioned above, object slicing also requires extra logic to support polymorphism and supplement the OOPL's method-selection mechanism. This extra requirement is not used for those subtyping partitions declared as static. When a partition is static, the normal polymorphic support of the OOPL can be used. In this way, object slicing can be selectively applied. The developer must choose according to the application's requirements.*

MAPPING FROM BASE FUNCTIONS   Two kinds of functions are presented in Chapter 19—base and computed. A base function defined on an object type is implemented in OOPLs as a *field* in a class. (The implementation of computed functions are presented in the following section.) In some OOPLs, fields are often referred to as *instance variables* or *slots.*

Fields are either references to other objects or data values stored within the object's data structure. The precise nature of a field depends on its implementation language. In Smalltalk, a field defining an integer value references an object that is an instance of the Integer class. In C++, strings and numbers can be contained by a class *or* referenced by a pointer.

To implement each function, a number of fundamental field operations are required to query values (sometimes referred to as *accessors* or *selectors*) and to change them (*modifiers*).

Minimum Cardinality Constraints

Cardinality constraints for functions are described in Chapter 19. The minimum cardinality constraint defines the minimum number of objects to which a given object must map. A minimum cardinality constraint of zero means that an object's minimum mapping is unconstrained. A minimum cardinality constraint of one means that an object must be mapped to at least one other object.

In order to enforce these constraints, the program must be able to distinguish when a field is *null* and when it has one or more values. Fields defined as pointers can be explicitly set to null. However, fields defined as data values have no explicit null designation. Since only a small number of operations directly access a field, the choice of the null representation is easily managed.

Maximum Cardinality Constraints

As mentioned earlier, base functions are implemented as fields that either reference other objects or stored data values. A function that maps to at most one

---

*Using flags in place of subclasses is another tactic and will be discussed in the following section.

object can be implemented as a field that stores a single object reference or data value. A function that maps to more than one object, however, requires some kind of *collection* to hold its various object references or data values. For example, Fig. 26.5 illustrates that each Organization object maps to a set of objects. The NASA Organization maps to a set containing two Person objects Paul and Jasper; IBM to a set containing one Jane Person object; ABC to a set containing no Person objects; and so on. In Smalltalk, these sets are generally implemented using a subclass of Collection. The inverse function does not require a Collection because each Person object has at most one employer.

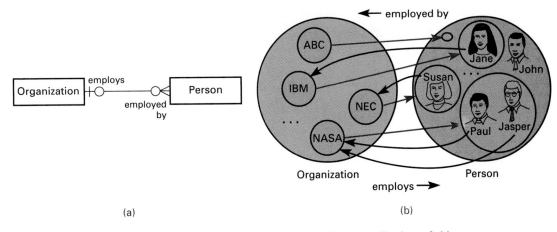

Figure 26.5   Pointer fields can point to single objects or collections of objects.

Fundamental Operations for Functions

As mentioned in the beginning of this chapter, each OOPL class should have four fundamental operations to maintain its objects. These are listed in Fig. 26.6. In a similar manner, fields also have fundamental operations.

Because of their simplicity, single-valued fields require only two fundamental operations: Assign and Get. The Assign operation establishes a field's object reference or data value. This means that the field can be set to contain a reference or value, be changed to a different reference or value, or be assigned a null designation. The Get operation returns the data value contained in, or the object referenced by the field. When there is no reference or value to return, a null condition is indicated. For example in Fig. 26.5(b), an employed_by_Get* operation for Susan would return NEC; for John it would return a null condition. An employed_by_Assign operation could change Susan's employer from NEC to

---

*A fully qualified name for this operation would be Person_employed_by_Organization_ Get. In order to avoid confusion and name duplication, the programmer should always use the full, qualified function name. It is abbreviated here for readability only.

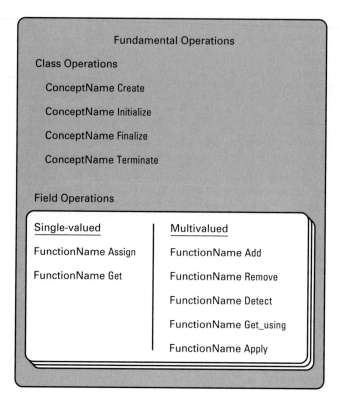

Figure 26.6   Fundamental operations for classes and functions.

another **Organization** object; for John it could establish an employer where previously no such association existed.

In contrast, multivalued fields require at least five fundamental operations. The operations are different because they are manipulating collections of fields, rather than just one. As mentioned above, a **Collection** is a class that is used for handling multiple similar objects. Smalltalk, for example, provides a variety of useful collections. The simplest of these is a **Bag** that holds multiple objects but does not check for duplicates. A **Set** class is a **Collection** without duplicates; while **Dictionary** and **Array** classes are **Sets** indexed by an explicit key and value. **Lists** arrange their elements in a particular order. More complex structures such as **Trees** and **Directed Graphs** are also available. Usually the **Collection** class has operations to insert and remove elements and a means to apply some operation to all elements (sometimes called *applicators* or *enumerators*). Often **Collections** will come with an *iterator* operation which acts as a cursor to work through the elements of the **Collection**.

The form of **Collection** chosen depends on how the function will be used and which subclasses of **Collection** are available. Languages that do not have a **Collection** class, such as C++, require the programmer to supplement the code.

Here, a common solution is to use an iterator and a macro to define a WHILE loop to iterate through the collection of elements.

The fundamental operations required for multivalued fields are Add, Remove, Detect, Get_using, and Apply. The Add operation adds a pointer or data value to its function's multivalued collection. The Remove operation deletes a pointer or data value from its function's multivalued collection. The Detect procedure tests to see if a given object is in the function's range.

The fact that such a variety of operations is required for Collections means that it is difficult to give a standard set of operations. These operations depend on which Collection subclasses are available and how they are applied. The Get_using operation, then, allows the programmer to select a specific method (among a possible many) that retrieves objects in the function's range. The Apply operation extends beyond the retrieval-only limitation of the Get_using. It allows the programmer to select a specific method that *updates* object associations.

Modification Constraint Checking

Whenever a field modification is requested, all specified constraints must be checked. The Add operation should check that the cardinality upper bound is not exceeded, and the Remove operation should check that the cardinality lower bound is not violated. For single-valued fields, the Assign operation should ensure that a null is not placed in it if the cardinality lower bound is greater than zero.

As discussed in Chapter 20, if a function is defined as immutable, no modifier operations should be allowed. Any setting of immutable values must be made when the object is created. In other words, only the Create operation sets immutable fields. In subsequent operations, only the Get, Get_using, and Detect routines are allowed.

Referential Integrity for Inverse Functions

Implementing functions also requires a consideration of their inverses. Use of pointers or unique object identifiers (OIDs) can ensure that references to objects do refer to objects that exist. However, when associating or disassociating mapped objects, correctly maintaining inverse mappings is important. For example in Fig. 26.7(a), if Peter leaves NASA, the reference from Peter to NASA must be removed. In addition—to maintain referential integrity—any inverse reference from NASA to Peter must also be removed.

Maintaining mappings and their inverses is commonly accomplished in two ways. In the first approach, depicted in Fig. 26.7(a), each object holds its own references to its mapped object(s). Therefore, whenever an Add, Remove, or Assign operation is invoked for an object's field, the same operation must be invoked for the inverse. For instance, if the employed_by_Assign operation is invoked to remove Peter's **employed by** reference to NASA, the **employs_ Remove** operation is invoked to remove NASA's **employs** reference to Peter.*

Another approach to maintaining mappings and their inverses is to define an association object. This new object, illustrated in Fig. 26.7(b), is a tuple that only holds references to its linked objects. In this way, only one object needs to be added or removed to maintain mapping integrity. However, cardinality-constraint checking can be more difficult if upper bound constraints exist in either direction. If this is the case, all association objects must be accessed to ensure the bounds are not violated. Additionally, queries across the functions can be cumbersome unless indexes are added. In short, the designer must choose on the basis of performance and space requirements.

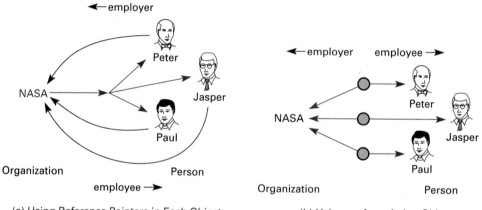

(a) Using Reference Pointers in Each Object   (b) Using an Association Object

Figure 26.7   Two ways of maintaining mappings and their inverses.

When Not to Maintain Inverses

Referential integrity is not an issue when inverse references are not maintained. For example in Fig. 26.8(a), each **Person** can possess a primary skill. While many functions have an inverse, the inverse is not always implemented. For example, the inverse function in Fig. 26.8(b) is not implemented. In this example, all **Person** objects will have a pointer field to **Skill**, but **Skill** objects will have no inverse pointer field to **Person**. Therefore, whenever a person's primary skill changes, only the primary skill pointer needs to be changed.

By not implementing an inverse pointer field, there is no referential integrity to maintain. However, the time and effort to determine which people have a specific skill is greatly increased—making queries and cardinality constraint checking costly. (However, when the inverse is not constrained, no cardinality

---

*Obviously, the programmer would have to construct the code so that the invoked operation would not recall the original operation. This infinite recursion could easily be prevented by defining an extra request parameter on each operation in order to prevent the recall step.

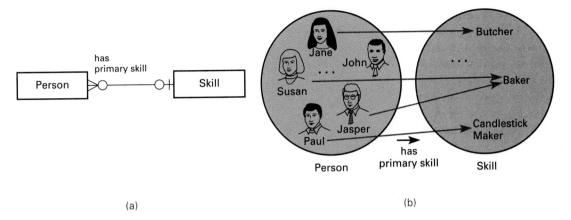

(a)   (b)

Figure 26.8   Functions do not require implemented inverses.

constraint checking is necessary. This is the case with the Skill to Person mapping in Fig. 26.8.)

**MAPPING FROM
GENERALIZATION
HIERARCHIES**

Generalization and specialization is a fundamental notion in object-oriented analysis. In object-oriented programming languages class/subclass hierarchies are typically implemented using an inheritance mechanism. For example, in Fig. 26.9 all the fields and permissible operations of Person are inherited by all of its subclasses: Customer, Employee, Manager,

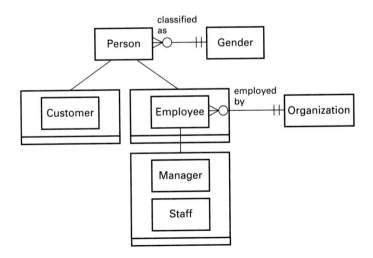

Figure 26.9   A generalization hierarchy of object types can be implemented as class/subclass hierarchies using inheritance.

and Staff. In turn, all the fields and permissible operations of Employee are inherited by its subclasses Manager and Staff.

Using Flags in Place of Subclasses

However, while mapping each subtype to a subclass produces technically correct coding, the result may not be efficient. For example, if Manager and Staff have no fields and operations defined for their classes, the OOPL overhead of the two subclass implementations may not be justified. In this situation, a *flag* field could be added to the superclass *in place of* actual subclasses. In the example above, this would mean not implementing Manager and Staff as subclasses, but instead adding a Manager_Staff_Flag to the Employee class. In other words, the flag field alone would indicate whether an object is a Manager or a Staff instance.

Using flags instead of actual subclasses facilitates changes in classification. For instance, when an Employee is promoted to Manager, the object's classification changes from Staff to Manager. In most OOPLs, an object's classification is static and such changes are not directly supported. However, when a system requires dynamic classification, using flags is one such mechanism—two others will be presented later in this section.

When flags are used in place of subclasses, all fields and permissible operations defined for the subclasses must be relocated to their superclass. In addition, control conditions must be placed on the usage of these fields and operations. For instance, the operation that reclassifies a Staff object to Manager must now ensure that the object is a Staff object prior to its promotion. Or, if the Employee class were to be represented as a flag in the Person class, a guard would have to be placed on using the employed_by field. In other words, the Person class must ensure that an object is an Employee in order to access and change employed_by information.

Using Private Subclasses Instead
of Public Subclasses

In the flag approach, all fields belonging to the replaced subclasses must be relocated to their superclass—whether used or not. For example, if the Employee class were to be represented as a flag in the Person class, every Person object must have a field for employed_by—even if the person is never employed. Therefore, if the number of fields defined for the various subclasses is large, the flag approach can be very wasteful of storage. In this case, a different mechanism can be used where the subclass is defined as *private* to its class (rather than *public* for access by any class). For example, if Employee class were defined in this way, it would be accessible only by the class Person. In short, no other class can be aware of the Employee subclass, except Person. The Person class alone has a pointer reference to Employee, where a null pointer means that the person is not an employee.

An additional feature of private subclasses is that while the subclass retains its fields, its operations are placed and *guarded* in its superclass. In the example above, all **Employee**-related functions are defined as fields in the **Employee** class, while all **Employee**-related operations are defined for the **Person** class. This retains the simplicity of the flag method without wasting any storage for **Person** objects that are not **Employee**s.

Object Slices, Revisited

Another mechanism for supporting dynamic classification is object slicing. Object slicing, discussed earlier in this chapter, supports the ability of an object to be classified in many ways—and to do so dynamically. With object slicing each subtype can be implemented as an OOPL subclass. An object's classification, then, can change from **Staff** to **Manager** through the object slicing technique. At the same time, this technique can take advantage of the inheritance from **Employee** and **Person** superclasses.

MAPPING FROM COMPUTED FUNCTIONS

The mapping from base functions is presented earlier in this chapter. Since base functions assert associations between objects, they are typically implemented as fields. Computed functions, however, derive or calculate their associations using other functions. A way of expressing computed functions is presented in Chapter 19 and Appendix C.

Each function expression is specified in terms of one or more processing steps. For example, Fig. 26.10(b) depicts the has parents function graphically

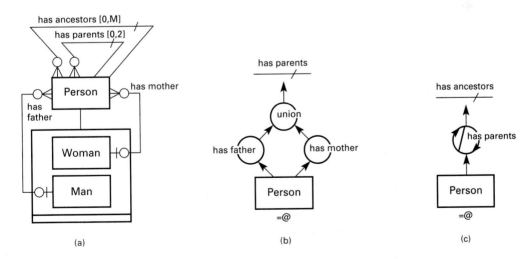

Figure 26.10   Function expressions are reusable operations.

expressed in terms of the two functions has mother and has father, and a union operator. In other words, the parent function uses the has mother and has father functions and returns the resulting objects. As depicted in Fig. 26.10(c), the computed function can serve as a processing step within another function expression. In this way, the function expression can be treated as an operation in its own right. In most OOPLs, then, computed functions are implemented as operations.

Figure 26.10(b) expresses a computed function for has parents. Since has parents is a multivalued function with an upper-bound cardinality constraint of two, its mapping could be implemented as a collection of two pointers to Person objects. Additionally, since its domain is Person, the has parents function would be implemented for the Person class as a has_parents_Get_using operation. The implementation could simply entail returning the has_mother and has_father field values as the two parents.

Function Expressions are Reusable

As mentioned earlier, computed functions can employ other computed functions in the process of calculating its result. Computed functions, therefore, must be reusable implementations. For example, the has ancestors function in Fig. 26.10(c) can be expressed as a transitive closure invocation of a reusable has parents implementation. In the case of the has ancestors and has parents functions, both will be implemented as operations for the Person class.

Function Expressions Can be Eager
or Lazy

When an operation should occur for a computed function is a design decision—it can be *eager* or *lazy*. An eager calculation evaluates its results whenever a change in one of its component mappings occurs. For instance, if the has parents function were eager, it would calculate the has parents whenever the mother or father of a Person were changed. A lazy calculation, on the other hand, does not evaluate its results whenever a change occurs. Instead, it calculates the results only when a specific request is made. For instance, if the has ancestors function were lazy, it would evaluate the has ancestors only when a request is issued.

Function Expressions and Cardinality
Constraints

The choice between eager and lazy functions is often based on performance criteria—particularly if the computed function is used as a query. However, if a computed function has any constraints on it, the operation should be eager. The reason for this is that if any component mappings change, the computed function can be immediately checked for constraint violations. If any violations are detected, the component mapping change should not be allowed to occur.

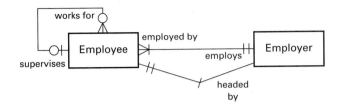

Figure 26.11   Cardinality constraint on computed functions must be enforced.

This can be illustrated by way of the example in Fig. 26.11. Here, the headed by function is a computed function where each Employer maps to exactly one Employee. As the function name suggests, this one Employee is the organization's most senior person. As such, this employeee has no supervisor. The one-and-only-one cardinality constraint on the headed by function ensures that only one Employee without a supervisor exists for any one Employer.

The headed by function is computed by locating only those employees for a given Employer that have no works for association. As stated above, the result of the headed by computation is constrained to yield one Employee. However, when should this restriction be enforced? If it is enforced only when some application wants to determine an organization's headed by:Employee, it is too late to prevent any improper causes. Therefore, it should be enforced whenever any supervises or works for associations change. For instance, adding a new Employee that has no supervisor to an organization could cause a violation. Unless the new Employee also becomes the supervisor of the preexisting head employee, two head employees would result. If the headed by function is defined as eager, situations such as this would not be allowed to occur, because it would be invoked whenever the supervises or works for associations change. In this case, each new Employee would either be required to have a supervisor or would become the supervisor of the previous head employee.

Controlling Redundancy

Since computed functions are derived using other functions, field operations such as Assign, Add, and Remove are not necessary. Such operations are necessary only when the results of a computed function will actually be stored. Storing the results of a computation reduces the access time for those applications requiring the information. Instead of reevaluating a function each time it is requested, its result is always precomputed at some point in time and stored in a field (or collection of fields).

Such storage, however, is redundant because its information is derived from already existing base functions. While redundancy is a useful technique for many applications, it must be managed properly. Without proper management, information may be lost. For example, if a Person's mother or father were changed for any reason, the Person's parents, ancestors—and any other function based on the mother or father—would also change. Therefore, a redundantly stored function must be reevaluated whenever one of its component functions has changed.

Hybrid Functions

To this point, functions have been implemented either as base or computed. Some applications may require a function to accommodate both modes. For instance, a particular ancestor of a **Person** may be known and explicitly asserted by an application. Yet, the remaining ancestors may still need to be derived. In both cases, the **has ancestors** function is a mapping from a given **Person** to the **Person**'s ancestors. However, different methods are selected to access them.

MAPPING FROM COMPUTED OBJECT TYPES   As discussed earlier in this chapter, each class contains the basic operations that construct and destruct the instances of a class. However, classes based on computed object types (discussed in detail in Appendix C) determine their own set membership. For example in Fig. 26.12, **Female Person** and **Adult Person** are expressed as *base* object types whose membership is asserted. The **Woman** object type, however, is computed as an intersection of the two object types **Female Person** and **Adult Person**. In other words, the set of all **Woman** objects is derived from those objects that are both **Female Person** and **Adult Person** objects. Furthermore, the set of all **Man** objects is defined here by excluding **Woman** and **Child Person** objects from the set of all **Person** objects.

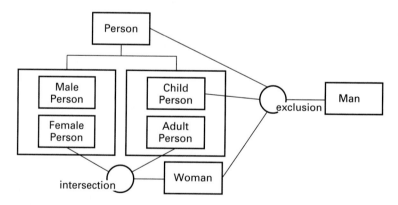

Figure 26.12   Object-type expressions are also implementable and reusable.

As with the computed functions, the object-type expression is implemented as an operation of the class whose membership it derives. For instance, the **Woman** class has an operation that implements the expression in Fig. 26.12. As with the function expression described in the previous section, the object-type expression also can be eager or lazy. A lazy object-type expression implies that the operation is invoked when access to its membership is required. For example, to request any operation for a Woman class requires that the computation operation be invoked first. An eager object-type expression implies that the computation operation is invoked every time the membership of its component classes changes. For example, the Woman object-type computation is invoked whenever an object is added or removed from either the Female Person or Adult Person class. Class expressions are usually eager when their class membership is redundantly stored. The above discussion of redundancy management, reusability, and hybrid operations for computed functions applies to object-type expressions as well.

REFERENCES

1. Booch, Grady, *Object-Oriented Design with Applications,* Benjamin/Cummings, Redwood City, CA, 1991.

2. Budd, Timothy, *A Little Smalltalk,* Addison-Wesley, Reading, MA, 1987.

3. Khoshafian, Setrag and Razmik Abnous, *Object Orientation: Concepts, Languages, Databases, User Interfaces,* John Wiley & Sons, New York, 1990.

4. Lippman, Stanley B., *A C++ Primer,* Addison-Wesley, Reading, MA, 1989.

27   OBJECT-ORIENTED DESIGN: MAPPING TO OOPL BEHAVIOR

The previous chapter presented ways of mapping the elements of object schemas to OOPL constructs. This chapter continues the presentation of object-oriented design issues by discussing how event schemas can be mapped to components of OOPL behavior.

MAPPING FROM OPERATIONS

An operation expressed in an event schema can be implemented by a construct of OO programming languages also called an *operation*. The two categories in which OOPL operations typically divide are accessors and modifiers. Accessor operations access objects without changing the states of those objects (i.e., accessors do not have *side effects*). In a sense, then, accessor operations are often thought of as OOPL components that are more structural in nature than behavioral. In the previous chapter, the accessors discussed are field operations (like get and detect), computed functions, and computed object-types.

In contrast, modifier operations *do* change the state of an object. They implement constructs like the state-changing operations expressed in event schemas. For example, in Fig. 27.1(a) the *modifier* operations Dispense Product, Take Money, Give Change, and Complete Sale could be implemented as OOPL operations called dispense_Product, take_Money, give_Change, and complete_Sale, respectively. The likely classes to which these operations associate are listed in Fig. 27.1(b).

MAPPING FROM TRIGGER RULES

A trigger detects an event, fills the arguments for its operation, evaluates the operation's control condition, and finally invokes the operation. At this time, trigger rules have no direct equivalent in OO programming languages. However, each of

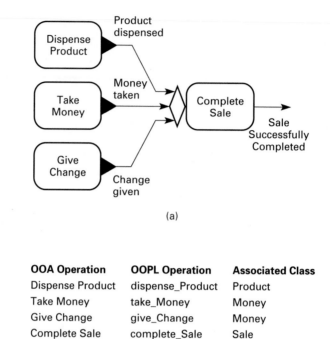

(a)

OOA Operation	OOPL Operation	Associated Class
Dispense Product	dispense_Product	Product
Take Money	take_Money	Money
Give Change	give_Change	Money
Complete Sale	complete_Sale	Sale

(b)

Figure 27.1 State-changing operations are implemented as OOPL operations.

the components in a trigger rule's procedure can be implemented as follows (starting from the end of the trigger process):

- **Invoke operation.** Operations are invoked in OOPLs by sending a request (or message) for a specific operation. This portion of the trigger, then, can be implemented simply as an OOPL *request.*

- **Evaluate control condition.** Condition testing is just a separate operation that either returns a "true" or "false" (or Boolean) value. When the condition is "true," the operation-invocation portion is executed. For instance, the control condition in Fig. 27.2(a) could be implemented by an operation called Decide_if_Job_is_completed or Send_Job_Bill_precondition. If this operation returns a "true" evaluation, the Send_Job_Bill operation can be executed.

- **Fill operation arguments.** Triggers must also provide those arguments required by an operation for invocation. Unless the requested operation's argument is the same as the event's, one or more functions must be invoked. The functions, then, will fill the required arguments. For example in Fig. 27.2(a), the Send_Job_Bill operation requires a Job object. Here, the trigger must map the Task object from the Task completed event to its associated Job using the part of:Job function depicted in Fig. 27.2(b). These functions should be implemented as operations in their own right (as described in the previous chapter).

- **Detect event.** Event detection is usually implemented either by actively polling the system environment for some predefined event to occur or by using a *demon* to activate the triggering mechanism. OO programming languages, in general, do not yet support event detection in any direct way.

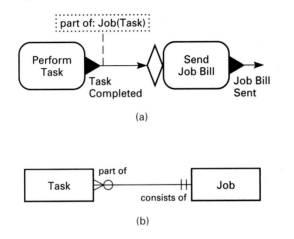

(a)

(b)

Figure 27.2   Triggers use functions to fill arguments before operations are invoked.

Typically, most OO designers and programmers do not use a separate triggering mechanism like that described above. Instead, it is incorporated into the code of a preceeding operation. For example, the **Perform_Task** would fulfill most of the trigger-rule's procedures, listed above, just before requesting the **Send_Job_Bill** operation. In other words, it would fill the **Job** argument, evaluate the control condition, and, if the condition is "true," request the **Send_Job_Bill** operation. While this implementation will work correctly, it increases the maintenance required for an operation's code. For instance, if any **Task** completed trigger rules are added, removed, or changed, the **Perform_Task** code would require modification. Therefore, by embedding trigger logic in an operation, the code is stable only as long as its trigger logic is stable.

On the bottom line, operations should be treated as black boxes. No operation should need to know what triggered it and what operations it triggers after completion. This is just good, sound modular thinking. In fact, without the separation of trigger-operation logic, reusable library of stable, building block modules will not be possible. How trigger rules can be implemented separately from operation code will be discussed later in this chapter.

MAPPING FROM EVENT TYPES

Events mark points in time when particular state changes occur. These points in time are marked, so that an appropriate reaction can be affected, they can be referenced later, or both. Event types, then, express the kinds of events to which an application must react or reference. While user-interface environments must implement some form of event processing, OO programming languages have no direct support. One way to implement event types for OOPLs is by constructing an event-scheduler mechanism. This will be discussed later in this chapter.

MAPPING FROM
EVENT SCHEMAS

Each event schema is a process specification for an operation. In other words, it specifies an operation's *method*. For example in Fig. 27.3, the method that results in event X is specified in terms of an event schema. Each of the operations requested within the method, in turn, can be specified in terms of another event schema.

Event schemas can be implemented in many ways. One approach is to code the event schema in a single-threaded manner—performing each action in a prescribed order. In a single-threaded language, the implemented method specified in Fig. 27.3 could be specified in the following manner:

```
OPERATION X_ACTION (...);
BEGIN:
    A_ACTION (...);
    B1_ACTION (...);
    D_ACTION (...);
    IF H_CONTROL_CONDITION (...) = FALSE
    THEN
        C_ACTION (...);
        IF H_CONTROL_CONDITION (...) = FALSE
        THEN
            E_ACTION (...);
            IF H_CONTROL_CONDITION (...) = FALSE
            THEN
                /* ERROR CONDITION?*/;
            ENDIF;
        ENDIF;
    ENDIF;
    H_ACTION (...);
    RETURN;
END;
```

Each operation requested above requires the name of the requested operation, the arguments required by the operation, and the specification of the object returned by the operation. The types of input and output objects required by an operation are often called the *signature* of an operation. This signature can be

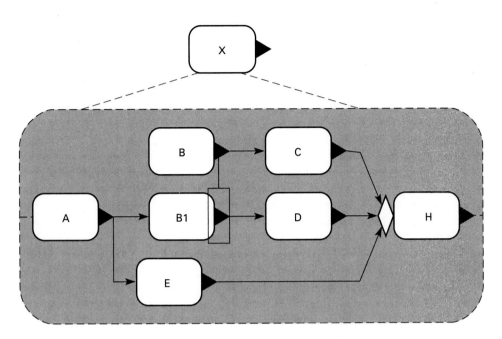

Figure 27.3   Event schemas express methods of operation.

determined from event schema and object schema specifications. The actual filling of the arguments is accomplished by the trigger-rule mechanism.

In concurrent OO programming languages, such as Concurrent C, the code can be implemented closer to that expressed in event schemas. Parallel processing paths can be followed and synchronization points can be enforced. In single-threaded languages, however, the designer must assign a processing sequence where none is dictated—checking for synchronization along the way.

Another approach employs an event-scheduling mechanism and is described in the next section.

AN EVENT SCHEDULER

One of the strengths of event schemas is that they have the potential to be complete and executable, providing a full description of application code. These event schemas are best implemented with code that is written in an event-driven manner. This style of programming is used by user interfaces—particularly Graphic User Interfaces (GUI)—and is becoming increasingly popular as a way to structure complex programs.

In this approach, the application is controlled by an *event-scheduler* program. Basically, the event scheduler *pops* an event from an event queue and performs the appropriate processing before going around for the next event. In a GUI, the events are usually prompted by the user (for example, by mouse and

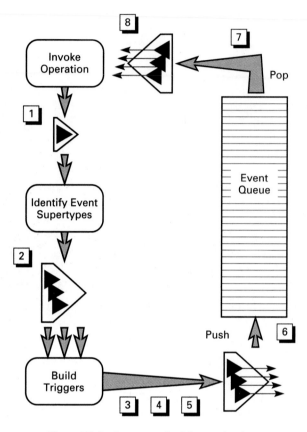

Figure 27.4   An event scheduler mechanism.

keyboard). The technique is extended by having operations generate events. In this way, when an operation completes, it generates an event whose triggers evaluate control conditons and invoke further operations. This event-trigger-condition-operation approach clearly fits in very well with event schemas.

An Event-Scheduler Loop

One implementation of an event scheduler is illustrated in Fig. 27.4. Its logic is based on event schema specifications and employs object schema specifications. Its processing is described in the following steps:

1. Each time an operation defined on an event schema completes, an event occurs. The event is created by the event scheduler when an operation ends successfully.

2. Each instance of a particular event type is also an instance of its supertypes. This step identifies all of the event supertypes and creates an event for each. (Since multiple events are really different facets of the same event, they are called *event slices*.)

3. For each event slice, the associated trigger rules are identified.

4. For each trigger rule, invoke the functions that supply those argument objects required by the triggered operation.

5. In addition, the control condition of each to-be-triggered operation is evaluated. If the evaluation is true, the triggering will be allowed.

6. The event, together with all its component event slices, triggers, and argument objects are placed, or *pushed,* onto the event queue.

7. A queued event is pulled, or *popped,* from the event queue.

8. The operations for each of the triggers are requested. If the environment supports multitasking or parallel processing, the scheduler can invoke several processes to run concurrently at this point. In single-threaded environments, the operations will be scheduled on a one-at-a-time basis.

An Event-Scheduler Loop Example

Consider the portion of the event schema depicted in Fig. 27.5. When operation A completes successfully, an event that is an instance of the A occurred event type is created. The A occurred event has no supertypes, and therefore only one event slice is required. The event slice, however, has two triggers and so both triggers are built. Each trigger contains a reference to operations B and C. At this point, all of the necessary argument objects are determined via the functions specified for the trigger rule (not shown). All these event components are then placed, or *pushed,* on the event queue. Some time later, the A event will be *popped* from the queue. Its two trigger rules are now dealt with, but the order is not defined. One trigger invokes operation C. An event of type C occurs, any corresponding triggers are built, and the C event is placed in the queue along with its triggers and associated argument objects. With the other trigger, opera-

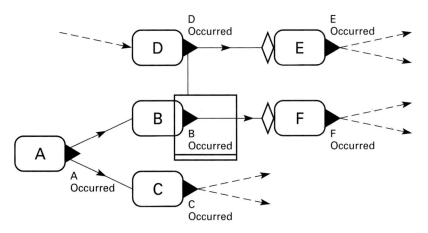

Figure 27.5   An example for an event-scheduler description.

tion B is invoked. When it has completed, the B occurred event is created. An event supertype D occurred is identified, and its event slice is attached to the event. Triggers are added for the B and D event slices, and the associated argument objects are determined. Since control conditions are specified for operations E and F, these must be evaluated before proceeding. If an evaluation is "false," the appropriate trigger is removed from the event slice. Finally, the whole event *package* is placed in the queue for later processing.

The Event-Scheduler in Pseudocode

The following pseudocode summarizes how an event-scheduler mechanism can work:

```
REPEAT UNTIL EVENT QUEUE IS EMPTY
  POP AN EVENT
  FOR EVERY EVENT SLICE ON THE EVENT
    FOR EVERY TRIGGER ON THE EVENT SLICE
      EXECUTE THE OPERATION DEFINED IN THE TRIGGER
      CREATE A NEW EVENT AND ITS INITIAL EVENT SLICE
      CREATE ALL OTHER EVENT SLICES FOR EVENT SUPERCLASSES
      FOR EVERY EVENT SLICE
        FOR EVERY TRIGGER ON THE NEW EVENT SLICE
          RUN FUNCTION(S) TO DETERMINE ARGUMENT OBJECTS FOR
            TRIGGERED OPERATION
          IF CONTROL CONDITON FOR TRIGGERED OPERATION IS FALSE
          THEN
            REMOVE THIS TRIGGER FROM THE EVENT SLICE
          ENDIF
        END FOR
      END FOR
      PUSH NEW EVENT
    END FOR
  END FOR
END REPEAT
```

The process described above will work in an OO environment using OO and non-OO languages.

ONE LAST THOUGHT ON OO PROGRAMMING   This book has concentrated on looking at object-orientation from the point of view of analysts and experts. This view raises some interesting questions about the current state of object-oriented technology and suggests some pointers for its future.

Support for multiple and dynamic classification is essential. Currently, very few commercial OO systems fully support this, yet our experience finds these object types extremely valuable during analysis. They represent a desirable extension of the OO paradigm.

Even with single, static classification, the concept of class inheritance has many subtleties. The fact that several different forms of inheritance exist indicates its evolution is still in progress. Currently, inheritance is a low-level notion that allows varied effects—not all of them desirable. In the future, a higher-level use of inheritance could give it a structure in the same way that structured programming organizes flow of control. Until then, inheritance—particularly multiple inheritance—remains a tool that must be used carefully.

28 OBJECT-ORIENTED DESIGN: NON-OOPL CONSIDERATIONS

OO MAPPINGS FOR IMPERATIVE PROGRAMMING LANGUAGES

Object-oriented designs do not require an object-oriented programming language to implement them. As stated in Chapter 10, the requirements for an object-oriented implementation can be summarized in the following way:

OBJECT-ORIENTED IMPLEMENTATION =
ABSTRACT DATA TYPES + TYPE INHERITANCE + METHOD SELECTION

Therefore, while OOP languages make it easier to implement OO designs, *imperative* languages such as FORTRAN, COBOL, and PL/I can be coded in an OO manner. This section gives an outline of how to do this with event schemas and object schemas. Those interested in more detailed aspects should consult Rumbaugh [2].

Abstract Data Types (ADTs)

ADTs are based on kinds, or types, of data. Therefore, each object type can be mapped to an ADT record structure in the same way as it is mapped to a class in OO programming languages. In addition, each ADT protects its data from improper use by offering a number of permissible operations. A set of procedural *sections* or subroutines should then be defined in the same way that operations are defined for classes in Chapters 26 and 27. In OO programming languages, these operations provide a protective wall that shields objects from improper use. The notion of encapsulation, however, can not be enforced in non-ADT languages. Under these conditions, then, data access is at the mercy of programmers' sense of honesty and fair play.

Type Inheritance

Type inheritance provides code and data reuse through generalization hierarchies. Conventional imperative languages, however, have no notion of subtypes and supertypes whatsoever. Therefore, what is automatically built into the OO environment now requires an explicit programmer code. Some of the ways for implementing inheritance are as follows:

- Physically copying the code from supertype modules. This can be accomplished by copying-and-pasting the code or by using COPYLIB statements. While this results in redundant code, it can be controlled with proper maintenance procedures.

- CALLing the routine in supertype modules. Instead of copying code, the operations could be CALLed from a module to its supertype module. For example, the change-phone-extension section in a Manager COBOL program may not contain the code or data to change a phone extension. Instead, the section would CALL the Employee program that has the change-phone-extension code and data. In this way, a manager object could still be handled by the Manager program, yet inherit the code from the Employee program. This approach will work as long as the programs are kept up-to-date with what they are supposed to inherit. As with the previous approach, proper maintenance procedures are important.

- Build an inheritance support system. Instead of building the reuse into individual program modules, construct an inheritance mechanism that is external to the programs. This mechanism would route requests to their appropriate modules based on object schema and event schema information. In this way, a change-phone-extension request for a Manager object could be automatically routed to the Employee module—as long as the Manager subtype does not have its own overriding routine. Since no inheritance-related logic would need to be built into the programs, the modules are much more stable. In addition, since the inheritance support system is based on object schemas and event schemas, it is *model* driven instead of *hard-coded.*

Method Selection

With method selection, the user need only specify which operation should be applied to one or more objects. The system will then choose the method appropriate for the specified parameters. However, non-OO languages do not recognize operation requests and method selection. Two ways for implementing method selection are as follows:

- Hard-code the selection logic within the requesting routine. This approach will work as long as the programs are kept up-to-date with all of the request and selection criteria (a monumental task).

- Build a method-selection support system. This mechanism would first enable modules to make requests for operations without knowing where the appropriate code, or method, is located. It would be driven by a table that matched selection criteria to the physical location of the code. In addition, the selection mechanism would be integrated with the inheritance support system described above—taking advantage of the object schema and event schema information.

The Event Scheduler, Revisited

An event-scheduler mechanism was described in the previous chapter. This mechanism could be expanded to include the inheritance and method selection support described above. Such a system would create a true object-oriented environment: an environment that would support OO and non-OO languages. This hybrid approach would bridge the gap between past, present, and future development.

OO MAPPINGS FOR RELATIONAL DATABASES

Relational databases (RDBs) are a common form of implementation that presents some additional issues for implementing an OO model. These issues involve database design, the use of triggers within the conceptual model, and the interface to application code.

The database design is, of course, driven by the object schema. At the very least, each concept can be implemented as a table, with each function implemented as an attribute within the table. As with OOPLs, attributes are either references to other tables or to internally stored data values. For example, using the object schema in Fig. 28.1, the Employee table could be expressed as

EMPLOYEE (..., SALARY, NO_OF_DEPENDENTS, EMPLOYER)

Since salary and no_of_dependents* map to fundamental data types provided by relational databases, they could be implemented as internally stored data values. (The double underline indicates the primary key.)

The employer attribute is a different situation. If you do not want to embed the Organization information in the Employee table, this attribute serves as a pointer. Pointers in RDBs are typically implemented as *foreign keys*. In other words, they contain the unique identifier of the table to which it points. So, the next step for an RDB designer is defining the unique identifier, or primary key, for each table. For Organization, the natural choice would be organization id. The Organization table could then be expressed as

ORGANIZATION (<u>ORGANIZATION_ID</u>, ORGANIZATION_NAME)

The Employee table could then be expressed as

EMPLOYEE (..., SALARY, NO_OF_DEPENDENTS, EMPLOYER. ORGANIZATION_ID)

---

*For clarity, nouns will be used for function names here.

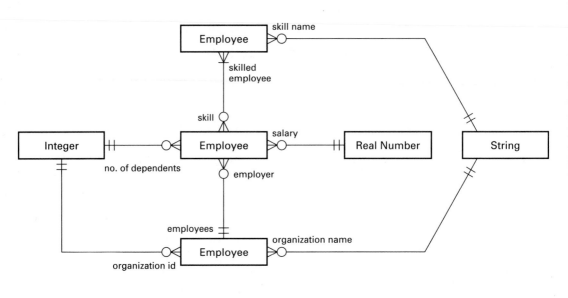

Employee (<u>employee_OID</u>, salary, no_of_dependents, employer.organization_OID)

Organization (<u>organization_OID</u>, organization_id, organization_name)

Employee Skill (<u>skilled_employee.employee_OID</u>, <u>skill.skill_OID</u>)

Skill (<u>skill_OID</u>, skill_name)

Figure 28.1   An object schema and a translation to a relational structure.

Instead of choosing a primary key from a table's attributes, another technique is assigning a single unique identification attribute to every table, called the *object identifier* (OID). The OID value for each table record would be system generated and unchangeable. If the record is deleted, the OID could never be reissued to any other record. Some RDBs already have a facility to assign *surrogate keys*. While these correspond to the notion of OIDs, surrogate keys are not accessible to programming languages. With an OID mechanism, the Employee and Organization tables can be expressed as

EMPLOYEE (<u>EMPLOYEE_OID</u>, SALARY, NO_OF_DEPENDENTS, EMPLOYER.ORGANIZATION_OID)

and

ORGANIZATION (<u>ORGANIZATION_OID</u>, ORGANIZATION_ID, ORGANIZATION_NAME)

While every table has a primary key, other attributes may also serve as secondary unique identifiers. For instance, in the Organization table the organization_id can serve as an alternate key via the indexing mechanism offered in most RDBs. The OID, however, helps to alleviate the immense problem of referential integrity inherent in RDBs.

1:M and M:M Situations

Tables in relational databases can only contain single values, not sets of values called *repeating groups*. This affects the storing of multivalued functions. Many-to-many relationships, like that between Skill and Employee, require an additional table to maintain the linkage. This Employee Skill table could be expressed as

EMPLOYEE SKILL (<u>EMPLOYEE.EMPLOYEE_OID</u>, <u>SKILL.SKILL_OID</u>)

However, one-to-many relationships, like that between Organization and Employee, do not require an additional table to maintain the linkage. In this situation, the Employee table will contain a reference to Organization, but the Organization table will not contain a reference to Employee. While a separate Employment table could be defined to handle the two-way linkage, one-way references are all that are needed. Relational databases can still retrieve all of an Organization's employees by choosing all of the Employee records for a given Organization.

Generalization Hierarchies

Generalization hierarchies are not currently supported by RDBs. Instead, the designer can implement the subtype relations as separate tables. Or, the subtype attributes can be incorporated into their subtype table along with *flag* fields indicating the subtypes that applied. In the end, though, the RDBs will not provide any inheritance capability.

Implementing generalization hierarchies requires a similar approach to implementing dynamic classification in a static classification language (described in the previous chapter). The same approaches can be used—flags and guards, private objects, and object slicing.

Compromises and Normalization

Other RDB design issues are resolved similarly to that of non-OO programming languages. However, special design attention must be given to the high overhead involved in joins. Supporting joins means that following an object reference from one table to another can be cumbersome and slow—especially if the function is multivalued. This alters the performance and integrity trade-off, making it more desirable to collapse what would be separate classes into single tables. Performance tuning is particularly important for databases and should be done to test the design at an early stage.

In discussing relational databases, the issue of normalization is worth mentioning. The basic principal of normalization—that data should only be stored in a stable, nonredundant fashion—is as valid for OO implementation as any other. However, if the *first cut* database is defined by mapping an object schema's concept and functions to relation and attribute, as described above, the design is already normalized. Therefore, any deviations from the *first cut* database mapping should be examined in light of the performance and integrity trade-offs. Such deviations typically dictate the need for additional code to control any ensuing redundancies.

Integrity

Relational databases store data and do not store the operations that permit access to the data. Ideally, operations should be placed in the database so that whenever an application wishes to alter the database, the appropriate operations can be invoked. Since RDBs do not yet support embedded operations, the application code must ensure the integrity of the data. In fact, one major breakthrough of OO data management is moving application logic out of the programs and into the database. (Relational and object-oriented databases were discussed in more detail in Chapter 13.)

Program-Database Interface

As demonstrated above, relational database designs can be generated directly from an object schema:

- each concept becomes a table
- every attribute of a fundamental data type is stored as an internal attribute
- all other attributes become foreign key *pointers* to the associated table's OID
- extra tables are defined to support many-to-many associations

While this approach will create a database design that conforms to conceptual specifications, it will most likely not perform very efficiently. Performance tuning is the next step in RDB implementation—resulting in a design that differs from that specified in analysis. Over time, this design will change many times based on performance and storage considerations. Therefore, having a set of classes that handle only database manipulations would be wise. In this way, the conceptually designed classes would be insulated from any database change—only the DB *server* classes would change. The conceptually designed classes should only change when the conceptual model changes. Further detail on this approach can be found in Booch [1].

With relational databases, server classes have another benefit. In the example depicted in Fig. 28.1, each Employee object is related to an Organization object. To determine the organization_name of an Employee's employer, the

Employee class would send a request to the Organization class. The Organization class would then obtain the related employer object and return its organization_name.

However, when data-related requests are made from one class directly to another class, the call is essentially hidden from the database performance analyzer. As a consequence, the performance analyzer will be unable to consider that call when planning the access—possibly resulting in poor performance. A preferable approach is to implement a *virtual column* that relates the required data through an SQL view. This will enable the optimizer to plan for the access and insulate the application from database changes. Views, then, can be considered *virtual object* classes defined at the query language level [3, 4].

REFERENCES

1. Booch, Grady, *Object-Oriented Design with Applications,* Benjamin/Cummings, Redwood City, CA, 1991.

2. Rumbaugh, James, *Object-Oriented Modeling and Design,* Prentice-Hall, Englewood Cliffs, NJ, 1991.

3. Stonebraker, Michael, "An Interview with Michael Stonebraker: Part I," *Data Base Newsletter,* 19:1, Jan/Feb 1991, pp. 1,12–16.

4. Stonebraker, Michael, "An Interview with Michael Stonebraker: Part II," *Data Base Newsletter,* 19:3, May/June 1991, pp. 1,13–19.

29 MANAGING THE OO PROJECT

**KEY PLAYERS
IN OO ANALYSIS
AND DESIGN
PROJECTS**

An OO project team requires certain critical players who must know their role and perform it well. Together, these people form a special and highly trained team. From the user community, the following people are included:

- executive owner
- system champion
- user analysis and design team

From the I.S. community, a project team involves the following roles:

- project manager
- workshop leader
- scribe
- rapid prototype builder
- modeling expert

The roles above can be assumed by one person or several persons, depending on the application size and development approach. For example, in a Rapid Application Development (RAD) project, the group will number between two and five at any one time. In addition, because the development lifecycle of any project should not exceed six months, the same individuals are involved throughout the project [2].

Support and directing the efforts of each project team is a project-administration group. This includes the following roles:

- repository director
- chief information engineer
- methodsmith
- toolsmith

In addition to the project team and its administrative group, a third team is recommended to ensure the continuity of project development and the integrity of its products. This involves expert users and a modeling expert.

USER COMMUNITY

Executive Owner

One of the most important players is the executive owner. (Some organizations use the term executive sponsor.) This person is a high-level user executive who wants the system and is committed to it. The executive owner makes the business decision that the system is needed and provides the money for it. This person *owns* the system and is ultimately responsible for it.

Committed to the fast development of the system, the executive owner must be responsible for cutting through any bureaucracy or politics that might slow down development of the system.

System Champion

A champion of an idea is the executive who perceives the value of that idea and becomes determined to introduce it into an organization. The champion relentlessly pursues the idea, persuading people of its value, until it becomes a reality.

The champion of a system is sometimes the executive owner of that system, sometimes not. The champion may persuade a different executive of the system's value.

User Experts

The quality of object schemas and event schemas is absolutely dependent on the quality of knowledge available in the analysis and design workshop. Therefore, expert users must be involved at every stage of a development project. Because the lifecycle is short, they can see the results of those activities they start. They are, therefore, more interested and more committed. In lengthy traditional projects, users see the specification for a system and then forget about it for 18 months.

Over the entire project, groups of expert users are selected to participate in every phase. In addition to the user analysis and design team, they may form other groups, such as the construction assistance team, the user-review board, and the cutover team. To a large extent, the same people play successive roles; a large number of people is not required.

I.S. COMMUNITY
PROJECT TEAM

Project Manager

The project manager is the person responsible for the project and can be responsible for more than one project simultaneously. This person manages the project lifecycle to ensure that its phases are well planned and executed on time, with no essential component missing.

With lengthy traditional development, the project manager who initiates the application will often have left by the time it is placed into production. If the application fails or appears ill-thought-out, the new managers can happily blame the previous regime. With the shorter lifecycle, the managers who start the project are more easily held accountable for it. They will be there when it becomes operational, and will, therefore, have a strong incentive for its success.

Workshop Leader

Analysis and design sessions are best conducted using workshops. These workshops should be run by a specialist who organizes and conducts analysis and design workshops. This person is particularly needed to conduct the intensive analysis and design workshops of Rapid Application Design (RAD). The progress and quality of the workshop deliverables depend heavily on the skills of its leader. The workshop leader is regarded as a professional in this activity—having both the credibility and capability to play such a role.

Scribe

The scribe records what is decided in workshop sessions. This person should use an I-CASE toolset and, wherever possible, record the workshop information in I-CASE format. The scribe uses the I-CASE tool during the session to document and validate its results, remove inconsistencies, generate screen and report designs, and illustrate the emerging design to the participants. Often this activity is assisted by a prototyper. Outside of the sessions, the scribe can polish it, possibly adding to it, or raising questions for further discussion.

Rapid Prototyper

Constructing working prototypes provides a proof-of-concept for decisions made during analysis and design sessions. The ability to make fast adjustments to the prototype ensures that the analysis is correct and the design will meet the user's need. In this way, the application can be tested for usability with end users to minimize difficulties that could be encountered in the production system. The rapid prototyper is responsible for creating prototypes that can be quickly reviewed by end users.

Modeling Expert

The modeling expert works with the expert users to produce models that accurately reflect the application area. This specialist can create models rapidly and competently. The modeling expert is typically part of the data-administration staff. However, in an object-oriented environment, model administration is not limited to data. It includes processes as well. In this way, the data-administration function is expanded to become knowledge administration or repository management.

PROJECT ADMINISTRATION

Repository Manager

The person responsible for the I-CASE repository and its integrity is called the repository manager. A repository is the heart of the I-CASE environment. All projects share information from a central repository. The repository manager oversees the repository and coordinates the information in it.

Chief Information Engineer

The best examples of rapid systems development are often found in an information-engineering environment, especially one designed to maximize reusable design. In such an environment, an executive is needed to take charge of the overall IE effort. Sometimes, this executive has the title chief information engineer and reports to the chief information officer.

Methodsmith

A person who develops and evolves methods for an organization is called the methodsmith. The methodsmith should be experienced in many different methods and skillful at customizing and applying them to the organization.

Toolsmith

Automated tools that enable IE activities must be selected for the organization. In order to support the organization's methods, these tools often need customization and the construction of other supporting tools. The toolsmith performs and administers these activities.

SYSTEM EVOLUTION

The most impressive of complex systems are not created with a single design and implementation. They evolve, being improved in many steps at different times and places.

A system designer looks at the works of nature with awe. A cheetah watching for prey at dawn suddenly races through scrub at 70 miles per hour with astonishing grace to kill a leaping antelope. A hummingbird, which engineers once *proved* was an aerodynamic impossibility, flits from flower to flower and then migrates to South America. The human brain, full of diabolical schemes and wonderful poetry, has proved to be far beyond our most ambitious artificial-intelligence techniques. These are not systems for which God wrote specifications; they are systems that *evolved* over millions of years.

The future will bring impressive software and corporate computer systems, and these will also be *grown* over many years, with many people and organizations adding to them. It is difficult or impossible to *grow* software that is a mess. To achieve the long-term evolution of software, we need structured models of data and structured models of processes. Designs too complex for one human to know in detail must be represented in an orderly fashion in a repository, so that many people in many places can add to the design. The design needs standards and reusable components, plus an architecture that facilitates the incremental addition of new functions. The behavior should be expressible in rules and diagrams that executives understand, so that they can control the behavior of the computers that automatically place orders, select suppliers, make trades, and so on.

When development tools are designed to enable systems to evolve easily, the development lifecycle truly becomes a cycle, as shown in Fig. 29.1.

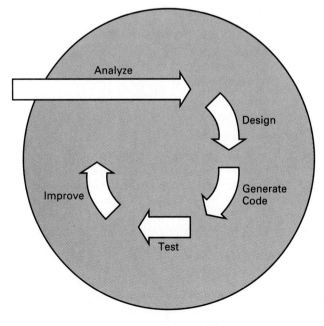

Figure 29.1   Evolutionary lifecycle.

With repository-based I-CASE tools, maintenance in the future will probably consist mainly of adding features to systems or changing them in an evolutionary fashion. Applications will grow and grow, and their details will be represented in the repository—until, in some cases, they become uniquely valuable corporate resources that competitors could not replicate quickly.

In order to achieve long-term evolutionary growth, various facilities are desirable:

- An application architecture designed to facilitate change over a long period.
- Representation of the architecture and design in an I-CASE repository that facilitates input by different people in different places at different times.
- An I-CASE environment that enforces fully structured design and uses a comprehensive, rule-based facility to ensure complete coordination of different parts of the design, guaranteeing overall design integrity among inputs from different developers.
- Code generated directly from the I-CASE design. A toolset that gives the fastest possible cycle of *design, code generation, testing,* and *modification.*
- An information-engineering environment with
  - an object schema
  - an event schema
  - object-oriented design showing reusable processes
- An I-CASE toolset that permits easy modification of the system within the information-engineering framework.
- Standards and templates for user-dialog design.
- Application standards such as IBM's SAA (Systems Application Architecture), DEC's AIA (Application Integration Architecture) or others.
- Reusable modules in an I-CASE repository in an object-oriented information-engineering environment.
- Design that is expressible in diagrams (and possibly rules) that business executives and end users understand.
- Design that is logically independent of the technology environment so that it remains valid when the technology (hardware or software) changes and, hence, can be used to generate code for environments of different technology.

**ONE SAMPLE
OF INDUSTRY
EXPERIENCE**

For most organizations, the move to object orientation is not a matter of *if* they will, but *when* they will. Numerous companies are already applying an object-oriented approach to planning, analysis, design, and implementation. One such company is Automation Research Systems, Limited (ARS) [1]. ARS uses the basic theory presented in this book. However, they have found that developing systems requires more than theory—

an application methodology and project implementation capability is required as well. To ARS, OO theory is of little value if the application method is inadequate. Furthermore, the best method devised is useless if it is not cost effective in terms of time, people, and money. The lessons, then, that ARS has learned fall under four categories:

- **Enterprise project definition.** ARS has found that the new wave of enthusiasm for the OO approach tends to focus on getting to code generation as quickly as possible. While this is a worthy objective, it ignores the business aspects of an organization such as: objectives, policies, structure, physical layout, and so on. Without these business aspects, project definition and planning is inadequate. And, without adequate project definition and planning, the results are—at best— ad hoc.

- **Methodology.** The ARS method is not limited to modeling object structure and behavior. The company is committed to object orientation. However, as indicated above, they realize that their method should also model the business aspects of an organization. Their approach, then, considers environment, objectives, functions, people, organization, and physical layout.

- **Tools.** ARS uses its methodology with a CASE tool set to support US Army and Federal government agencies in their system development needs. They believe that CASE tools are essential to system quality and timely development. For ARS, they find that the power of CASE lies in its ability to capture quickly those complex relationships that would be lost to the human mind. In addition, they believe that a CASE tool should automatically identify inconsistencies in their models and highlight them for resolution. Last, the CASE tool should be integrated with a code generator producing fully executable code.

- **Training.** ARS firmly believes that a method and tool are only as good as the developer's ability to use them.

OO Experience

In their first pilot project, ARS estimates that 50 to 70 percent of the code was reused among its three applications. They found that this was a vast improvement over conventional methods where the reused code was only 5 to 10 percent.

This same reusability also applies to their analysis and design models. Where models exist, the developers can concentrate more on the user's requirements and the way they differ from existing models. The staff at ARS was astonished at the speed with which individual models could be developed from existing basic models.

Benefits of object orientation have already been experienced by ARS. However, the real benefits come in subsequent application development and maintenance. ARS considers its experience to date as just a spark within a tremendous technological explosion—one that will occur as object-oriented methods and tools are refined.

REFERENCES

1. ARS, *Industry Experience with Object-Oriented Analysis, Design, and Programming,* Automation Research Systems, Limited, 4480 King Street, Alexandria, VA, 22302, October 2, 1991.

2. Martin, James, *Rapid Application Development,* Macmillan, New York, 1991.

PART **VI** APPENDIX

Appendix

A GLOSSARY OF TERMS

ABSTRACT DATA TYPE (ADT). A type of object that contains the definition of its data structure and permitted operations. ADTs give objects a *public* interface through its permitted operations. However, the representations and *method*s of these interfaces are *private*. Also referred to as an *object type* and implemented in OOPLs as a *class*.

ABSTRACTION. The act or result of removing certain distinctions between objects so that we can see commonalities. The result of the abstraction process is a *concept* (or *object type*).

ACTIVITY. A process whose production and consumption are specified. Its *product* is a function of those products it consumes.

ARGUMENT. The subject, or independent variable, of a *function* or *operation*. Any object that is a parameter value. When an argument is filled, the value of a function can be returned, or the results of an operation can be produced.

ARGUMENT-FILLED FUNCTION. A *function* supplied with a specific object. For example, the function employs(Organization) maps each Organization object to the set of Person objects it employs. When a specific object fills the Organization *argument*, such as employs(IBM), the result is a specific subset of Person objects that are employees of IBM. In this way, an argument-filled function is an object type in its own right. Its *extension* is the set of objects to which the given object maps.

ASSOCIATION. A means to link *object types* meaningfully. Two principal ways of associating are the *relation* and the *function*.

ATTRIBUTE. An identifiable association between an object and some other object or set of objects. Each attribute is an instance of an *attribute type*.

ATTRIBUTE TYPE. A kind of association that links a given set of objects to another set of objects. (Synonymous with *function*.) In an OOPL, attribute types associate objects of one class with either a value or a pointer to objects of another class. The OOPL implementation of an attribute type is called a *field* or an *instance variable*.

BASE FUNCTION. A function whose mapping is fixed by assertion. It contrasts with *computed functions* whose mappings are derived.

BEHAVIOR. A metaphor referring to the way objects change over time within a defined *structure*.

BINDING. (See *method binding*)

CARDINALITY CONSTRAINT. A constraint on the number of objects that must participate in the mapping of a *function*. This constraint is typically expressed as a minimum and maximum number. The minimum cardinality constraint indicates the least number of objects to which a given object must map. The maximum indicates the greatest number of objects to which a given object must map.

CLASS. An implementation of a *concept* or *object type*. In OO programming languages, *abstract data types* are called classes. In mathematics, the meaning of class is similar to that of *set*. The meaning of the OOPL definition of class arose from the mathematical definition.

CLASSIFICATION. The act or result of determining that a *concept,* or *object type,* applies to a specific object. When an object is classified, it becomes an instance of a specific object type. Classification defines a relation between an object type and its instances.

CLOCK OPERATION. An *operation* that emits a specified pattern of clock-tick events. A clock operation may run indefinitely or tick an exact number of times as requested at invocation. In this way, a clock may be invoked to emit a tick indefinitely every 15 days, or invoked to tick just once after 15 seconds.

COMPLETE PARTITION. A *type partition* that expresses a full list of its partitioned subsets.

COMPLEX OBJECT. (See *composite object*)

COMPONENT OBJECT. An object that is a part of a *composite object.*

COMPOSITE OBJECT. An *object* that is configured from or formed by one or more objects. It is the result of *composition*. For example, a Boat object is a composite object consisting of Hull and Motor objects; a Marriage object consists of Man and Woman objects. Composite objects are sometimes referred to as *complex objects.*

COMPOSITION. The act or result of forming an *object* configured from its component parts. An immutable composition treats one or more objects as invariant components of a *composite object*. The invariant components of a composite object define a *tuple*. *Object types* based on immutable compositions are called *relations*. A changeable composition allows its components to change. For example, the component objects of Man and Woman that compose a Marriage cannot change without changing the composed object. However, Wheel or Radiator objects that compose a Car object are changeable. Marriage objects, then, are immutable compositions, and Car objects are changeable compositions. Composition is not a form of *abstraction*. Abstraction removes distinctions between objects to form *concepts* (or *object types*). Composition removes distinctions between objects to form other objects.

COMPUTED FUNCTION. A function whose mapping is derived or computed. It contrasts with *base function*s whose mappings are fixed by assertion.

COMPUTED OBJECT TYPE. An *object type* that is fully derived or computed in terms of other object types. For example, the object type called Tall Woman could be derived from the intersection of Tall Person and Woman object types. Compound object types can be specified with *object type expressions.*

CONCEPT. An idea or notion we share that applies to certain things (i.e., *objects*) in our awareness. A person has a concept if the person understands when the concept applies and when it does not. Also called an *object type.*

CONCEPTION. A privately held *concept.*

CONTROL CONDITION. A process that determines whether a certain set of conditions is true or false. Processing continues beyond this point only when the result is true. Control conditions can be employed as *preconditions* or *postconditions.* Since each control condition is a processing unit, it can be thought of as an *operation* in its own right.

CONTROL-CONDITION EVALUATION. An instance of a *control condition.* If the control condition is *true,* the process that follows begins.

DECLASSIFICATION. The act or result of determining that an object type no longer applies to a specific object. When an object is declassified, it is removed as a member of a specific set.

DIAGRAM. A graphic depiction. A formal depiction is called a *schema.*

DOMAIN. The collection of all objects mapped by a *function.* Various analysis approaches use the word domain differently. For example, some entity-relationship modelers refer to the *domain* of an attribute type. This book uses the word *range* instead. Domain also refers to a delimited sphere of knowledge or activity. This book uses the word *realm* instead.

DYNAMIC BINDING. *Method binding* that is performed at the time a *request* is issued. It is also known as late binding. Dynamic binding is the opposite of *static binding.*

DYNAMIC CLASSIFICATION. *Classification* that is performed at runtime. With dynamic classification, the classification of an object can change over time.

ENCAPSULATION. A protective encasement that hides the implementation details of an object, making its data accessible only by operations put there to mediate its access. It is often used interchangeably with *information hiding.*

EVALUATE. Literally, to determine or calculate the value of something. For example, the square function evaluates the number 5 to be 25; or 2 plus 2 is evaluated to be 4. Evaluation results, however, should not be limited to Numbers. Instead, they can be mapped into any set of objects. For example, determining the employees that work for a given company is an evaluation. Evaluation, then, is another name for the process of mapping an object to a set of objects. Another example is evaluating conditions, which means that a process that tests for certain conditions will result in (i.e., map to) either the values *true* or *false.*

EVENT. A noteworthy change in object *state*. The successful completion of an *invoked operation*. An invoked operation, then, is the potential for *state change:* its actual state change is its event. The change is stated in terms of an *event prestate* and an *event poststate.*

EVENT POSTSTATE. Specifies those object types that *must* apply to an object after a particular change in state (i.e., *event*) occurs.

EVENT PRESTATE. Specifies those object types that *must* apply to an object before a particular change in state (i.e., *event*) occurs.

EVENT TYPE. A kind of *event*. The set of all state changes of a kind resulting from an *operation*. An **Order accepted** event type defines a set of all events when orders were accepted.

EXTENSION. The collection of all objects to which the *object type*, or *concept*, applies. (Used interchangeably with *set.*)

FEATURE. A data structure field or a permitted operation in an *abstract data type*. The data structure and operations of an ADT are its features.

FIELD. An implementation of an *attribute type*. (Synonymous with *instance variable.*)

FUNCTION. A mapping process that—given an *object* of one *set*—returns a set of objects in the same or a different *set*. Functions are *operations* that do not change object state. A function that always returns a set containing a single object is called *single-valued.* For example, each **Person** object maps to exactly one **Biological Mother** object. Functions are *multivalued* when they return a set containing an unspecified number of objects, rather than just a single instance. For example, the multivalued function in Fig. 18.1(a) maps NASA to a set containing Jasper and Paul, and IBM to Jane. The actual number in the set is restricted by a *cardinality constraint.* An alternate definition of function is a mapping from one set into a *power type* or set of all subsets of another. A function whose mapping is fixed by assertion is called a *base function.* A function whose mapping is not fixed, but is derived or computed, is called a *computed function.* The definition of function can also be extended to be a *multiple-argument function.* A multiple-argument function is defined as a function that—given multiple objects of one or more sets—returns a set of objects. For example, the **subtract** function takes two arguments to determine the difference. In order to determine a **Marriage** object, the **marriage** function requires three arguments: a husband, a wife, and a marriage date. Some OOPLs, such as Eiffel, differentiate between an operation that changes object state and an operation that does not. In these approaches, the former is called *procedure* and the latter *function.*

FUNCTION EXPRESSION. An expression that specifies the way in which functional mappings are derived or computed. A function whose mapping is not fixed, but is derived or computed, is called a *computed function.*

GENERALIZATION. The result (or act) of distinguishing an *object type* as being more general, or inclusive, than another. The specifying of a *supertype*. For example, **Person** is a generalization of **Man**. Generalization is not a form of *abstraction;* it is a comparison between different abstractions. Generalization defines a relation between two object types: one that is more general than another.

HYPER-MODEL. A *meta-model* that serves as a conceptual foundation. It is a starting point for defining other modeling approaches.

IMMUTABLE COMPOSITE OBJECT. (See *composite object*)

IMMUTABLE COMPOSITION. (See *composition*)

INCOMPLETE PARTITION. A *type partition* expressing a partial list of subtypes.

INFORMATION HIDING. The notion of hiding the implementation of an object, while allowing a public interface through its permitted operations. Often used interchangeably with *encapsulation.*

INHERITANCE. Class inheritance is an implementation of *generalization.* It permits all of the *features* of an OOPL *class* to be physically available to, or reusable by, its *subclass*es—as though they were the features of the subclass. Object-class inheritance allows instances of a class to inherit default values. Object-object inheritance, also called delegation, transfers the *state* of one object to another.

INSTANCE. (Synonymous with *object*)

INSTANCE VARIABLE. (See *field*)

INSTANTIATION. Object creation.

INTENSION. The complete definition of a *concept* or *object type.* The intension defines when a concept applies (and does not apply) to an object. For example, an intension for Man could be stated as an adult Person of the male gender. The word intension is used rather than intention. Intension reflects more that intent: it implies a thorough and intensive definition.

INVOKED OPERATION. An actively running process. An instance of an *operation.*

MAPPING. (See *function*)

MAPPING INSTANCE. A function whose mapping is restricted to a given object. The mapping of a single object.

MESSAGE. (See *request*)

META-MODEL. A *model* that expresses those object types whose objects are also object types. A model that defines other models.

METHOD. A specification of the steps by which an *operation* will be carried out. It is an implementation script for an operation. Different methods can be used to carry out the same operation. For example, the method of an addition operation would be different for an integer than for a floating-point number. In OOPLs, it is the code that is executed.

METHOD BINDING. An OO implementation term that refers to the selection of a *method* to perform a requested *operation.*

MODEL. An *abstraction* device. It expresses our *concept*s.

MULTIPLE-ARGUMENT FUNCTION. A *function* that—given multiple objects of any number of sets—returns a set of objects in another *set.* For example, the subtract function takes two arguments to determine the difference. In order to determine a Marriage object, the **marriage** function requires three arguments: a husband, a wife, and a marriage date. It extends the common notion of function and is closer to programming language practices.

MULTIPLE-ARGUMENT OPERATION. An *operation* that requires multiple objects as arguments. For example, the **subtract** operation takes two arguments to determine the difference. The **Marry** operation requires three arguments: a husband, a wife, and a marriage date.

OBJECT. Anything to which a *concept,* or *object type,* applies—an instance of a concept or object type. In OOPLs, it is any instance of a *class.*

OBJECT SLICING. A metaphor that describes how an object can be an instance in more than one OOPL class by *slicing* it into multiple *pieces.* Each *piece* is implemented as an instance of one of the multiple classes. The object-slicing mechanism does this by maintaining one *whole* copy of an object as a **Conceptual Object** linked to its many **Implementation Object** *pieces.*

OBJECT STATE. (See *state*)

OBJECT STATE CHANGE. (See *state change* or *event*)

OBJECT TYPE. Usage differs. It can mean the same as *concept* or *abstract data type.* In this book, it is used synonymously with *concept.*

OBJECT TYPE EXPRESSION. An expression that specifies the way in which instances of a specific *object type* are derived or computed from other object types.

OPERATION. A process that can be requested as a unit. A single step that is performed in a series of steps. Operations may or may not change the *state* of an object. *Functions* are operations that do not change state. However, in an event schema, the operations that result in events do change states (and could more properly be called *state-changing operations*). Each state-changing operation can be thought of as a transaction. A transaction is a process or a series of processes acting as a unit to change the state of an object. Instances of operations are called *invoked operations*. The specification of how an operation must be carried out is called the *method.* Some approaches, such as Eiffel, differentiate between an operation that changes object state and an operation that does not. In these approaches, the former is called a *procedure* and the latter, a *function.*

PARTITION. The act or result of decomposing something into its disjoint subparts. For objects, this is also known as *decomposition* (see *composition*). In this book, the meaning of the word *partition* is restricted to decomposing a *set* of objects into subsets. (See *type partition*)

PERSISTENT OBJECT. An object that survives the *invoked operation* that creates it.

PLACE. An object type associated by a *relation.* For example, **Employment** is a relation between the object types **Person** and **Organization**. Employment, then, is a 2-place relation, where **Person** and **Organization** are its places. The word *place* is used, because it refers to a specific position in a relational expression, as in **Employment (Person, Organization)**.

POSTSTATE. (See *event poststate*)

POWER TYPE. An object type whose instances are the subtypes of another object type. For example, the object type of Product Type can be expressed as all of the subtypes of Product. Here, Product Type is said to be the power type on the object type Product.

PRESTATE. (See *event prestate*)

PROCESS. An orderly sequence of acts. Something done leading to a particular result.

PRODUCT. The end result that fulfills the purpose of an *activity.*

PROPERTY. (Synonymous with *attribute*)

RANGE. The collection of all objects to which a *function* maps.

REALM. A distinctly delimited sphere of knowledge or activity. A focus or scope of examination. Also called a *problem domain, space,* or *universe of discourse.*

REALM SPECIFICATION. A set of object types relevant to a *realm* of interest.

RELATION. An *object type* whose extension is a set of *tuples.* An object type with *places.* For example, Employment is a relation between the object types Person and Organization. Employment is a 2-place relation.

REQUEST. An invocation for a specific *operation.* It consists of an operation name and zero or more actual parameters. A request is issued to cause an operation to be performed. This notion is often referred to as a *message.* Messages, however, are a more restricted case of requests. A message supplies only one object in its request for an operation along with any number of object parameters. A request is not limited to one object it requests for an operation. For example, a message to a robot vehicle might be: Vehicle71 Move To Bin 17. Here the object is Vehicle 71, the operation is Move To, and the parameter for that method is Bin 17. A request would be stated in a different manner: Move To (Vehicle71, Bin 17). In this way, a request is not a message restricted *to* one recipient object but *for* multiple objects. Therefore, the user is not required to know which object is the recipient and which are the supporting parameters. For instance, in the request Attach (Engine, Boxcar) the recipient object is not clear. The request mechanism, then, is responsible for selecting the appropriate method based on its parameters.

REQUEST TYPE. A kind of *request.* For example, a request could be made to fulfill a particular Order. The request type defines the properties of every order-fulfillment request.

SCHEMA. A formal diagrammatic representation. A diagram is considered formal when it consists of a set of defined symbols together with a set of rules governing the formation of diagrams using these symbols. Additionally, supporting this schema should be a means of manipulating the symbols to reason about and transform their constructs to other constructs.

SET. The collection of all those objects to which an object type applies. (It is used interchangeably with *extension.*)

SIDE-EFFECT. A change that is noticeable or detectable outside of an operation. (Synonymous with *state change* or *event.*)

SPECIALIZATION. The result (or act) of distinguishing an *object type* as being more specific than another. The specifying of a *subtype*. The inverse of *generalization*. For example, Man is a specialization of Person.

STATE. The collection of object types that applies to an object. An alternate, but equivalent, definition is that the state of an object is the collection of associations that an object has with other objects.

STATE CHANGE. A change in the collection of all object types that apply to an object. A change in object *state*. (Synonymous with *event*)

STATIC BINDING. *Method binding* that is performed prior to the time a *request* is issued usually at compile time. Also known as *early binding*. OOPLs employ *dynamic binding*.

STRUCTURE. A metaphor that refers to a static expression of how objects are laid out in space. Object schemas are one way of expressing structure. (See also *behavior*)

SUBCLASS. A *class* that is a *subtype* of one or more classes (called *superclass*es). As such, it inherits all the *features* of its superclasses (See *inheritance*). In other words, all the features of a class are reusable by its subclasses.

SUBSET. A *set* whose members are all included in another set. For example, the set of all Person objects is a subset of Mammal objects. A subset is not merely a set within a set: the subset must be an extension of an object type with properties of its own.

SUBTYPE. A specialized *object type*. All the properties that apply to an object type apply to its subtypes. A subtype, however, has additional properties. For example, all the properties of Person apply to Man and Woman. Furthermore, Man and Woman will have properties in addition to those of Person. The extension of a subtype is a *subset* of a given object type's set. (A more general object type is called a *supertype*.)

SUPERCLASS. A *class* that is a *supertype* of one or more classes (called *subclass*es). As such, it is a class from which all of its *features* are inherited by its subclasses (see *inheritance*). In other words, all of the features of a superclass are reusable by those classes that are its *subtypes*.

SUPERSET. A set whose members include all the members of one or more other sets. For example, the set of all Mammal objects is a superset of Person and Kangaroo objects.

SUPERTYPE. A generalized *object type*. An object type with properties more general than its *subtype*s. All the instances of an object type are instances of its supertype—but not the other way around.

TRANSIENT OBJECT. An object the existence of which is limited to the lifetime of a running process.

TRIGGER RULE. A process that invokes a specific *operation* when a specific *event type* occurs. It also specifies the way in which objects are filled as arguments to the operation. An instance of a trigger rule is a *trigger*.

TRIGGER. A linkage between cause and effect. It responds to *events* and determines the objects necessary as arguments for the *operation* it invokes. In addition, it causes an evaluation of the operation's *control condition*. If the evaluation is *true,* only then does the operation begin.

TUPLE. A configuration of objects that are the invariant components of a *composite object* (see also *composition*). For example, if Bob and Maddy are the invariant components in a Marriage object, the tuple for Bob and Maddy's Marriage can be expressed as: (Bob, Maddy). The *object type* that applies to a set of tuples of this kind is a *relation* called Marriage and relates two object types, Man and Woman, as husband and wife respectively. Each object in a tuple, then, is an instance of a specific *object type*. Tuples composed of two objects are called *couples;* with three, *triples;* or with any other number, *n*-tuples.

TYPE. (Synonymous with *object type* in this book.)

TYPE PARTITION. A division or partitioning of an *object type* into disjoint *subtypes*. Partitioning is best explained in terms of an object-type's *extension*. For example, the set of Person objects can be partitioned into the disjoint subsets Man, Woman, and Child. The same set can also be partitioned into Employed Person and Non-Employed Person subsets. A type partition (referred to as just *partition* in this book) specifies a set of mutually exclusive object types—which are *subtype*s of a more general object type.

UNIQUENESS CONSTRAINT. A constraint that all objects of a particular kind are subject to a specific unique identifier.

B OBJECT SCHEMAS AND ENTITY-RELATIONSHIP DIAGRAMS

What is the difference between object schemas and entity-relationship (ER) diagrams? This book introduces several notions that are not included in many conventional ER diagramming approaches, such as subtypes, subtype partitions, composition (immutable and changeable), computed functions, object-type expressions, and associating types to instances. These notions, however, are not what differentiate object schemas and ER diagrams. Instead, any ER diagramming approach can be extended to express these ideas—using the same or different symbols. The major difference between object schemas and ER diagrams is that ER diagrams can express attribute types that are *within* an entity type—object schemas do not.

OBJECT SCHEMAS VERSUS ENTITY-RELATIONSHIP DIAGRAMS

Object Schemas

In object orientation, attributes are defined as an identifiable association between an object and some other object or set of objects. An *attribute type,* then, is an identifiable association between one *type* of object and another *type* of object (also know as a function). This is why object structure analysis (OSA) models object types and their associations—without any notion that these associations are *within* or *outside of* object types. The notion is useful in *design,* however, where an association can be a physical value *within* and a pointer to something *outside of* a data structure. Since analysis does not make implementation distinctions, objects only have attributes that are *with* other objects—not *within* or *outside of* other objects. (This should not be confused with the notion of object composition, where objects are defined as *containing* other objects.)

An example of an object schema depicting object types and associations is illustrated in Fig. B.1. Here, nouns are used to name the functions. (Functions were presented in Chapter 18.) Instead of indicating the function from Car to Day with the name registered on, the function is named car registration day. They are named in this way to indicate the kinds of objects to which the function maps. There are several reasons for doing this. First, the mapping from object schema and ER diagrams can be clearer with nouns than verbs. Additionally, since functions are implemented as fields, fields specified with noun names are more conventional than fields with verb names. Lastly, functions as nouns are easier to comprehend in formal notations like the functional expressions in Appendix C. For a comparison, the mapping from object schema and ER diagrams is expressed with verbs at the end of this section.

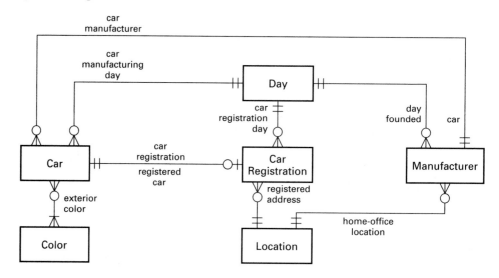

Figure B.1   An object schema representing a car-related example.

Entity-Relationship Diagrams

For ER diagrams, associations are expressed either *within* or *outside of* entity types. Those *within* are called *attribute types*. Those *outside of* are represented in terms of *relationship types* with other entity types. Technically, then, the object types and associations in an object schema can be expressed as an ER diagram depicting entity types with ER attribute types and relationship types.

Figure B.2 illustrates two ways of diagramming the object schema in Fig. B.1. The ER diagram in Fig. B.2(a) employs a mixture of ER attribute types and relationship types. For instance, car manufacturer and car registration are two functions on two different relationship types. They are those portions that map from the Car entity type to the Car Manufacturer and Car Registration entity types—as they are in the object schema. In contrast, manufacturing

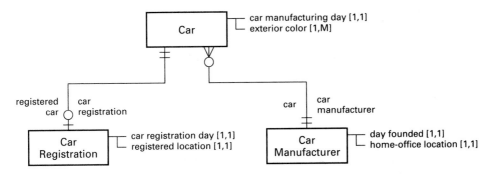

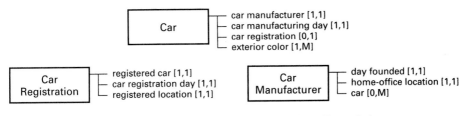

(a) Entity-Relationship Example with ER Attribute Types and Relationship Types

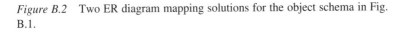

(b) Entity-Relationship Example with ER Attribute Types Only

Figure B.2   Two ER diagram mapping solutions for the object schema in Fig.
B.1.

day and exterior color have become ER attribute types *within* the Car entity
type.

In actuality, the diagram in Fig. B.1 could also be an ER diagram—one with
no ER attribute types. Another extreme is illustrated in Fig. B.2(b). This diagram
represents all of the object schema functions solely as ER attribute types. With
Fig. B.1 and Fig. B.2(b) being two extremes, Fig. B.2(a) is just one of the possible
interim solutions. The solution selected is determined by the ER analyst and the
end user in an analysis session—or based on some adopted modeling guideline.

Identifying the right object types is vital to achieving sound OO design.
However, when ER attribute types are specified as they are in Fig. B.2, fewer
object types are identified than in a corresponding object schema. The ramifications of using ER diagrams for OO analysis and of having fewer object types for
OO design is discussed in the next section.

Using Verbs as Function Names

Using nouns to name functions is helpful, because ER attribute types convention-
ally use noun names. However, relationship types use verb names. In contrast to
Fig. B.1, the object schema in Fig. B.3(a) uses verb function names. Figure
B.3(b) illustrates one possible mapping to an ER diagram.

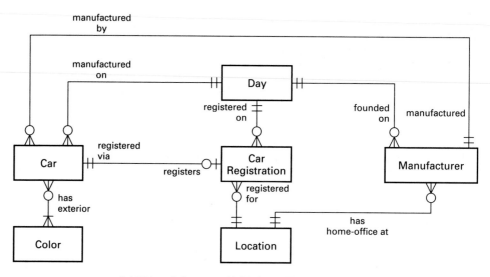

(a) Object Schemas with Verbs as Function Names

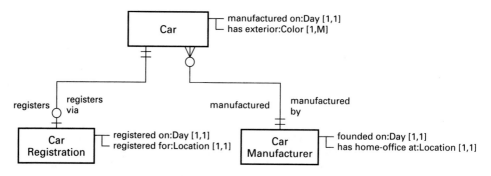

(b) An ER Diagram Mapping from the Object Schema Above

Figure B.3   Using verbs for function names maps to verbs as ER attribute type and relationship type names.

While verbs are standard for relationship types, they are not for ER attribute types. Therefore, using only verbs or only nouns to name object schema functions produces *nonstandard* results when mapping to ER diagrams. Basically, the analyst has two choices:

1. Define both a verb and a noun form for each function, so that when the function is mapped, the standard naming form can be chosen.

2. Use only nouns or only verbs on object schema functions and accept that ER attribute types and relationship types will have the same naming convention.

<table>
<tr><td>THE
RAMIFICATIONS
OF OBJECT TYPES
FOR OO DESIGN</td><td>In object-oriented programming languages (OOPLs), object types are generally implemented as classes. Each class determines a set of objects. In addition, each class defines the structure of its objects and the operations that are permitted on them.</td></tr>
</table>

Classes Determine Sets of Objects

Figure B.4 is an example that illustrates the associations between two types of objects: Car and Day. As expressed in Fig. B.1, the car manufacturing day function defines a mapping from each Car object to exactly one Day object. This same specification could be implemented in an OOPL as Car and Day classes, where each Car object would have a pointer to a Day object. The set of all Car objects are those that are manufactured on a specific day. The Day set would comprise only those objects that are valid days. For instance, the Day object named June 30, 1991 could be a member of this set, June 31, 1991 could not.

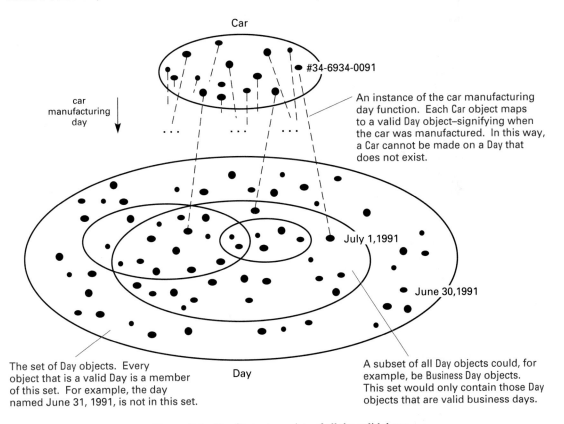

Figure B.4 The Day set consists of all the valid dates.

Moreover, the car manufacturing day function ensures that a given Car maps to a valid Day. When implemented in this way, the Day set acts like a calendar to which other objects can relate.

The Day object type, however, does not have to be implemented as a Day class. Instead, a table of valid days—or a mechanism to compute them—could be placed in those classes relating to the notion of Day. In other words, instead of organizing Day information once via a single class, it would be redundantly specified within those classes that require it. The OO designer chooses the implementation based on performance and space considerations. To assist the designer in making correct implementation decisions, the OO analyst should make certain that all object types are clearly specified. For instance, if the Day object type is not specified during analysis, the designer may not implement its functionality.

Classes as the Index for Structure and Operations

As mentioned earlier, each class defines the structure of its objects along with the operations permitted on each of its objects. For instance, the Day class would define the structure of each Day object along with the various operations that access and maintain this structure. In this way, the Day operations could include such services as

- validation—validating a given day to be correct. For example, if the Day class were requested to create or associate to a Day object for June 31, 1991, the validation operation would reject the request.

- incrementing/decrementing—increasing or decreasing a date by a specific number of days, months, or years.

- comparison—comparing whether one day is earlier, later, or equal to another.

- determination of weekday names—given a particular Day, like June 30, 1991, returning Sunday as the name of the weekday.

- computation of shopping days until Christmas—given a specific day, computing the number of days remaining until Christmas.

- calendar date conversion—given a specific day, returning the date in terms of a given calendar such as Gregorian, Julian, Arabic, Hebrew, Hindi, and sidereal.

If the Day object type is implemented as a class, operations like those above can be requested by those classes requiring date-related information. For instance, the day founded of a particular Car Manufacturer must be a bona fide date before the association can be made. Typically, the Day class would ensure this. Without a Day class, the responsibility for a validation of this kind resides with the Car Manufacturer class. If the only time such validations occur are with Car Manufacturers, this presents no problems. However, if any other class requires the same Day operations, they must either reference the code in the Car

Manufacturer class or write redundant code. Referencing code in an existing module is the goal of good modular programming. However, the programmer must know which module contains the code and where it is located. In very small systems, this is easy. In highly automated companies, it is virtually impossible—unless an OO approach is adopted. In OOPLs, each operation is associated with the class of objects on which it operates. Validating a date would be associated with the **Day** class, registering a **Car** would be associated with the **Car Registration** class, creating or destroying a **Car** the **Car** class, and so on. In short, the class acts as an index for both structure and operation in the OO world.

ENSURING ER DIAGRAMS SUPPORT OO DESIGN   The entity-relationship diagrams in Fig. B.2 do not contain nor indicate the need for a **Day** entity type. Yet in actuality, three of the entity types have attribute types that are **Day**-related. Since the specification does not explicitly make this fact clear, the designer (or code generator) has no way of knowing that a **Day** class should even be considered as a useful OOPL implementation.

Does this mean that analysts can no longer use ER attribute types if they wish to produce object-oriented designs? Some analysts find that making the distinction between ER attribute types and relationship types is highly useful. On the other hand, some analysts prefer the object schema approach which does not make the distinction. Can both approaches be accommodated in an OO environment?

A Solution

Every function maps to an object type. Therefore, *every* ER attribute type and relationship type maps to an entity type. For example, in Fig. B.2(a), the **Car Registration** entity type is associated via a relationship type containing a **registered car** function. This function maps to the **Car** entity type. **Car Registration** also defines an attribute type named **car registration day**. However, this function does not specify the entity type to which it maps. Without this specification, the notion of **Day** cannot be communicated to the OO designer. In Fig. B.2(a), this same omission also applies to those attribute types related to color and location. Without explicitly specifying the entity types to which these attribute types map, **Color** and **Location** could easily be overlooked as possible classes.

Many ER practitioners already specify this by documenting what they call the *domain* or *class word* of the ER attribute type (although in mathematics, the term for this would be *range,* instead). Figure B.5(a) illustrates how Fig. B.2(a) might be more completely expressed so that *all* types are identified. When specified in this way, the *domains* are types in their own right. Furthermore, if the analyst wishes, these same *domains* can also be represented as entity types, as depicted in Fig. B.5(b).

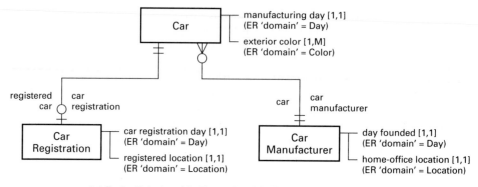

(a) Entity-Relationship Example with ER "Domains" Specified

(b) ER "Domains" from Part (a) Expressed as Entity Types

Figure B.5   ER *domains* identified and represented as entity types.

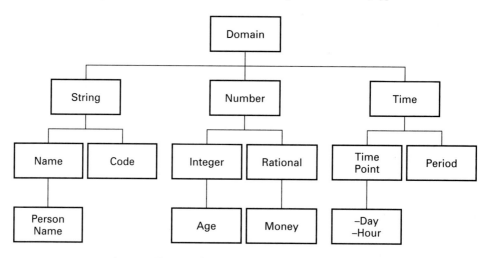

Figure B.6   An ER domain hierarchy.

An example of the *domains* commonly employed in ER modeling are illustrated in the *domain hierarchy* in Fig. B.6 [1].

SUMMARY

This appendix discusses the difference between object schemas and entity-relationship (ER) diagrams. Several notions expressed in object schemas are not included in many conventional ER diagramming approaches. These notions, however, are not what differentiate object schemas and ER diagrams. Any conventional ER diagramming approach can be extended to express these ideas. The major difference between object schemas and ER diagrams is that ER diagrams can express attribute types that are *within* an entity type. Object schemas have no such notion.

The ER attribute type is a function. However, object-oriented design problems can result if the ER attribute type is not properly specified as a function. To avoid these problems every ER attribute type identifies the object type to which it maps. (This is defined as the *range* in Chapter 19 and called the *domain* by some ER analysts.) Every ER *domain* is an object type in its own right.

REFERENCE

1. Van Assche, Frans (1991) personal communication.

 COMPOUND CONCEPTS

At some point, all object types in a system must be specified by a developer. This appendix contains advanced material that presents ways of specifying object types in terms of other object types. Such specifications allow us to readily automate these object types, so that they can be derived or *computed* from already existing object types.

OBJECT TYPES IN TERMS OF OTHER OBJECT TYPES
When we form concepts, we almost always define them in terms of other concepts. Or, to put this in OO standard terminology, when we form object types, we almost always define them in terms of other object types. Howeveɪ, precise object-type definitions are not always easily produced or not worth the effort. For example, object types such as Truth, Beauty, Human, and Chair are among these. Definitions of Truth or Beauty have been debated for thousands of years. Human, on the other hand, is more tangible, yet its definitions usually address only what is *prototypically* Human. For example, zoology textbooks [6] tend to define Human (Homo sapiens) as follows:

5. Order Primate in having 4 generalized limbs each with 5 digits bearing nails.

6. Superfamily Hominoidea in lacking cheek pouches and a tail.

7. Family Hominidae (as distinguished from the Family Pongidae, or anthropoid apes) in the possession of many features, including:

   a. Brain with far greater functional ability and of larger size (minimum… 1000cc…); brain case larger than face.

   b. Face flatter and more vertical, brow ridges reduced, lower jaw less protruding, teeth more evenly sized.

    c. Hair long and of continuous growth on head, but sparse and short on body.

    d. Hands more generalized, thumbs better developed; leg 30 percent longer than arm, and straight; big toe not opposable to other toes.

    e. Skeleton and soft parts of different configuration and proportions.

The Human species habitually walks erect on two feet, is terrestrial in habits, highly gregarious, and omnivorous in diet, and commonly uses cooked food.

Clearly, if **Humans** are bipeds, one-legged people fail the definitional test. In fact, using the above as a true specification, people who are vegetarian, bald, or even missing a fingernail would not qualify as **Human**.

Constructing a statement for the object type **Chair** is similarly complicated. Webster defines a **Chair** as a seat with four legs and a back, used by one person. However, modern designers do not always follow Webster's paradigm, giving **Chair** variable numbers of legs. Again, if an object has a seat and back-support typical of a chair, but is too old and fragile to support the weight of a person, is it still a **Chair**?

Computed Object Types

Some object types, however, can be readily and usefully specified in terms of other object types. For example, the object type of **Managing Salesperson** may be specified in terms of the **Manager** and **Salesperson** object types. The object type of **Boy** can be determined from the object type of **Child** and **Male Person**. The object type of **Parent** is expressed in terms of **Father** and **Mother**. **Grandparents** can be expressed as the **parents** of **Parents**.

Specifying such *computed object types* is useful, because they can be easily automated using existing object types. This means that not only are object types reused to form other object types, but the computed object types themselves can be reused. The next section is devoted to presenting ways of expressing these computed object types with *object-type expressions.*

EXPRESSING COMPUTED OBJECT TYPES

Figure C.1 displays three basic ways of expressing computed object types.

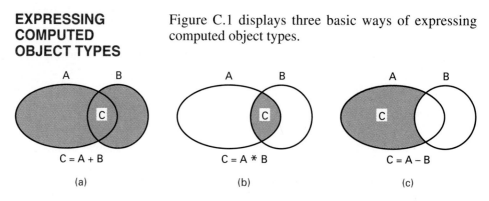

$$C = A + B$$
(a)

$$C = A * B$$
(b)

$$C = A - B$$
(c)

Figure C.1   Three basic expressions of object type.

Object-Type Union

In Fig. C.1(a), object type **C** is expressed as a union of the two object types **A** and **B**. As mentioned in Chapter 15, each object type has an intension (its complete definition) and an extension (its set of objects). The expression **C = A + B** represents both aspects. Interpreted as an intensional specification, this expression would read: the definition of **C** is true for an object if, and only if, the definition of **A** *or* the definition of **B** is true. Another example of an object-type specification is **Parent = Father + Mother**. When considering this expression *in intension,* it means that whenever the definition of **Father** *or* **Mother** applies to an object, the definition of **Parent** also applies. Object-type union, then, is an *inclusive or* when expressing intension.

The distinction between object-type intension and extension is important. However, applying object-type specifications *in extension* is often more practical for the OO developer. It is more tangible, because it directly applies to sets of objects. Here, the object-type union actually computes the addition of sets. For example, in **Parent = Father + Mother**, the set of all **Parent** objects is unambiguously computed to be all those objects contained in the **Father** set, as well as the **Mother** set. When an expression is specifically restricted to an object type's extension, they are called *set expressions.** In addition, different symbols are often employed to express a union, such as **C = A ∪ B**.

Figure C.2(a) represents two ways that graphically express object-type union: partitions and union operators. The first expresses **Person** as a union of

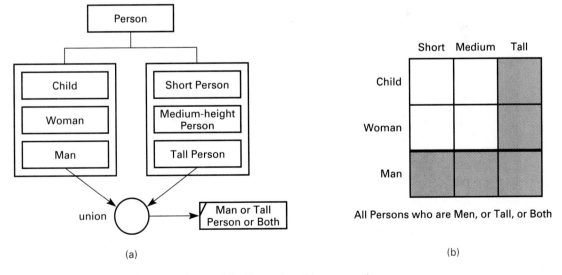

(a)   (b)

Figure C.2 Expressing object-type unions.

*These expressions are usually called *class expressions* by mathematicians [7].

object types within a partition. The partition on the left is one graphic expression of Person and can be written in the form

Person = Child + Woman + Man

The partition on the right expresses

Person = Short Person + Medium-height Person + Tall Person

However, partitions, by definition, only include nonoverlapping, or disjoint, object types. Expressing a union of overlapping object types requires a different representation. The circle in Fig. C.2(a) is an operation symbol. The function name union next to it defines the operation as a union operation. In this example, the Man or Tall Person or Both object type is computed from the union of Man and Tall Person object types. (The slash mark in the rectangle indicates that the object type is computed.)

Fig. C.2(b) illustrates the result of the union expressed in Fig. C.2(a). The rows and columns are the partitioned object types represented in Fig. C.2(a). Each Person object can be classified in any one of these cells depending on its gender/age and height. The objects to which Man or Tall Person or Both applies are in the shaded areas of "man," or "tall," or both.

Object-Type Intersection

In Fig. C.1(b), object type C is calculated as an intersection of the two object types A and B. C is what is common to both object types. In intension, this specification would read: the definition of C is true for an object if, and only if, the definition of A *and* the definition of B are both true. In another example, Boy = Male Person * Child Person means that whenever the definition of a Male Person *and* the definition of a Child Person applies to an object, the definition of Boy applies also. In short, object type intersection is an "and" when expressing intension.

In extension, object-type intersection computes the overlap of sets. For example, in Boy = Male Person * Child Person, the set of all Boy objects can be unambiguously computed to contain whatever is *both* in the set of all Male Person objects *and* in the set of all Child Person objects. When an expression is restricted to a object type's extension, different symbols are often employed to express intersections, such as C = A ∩ B.

At the bottom of Fig. C.3(a), the intersection operator is depicted. In this example, the object type of Both Man and Tall Person is computed from the intersection of Man and Tall Person. Figure C.3(b) illustrates the calculation result. The objects to which Both Man and Tall Person apply are the shaded area common to both "man" and "tall."

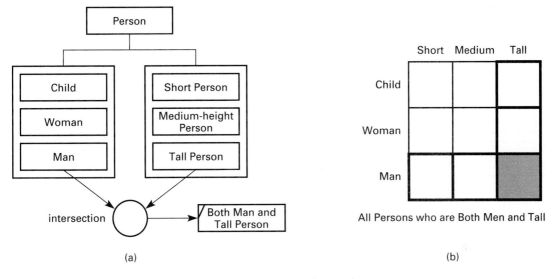

Figure C.3   Object type intersection.

Object-Type Exclusion

Last, in Fig. C.1(c) object type C is calculated as the exclusion of object type B from object type A. In intension, this specification would read: the definition of C is true for an object if, and only if, the definition of A is true, and the definition of B is *not* true. In another example, Man = Male Person – Child Person means that whenever the definition of a Male Person applies to an object—yet the definition of a Child Person does not—the definition of Man also applies. Object-type exclusion, then, is a "not" when expressing intension.

In extension, object-type exclusion computes the subtraction of sets. For example, in Boy = Male Person – Child Person, the set of all Boy objects can be unambiguously computed to contain whatever is in the set of all Male Person objects *minus* whatever is in the set of all Child Person objects.

At the bottom of Fig. C.4(a), the intersection operator is depicted. Here, Man is the minuend or the object type from which the Tall Person subtrahend is excluded. Every operation requires one or more arguments to be filled prior to invoking the operation. The required argument types are defined by *argument-fill rules*. In Fig. C.3(a), the intersection operation has two argument-fill rules represented as lines drawn from the object types Man and Tall Person. The role of these two argument-fill rules is not important to the intersection function: it intersects one argument set with another without regard for which is which. However, the exclusion operation has multiple arguments that are employed by the function in different ways. The result is computed by excluding the subtrahend from the minuend. The argument-fill rules, then, must clarify which is the subtrahend and which is the minuend. With the argument-fill rule lines annotated,

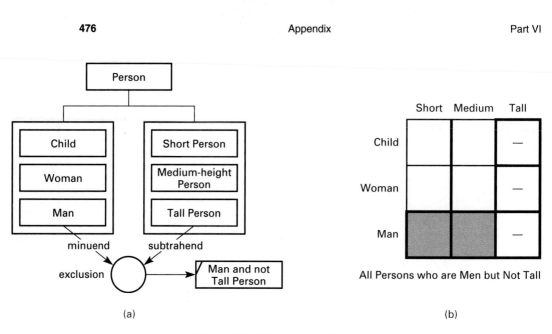

(a)

(b)

Figure C.4   Object-type exclusion.

Fig. C.4(a) clearly expresses that the object type of Man and not Tall Person is computed as the exclusion of Tall Person from Man. Figure C.4(b) illustrates the calculation result. The objects to which Man and Tall Person apply are in the shaded areas of "man" minus that of "tall."

Multistep Object-Type Expressions

Object-type expressions often require more than one step. Figure C.5(a) indicates an intersection that derives the object type Woman. From this, the object type of

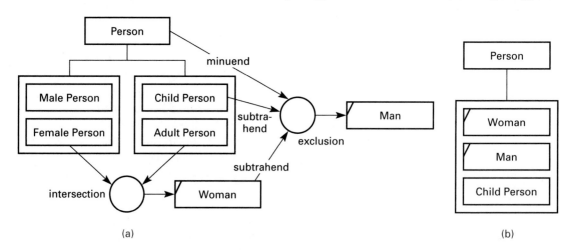

(a)

(b)

Figure C.5   Object-type intersection and exclusion.

Man can be derived by excluding the **Woman** and **Child Person** object types from the object type **Person**.

Once specified in this manner, compound object types can be used in other object schemas and calculations. For example, Fig. C.5(b) contains two compound object types. Once a calculation is expressed, expressing it again in subsequent diagrams is not necessary. In short, these expressions can be automated and reused.

Figure C.5(a) specifies an object-type expression graphically. Depending on the complexity of such diagrams, it may be easier to express the calculation in a written form. Figure C.6 depicts a written alternative for expressing the object type of **Man**. The definition of **Man** in Figs. C.5(a) and C.6 is the same—only the representation is different. In other words, while there are many syntaxes, the underlying semantics are the same.

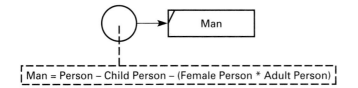

Figure C.6   Nongraphic alternative to object-type expression.

Figures C.5(a) and C.6 present one way of deriving the object type **Man**. However, multiple ways of deriving the same object type may be expressed. Figure C.7 represents another. Here, the set **Man** is computed from the intersection of **Male Person** and **Adult Person**.

While both derivation *methods* of **Man** are different, their net result is the same. In fact, their equivalence can be deduced. For example, the object type can be initially expressed as

Man = Male Person * Adult Person

The terms on the right can be substituted by solving the partition-implied expressions **Person = Male Person + Female Person** and **Person = Child Person + Adult Person**, to yield

Man = (Person – Child Person) * (Person – Female Person)

followed by

Man = Person – Child Person – Female Person

Incorporating the fact that **Woman = Female Person * Adult Person**, also implies

Man = Person – Child Person – (Female Person * Adult Person)

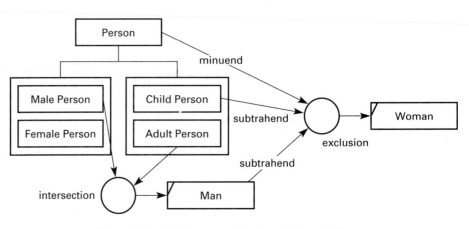

Figure C.7   A different specification of Man and Woman.

However, the **Adult Person** term neither adds meaning nor alters the calculation results. Therefore, while technically equivalent to Figs. C.5(a) and C.6, Fig. C.7 may be regarded as an inefficient computational expression.

EXPRESSING FUNCTIONS

The previous section introduced ways of expressing compound object types, by employing object-type union, intersection, and exclusion. Because functions are specialized forms of object types, these same expressive elements used above play a role in expressing functions. This section presents ways of expressing functions.

Simple Function Expression

In Fig. C.8(a), **Person** has four labeled functions that indicate biological associations: **mother, father, children,** and **parents.*** The functions **mother** and **father** are not calculated, because they are base functions. The **mother** and **father** functions can be expressed in either graphic or written form. For instance, a person's father might be written as, **father(Person)** or **father(Person=@)**, and interpreted as father of a yet-to-be-specified **Person** object. The @ symbol indicates that the function is expecting a value, or argument; and if omitted, its presence is always understood. Once a **Person** object fills an argument, it is mapped via the **father** function.

---

*For the sake of simplicity, all of the function names in this chapter will be presented in a noun form. Instead of writing **has father**, **father** will be written, and so on. The reason for this is that function expressions are not only easier to understand, but are traditionally written as nouns in most disciplines (e.g., the function name to square a given number is not written **has square** or **is squared to be**, but simply **square**. In fact, many OO analysts employ nouns instead of verbs as object schema function names.

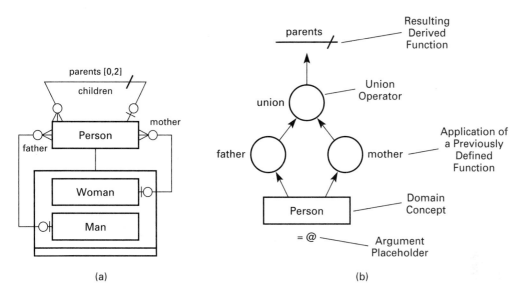

Figure C.8   Object schemas and function expressions complement each other.

The function could also be expressed as father() or father(@)—or even father(x) as typically expressed in mathematics. However, a function often requires qualification, because its name is not always unique. Here, the domain Person can be added as a qualifier. When represented like Fig. C.8(a), father is graphically visible as a function of Person. However, in the grand scheme of things, the name father may also be associated with other object types, such as a father of an Idea, a father of a Colony, and so on. Using the domain name, here, provides a unique qualification.

Function expressions written where an object name is substituted for the @ indicate that the function's argument is filled. For example, the father of Fred would be written father(Person={Fred}), or simply father({Fred}) when the domain is understood. This argument-filled function would return the Man object who is Fred's father. The Person=@, or just Person, symbol is used above as a placeholder until an actual Person object is known and specified.

Computed Functions

In Fig. C.8(a), the mother and father functions are depicted as *base functions.* As presented in Chapter 19, base functions define mappings that are fixed by assertion. In other words, an external source explicitly declares those Persons that are mothers and fathers. In contrast to base functions, *computed functions* are those whose mapping results can be derived or computed. The slash mark on the function line in Fig. C.8(a) indicates that the parents and children functions are computed.

A parent can be either a mother or a father. Therefore, the parents function can be unambiguously calculated as a union of the mother and father functions:

$$parents(Person=@) = father(Person=@) + mother(Person=@)$$

Computed-function expressions (or *function expressions* for short) work like the object-type expressions described above, because argument-filled functions are also object types. Therefore, when the Person argument for parents is filled, the same basic expressions depicted in Fig. C.1 can be used to express computed functions.

The diagram in Fig. C.8(b) expresses the parents calculation graphically. Each labeled circle represents an application of a previously defined function. Here, both the mother and father functions are simultaneously applied to any given Person object. As defined in Fig. C.8(a), the outcome of the mother function is a Woman object; the outcome of the father function is a Man object. Both outcomes are presented to a union operator and become members of the same set. The net effect of the parent function is that it calculates the mapping of a given Person object to its parent objects—which are also Person objects.

Reusing Function Expressions

The function expressions presented so far involve base functions. However, function expressions may also incorporate computed functions. For example, the calculation expressed in Fig. C.8(b) is defined as the parents function. This implies that, whenever the parents function is applied to a Person object, its parents will be calculated. The name parents labels the newly constructed expression and can be referred to thereafter by other expressions. The function expression in Fig. C.9, for instance, reuses the parents function to calculate the first cousins of a given Person.

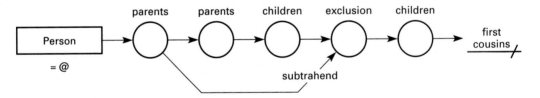

Figure C.9   Function calculation for first cousins.

The first cousins function can be derived in the following manner. First, the given person's grandparents are determined. Then, the children (the inverse of parents in Fig. C.8) of the grandparents are determined. The objects, at this point, are the aunts, uncles, and parents of the given Person object. If the children function were applied one more time, it would yield not only cousins, but brothers and sisters as well. Therefore, the original parents must be subtracted just before the last children function—permitting only first cousins to be computed. A nongraphic expression for this same calculation could be written

first cousins (Person=@) = children(children(parents(parents (Person=@)))–
parents(Person=@))

Transitive Closure

In Fig. C.9, a Person's grandparents are determined by applying the parents function twice in sequence. In order to apply the parents function to the results of a previous parents application until no more parents can be determined, another mode of operation is required. It is called *transitive closure*. Transitive closure is an iterative operation that reapplies its function until no more objects can be determined. When the set of evaluated objects grows no larger, closure is reached.

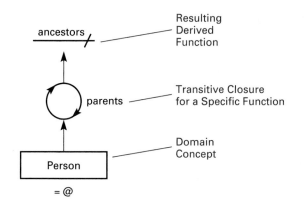

Figure C.10 Using constructed function expressions.

The most widely used application for transitive closure is the bill of materials parts *explosion*. Here, transitive closure is applied to a Part object to determine its subassemblys, its subassemblys' subassemblys, and so on. In Fig. C.10, transitive closure is applied to the previously defined parents function. The two-arrowed circle symbolizes a transitive closure operation. A nongraphic expression for this same calculation could be written

ancestors(Person=@) = transitive closure application(parents,Person=@)

Function Filters

Thus far, function specification requires a facility to compute a result using a series of basic set operators (like union, intersection, and exclusion) and user-defined function applications. Function calculation also requires the capacity to

specify conditional statements. Conditional statements support function calculation by determining whether or not a given object passes a certain condition.
These conditions are Boolean, because their result is limited to a "true" or "false"
evaluation. If the result is "true," the object passes the filter's condition test; otherwise, it does not.

In Fig. C.11(a), the function expression begins by calculating children for a
given Person. Each of the objects mapped by the children function is then tested
for Location, via the residence attributed to each Person. If the child's residence function maps to the Location object named Basingstoke, the child passes
through the filter operation to the next step. In this case, the step determines that
the child is one of the children living in Basingstoke. In this way, the children
living in Basingstoke function specification maps each parent Person to its associated children residing only in the location named Basingstoke.

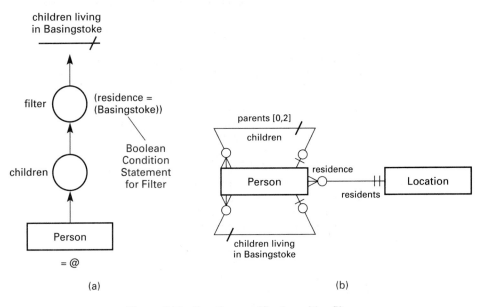

Figure C.11   Function specification with a filter.

Computed Functions as Constraints

By using a computed function in conjunction with a cardinality constraint, certain
kinds of object associations can be restricted. For example in Fig. C.12(a), the
chief employee is a computed function constrained to map to exactly one
Employee. The computation, expressed in Fig. C.12(b), begins by determining
the employees for a given Employer. The resulting set is passed to a filter that
allows only those Employee objects having no boss associations to pass through.
The result, then, is a set consisting of only those employees without a boss.

Since its cardinality is constrained, the chief employee must map to exactly

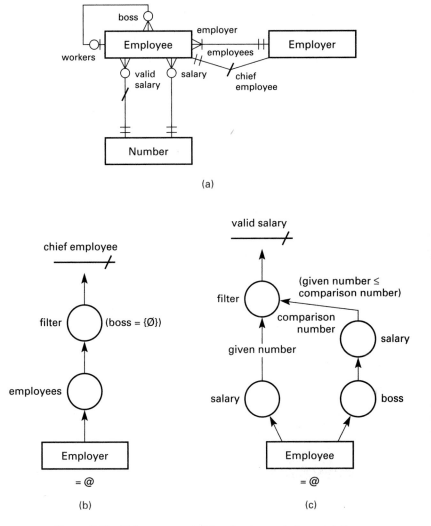

Figure C.12   Using a computed function to constrain associations.

one **Employee** object. If the cardinality constraint is violated, the problem of structural integrity exists. In order to avoid this, computed functions used conjunction with a cardinality constraint must be reevaluated whenever their component functions change. In the example above, this means that whenever an **employees** or **boss** association changes, the **chief employee** function must be computed and its constraint checked. If the **chief employee** constraint is met, the change is permitted to remain. If the constraint is violated, the change is disallowed. In this way, an **Employer** will always have exactly one **employee** at the *top* of an organization chart.

Figure C.12(c) expresses another computed function: valid salary. This function begins with a specific Employee object and determines not only the Employee's salary, but the boss's salary as well. The filter allows only those Employee salary objects that are less than or equal to the boss's salary object to pass. The cardinality constraints require that the mapping always result in exactly one Number. In other words, if no Number object results, a structural integrity problem exists—the Employee's salary is too high. Therefore, whenever a salary association is made, the valid salary function must be evaluated and its constraint checked. If the valid salary constraint is met, the salary change remains. If the constraint is violated, the change is disallowed.

Computed Functions that Use Numeric Operations

The filter in Fig. C.12(c) checked for one object to be less than or equal to another object. Yet, how can two objects be compared in this way? What would it mean if we asked whether a Puce object is greater than a Chartreuse object? However, we know exactly what it means to ask whether one salary figure is less than or equal to another, because Numbers can be regarded in this manner. In order for function expressions to handle Number objects, numerically oriented operations are required. These include arithmetic computations like addition and subtraction, and numeric comparisons like greater, less than, or equal to.

EXPRESSING OBJECT TYPES AS ARGUMENT-FILLED FUNCTIONS

As discussed previously, object-type expression used only object types. However, as already mentioned in Chapter 19, argument-filled functions are object types. For example, the Muscovite object type in Fig. C.13 is derived by filling the argument for the residents function that maps Location to Person. In this way, a location-specific object type is unambiguously defined with the argument Moscow. Its extension is the set of all Person objects whose Location is Moscow. Once defined in this manner, the Muscovite object type can be represented in other diagrams without further elaboration. With a formal OO approach to modeling, attributes of specific objects *are* object types.

Without the supplied argument, the residents function can be regarded as an incomplete object type. The incomplete expression can be written as residents(Location=@) to indicate where the argument would be supplied.

Multi-Argument Object Types

Figure C.14(a) specifies an object type that requires two argument-filled functions. In the lower left, the argument-filled function is similar to that in Fig. C.13—it maps to the set of all Person objects whose residence is Paris. The other argument-filled function maps to all Person objects whose employer is the

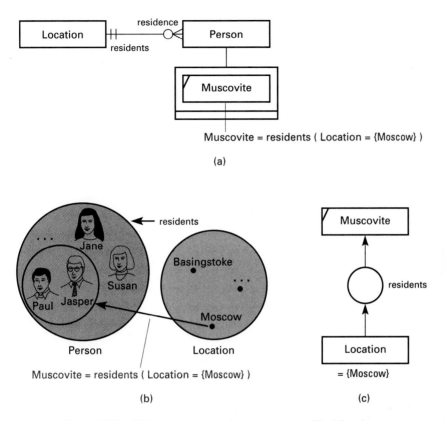

Muscovite = residents (Location = {Moscow})

(a)

Muscovite = residents (Location = {Moscow})

(b)

= {Moscow}

(c)

Figure C.13 Object type expressed as an argument-filled function.

NEC. Each of the argument-filled functions defines a subset of **Person** objects, which could be named **Parisian** and **NEC Employee**, respectively. By intersecting these two object types, a new object type is defined. The **Parisian NEC Employee** object type is based on joining **Parisian** and **NEC Employee** objects.

Similarly, by changing the **Organization** argument to IBM, a **Parisian IBM Employee** object type would be constructed. Both object types are disjoint on account of employer, yet both are types of **Person**. **Parisian NEC Employee** and **Parisian IBM Employee** can also be expressed as members of the same partition, as depicted in Fig. C.14(b). If two objects such as NEC and IBM were supplied (specified as ={NEC, IBM}), all **Person** objects that are employed in Paris by both companies would be determined as **Parisian NEC or IBM Employee**.

For All Objects in a Domain Object Type

Previously, function expressions were defined using either a variable or fixed argument. The variable argument (expressed by =@) denotes that an object is supplied at the time the function is evaluated. The fixed argument (expressed in

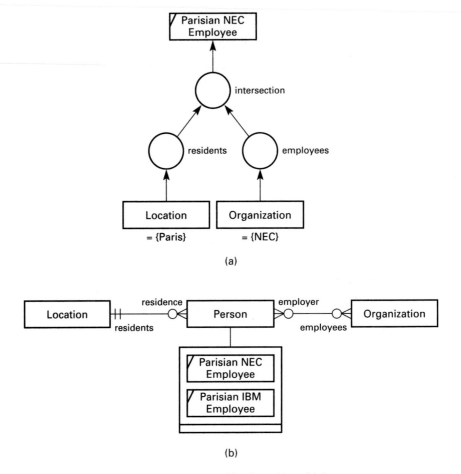

Figure C.14   Object-type specification with multiple arguments.

the form ={object name-1, object name-2,...}) is supplied when the function is defined. Often, however, having a function computation involving *all* of the objects in a domain is desirable.

For example, in Fig. C.14(a) the Organization argument to the employees function is limited to the NEC object. To indicate that all Organization objects should (separately) be supplied as arguments to the employees function, a different designation is needed. An "= all" or "for all" could be placed next to the domain object type to indicate this. For simplicity, this book omits the "=" designation altogether to mean "for all." (Such an approach is consistent with the object-type expressions presented earlier.) In Fig. C.15(a), the Organization object type has no "=" designation. Therefore, the instances of the computed object type Employee are the employees of *every* Organization. Figure C.15(b) depicts this computed object type as part of an object schema.

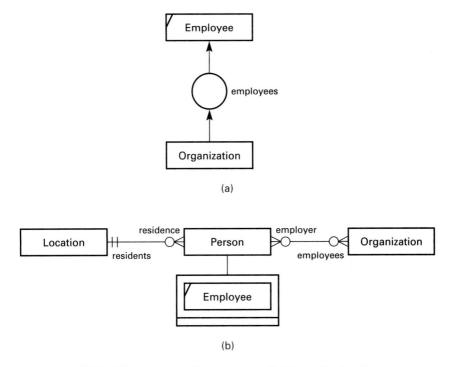

Figure C.15 Object-type specification using all objects of a domain as arguments.

SUMMARY   During OO analysis, the analyst will find that some object types can be expressed in terms of other object types. Three basic expressive devices of an object type are union, intersection, and exclusion. When applied in extension, these three calculate set membership. The *union* combines two or more sets as one set. The *intersection* includes only that portion common between two or more sets. The *exclusion* specifically excludes the objects of one set from another.

Object-type expressions employ other object types in their construction. Once defined, in a graphic or written form, these *computed object types* can be reused in other representations without having the specification reexpressed. For most applications, object-type expressions will be used *in extension.* In this context, they are called *set (or class) expressions.*

Expressing *computed functions* builds on the three expressive devices of object types by

- adding the ability to employ user defined function applications
- supporting transitive closure
- employing *filters* to allow objects through when the condition is "true"

Finally, since argument-filled functions are also object types, their expressions can be incorporated into object-type expressions. In this way, object-type expressions involve object-type instances.

This chapter presents ways for expressing compound object types and computed functions. An example of a nongraphic specification language for functions is DAPLEX [5]. However, no one notation, or syntax, need be used to communicate the underlying meaning, or semantics. As long as the meaning can be expressed in a clear, concise, and consistent manner, the notation is a matter of aesthetics and usability.

REFERENCES

1. Beech, David, "Intensional Concepts in an Object Database Model," *Proceedings of OOPSLA 88,* OOPSLA 88 (San Diego, Calif.), Norman Meyrowitz ed., ACM Press, New York, 1988, pp. 164–175.

2. Joy, Mike and Tom Axford, "A Standard for a Graph Representation for Functional Programs," *ACM SIGPLAN Notices,* 23:1, Jan. 1988, pp. 75–82.

3. Kim, Kyung-Chang *et al.,* "Cyclic Query Processing in Object-Oriented Databases," *Proceedings of Fifth International Conference on Data Engineering,* Data Engineering (Los Angeles), IEEE Computer Society Press, Washington, DC, 1989, pp. 564–571.

4. Manola, Frank, *PDM: An Object-Oriented Data Model for PROBE,* Computer Corporation of America, Technical CCA-87-03, September 1987.

5. Shipman, David, "The Functional Data Model and the Data Language DAPLEX," *ACM Transactions on Database Systems,* 6:1, 173, 1981, pp. 140.

6. Storer, Tracy I. and Robert L. Usinger, *General Zoology* (3rd edition), McGraw-Hill, New York, 1957.

7. Whitehead, Alfred North and Bertrand Russell, *Principia Mathematica,* Cambridge University Press, Cambridge, 1910.

D MODELS AND META-MODELS

Models are an abstraction device. They help us differentiate the forest from the trees. As such, they must be sufficiently powerful to give us some understanding of the objects in our world and how they relate. Models are not used just to enhance understanding and abstract detail. When automated, they define our reality. This appendix contains advanced material that describes how object schemas can represent models—and, our models of models.

MODELING LEVELS   The conventional approach to modeling is through levels similar to those illustrated in Fig. D.1. A *meta-model* is a model that defines other models. For example, if an enterprise adopted the approaches of entity-relationship and data-flow diagramming, the meta-model would define instances of object types such as Entity Type, Relationship Type, Attribute Type, Process Type, Data Store, and Data Flow. These object types would then dictate the way in which the next level would be expressed. For example, a meta-model with an object type called Process Type would allow the

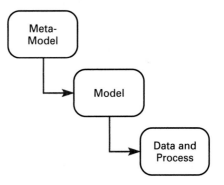

Figure D.1   Conventional modeling levels.

model level to instantiate types of processes such as Assemble Part or Pay Employee. The meta-model object type called Entity Type would instantiate *model* level occurrences such as Part or Employee.

Continuing down, the *model* level object types determine the types of *data and process* instances that can occur in an enterprise. For example, Pay Employee at the model level instantiates all the various processing moments when an enterprise pays its employees. An Employee object type at the model level instantiates all the instances of enterprise employees.

Maintaining Modeling Levels

In order to change the kinds of object types that can be defined at the model level, a meta-model must be modified. For example, if an organization decides to support the function decomposition of activities, the meta-model must be changed to allow a tree structure of Activity Types. While this separation of model and meta-model is sensible, it can be troublesome. First, each level is its own self-contained unit that represents just one portion of an organization's total modeling needs. Such fragmented models also mean fragmented maintenance. Second, modifying meta-models is often impossible. The software vendor may consider the contents of its meta-model to be proprietary. In addition, the software vendor may provide no customization features, or may implicitly define the meta-model in the form of program code.

Model Levels that Cannot Reference Each Other

Figure D.1 depicts each modeling level as a distinctly separate group, because that is how levels are typically developed and applied. In practice, modeling is too often performed in a *downward* direction only. For example, if Entity Type appears as a meta-model object type, instances of Entity Type, such as Person or Product, could be defined at the model level. However, if Entity Type also appeared at the model level, it would be understood as a different object type than the Entity Type in the meta-model. Here, the meta-model level can instantiate the model level, while the model level has no knowledge of its meta-level.

Even a simple statement, such as Person is an instance of Entity Type, cannot be explicitly represented in this arrangement. Entity Type is located in the meta-model level, and Person is located in the model level. Since neither object type resides in both models, the *instance* association is lost to the model level.

When one modeling level cannot reference its previous level, knowledge is lost—even though the levels are meant to fit together. One remedy allows a selective *overlap* in levels. However, this offers only limited help. Unless each level of a model is propagated to the next, some meaning will be lost.

Model Levels as Object-Type Instance Boundaries

The three levels depicted in Fig. D.1 might, on first glance, seem to reflect a natural division in model building. However, each level is supposed to define the basis for instantiating the next. Three levels are not enough. For example, the levels in Fig. D.2 correspond to the same three levels presented in Fig. D.1. The model level contains several instances of Entity Type. The Entity Type named Product applies to several instances at the data and process level, such as Sony CD Player and B&O Turntable. As far as the salesperson at a hi-fi store is concerned, these are most certainly two instances of the products offered.

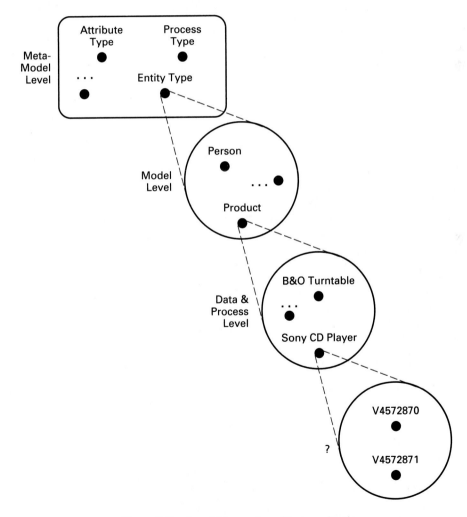

Figure D.2　A variable number of instance levels.

However, for the inventory clerk in the hi-fi store, the Sony CD Player is a *type* of product for sale. The clerk and salesperson may even agree to rename Product as Product Type. Yet, to the inventory clerk, the important objects are really instances of the instances of Product Type. For example, if Sony CD Player is an instance of Product Type, the clerk may have two instances of a Sony CD Player identified by the serial numbers V4572870 and V4572871. In other words, the salesperson's object is the clerk's object type; instances of the clerk's object type are a level *below* the data and process level.

Should a new modeling level then be added to accommodate these instances? If ability to instantiate at the data and process level were allowed, any number of levels could be defined within it. This ability could be supported by defining (within the meta-model) that every Object Type can map to an Object via an instantiates function. Such a definition is expressed in Fig. D.3.

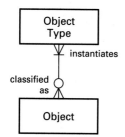

Figure D.3   Each instance of an Object Type instantiates any number of Objects; each Object instance is classified as one or more Object Types.

The example in Fig. D.2, then, would allow the Product object type to have instances such as Sony CD Player and B&O Turntable at the model level. In addition, this would allow object types at the data and process level, like Sony CD Player, to have instances like V4572870 and V4572871. In other words, by defining the instantiates function at the meta-model level, all levels can have instances. In fact, the only difference between the model and meta-model levels is that one has instances of the other. Why have these boundaries at all? If one person's object is another person's object type, rigidly maintaining separate levels of abstraction is not realistic for an analysis and design team.

Modeling in One Framework

As seen above, modeling in levels can create problems. These can be remedied by modeling within a single framework—or conceptual system—instead. In this way

- Model maintenance is performed on one coherent and integrated model, not fragmented by levels.

- Object types and instances share the same model, so that a two-way knowledge of their association is not lost between segregated levels.

- Any number of instantiates *levels* is possible since the number of levels is not required to be rigid.

Such an approach has another major advantage. A single framework model can be used to describe itself, as well as the enterprise. If a model is sufficiently descriptive, it should be able to specify its own object types. A small subset of the model can then describe a much larger subset, which can be propagated to an even larger subset, and so on. Furthermore, any changes to the model can be rigorously specified by and within the model. If a model can be a meta-model to describe itself, it can be a meta-model to describe other models. An approach of this kind can both describe different models and provide a common framework for expressing and comparing models [1].

Figure D.4 illustrates this idea. The kernel subset with which the model describes itself is called a *hyper-model*. It would contain such *primitive* object types as Object Type, Object, Relation, and Function. In order to support processing requirements, it would also contain object types like Operation, Trigger Rule, Control Condition, and Event Type. Primitives, such as these, can be used to form foundational constructs for other structures—which, in turn, may be used as constructs. From here, thinking in terms of meta-models, models, and instances is a personal choice. As mentioned earlier, the conceptual and physical boundaries between these are tenuous. In a single framework model, the boundaries are nonexistent. The only reason for inhibiting *changes* to the hyper-level or meta-level is to maintain standardization.

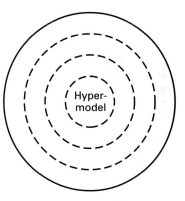

Figure D.4   Single framework modeling.

REPRESENTING OBJECT TYPES

The single framework approach described above only works when hyper-model *primitives* are defined in a precise and consistent fashion. Without agreed-upon sets of symbols, well-formed rules, and axioms, the results would be an informal hodgepodge, at best. While the theoretic formalism will not be presented in this book, this section shows how a formal foundation can be applied to OO model building.

Meaning and Representation

As mentioned above, the modeling foundation in this book begins with notions, such as Object Type, Object, Relation, and Function. These notions provide the basis for the meaning, or semantics, on which a meta-modeling effort builds.

Once the semantics are established, they can be depicted in any way their user finds meaningful. For example, Fig. D.5 represents three ways of depicting the same association between the two object types, Person and Desk. As long as meaning is preserved, its depiction can differ. The underlying model provides this meaning; its depiction is a matter of useful aesthetics.

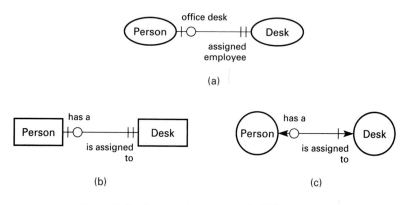

Figure D.5 Representing meaning in different ways.

Representing Subtypes and Supertypes

For example, in Fig. D.6(a), the object type Object Type is represented with a supertypes function and its subtypes inverse. Based on these two functions, *all* object types can now have subtypes and supertypes. The resulting Super/Subtype relation is also important, particularly if you want to depict instances of subtypes and supertypes. Each instance of the Super/Subtype relation is a couple whose form can be written

Super/Subtype(supertypes:Object Type, subtypes:Object Type)

In other words, each Super/Subtype is a couple where one object supertypes another; and, inversely, the latter subtypes the former. Since an object can be symbolized in any way, each Super/Subtype instance can be represented by a line with a dark arrow in the middle (see Fig. D.6(b)). For example, Salesman is represented as a supertype of Managing Salesman and a subtype of Employee. These are two Super/Subtype relations.

This can be further extended so that subtypes can be placed in a round-cornered box, as shown in Fig. D.6(c). In this way, only one arrowed line is needed to point to the supertypes.

Again, these representations are arbitrary, but their basis is formal. If other representations are preferred, the conceptual foundation can support them. If no device is useful for depicting an object of this (or any other) kind, do not adopt one.

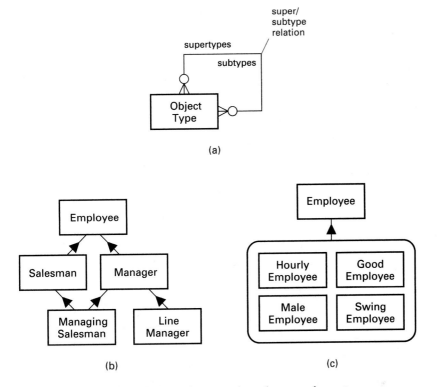

Figure D.6   Defining and representing subtypes and supertypes.

The conceptual foundation can be extended further to define type partitions. In Chapter 21, the type partition was defined as a division of an object type's extension, or set, into disjoint subsets. Figure D.7 contains a schema that defines this. The symbol chosen for instances of **Complete Partition** has been the square-cornered box. **Incomplete Partitions** are indicated in the same manner with an additional trailing bar.

In addition to the notation, the meta-model can be extended to incorporate additional partition-related object types. Figure D.8 depicts the result of three such extensions. The first representation specifies an immutable partition for the object type **Person**. The thick arm is chosen here to indicate that once a particular subtype is chosen for an object, that object may not be reclassified to any other object type within the partition. Figure D.8(a) specifies that a **Person** object, once classified as a **Female Person**, may never be reclassified as a **Male Person**, and vice versa.

The notions of mandatory and optional can also be applied to partitions. For example, the short-bar representation above the partition in Fig. D.8(b) indicates that any object classified as **Customer** *must* also be classified as either an **Individual Customer** or a **Corporate Customer**. Whereas, the representation on

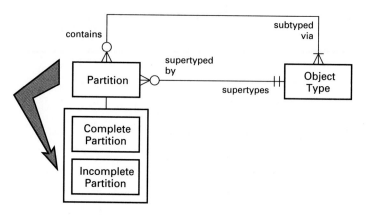

Figure D.7   Defining and representing partitions.

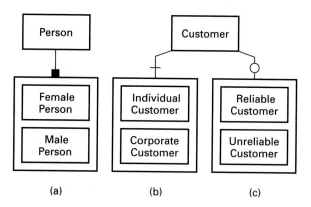

Figure D.8   Extending partition representations.

the right indicates that its subtypes are optional. In this case, the determination of whether a Customer is a Reliable Customer or an Unreliable Customer can be deferred until some future point.

    Even the idea of minimum and maximum cardinality can be applied to subtypes. The example in Fig. D.9(a) shows one way that an Employee can be classified as zero, one, or many of the subtypes enclosed in the round-cornered box presented earlier.

    Last, Figs. D.9(b) and D.9(c) depict a different way of representing generalization hierarchies. They employ a fern-like representation. In Fig. D.9(b), instead of the round-cornered box of Figs. D.6(c) and D.9(a), the subtypes of Employee are listed along a vertical line. Here, the implication triangle is not filled in to indicate a nondisjoint list. In contrast, the filled-in triangle of Fig. D.9(c) indicates that the list is disjoint. This representation is known in this book as an incomplete partition.

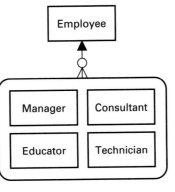

(a)

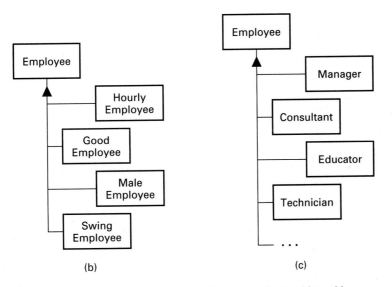

(b)   (c)

Figure D.9   Other techniques describing generalization hierarchies.

Representing Instances

The examples above show how a formal foundation can be employed to support and represent generalization. This foundation can also be used to support and represent abstraction. The Classification/Instance relation between Object Type and Object is an important *primitive* for any modeling effort. Without it, no formal foundation exists for displaying objects of any kind. Even object types and their associations would have no basis for existence, because they depend on the instantiates function. After all, each object type is an Object that is classified as an Object Type.

Figures D.10(b) and D.10(c) indicate two popular representations of Classification/Instance relations. Both diagrams signify that Operations and Personnel are objects which are classified as Organization Unit. Here, the representation for each Organization Unit object is the small, dark circle. Again, the symbols chosen for each of the objects is determined by the user. Schemas, such as Fig. D.10(a), provide the foundation for object identification.

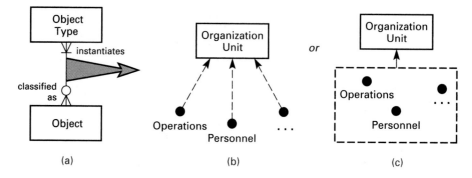

Figure D.10   Defining and representing instances.

Representing Components

Representing components is another notion that analysts find useful. Chapter 16 introduces composition as a way of expressing how objects can consist of other objects. One definition of composition is expressed by the schema in Fig. D.11(a). Figure D.11(b) extends this to support two kinds of composition: changeable and immutable.

Figure D.12(a) depicts an example of a changeable composition. Each Boat object is an instance of Composite Object. Its Hull and Motor objects are its contained by a Boat object. In Fig. D.12(a), the contained by/contains associations are signified by the large clear triangle symbols. In other words, because the Hull and Motor are changeable components, each Boat instance can change Hull or Motor components and still be the same boat. If it is later decided that only the Motor components can change while the Hull is an immutable component, the schema can be changed. In this situation, the Boat object type will have one changeable and one immutable component.

Relations are subtypes of Composite Object Types. Tuples, which are instances of Relations, are subtypes of Composite Objects. Each Tuple is a specialized form of Composite Object, because its components cannot change. The large clear triangles with the "I" in Fig. D.11(b) indicate that each Employment object has two immutable components: an Organization object and a Person object. In other words, each instance of Employment is immutably composed of Organization and Person objects. If either the Organization or the Person object is removed or replaced, a different Employment object results.

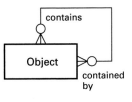

(a)

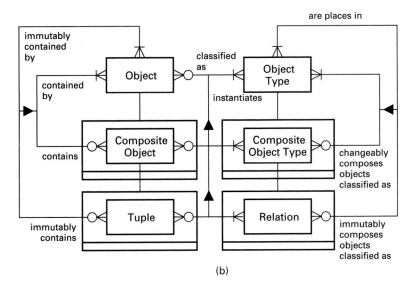

(b)

Figure D.11 Expressing composition.

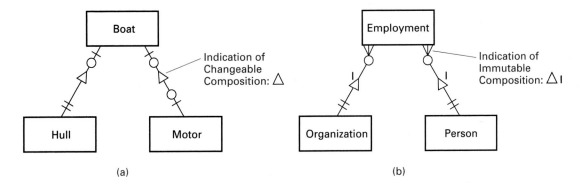

Figure D.12 Examples of representing changeable and immutable composition.

Object Types as Objects of Object Types

A conceptual foundation can also support the notion that object types can have instances that are also object types. For example, the object type **Object Type** applies to many different objects, one of which is **Product Type**. Product Type, in turn, is an object type that applies to many different objects. In Fig. D.13, it applies to such objects as Sony CD Player and B&O Turntable—which in turn are object types that apply to their own objects. For example, a **Sony CD Player** applies to the objects identified by serial numbers V4572870 and V4572871. Notice also that the **Sony CD Player** which is a subtype of **Product** is the *same* object to which the object type **Product Type** applies. In fact, the definition of **Product Type** can be expressed as all of the subtypes of **Product**. Another name for this relation is called the *power type*. In the example, **Product Type** is said to be the power type of **Product**.

Situations like that portrayed in Fig. D.13 wreck havoc for the analyst attempting to enforce the strict meta-modeling levels illustrated in Fig. D.1. When models have one framework, the **Power Type** relation is but one relation among many. Moreover, since the **Power Type** relation is important, many analysts wish to indicate them specifically. Fig. D.13(b) depicts the **Power Type** relation with a

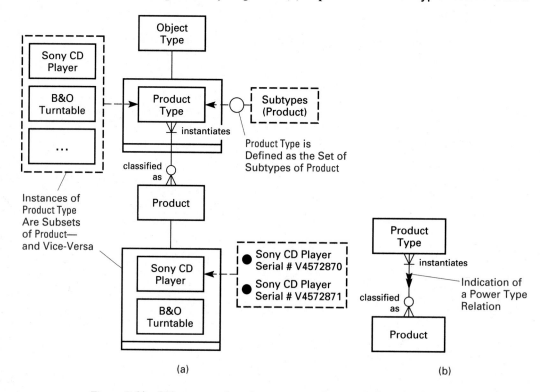

Figure D.13   Object types whose instances are subtypes of other object types.

double arrow. An arrow is chosen to indicate the direction of classification. In this case, the instances of **Product Type** classify the instances of **Product**.

Figure D.14 illustrates another way of expressing that the subtypes of one object type are instances of another. While this communicates the meaning more clearly, it can pose maintenance problems. For instance, if a company has many **Product** subtypes, expressing and maintaining them in partition form is not feasible. For situations like this, a special instance/classification relation notation like that depicted in Fig. D.13(b) would be preferable.

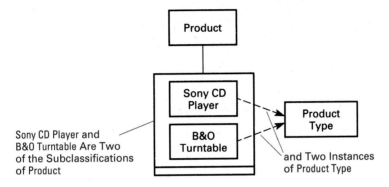

Figure D.14　　The subtypes of one object type can be instances of another.

Object-Type Reusability

Single framework modeling means one conceptual system and all of its defined structures can be employed in further modeling activities. For example, Fig. D.15 references basic terms such as **Object Type**, **Object**, **instantiates**, and **classified as**, as well as, instances of these **Object Type** and **Object**.

Building on these object types encourages further reusability. For instance, the object type of **Measurement** can be defined for **Objects** that are instances of **Measured Types**. For example, **Height**, **Weight**, **Density**, and **IQ** are all object types that may have measurements. **Measurement**, then, acts as a reusable template for various measurable object types. In this way, the same object can have different measurements within different conceptual contexts. Without a single, common modeling framework, schemas like this are not possible for the OO analyst.

SUMMARY　　　　　　A common approach for describing modeling structures employs physically and conceptually different modeling levels. This can create problems, which can be remedied by modeling within a single framework—or conceptual system. In this way

- Model maintenance is performed on one coherent and integrated model, not fragmented by levels.

- Object types and their instances share the same model, so that a two-way knowledge of their association is not lost between segregated levels.

- Any number of instantiates *levels* is possible since the number of levels is not rigid.

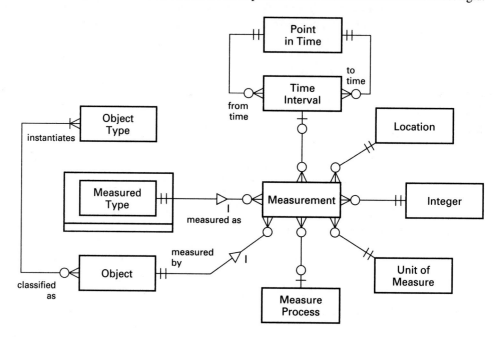

Figure D.15   Several meta-levels at once.

Such an approach has another major advantage. A single framework model can be used to describe itself, as well as the enterprise. If a model is sufficiently descriptive, it should be able to specify its own object types. Typically, this begins with hyper-model, or *primitive,* object types such as Object Type, Object, Relation, and Function. With these basic constructs, others can be defined, such as subtypes, supertypes, partitions, instantiates, classified as, contained by, immutably contained by, and so on. These *second generation* forms are part of what is often called the meta-model, because they define the constructs an enterprise model will contain. However, in a single framework model, an enterprise model consists of all object types: hyper-model, meta-model, or otherwise. The only reason to restrict access to such a model is to enforce some degree of standardization on project teams and to protect against unauthorized model changes.

REFERENCE

1. Tsichritzis, Dionysios C. and Frederick H. Lochovsky, *Data Models,* Prentice-Hall, Englewood Cliffs, NJ, 1982.

E STATE: A COLLECTION OF OBJECT TYPES VERSUS A COLLECTION OF ATTRIBUTES

In this book, *state* is defined in the following manner:

> The *state* of an object is the collection of object types that applies to it.

When implemented by an OO programming language, object state is recorded in the data stored about the object. The object state is determined by the classes and data-field values associated with the object. Therefore, an alternate definition of state is commonly used by OO programmers:

> The *state* of an object is the collection of associations for that object.

These two definitions do not conflict with each other. Instead, they are two ways of viewing the same object state.

State as a Collection of Associations of an Object

Figure E.1 depicts an object named Paul expressed in terms of its associations with other objects. Paul's current state, then, is a collection of four associations indicating that Paul is employed by NASA, has brown hair, and is classified as both a **Pet Owner** and a **Person**. If Paul becomes unemployed, changes his hair color, or no longer owns pets, Paul's state will change. His state will change, because his collection of associations will have changed.

From Fig. E.1 we know immediately that at least two object types apply to the Paul object: **Pet Owner** and **Person**. We know this because an object type *classifies* objects—and objects are *classified as* (or instances of) object types. For

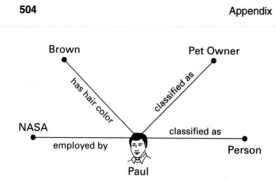

Figure E.1   The current state of the object named Paul is expressed in terms of its association with other objects.

example, in Fig. E.2 a set of objects are classified as **Person**. Here, the object named Person (which is an instance of **Object Type**) has an association that classifies the objects Susan, Jane, Jasper, Paul, and so on. In other words, mapping from a given object determines a set of other objects.

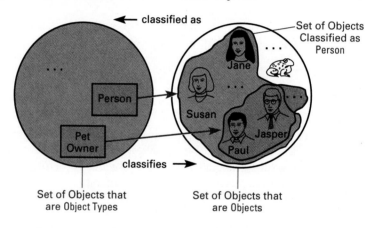

Figure E.2   Object types are objects that classify sets of objects.

Figure E.3 depicts a different kind of association. Here, objects that are *not* object types map to a set of objects. For instance, the NASA object maps to a set containing objects Paul and Jasper, NEC maps to a set containing Susan, and so on. As with the example in Fig. E.2, mapping from a given object determines a set of other objects. In this case, however, **Object Type** objects are not mapped to sets of objects: **Organization** objects are mapped to sets of objects.

What Are Object Types?

In Chapter 15, the term object type (i.e., concepts) is defined as an idea or notion we share that applies to certain objects in our awareness. So, thinking of objects like Person and Pet Owner as object types is quite natural. Yet, Brown and NASA are not considered to be types of objects.

Another way of thinking about object types is that they have extensions and intensions. The extension of **Person** in Fig. E.2 is the set of objects to which **Person**

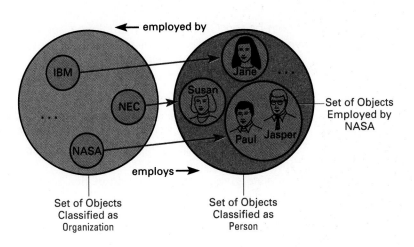

Figure E.3   Objects of one type *map* to sets of objects of another type.

applies—Susan, Jane, Jasper, Paul, and so on. The intension of **Person** is the complete definition of what it means for an object to be classified as a human being.

The same idea can be used for the mapping in Fig. E.3. Here, the extension is the set containing the objects Jasper and Paul. The intension is defined simply in terms of whether or not an object is one that NASA **employs.*** In other words, here is an idea or notion that applies to certain objects. In addition, this *idea* has both an extension and intension. If this is so, what should the object types based on these NASA and Brown associations be called? In Fig. E.4, they are named

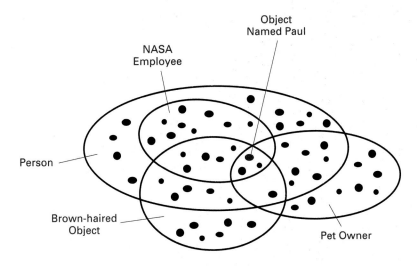

Figure E.4   Paul is an object that is an instance of four object types.

*In Chapter 19, this function is referred to as argument-filled.

NASA Employee and Brown-haired Object. NASA Employee applies to those objects that are employed by NASA. The object type named Brown-haired Object applies to those objects that have a hair color of Brown.

State as a Collection of Object Types

Figure E.4 illustrates the various sets of objects to which four object types apply: Person, Pet Owner, NASA Employee, and Brown-haired Object. In other words, the state of the Paul object introduced in Fig. E.1 is now defined in terms of a collection of object types that apply to it.

The two definitions of state given in the beginning of this appendix, then, are equivalent.

INDEX

A

Abstract data types (ADTs), 157-59, 167, 433
  cancelling inherited features, 165
  inheritance and polymorphism, 162, 164-65
  multiple inheritance, 165-67
  objects and requests, 160-62
  objects as encapsulations, 159-60
  object identification, 162
  objects relating to other objects, 162
Abstraction, 247-48, 297, 497
Accessors, 410, 423
Action diagrams, 11, 70, 125, 126, 174, 177, 178
Activities, 123, 125, 127, 128, 381, 382, 387-88
  activity leveling, 392-94, 395
  activity-product pairs, 389-90
  adding value, 389
  consumed products, 392, 393
  definition of, 387
  linking state changes and, 150, 151-53
  object flow diagrams and event schema leveling, 394, 396
  as object types, 396-98
  persistence of, 388-89
  products and by-products, 391-92
  value chains, 389
Activity schemas, 142, 143, 144
Argument-filled functions, 275-76
  expressing object types as, 484-86
Argument-fill rules, 475
Arrows, 129
Artificial intelligence, 4, 11
Associations, 259-60
  reading like sentences, 134
  state as a collection of, 503-4
  subsets of, 138
Attributes, 274-75, 461
Attribute types, 274-75, 462, 463, 467
  mutable and immutable, 286-88
  relations with, 286

B

Base functions, 278, 417, 479
  mapping:
    fundamental operations for functions, 411-13
    maximum cardinality constraints, 410-11
    minimum cardinality constraints, 410
    modification constraint checking, 413
    referential integrity for inverse functions, 413-14
    when not to maintain inverses, 414-15
Binary relation, 253
BLOBs (binary large objects), 21, 34, 203
Business area analysis (BAA), 224
By-products, 391-92

C

C, 11, 36, 38, 68, 70, 179
Candidate keys, 293
Cardinality, 125, 126
  relation, 281-82
  relational nodes and, 289-90
Cardinality constraints, 130-31, 139, 140, 141, 268-71, 413
  beyond zero, one, and many, 271
  computed functions as, 48284
  crow's feet, 131, 269, 270
  function expressions and, 418-19
  labeling of lines, 134
  minimum and maximum, 132-34, 410-11
  one-with-one, 131
  reading associations like sentences, 134
  specialization by, 310-11
  zero, 131-32
CASE (computer-aided software engineering), 4, 5, 10, 11, 35, 68

CASE tools:
  categories of, 172-73
  consistency among diagrams, 182-83
  consistency among different analysts, 183
  consistency among different projects, 183-84
  design synthesis and code generation, 174-76
  diagrams for OO development, 177-78
  insightful models, 173-74
  maximum reusability, 184-86
  OO repository for non-OO techniques, 181-82
  precision in diagramming, 176-77
  repository, 178-81, 208
  sources of reusable components, 186-88
  variety of, 171-72
CD-ROM, 44
Chief information engineer, 444
Chief information officer (CIO), 39-40
Class(es), 21-22, 23, 27, 32, 34, 108, 112, 113, 123, 158
  as index for structure and operations, 466-67
  determining sets of objects, 465-66
Class independence, 211
Class inheritance. *See* Inheritance
Class-instance inheritance. *See* Inheritance
Class libraries, 5, 8, 22
Client-server technology, 5, 8, 10
Clock events, 142
Clock operation, 341, 343-44
Clock time, 341
COBOL, 11, 36, 46, 68, 70, 172, 179, 199, 200, 433
CODASYL, 200
Code generation, 174, 175
Code generation from the enterprise model (CGEM), 60

THE JAMES MARTIN BOOKS

Information Systems Management and Strategy	Methodologies for Building Systems	Analysis and Design	CASE
AN INFORMATION SYSTEMS MANIFESTO	STRATEGIC INFORMATION PLANNING METHODOLOGIES (second edition)	STRUCTURED TECHNIQUES: THE BASIS FOR CASE (revised edition)	STRUCTURED TECHNIQUES: THE BASIS FOR CASE (revised edition)
INFORMATION ENGINEERING (Book I: Introduction)	INFORMATION ENGINEERING (Book I: Introduction)	DATABASE ANALYSIS AND DESIGN	INFORMATION ENGINEERING (Book I: Introduction)
INFORMATION ENGINEERING (Book II: Planning and Analysis)	INFORMATION ENGINEERING (Book II: Planning and Analysis)	DESIGN OF MAN-COMPUTER DIALOGUES	**Languages and Programming**
STRATEGIC INFORMATION PLANNING METHODOLOGIES (second edition)	INFORMATION ENGINEERING (Book III: Design and Construction)	DESIGN OF REAL-TIME COMPUTER SYSTEMS	APPLICATION DEVELOPMENT WITHOUT PROGRAMMERS
SOFTWARE MAINTENANCE: THE PROBLEM AND ITS SOLUTIONS	STRUCTURED TECHNIQUES: THE BASIS FOR CASE (revised edition)	DATA COMMUNICATIONS DESIGN TECHNIQUES	FOURTH-GENERATION LANGUAGES (Volume I: Principles)
DESIGN AND STRATEGY FOR DISTRIBUTED DATA PROCESSING	**Object-Oriented Programming**	DESIGN AND STRATEGY FOR DISTRIBUTED DATA PROCESSING	FOURTH-GENERATION LANGUAGES (Volume II: Representative 4GLs)
Expert Systems	OBJECT-ORIENTED ANALYSIS AND DESIGN	SOFTWARE MAINTENANCE: THE PROBLEM AND ITS SOLUTIONS	FOURTH-GENERATION LANGUAGES (Volume III: 4GLs from IBM)
BUILDING EXPERT SYSTEMS: A TUTORIAL	PRINCIPLES OF OBJECT-ORIENTED ANALYSIS AND DESIGN	SYSTEM DESIGN FROM PROVABLY CORRECT CONSTRUCTS	**Diagramming Techniques**
	OBJECT-ORIENTED METHODS	INFORMATION ENGINEERING (Book II: Planning and Analysis)	DIAGRAMMING TECHNIQUES FOR ANALYSTS AND PROGRAMMERS
	OBJECT-ORIENTED TOOLS	INFORMATION ENGINEERING (Book III: Design and Construction)	RECOMMENDED DIAGRAMMING STANDARDS FOR ANALYSTS AND PROGRAMMERS
			ACTION DIAGRAMS: CLEARLY STRUCTURED SPECIFICATIONS PROGRAMS, AND PROCEDURES (second edition)